RESEARCH IN REHABILITATION COUNSELING

Third Edition

RESEARCH IN REHABILITATION COUNSELING

A Guide to Design, Methodology, and Utilization

By

PHILLIP D. RUMRILL, Jr.

Kent State University
School of Lifespan Development and Educational Sciences
Kent, Ohio

and

JAMES L. BELLINI

Syracuse University
Department of Counseling and Human Services
Syracuse, New York

CHARLES C THOMAS • PUBLISHER, LTD.
Springfield • Illinois • U.S.A.

Published and Distributed Throughout the World by

CHARLES C THOMAS • PUBLISHER, LTD.
2600 South First Street
Springfield, Illinois 62704

This book is protected by copyright. No part of
it may be reproduced in any manner without written
permission from the publisher. All rights reserved.

© 2018 by CHARLES C THOMAS • PUBLISHER, LTD.

ISBN 978-0-398-09199-6 (paper)
ISBN 978-0-398-09200-9 (ebook)

First Edition, 1999
Second Edition, 2009
Third Edition, 2018

With THOMAS BOOKS *careful attention is given to all details of manufacturing and design. It is the Publisher's desire to present books that are satisfactory as to their physical qualities and artistic possibilities and appropriate for their particular use.* THOMAS BOOKS *will be true to those laws of quality that assure a good name and good will.*

Printed in the United States of America
MM-C-1

Library of Congress Cataloging-in-Publication Data

Names: Rumrill, Phillip D., Jr., author. | Bellini, James L., author. | Bellini, James L. Research in rehabilitation counseling.
Title: Research in rehabilitation counseling : a guide to design, methodology, and utilization / by PHILLIP D. RUMRILL, Jr., Kent State University, School of Lifespan Development and Educational Sciences, Kent, Ohio and JAMES L. BELLINI, Syracuse University, Department of Counseling and Human Services, Syracuse, New York.
Description: Third Edition. | Springfield, Illinois : Charles C Thomas, Publisher, Ltd., [2017] | Revised edition of the authors' Research in rehabilitation counseling, c2009. | Includes bibliographical references and index.
Identifiers: LCCN 2017032447 (print) | LCCN 2017036521 (ebook) | ISBN 9780398092009 (ebook) | ISBN 9780398091996 (pbk. : alk. paper)
Subjects: LCSH: Rehabilitation counseling--Research.
Classification: LCC HV1568 (ebook) | LCC HV1568 .B45 2017 (print) | DDC 362.4/0486--dc23
LC record available at https://lccn.loc.gov/2017032447

*For Amy, Brian, Doug, Nate, Phil Sr.,
Rick, Shirley, and Stuart*
                            PDR

For Hong Anh
                 JBL

PREFACE

This third edition was written as a primary text for graduate level students and practitioners concerning the role of research in contemporary rehabilitation counseling. As with the first two editions, our intent was to provide a comprehensive overview of the philosophical, ethical, methodological, and analytic fundamentals of social science research—as well as to specify aspects of rehabilitation research that distinguish it from scientific inquiry in other helping professions. Foremost among these distinctions are the clientele of people with disabilities and their role as valued partners in the research enterprise; the historical, philosophical, and legislative bases of rehabilitation counseling; and research utilization strategies.

This third edition represents the thorough revision that we believed necessary in order to accurately reflect the variation and wealth of research methodologies used in contemporary rehabilitation counseling research. We have added more than 300 new references to this edition, which represents a 30 percent revision of the second edition. Most of the research examples cited in this edition were published in peer-reviewed rehabilitation counseling journals over the past decade, and these examples represent the current status of research methods as well as the most relevant contemporary topic areas of research and scholarship in our field. Accordingly, this edition may be used both as a research textbook and as a general introduction to the current scholarship in our profession.

Like the previous two editions, the third edition of this book is divided into ten chapters. Chapter 1 establishes the theoretical underpinnings of social scientific inquiry; provides a foundation in the philosophical, epistemological, and methodological considerations related to the design and execution of rehabilitation research, and discusses the broad purposes of research in rehabilitation counseling. The updated Chapter 2 addresses issues that are preparatory to designing and evaluating rehabilitation research, such as sources of research ideas, translating research ideas into research hypotheses, identifying variables, and sampling issues. Chapter 3 discusses key measurement and statistical concepts used in the quantitative research tradition, including reliability and validity of measurement instruments, the purposes of descriptive and inferential statistics in analyzing numeric data, and an updated section on methods of statistical analysis. Chapter 4 reviews ethical issues and guidelines for the design, implementation, and reporting of rehabilitation research. Chapter 5 addresses key criteria for evaluating the quality of rehabilitation research, drawing valid inferences from results, and generalizing findings from the research sample to the target population.

Chapters 6, 7, and 8 review the wide range of different quantitative, qualitative, and integrative approaches to doing rehabilitation research, and they provide examples of these from the recent rehabilitation literature. Chapter 6 addresses intervention/stimulus, relationship, and descriptive studies in the quantitative paradigm. Chapter 7 discusses qualitative methods of rehabilitation research. Chapter 8 examines and categorizes a variety of narrative literature reviews according to their purposes. Chapter 9 presents a published research article section by section, annotates the components and composition of a research report, and provides a protocol that students and practitioners can use to evaluate the technical soundness and scientific merits of published research articles. The concluding chapter of the text addresses future trends in rehabilitation counseling research in relation to fruitful topic areas and methodologies and as they apply to a variety of stakeholders (e.g., counselors, administrators, policymakers, educators, researchers, people with disabilities, consumer advocates).

Because this book was written as an introductory research methods textbook for graduate students in rehabilitation counseling, we focus much of the information contained herein on the role of readers as "professional consumers" of rehabilitation research. In doing so, we not only introduce the reader to the fundamentals of research design, we also serve the purpose of introduction to the professional literature in our field. This book provides the "basics" that one would need to begin conducting a research investigation, but we would encourage that person to supplement this book with coursework in statistics and advanced research design before initiating an independent empirical study.

PHILLIP D. RUMRILL, JR.
JAMES L. BELLINI

ACKNOWLEDGMENTS

We would like to thank the individuals and organizations who made it possible for us to complete this third edition of our book. We begin by thanking Mr. Michael Payne Thomas of Charles C Thomas Publishers for the opportunity to accomplish this revision. Mr. Thomas and his associates have been supportive and encouraging throughout this project, and we appreciate the patience they accorded us as we put the finishing touches on this volume.

We are grateful to our faculty mentors and advisors at the University of Arkansas, who provided us with a strong foundation in both qualitative and quantitative research, introduced us to the rehabilitation research enterprise, and inspired us to proceed with our own research agendas. Our deep appreciation goes to Dr. Jason Andrew, Dr. Brian Bolton, Dr. Daniel Cook, Dr. George Denny, Dr. Reed Greenwood, Dr. Richard Roessler, Dr. Kay Schriner, and Dr. James Swartz.

We are indebted to a number of funding agencies who have provided support and sponsorship for our research over the years, thereby enabling us to draw from numerous examples of completed research projects in developing this text, in teaching and advising our students, and in providing consultation to other researchers in the fields of rehabilitation counseling and disability studies. These agencies include the National Institutes of Health; the National Institute on Disability, Independent Living, and Rehabilitation Research; the Rehabilitation Services Administration; the National Multiple Sclerosis Society; the Ohio Learning Network; and the United States Department of Education, Office of Special Education Programs and Office of Postsecondary Education.

For their editorial assistance, we thank Ms. Aundrea Gee Cormier, Ms. Cassidy Pittman, Mr. Stuart Rumrill, Mr. Nathan Rumrill, and Ms. Aliza Weiss, all of the Kent State University Center for Disability Studies. We gratefully acknowledge Dr. Lynn Koch of the University of Arkansas, Dr. Tricia Niesz of Kent State University, and Ms. Melissa Jones Wilkins of the University of Arkansas for contributing an outstanding chapter (Chapter 7) on qualitative research. We also thank Dr. Courtney Vierstra, Dr. Mykal Leslie, Mr. Rowan Blundell, and Ms. Sarah Davis–all of Kent State University–for their contributions to the chapter (Chapter 6) on quantitative research designs; and Ms. Aundrea Gee Cormier of Kent State University for her contributions to Chapter 4 on research ethics.

Finally, we thank our fellow rehabilitation researchers and educators throughout the United States for their ongoing efforts to build a comprehensive knowledge base that informs and shapes rehabilitation counselor training and practice. Since the first edition of our book was published in 1999, we have seen substantial improvements in the quality and quantity of methodologically rigorous, scientifically sound, and practically relevant research regarding all aspects of the rehabilitation counseling process. We are proud to call the researchers who have made such significant advancements in our field our friends and colleagues.

CONTENTS

Preface .... vii *Page*

Chapter
1. INTRODUCTION TO REHABILITATION COUNSELING RESEARCH 3

2. BEGINNING THE RESEARCH PROCESS: RESEARCH QUESTIONS, VARIABLES, AND SAMPLING ISSUES 36

3. MEASUREMENT AND STATISTICAL ISSUES IN REHABILITATION RESEARCH 61

4. ETHICAL ISSUES AND GUIDELINES FOR REHABILITATION RESEARCH (*with Contributions by Aundrea Gee Cormier*) 100

5. RESEARCH VALIDITY 125

6. QUANTITATIVE RESEARCH DESIGNS (*with Contributions by Courtney Vierstra, Mykal Leslie, Rowan Blundell, and Sarah Davis*) 145

7. QUALITATIVE RESEARCH DESIGNS–*Lynn Koch, Tricia Niesz, and Melissa Jones Wilkins* 186

8. NARRATIVE LITERATURE REVIEWS 228

9. ANATOMY OF A RESEARCH ARTICLE AND GUIDELINES FOR CRITIQUE 251

10. THE FUTURE OF REHABILITATION RESEARCH 278

References 295
Index 337

RESEARCH IN REHABILITATION COUNSELING

Chapter 1

INTRODUCTION TO REHABILITATION COUNSELING RESEARCH

INTRODUCTION

Rehabilitation counselors are professionals who "assist individuals with disabilities in adapting to the environment, assist environments in accommodating the needs of individuals, and work toward full participation of individuals with disabilities in all aspects of society, especially in work" (Szymanski, 1985, p. 3). Rehabilitation counseling research is directed toward (a) understanding the impact of disability on the social functioning of individuals, families, and groups, and (b) identifying effective practices that facilitate the successful accommodation of individuals with disabilities in their chosen environments. The fundamental aim of rehabilitation counseling research is to improve the lives of persons with disabilities by facilitating the achievement of their vocational and independent living goals (Bellini & Rumrill, 2009; Bolton, 1979). A large number of interrelated lines of inquiry have been pursued over the past five decades of rehabilitation counseling research, including (but not limited to): understanding the impact of disability on social functioning; understanding the characteristics of consumers of rehabilitation services (persons with disabilities) and their service needs; understanding the roles, functions, and professional practices of rehabilitation counselors; identifying consumer, counselor, and service provider characteristics that are associated with particular social and vocational outcomes; evaluating the impact of federal policy initiatives in the lives of individuals with disabilities; and evaluating the effectiveness of rehabilitation counseling interventions.

SCIENCE AND REHABILITATION COUNSELING RESEARCH

Science is not a set of definitive results; rather, it is a way of understanding the world around us. In other words, the purpose of science is to establish knowledge (Kazdin, 2003; Shadish, 1995). Research methods are the techniques that are used to establish scientific knowledge. Within the domain of research methods, the concept of research design refers to the specific plans or arrangements that are used to examine questions of interest. Thus, the terms research methods and research design both focus on the specific decisions, options, and practices that characterize research (Kazdin, 2003). The quality of the methodology and design of a given investigation forms the essential basis for the strength of the knowledge claims or conclusions that researchers may derive from the research findings. Understanding the strengths and limitations of particular research methods and research designs permits consumers (i.e., readers) of research manuscripts to evaluate the quality of the research and the warrant for the knowledge claim given the findings that are reported.

Two broad and distinct categories of rehabilitation research methods are qualitative and quantitative approaches. Qualitative methods are based in a subjective, phenomenological approach to knowledge, and they are typically directed to the discovery of how individuals ascribe meaning to phenomena, investigation of previously unexplored phenomena, or examination of complex social phenomena (Bogdan & Biklen, 1998; Hagner & Helm, 1994). Qualitative research methods have their roots in anthropology and sociology and may include ethnographic studies, participant observation, case studies, or discourse analysis. Qualitative research methods have a long history of application in disability issues and have been particularly valuable in providing in-depth understanding of the lived experience of disability. Moreover, these methods are becoming more prevalent in rehabilitation counseling research. Recent examples of articles that reported the use of qualitative methods in rehabilitation research include explorations of how individuals with traumatic brain injuries compensate for cognitive limitations through the use of assistive technology (Nardone et al., 2015), the meaning that people with multiple sclerosis ascribe to employment (Meade et al., 2016), and the perspectives of notable leaders in the disability community regarding the accomplishments and continuing challenges of the disability rights movement (McCarthy, 2003).

Quantitative research design features the numeric expression of information for purposes of summarization, classification, analysis, and generalization. Thus, quantitative methods involve the measurement of variables of interest and the use of statistical analyses to identify relationships among variables. With roots in nineteenth century philosophy of science and statistical methods largely borrowed from the physical sciences, the goal of quantitative research is the development of objective knowledge about nature and human nature. Contemporary quantitative researchers in the social sciences, like their colleagues who use qualitative methods, recognize that human experience is fundamentally subjective and that our knowledge about reality is embedded in particular social and cultural contexts (Phillips, 1987, 1992). However, post-positivist, quantitative researchers also assume that causal relationships exist outside the human mind, that humans are capable of discerning these causal connections among events in the world (albeit imperfectly), and that agreement among persons about the nature of these causal relationships forms the basis for the development of an objective knowledge of nature and human nature (Cook & Campbell, 1979; Manicas & Secord, 1983; Phillips, 1987; Strong, 1991). A more accurate term for the nature of this "objective" knowledge that highlights the subjective but public quality of consensus about what is "known" is intersubjective agreement, or agreement among members of the community of scientists and practitioners in a given field of study.

Quantitative research methods are widely used in rehabilitation research and include surveys, true experiments, quasi-experimental research in field settings, single-subject or small-N designs, and ex post facto (after the fact) designs. Quantitative research is important in evaluating the effectiveness of rehabilitation interventions, programs, and policies relative to the goals of rehabilitation; describing the characteristics of programs and program participants; needs assessment; and theory testing. One of the key advantages of quantitative research is that vast amounts of data from large numbers of people can be aggregated, analyzed, and summarized to provide program participants, administrators, policymakers, and other interested parties with key information about questions of interest.

Recent examples of articles that used quantitative research methods in rehabilitation counseling include the examination of patterns in perceived workplace discrimination among persons with multiple sclerosis (Roessler, Rumrill, Li, & McMahon, 2016); an exploration of the major job functions that are perceived as important for rehabilitation practice by certified rehabilitation counselors (Leahy, Chan, Sung, & Kim, 2013); and an analysis of client characteristics and vocational rehabilitation services received as determinants of competitive employment outcomes among transition-age youth with visual impairments and blindness (Cimera et al., 2015).

Although quantitative and qualitative methods have different historical roots, philosophical assumptions, approaches to discovering knowledge, techniques for ensuring researcher neutrality regarding the content of the research, and ways of evaluating the validity of knowledge claims, no research method is more valid than the other. Rather, each method is appropriate for answering certain types of questions and less appropriate for answering other questions. The choice of research methodology is largely a function of the nature of the phenomena we wish to understand and the types of research questions that are posed. Nor should qualitative and quantitative approaches be perceived as mutually exclusive. Rather, qualitative and quantitative methods can be effectively combined in a single study (or a series of studies) to enhance the validity of the knowledge gained (Cook, 1985; Cook & Campbell, 1979; Szymanski, 1993). Cook and Campbell (1979) maintained that "field experimentation (i.e., quantitative studies in community settings) should always include qualitative research to describe and illuminate the context and conditions under which research is conducted" (p. 93).

SCIENCE AND KNOWLEDGE CLAIMS

Knowledge comes from many sources, and the quality of the source of knowledge often determines whether the knowledge will be accepted. To gain an appreciation for the efficacy of knowledge claims based on scientific methods, it is useful to compare the scientific approach to establishing knowledge to other common approaches. The framework discussed below follows Krathwohl (1998) and includes knowledge gained from personal observation and experience, intuition, tradition, and authority.

Personal Observation and Experience

Personal observation and experience comprise the source of knowledge that we trust most. "I'll believe it when I see it" is an expression of this universal knowledge standard. Moreover, it appears to be an essential characteristic of human beings to seek order or patterns in their experience. To perceive a pattern means that we have already formed an idea of "what comes next." Thus, the ability to perceive patterns in our observations and experiences allows us to understand, predict, and possibly control what happens to us, thereby changing the outcome from what might have been.

So, personal experience, and particularly those experiences that can be organized into patterns, is a vital source of knowledge. In fact, it is the raw stuff of science, because the personal experience of the scientist is often the catalyst for research questions that the scientist may pursue. The personal experience of the scientist may also be the primary data for the investigation, particularly in qualitative methods such as participant observation and ethnographic research.

However, we have all learned from experience that sometimes our sense impressions are inaccurate. Also, knowledge claims based on experience are naturally limited to those things we personally experience and, sadly, our lives are too short and the opportunities for wide-ranging experience may be limited or carry a heavy cost.

Intuition

Knowledge claims based on intuition are those propositions that are so obviously true as to be self-evident. In many instances we infer these propositions from the world around us. For example, in medieval Europe, it was a self-evident "fact" that the sun revolved around the earth. To verify the proposition for oneself required only that one observed that the sun appears to move across the sky and the earth remains stationary under one's feet. Other "self-evident" propositions widely held in various cultures pertain to gender differences, racial differences, differences among persons of different classes, and so forth. These examples highlight the fact that what is self-evident (but unverified) may turn out to be grossly untrue and unfair. Without deferring to some other approach to knowledge it is difficult to distinguish those self-evident propositions that are true (i.e., accurate) from those that are false.

Tradition

Knowledge claims based on tradition are facts that are transmitted from generation to generation within families and cultures. It is a particularly important source of knowledge in less technologically developed cultures, and it becomes a less reliable source of knowledge in cultures that are experiencing rapid change. Facts based on tradition are often rooted in the world view of the given culture, and accepting the "fact" often means accepting the general world view in which the fact is embedded. Also, traditional knowledge, particularly of the religious variety, often tends to be transmitted by authorities, and acceptance of the tradition is linked to acceptance of the authority. In every case, "knowing" based on traditional knowledge relies on making a personal judgment to accept the tradition.

Authority

Given that individuals have limited personal experience; self-evident facts are often proved wrong and the most valuable lessons are unlikely to be self-evident; and tradition is a foundation for, but also a limitation on, the development of knowledge; we are most likely to believe something is true if a respected authority tells us it is true. Authorities may range from arbitrary to dogmatic to reasoned. In most cases, we are more likely to accept and have confidence in an authority's pronouncement if it agrees with reason and if previous assertions were proved true. Thus, it is the reputation of the authority, or in the case of reasoning authorities, the logical force of their arguments, that forms the basis for the knowledge claim. The history of science (and culture in general) is filled with examples of authorities of all kinds (i.e., arbitrary, dogmatic, and reasoning) who blocked the advancement of knowledge.

The reasoning authority is likely to be more authoritative to other reasoning individuals because he or she is more apt to be open to what is and is not known, more willing to reveal the weaknesses in the given case in question, and more likely to give a balanced presentation of pros and cons. In other words, the integrity of the reasoning authority makes it less likely that essential information is being hidden that might affect the judgment of the authority or others who depend on him or her.

How Scientific Knowledge Differs from Other Sources of Knowledge

Although science, throughout most of the nineteenth and twentieth centuries, had been conceived as the paragon of human knowledge, contemporary perspectives recognize that scientific knowledge is fundamentally rooted in a social process of consensus building (Anderson et al., 2014; Atherton & Toriello, 2012; Krathwohl, 1998; Phillips, 1987, 2000). In developing a consensus around a particular knowledge claim, scientists will draw on both empirical evidence and reason; however, neither empiricism nor rationality provides the ultimate foundation for the veracity or falsehood of any claim. Rather, scientific knowledge, like other forms of knowing, is a matter of social consensus. Acceptance or rejection of a scientific proposition or theory comes about because a community of scientists is persuaded or dissuaded. Also, research conclusions are rarely evaluated on an independent basis; rather, their veracity is assessed with reference to their compatibility to the network of previously verified knowledge and relevant theories. Thus, research conclusions and interpretations are issues on which reasonable people can and do disagree. However, scientific knowledge differs from other types of knowledge because: (a) ideally, scientific knowledge is based on the agreement of many individuals rather than one person's subjective experience or intuition, hence potential personal bias is removed; (b) it is provable by experience of others who are unrelated to the original researcher and who have no vested interest in the veracity of the particular claim; and (c) the knowledge claim is evaluated on its own merits rather than on the authority or prestige of the person who makes the claim. In other words, the consensus that develops around particular knowledge claims depends on the consistent application of a common, accepted set of rules or norms that governs the behavior of scientists (Goodwin & Goodwin, 2012; Merton, 1968).

Scientific knowledge represents an ongoing, self-corrective process of discovery and evaluation. Questions are asked, data are collected, and tentative conclusions are drawn. As more evidence is collected from subsequent research studies, a particular knowledge claim may gain more or less credibility in the community of scientists. There is no such thing as a final, definitive study in any scientific domain. The criterion for evaluating particular knowledge claims and the state of knowledge in any given area of research is the total weight of the empirical evidence (Bellini & Rumrill, 2009; Phillips & Burbules, 2000). It is quite possible (even likely) in the short term that reasonable experts may disagree as to the proper interpretation of a body of empirical evidence. The history of science also provides numerous examples of theoretical disputes that are settled conclusively over the course of time. Thus, few contemporary biologists dispute the Darwinian theory of natural selection in favor of a Lamarkian theory of inheritance of learned characteristics, although this was once a major disputation. In this view, science is a method for evaluating the veracity of different knowledge claims and permits the gradual development of a knowledge base that reflects the best possible approximation of the truth given the current evidence in an area of inquiry.

The validity of knowledge claims based on scientific methods follows directly from the fact that the evaluation of these claims is based on adherence to a specific set of rules, norms, or regulatory ideals governing the nature of the research enterprise, the behavior of individual researchers, and the discourse among them (Merton, 1968; Phillips, 1987, 1992). Moreover, the norms of science are fundamental to both quantitative and qualitative research methods. These norms include (a) universal standards for knowledge claims, (b) common ownership of information, (c) cultivated disinterestedness, and (d) organized skepticism (Merton, 1968).

The phrase *universal standards for knowledge claims* means that scientific conclusions are judged on the basis of the same set of standards rather than on different criteria for each separate claim. Thus, it is the quality and rigor of the work that should inform the judgment of the community of scientists rather than the characteristics of the research, the reputation or past accomplishments of the researcher, or the power of the financial supporter or home institution. This norm is exemplified in the anonymous, peer-review process used to evaluate publishable research in academic journals. Prior to publication, manuscripts are sent to several anonymous reviewers with the authors' names and institutional affiliations deleted. This permits the authors' peers to make judgments about the quality of the research paper and the veracity of the knowledge claim solely on the basis of the merit of the investigation and the rigor of the methodologies employed. Only those manuscripts that are judged worthy following the rigorous peer-review process will be accepted for publication in a scholarly journal. Universal standards for knowledge claims provide the foundation for the development of an objective knowledge, that is, agreement across individual researchers that a given knowledge claim has merit. The integrity of the scientific enterprise depends on the consistent application of a single set of standards for all claims.

Common ownership of information means that scientific norms reduce proprietary rights to a minimum. In other words, the ethos of science regards scientific findings as part of the public domain and a common heritage of humankind rather than the property of the individual scientist. Information is to be made available to other interested parties; indeed, there is a professional obligation to communicate findings. Progress in science is predicated on the availability of knowledge to all who wish to participate. This norm is best exemplified by Sir Isaac Newton's remark, "If I have seen farther, it is by standing on the shoulders of giants."

Common ownership of information provides the foundation for the replicability of research findings. Research findings should be able to be replicated by other researchers who use the same set of procedures to investigate the same phenomenon. Replicability of findings is a key to establishing a certified body of objective knowledge. For replication of a study to be possible, two conditions are necessary: (a) the procedures used must be public, and (b) the procedures used must be precisely described. Research reports, including those that are published in professional journals, typically include a section entitled "Method" in which the author describes the precise procedures used in the investigation.

The norm of *cultivated disinterestedness* means that, for knowledge claims to have merit, the researcher must demonstrate integrity in the gathering and interpretation of data. Science is fundamentally an empirical approach to knowledge production. Science depends on formulating a research question or hypothesis about how variables relate, then testing the formulation by gathering empirical data. Speculation is vital in the generation of ideas for research, but it is the confirmation or disconfirmation of these hypotheses by gathering data and interpreting the findings that provides the basis for building a consensus around a particular knowledge claim. The norm of cultivated disinterestedness means that data should be gathered, analyzed, and interpreted without regard to the researcher's personal predictions or bias about what it should be or what it should show.

Both qualitative and quantitative researchers are required to maintain an awareness of how their own biases and preconceptions can affect their interpretations of the data. Whereas quantitative research methods include more formal methods to ensure that the researcher maintains neutrality regarding the process of research (e.g., double-blind experiments and measurement instruments with established reliability and validity to guide the interpretation of results), qualitative researchers apply other methods (e.g., using multiple sources of data, sampling discrepant cases to try to disconfirm hypotheses, having a colleague who is not invested in the research project verify the themes that emerge in the data) to ensure researcher neutrality in the conduct of research. In each case, these methods support the application of the scientific norm of cultivated disinterestedness to ensure that researcher bias does not contaminate study findings.

The norm of *organized skepticism* refers to the responsibility of the community of scientists to be skeptical of each new knowledge claim, to evaluate it on its own merits, to test it, and to strive to think of alternate explanations for the same data and other limitations on its truth. This also means that one should interpret the results of a study with caution, making claims that are warranted based on the findings of the study rather than extending the findings into the realm of speculation. This norm is exemplified in the convention that each manuscript published in professional journals contains a section entitled "Limitations" wherein the author discusses the limits of the findings and the limitations inherent in the study's methodology.

The norm of organized skepticism reflects the self-correcting nature of science. Organized skepticism means that "it is the responsibility of the community of scientists to be skeptical of each new knowledge claim, to test it, to try to think of reasons the claim might be false, to think of alternative explanations as plausible as the one advanced" (Krathwohl, 1998, p. 54). Knowledge claims are only tentatively accepted, and then only when they have survived repeated challenges or attempts at disconfirmation over time.

Organized skepticism, however, can only operate effectively in a context in which the other scientific norms are accepted and observed. Thus, the findings and the process by which data were obtained must be public and freely available (common ownership of information). Researchers must expose their work to challenge and criticism on the part of the scientific community, and must know that their work will be judged fairly and appropriately (universal standards). The scientific community must be able to assume that the researcher exercised integrity in gathering and analyzing data if the report is to be accepted at face value (cultivated disinterestedness). By holding that all knowledge is only tentatively true until it is replaced by new, more substantive knowledge (i.e., organized skepticism), the influence of particular knowledge claims is checked and (hopefully) prevented from becoming dogma. The self-correcting nature of the scientific enterprise permits the steady accumulation of a solid knowledge base that is founded on the careful interpretation of empirical evidence. Ultimately, the integrity of the scientific enterprise in every discipline rests largely on the integrity of the community of peers and the social processes (e.g., peer review) by which knowledge claims are evaluated in those research communities.

THE GOALS OF SCIENCE

Historically, the scientific approach to establishing knowledge has two basic, interrelated functions. One goal of science is to advance knowledge, make discoveries, and learn facts to improve some aspect of our world. This is a practical purpose. Scientific research is designed to provide answers to pressing questions or practical problems. Often this purpose involves establishing a relationship between events that may prove useful to practitioners in their daily practice. Many of the technological advances that characterized the late nineteenth and twentieth centuries and provided for enhanced quality of life in the industrialized nations were made possible by the technological application of scientific discoveries. Given that scientific research is designed to provide answers to practical questions, one important criterion for judging the adequacy of research is whether the answers that research provides are useful to practitioners in resolving the practical issues they face. One of the essential criteria for the evaluation of rehabilitation research is how well it addresses questions and provides answers to the pressing issues of persons with disabilities and the rehabilitation counselors who work with them.

The second goal of science is to invent theories that represent the unseen realities posited to underlie and find expression in observed events. In building theories, scientists "represent this unseen reality with a network of constructs, construe how the constructs generate observed events, and identify how symptoms of the underlying processes are to be measured" (Strong, 1991, p. 205). Theory building has a central role in the scientific approach to establishing knowledge because theories allow us to attain a better understanding of the relationships among persons and events and the conditions in which these relationships take place.

Theory is both a tool and a goal of science (Goodwin & Goodwin, 2012; Phillips, 1992). Theory is a conceptual tool for scientific research in that it can explain what variables are related, how they are related, and why. Moreover, it is particularly a vital tool of science because speculative theory may leap well beyond the sum of what is known in a given area and time, and establish propositions with which empirical research may be fruitfully engaged for many years. Darwin's theory of natural selection exemplifies this transformative power of theory to exhibit connections between matters of observation that would otherwise be regarded as unrelated and, thereby, effectively guide future scientific inquiry.

Theory is a goal for research because we strive to build and revise theories of human behavior on the basis of careful observations in the world. Speculation is a key source of theory, but the evaluation and confirmation of a theory's veracity (and its revision) is based on how well it explains and predicts empirical data. Thus, one key purpose of doing research is to test the assertions of theory (Strong, 1991). Research is often guided by theoretical issues within a line of inquiry and seeks to establish general relations, conditional statements, and categories among events that help practitioners understand phenomena, organize knowledge, and predict future events. Thus, theory development also has a fundamental practical purpose.

Theories are developed, tested, and revised through an interplay of inductive and deductive logic. Inductive logic is characterized by a movement from making specific observations to articulating general statements based on these observations. Theory development is largely an inductive process. Classic examples of inductively derived theories in psychological research include Freud's theory of repression, which was developed on the basis of careful scrutiny of a small number of case studies, and Piaget's theory of childhood development, which was rooted in his observation of developmental processes in his biological children. Deductive logic is characterized by a movement from the general to the specific case, and is fundamental in the empirical hypothesis testing that characterizes the scientific method. Often the purpose of research is to test the elements, propositions, or lawful relationships among variables that are specified by a particular theory against empirical data that are gathered by the researcher. To set up an empirical test of a theory, it is necessary to deduce the particular relationships among variables that are expected in the data. The empirical test is then a confirmation or disconfirmation of the specific deductions of the investigator, and, by extension, a test of the theoretical propositions. "In theory-driven science, scientific work cycles from constructing theory to generating observations with which to test the theory and then returns to reconstructing theory in light of the findings" (Strong, 1991, p. 207).

SCIENCE AND CAUSALITY

The two fundamental goals of science–to advance knowledge and build theory–serve to enhance our understanding of *causality*. In this view, the purposes of science are to (a) establish the presence or absence of causal relations among relevant variables, and (b) provide explanations (i.e., theories) for how causal relations account for our experience of the natural and social worlds. The philosophical basis for causality is largely drawn from the eighteenth and nineteenth century philosophers David Hume and J. S. Mill (Cook, 1985; Phillips, 1987, 1992). However, the twentieth century saw the development of more sophisticated views of causality, particularly as these pertain to the social sciences. Earlier, more deterministic representations of causality are clearly inadequate to explain relations among phenomena in the social sphere where human beings are both objects of study and active, intentional agents, where effects are likely to be collectively determined rather than the result of a single, identifiable source, and where measured variables are imperfect representations of the underlying variable that is the presumed causal agent of actual interest to the researcher (Cook, 1985; Shadish, 1995).

We endorse an evolutionary perspective of causal explanation articulated by Cook and Campbell (1979). From an evolutionary perspective, human beings show a stubborn and strong psychological disposition to infer causal relations from the sense data that we gather in everyday experience. It is an evolutionary perspective because the tendency to infer cause is closely linked to humanity's propensity to manipulate the environment to accomplish tasks that enhance adaptation and because it assumes a special survival value in knowing about causes that can be manipulated to advantage. A classic example is the agricultural revolution that occurred in the Neolithic era (Conner, 2005). We can infer that the process unfolded as follows: First, during the long millennia proceeding the Neolithic era, human beings observed where and how plants grew. This led in turn to purposeful pruning or manipulating of naturally-occurring plant resources, then to the planting of seeds, then to purposeful manipulation of the characteristics of plants so as to increase yields. Moreover, the archeological record shows that this process of plant domestication unfolded similarly on different continents, at different times, and with a wide range of naturally occurring plants (Diamond, 2005). Altogether, the development of agriculture indicates that human beings over time developed a practical understanding of the causal mechanisms at work in naturally occurring flora. As these mechanisms came to be understood, humans intervened in these natural processes and put these to work in ways that made life better.

In this view, the mental framework that supports causal thinking is not a new development or a characteristic of scientific societies only. Rather, it is as old as humanity itself, and was present, at least in rudimentary form, from the earliest phases of the genus Homo and in varying degrees in all prescientific and scientific cultures. However, science represents an advance in knowledge production from earlier cultures in that the framework for causality is systematized and made explicit in science.

Contemporary perspectives on causality are based on the work of J. S. Mill, the nineteenth century British philosopher. Mill stated that causal inference depends on meeting three key criteria: (a) the cause and effect are related, (b) the cause must precede the effect in time, and (c) other explanations of the cause-effect relationship must be eliminated. In addition, contemporary philosophy of science highlights a fourth criterion for firmly establishing that a causal relationship exists: the need for a causal explanation that specifies how the variables are related and what mechanisms are at work (Abelson, 1995; Miles & Shevlin, 2001; Phillips, 1987, 1992). We will address each of these key criteria in the following discussion, and we will provide examples for how research design and statistical analysis can contribute to establishing a strong warrant for causality.

The first condition for verifying that a causal relationship exists is to establish that *the cause and effect are related* (i.e., covary). In other words, a change in the value of the presumed cause must produce a change in the value of the presumed effect. In quantitative research, covariation is demonstrated by a statistically significant association (e.g., correlation, t-test, or other statistical test) between the presumed cause and effect. However, it is a truism in statistics that correlation does not equal or necessarily imply causation; a statistically significant association between variables may be the result of other variables that are not taken into account. For example, day and night covary, but are not causally related. Rather, both are caused by the earth's rotation. Height and weight also covary, because both are causally related to genetics and nutrition. In each of these cases, a third force impinges on both the presumed cause and effect and makes them covary. Therefore, statistical association is necessary but it is not sufficient to make a strong claim for a causal relationship between variables.

When we speak of causality, we also must specify the direction of the variable relationship. The second condition for establishing that a causal relationship exists is known as temporal priority: *The cause must precede the effect in time.* In other words, changes in the presumed effect must be observed after making or observing a change in the presumed causal variable.

The third and perhaps most difficult requirement for establishing a causal relationship between variables is that *other explanations of the cause-effect relationship must be eliminated.* To be certain that variables are causally related, it is necessary to *isolate* the presumed effect from all influences other than the hypothesized cause. Isolation is the goal of experimental design. In the classic experiment, random assignment of subjects to treatment or intervention groups ensures to a large degree that the groups are equivalent on all extraneous variables other than the variable under investigation (i.e., the presumed cause or independent variable). Then, the causal (i.e., independent) variable is manipulated, with one treatment group receiving the intervention and the other, control group receiving no intervention. One of the great breakthroughs in experimental design was the realization that experimental manipulation of the presumed causal variable coupled with random assignment provides the strongest warrant for establishing causality (Cook & Campbell, 1979). The randomized clinical trial is the "gold standard" for establishing causality in the social sciences because it incorporates all three essential conditions: temporal priority (i.e., manipulation of the presumed cause precedes the measurement of the presumed effect); covariation (demonstrated by an appropriate statistical test); and logical elimination of alternative explanations for the observed variable relationship (via manipulation and random assignment). The manipulation of the independent variable is known as *experimental control*.

Although experimental control can be used to ensure temporal priority and to isolate the effects of the presumed cause on the presumed effect, in many research circumstances it is not possible to experimentally manipulate the presumed cause and/or randomly assign participants to intervention groups. For example, a researcher may hypothesize that social support influences (i.e., causes) the psychosocial adjustment of persons with traumatic brain injury (TBI). In this circumstance, there is no way to experimentally isolate the presumed cause-effect relationship from all the other variables that also may influence both social support and psychosocial adjustment (e.g., social skills, degree of impairment, level of accessibility in the person's environment). What the researcher can do is isolate the variable relationship under investigation by using statistical methods for controlling the influences of these other potential causal variables. Multiple regression analysis is one method for ensuring *statistical control* when experimental control is not feasible (Miles & Shevlin, 2001). In this case, statistical control is exercised by holding constant the influences of all other predictor or presumed causal variables in the regression equation so that the influence of the target causal variable on the presumed effect can be assessed. Statistical methods provide inherently weaker warrants for causality than experimental methods do, because statistical control depends on the inclusion of all of the important extraneous variables in the model as independent variables, and it is difficult to be certain that all relevant variables have been identified and isolated in this way (Keith, 2006). Nonetheless, statistical methods of control are valuable because they permit scientists to begin to isolate the presumed cause-effect relationship from other relevant variables. In this way, the justification for causality may be supported, although the knowledge claim remains weaker than the warrant that can be obtained by means of a true experiment.

The fourth criterion needed to conclusively establish causality is the need for a *causal explanation* that specifies how the variables are related and what mechanisms are at work. In other words, we need to apply a theoretical framework to explain the causal relationships and evaluate the total body of research evidence that has been obtained in all the relevant studies (Abelson, 1995; Phillips, 1987, 1992). The theoretical framework may serve as a primary source of research hypotheses, and, in turn, the theoretical framework may be modified or revised based on the empirical evidence that exists in a given area. The importance of theory as a necessary framework with which to evaluate the warrant for causality in a body of empirical findings is highlighted in most contemporary approaches to social science (Abelson, 1995; Goodwin & Goodwin, 2012; Phillips, 1987; Serlin, 1987; Tracey & Glidden-Tracey, 1999).

Given the logical criteria needed to conclusively establish causality, it is highly unlikely that any single study will be sufficiently rigorous on all dimensions to permit a strong warrant for a given knowledge claim. For example, most of us would readily accept that there is a causal relationship between smoking and lung cancer. However, there is no single study that conclusively establishes this causal relationship. In fact, most of the evidence that smoking causes lung cancer is correlational data, and for many years apologists (such as tobacco company executives) claimed that there was insufficient evidence to conclude that the link was causal. In reviewing this body of research, Abelson (1995) noted that the causal explanation that links smoking to lung cancer is based on the fact that, when tobacco smoke comes into contact with lung tissue, the smoke damages the tissue. Moreover, numerous empirical findings from a number of separate research studies on smoking are tied to this hypothesis:

1. The longer a person has smoked cigarettes, the greater the risk of cancer.
2. The more cigarettes a person smokes over a given time period, the greater the risk of cancer.
3. People who stop smoking have lower cancer rates than those who keep smoking.
4. Smokers' cancers tend to occur in the lungs, and be of a particular type.
5. Smokers have elevated rates of other diseases.
6. People who smoke cigars or pipes and do not usually inhale have abnormally high rates of lip cancer.

7. Smokers of filter-tipped cigarettes have lower cancer rates than other cigarette smokers.
8. Non-smokers who live with smokers have elevated cancer rates. (Abelson, 1995, pp. 183–184).

If there were some other variable or variables that plausibly accounts for the relationship between smoking and lung cancer, then it would be very difficult to explain why all of these findings were obtained. In addition, for the hypothesized causal explanation to be plausible, there can be no anomalous results in the research literature. In other words, there should be no findings that are not explained by the causal relationship. Abelson (1995) referred to this approach as the *method of signatures.* It is this total body of positive and negative findings, taken together and linked to a plausible, causal explanation, that represents the signature of the causal relationship or process.

Building on the work of Mill, Sir Karl Popper (1959, 1976) made important contributions to causal analysis in the twentieth century. His contribution included a systematic focus on the necessity of basing the warrant for knowledge on ruling out all alternative explanations of a phenomenon so that only a single, conceivable explanation will remain. Popper termed this a *falsificationist* approach to knowledge production. According to Popper, even after the most impressive validation or confirmation of a given prediction related to causal relationships, the status of the causal proposition is that it is *not yet disconfirmed* rather than that it is *true* (i.e., confirmed). Most experts (Cook, 1985; Kincaid, 1996; Phillips, 1987; 1992; Shadish, 1995) agree with Popper that science is not ultimately capable of positively confirming causal propositions. Rather, what scientific methods can do is eliminate (using logic, research design strategies, and statistical methods) as many rival explanations as possible and, using strong tests, fail to disconfirm the causal proposition. In this way, scientific knowledge is best regarded as tentative, as the "best we know at this time." Scientific conclusions always remain subject to revision pending future attempts at disconfirmation.

STATUS OF THE SOCIAL SCIENCES

The goal of the social sciences is to develop theories of human behavior, which consist of an interrelated network of knowledge statements that are internally consistent and grounded in observations (Heppner et al., 2015). Throughout most of the twentieth century social scientists used a quantitative model of investigation borrowed from the physical sciences. The hope was that using these methods and assumptions would lead to comparable advancement in the social sciences as had been demonstrated in the physical sciences. One of the primary assumptions borrowed from the physical sciences and adapted to the social sciences was the assumption of "correspondence," that the veracity of theoretical propositions could be evaluated according to how well they correspond to objective observations (Heppner et al., 2015; Phillips, 1987).

However, as social scientists adopted more sophisticated models of human behavior that are consistent with observation, they came to realize the extent to which human perception, motivation, and behavior depend on the subjective experience of the person in the context of his or her living and relating to others (Heppner et al., 2015; Livneh, 2016). In other words, the social realities that are studied by social scientists, including rehabilitation researchers, are constructed out of the values and experience of a given culture, including, in the West, the values and ideals of science. The notion that human perception is a passive process by which we apprehend an objective, unchanging reality has been replaced by the understanding that perception is an active, interpretive process that is linked to personal, historical, and cultural contexts and goals (Bishop, 2012; Goodwin & Goodwin, 2012; Phillips, 2002; Polkinghorne, 1991). As Phillips (1987) stated, "the theory, hypothesis, or background knowledge held by an investigator can strongly influence what is observed" (p. 9). Most contemporary philosophers of science question the so-called objective stance of the observer and maintain that value-free, objective observation is not possible. Thus, there is less faith today that an objective, social reality is lawful in the same sense as the natural world and is capable of yielding its secrets using the methods borrowed from the physical sciences.

The development of the social sciences in the twentieth and twenty-first centuries reflects the interplay of theory building, observation, and consensus-making in the scientific enterprise. Theories or models are developed to explain increasingly large "chunks" of observational data. In turn, the propositions of a given theory are tested by new research, and the theory is revised according to the new findings. As a theory or model becomes less viable (that is, subject to more caveats, exceptions, and disconfirmation by observation) it is revised or superseded by a new, more inclusive theory. In the social sciences, it is widely appreciated that human behavior is multidetermined, that is, results from the complex interplay of numerous person and environmental variables (Heppner et al., 2015; Rosnow & Georgoudi, 1986). The nature of the subject matter in the social sciences, human behavior and volition, does not currently permit theories of sufficient complexity to account for the totality of human experience and observation. What we are left with is a much more complex view of the social science enterprise: human behavior in context, which is rooted in subjective perception but which also has objective elements that are capable of being tested and yielding unbiased knowledge about human nature (Cook & Campbell, 1979; Polkinghorne, 1991).

Rather than leading to abandonment of the quest for objective or verifiable knowledge, the "creative chaos" that has characterized social science research over the past four decades has led to renewed efforts to understand the limits of human subjective perception and its effects on science (see, for example, MacCoun, 1998). Moreover, by examining the implications of experimentation in science, social scientists have clarified many issues that are fundamental to testing hypotheses and generating credible findings in real world settings where experimental controls are often not possible (Cook & Campbell, 1979). The creative ferment in the contemporary social sciences has led to renewed attention to the implications of philosophy of science for providing a framework for understanding the distinct contributions of quantitative and qualitative methods to a research program, the role of theory and the purpose of experimentation in science, and the basis for knowledge consensus in the social sciences (see Cook & Campbell, 1979; Manicas & Secord, 1983; Phillips, 1987; Shadish, 1995) and in counseling (see Polkinghorne, 1991; Serlin, 1987; Strong, 1991). Contemporary philosophers of science acknowledge that there is no ideal source of knowledge or absolute foundational criteria (e.g., sense data, reason) for judging or demonstrating that a particular knowledge claim is sound (Goodwin & Goodwin, 2012; Harre, 1986; Phillips, 1987). Rather, knowledge claims are defended by making the best case possible by marshaling good arguments, explanatory theory, and empirical evidence (relevant observations and solid experimental results).

THE PURPOSES OF REHABILITATION COUNSELING RESEARCH

Rehabilitation counseling research has the fundamental practical goals of improving the lives of people with disabilities and enhancing their participation in society. Moreover, the preceding discussion of science as a method of establishing the validity of propositions about human realities should make it clear that a helping profession based on objective and verifiable information is more likely to result in practical benefits than a profession based on personal experience, tradition, intuition, or authority (Heppner et al., 2015; Rubin, Roessler, & Rumrill, 2016). Also, realizing the practical benefits of a scientific approach to knowledge in rehabilitation counseling is contingent on the ability of rehabilitation counselors to translate scientific principles and research-based findings to their practices.

Unfortunately, many graduate students in rehabilitation counseling and practicing rehabilitation counselors question the value of learning about rehabilitation counseling research or doing research within their work setting (Bolton & Parker, 1998; Roessler, Rubin, & Rumrill, 2017). Students prefer that graduate instruction focus exclusively on techniques of rehabilitation counseling service delivery (Bellini & Rumrill, 2009; Rubin & Rice, 1986), and typically feel that, in their future role as rehabilitation counselors, they will not engage in research or utilize research findings in their practice (Leahy et al., 2013). Many professional rehabilitation counselors do not consider research to be relevant to the practical, everyday issues of serving individuals with disabilities. For example, in an investigation of the perceived competencies and training needs of practicing rehabilitation counselors, Leahy et al. (2013) reported that, among 15 professional competency areas, practitioners considered knowledge of program evaluation and research to be least important to their professional roles.

This negative attitude toward research is not specific to rehabilitation counseling. Rather, it is a common attitude of counselors and counseling students of all varieties (Anderson & Heppner, 1985; Heppner et al., 2015). Despite this, course work in research is a standard part of graduate instruction for counselors including rehabilitation counselors. Research instruction is also a key requirement for graduate rehabilitation counseling programs that are accredited by the Council on Rehabilitation Education (CORE, 2017).

We believe that the responsibility for the negative attitudes of students and practitioners falls squarely on the shoulders of rehabilitation counselor educators rather than students or practitioners. To become competent practitioners, students need to know the principles and methods of research design as well as how to utilize research findings in their everyday practice. To engage in relevant research, rehabilitation researchers need to collaborate with rehabilitation practitioners, administrators, and persons with disabilities in the design, implementation, and analysis stages of the research process (Bellini & Rumrill, 2009; Seelman, 1998). Educators need to teach rehabilitation research concepts within the context of professional practice so that students and practitioners are able to understand and utilize research findings to improve their practice (Koch & Rumrill, 2016; Schaller & Parker, 1997; Syzmanski, Whitney-Thomas, Marshall, & Sayger, 1994). Heppner et al. (2015) provided a number of valuable recommendations for enhancing the efficacy of research instruction in graduate counseling programs.

It is important for students to develop an appreciation for rehabilitation counseling research by understanding the contribution of scientific research in the development of the rehabilitation counseling profession. Several interrelated purposes of scientific research as applied to rehabilitation counseling include (a) build the professional knowledge base of rehabilitation counseling, (b) develop theory to guide rehabilitation counseling practice, and (c) identify effective rehabilitation counseling practices.

Build the Professional Knowledge Base

Rehabilitation research is a young field of inquiry, having its formal genesis in the 1954 Amendments to the Vocational Rehabilitation Act (Bolton, 1979). Partly as a function of this relative youth, rehabilitation counseling research is a hybrid, multidisciplinary field of inquiry that draws many of its essential concepts, theoretical models, and new technologies from other areas of social science (Roessler et al., in press), particularly medical science, psychology, and sociology. For example, continuing advances in medical technology since World War II have resulted in significant reductions of mortality following severe traumas such as spinal cord injuries. Greater survival rates following spinal cord injury led, in turn, to better understanding of the psychological and social processes of adjusting to an acquired, severe physical disability and a new focus on the role of rehabilitation services in promoting employment and community integration. The application of new technologies in rehabilitation has permitted many individuals with severe physical disabilities to attain greater independence and social participation than was possible in earlier decades. Medical advances led, in turn, to conceptual advances in rehabilitation counseling and new models of service delivery. The recent attention in the professional literature to psychosocial and service delivery issues in the rehabilitation of individuals with traumatic brain injuries is an example of this process of "cascading advancement" in rehabilitation that begins in the medical domain and extends to the areas of service delivery and community integration.

In addition to borrowing many of its fundamental concepts, models, and assessment approaches from related fields, rehabilitation counseling research has built a significant base of knowledge that is specific to the unique issues, concerns, and needs of persons with disabilities, rehabilitation counselors, and administrators. It is this combination of a multidisciplinary focus and domain-specific knowledge exemplified by rehabilitation counseling that can develop a knowledge base of sufficient breadth and depth to respond adequately to the complexity of issues facing people with disabilities (Koch & Rumrill, 2016; Stubbins, 1984). The multidisciplinary nature of rehabilitation counseling places heavy demands on rehabilitation counselors to keep pace with technological and conceptual advances as a means of effectively serving the changing needs, goals, and perspectives of people with disabilities (Rubin et al., 2016).

Research has also served to build the professional knowledge base by identifying the specific professional competencies, knowledge, and job functions that are unique to rehabilitation counseling (Leahy et al., 2003, 2013; Rubin et al., 2016). The long and distinguished history of research on the roles and competencies of rehabilitation practitioners (Muthard & Salomone, 1969; Rubin, Matkin, Ashley, Beardsley, May, Onstott, & Puckett, 1984) has served as an empirical basis for curriculum development in graduate rehabilitation counseling programs. By applying research findings, graduate programs constantly revise their curricula to reflect advances in the theory and practice of rehabilitation counseling. This body of knowledge has also helped to refine and distinguish the profession of rehabilitation counseling from other helping professions that in some aspects may overlap with rehabilitation counseling but that have different orientations (e.g., social work, occupational therapy).

Develop Theory to Guide Rehabilitation Counseling Practice

Numerous authors have stressed that rehabilitation counseling needs to develop a comprehensive theoretical base to guide professional practice (e.g., Arokiasamy, 1993). According to Patterson (1986), a comprehensive theory:

> organizes, interprets, and states in the form of laws and principles the facts and knowledge in an area or field. The organization or arrangement of what we know makes possible a systematic description from which explanations and predictions can be derived that can then be systematically tested. . . . An explanatory theory gives a sense of understanding, direction, and rationality to practice. It provides a guide to application, extension, extrapolation, and modification in new and different situations. (p. xix)

A systematic body of theory is one factor (along with professional ethics, standards of credentialing and licensure, and academic respectability) that distinguishes a profession from other groups of skilled workers (Arokiasamy, 1993). In other words, an appropriate and unique theoretical foundation lends credibility to the claim that a particular occupational group is an independent profession, and it is the chief factor that distinguishes a profession from a highly skilled occupation (e.g., gem cutters, draftspersons, etc.). Theory plays a pivotal role in the development of consensus and the organization of knowledge within a given profession. A comprehensive theory articulates the unifying philosophy, organizes principles and facts into a unifying framework, provides a recognizable identity to practitioners and other stakeholders, and enables greater consensus on what constitutes valid processes, models, and outcomes.

Rehabilitation counseling, like the social sciences in general, currently lacks a fundamental, comprehensive theory. Criteria by which the value of a theory is evaluated include simplicity (parsimony), interpretability, usefulness, generalizability, testability, and logical consistency (Forsyth & Strong, 1986). Of these characteristics of "good" theory, explanatory power (interpretability; generalizability) and practical application (usefulness) are among the most important criteria to practitioners.

Over the past few decades, several general theories have been advanced as a basis for understanding and organizing the professional knowledge base of rehabilitation counseling, including the psychomedical (Cottone & Emener, 1990), systems (Cottone, (1987), systems/ecological (Hershenson, 2010), minority-group (Hahn, 1985), and work adjustment theories (Dawis, 2005). These general frameworks have considerable heuristic value for educators, students, and practitioners, but they have not been especially fruitful for generating theory-based research in rehabilitation counseling (Bellini & Rumrill, 2009). Given its strongly pragmatic orientation, rehabilitation counseling research has focused primarily on providing answers to pressing practical issues related to providing services to people with disabilities.

The view that rehabilitation counseling has a deficient theoretical foundation may also be a consequence of a failure to adequately distinguish between theories and models (Mpofu, 2000). These terms are often used synonymously but may be distinguished in terms of their generality. Theories are more general than models, and models typically operate at an intermediate level of conceptualization (Bellini & Rumrill, 2009). Also, a single theory may spawn several, competing models (e.g., the theory of evolution has produced several competing models to account for the dynamics of evolutionary change). A theoretical model may be regarded as "mini-theory," or a simplified version of events, variables, and processes.

A number of theoretical models or frameworks of varying degrees of specificity and generalizability have guided rehabilitation research efforts and informed practice, and they reflect the valuable interplay between theory development and resolution of practical issues in rehabilitation counseling research. For example, Wright (1983) theorized, based on a synthesis of social psychological research and clinical observations, that the process of adjustment to disability is facilitated when the individual can modify personal values to accommodate capabilities and limitations associated with the disability. Wright's theory of value changes provides practitioners with tools for understanding the relationships among personal values, beliefs about disability, and subsequent adjustment of persons with acquired disabilities.

Alston (1992) showed how Wright's theory of value changes and adjustment also explains adjustment processes experienced by individuals with substance abuse disorders. Thus, Wright's theory was shown to be applicable, or generalizable, to other populations of people with disabilities besides people with acquired physical disabilities.

The development of theoretical models has been and continues to be a rich source of research propositions in rehabilitation counseling, and the interplay between model development and empirical tests of these propositions reflects the vitality of the research tradition in our profession. As Phillips (1992) noted, the presence of dynamic theory–or model-based research programs is an important indicator of the viability of a research tradition.

In recent years, a number of new or revised theoretical models of disability and related constructs have been proposed, including the International Classification of Function (ICF) model of disability (World Health Organization, 2001), the empowerment model (Koscielek, 1999), the poverty disability model (Lustig & Strauser, 2007; Strauser, 2013), the quality of life/disability centrality model (Bishop, 2012), and models of vocational rehabilitation service provision (Bolton, Bellini, & Brookings, 2000; Kosciulek, 2004). Each of these models frames disability and the rehabilitation process as a complex interaction of personal, environmental, and systems variables, and each model serves to organize and explain hypothesized relationships among personal, environmental, and experiential phenomena in the lives of people with disabilities and/or service providers. It is more common than in previous decades for rehabilitation investigators to utilize these and other model-driven frameworks to guide the development of their research programs and to design individual studies to test, either wholly or in part, specific theoretical propositions. A large body of rehabilitation counseling literature is devoted to applying theoretical or conceptual models to rehabilitation counseling practice. One of the most vital purposes of rehabilitation counseling research is to empirically verify the validity of these conceptual models for rehabilitation practice by testing theory generated propositions against real world observations.

Identify Effective Rehabilitation Counseling Practices

A third key role of rehabilitation counseling research is to identify effective rehabilitation counseling practices. A large body of rehabilitation counseling research is devoted to the development and evaluation of rehabilitation interventions. Many intervention studies are published in rehabilitation counseling journals such as *Rehabilitation Counseling Bulletin, Journal of Applied Rehabilitation Counseling, Journal of Rehabilitation,* and the *Journal of Vocational Rehabilitation, Work,* and *Rehabilitation Psychology.*

However, availability of research is not the same thing as accessibility of research. For practicing rehabilitation counselors to access and use the professional literature, they must have a working knowledge of research design and methodology. At a minimum, it is important for rehabilitation counseling practitioners to have the research utilization skills needed to evaluate findings from published research and apply these to their professional practice, so that they stay current with developments in the field of rehabilitation counseling and can use the most valid and effective practices and technologies available in their daily work with people with disabilities.

Professional rehabilitation counselors are often routinely required to collect and record data on clients, services, and outcomes that are used to demonstrate the effectiveness of the services the agency provides (Roessler et al., 2017). In the present era of tightened funding, agencies and practitioners alike are being called upon to demonstrate that the services they provide are cost-effective and result in successful outcomes. Because of changes in the manner in which medical and social services are delivered, it is likely that professionals in the field will need to be more competent in the principles of the scientific method and their application to service provision (Crystal & Espinosa, 2012; Dellario, 1996). In other words, rehabilitation counselors need to acquire the skills needed to understand and apply scientific methodology in their daily practice to complement their skills as practitioners and demonstrate the effectiveness of rehabilitation services.

THE SCIENTIST-PRACTITIONER MODEL OF REHABILITATION COUNSELOR EDUCATION

Most graduate training programs in psychology, counseling, and rehabilitation counseling are founded, at least implicitly, on the scientist-practitioner model of training, known as the Boulder model (Dellario, 1996; Goodyear & Benton, 1986; Heppner et al., 2015), which consists of graduate training in both scientific and practitioner activities. The model is typically conceived as a continuum of emphasis in graduate training. Graduate training at the doctoral level focuses more heavily on the scientist end of the scientist-practitioner continuum, whereas practitioner activities and research utilization skills are emphasized in master's level programs (Dellario, 1996; Heppner et al., 2015). In rehabilitation counseling, knowledge standards related to understanding and using research are articulated in the CORE standards of accreditation for masters' level graduate programs and the Commission for Rehabilitation Counselor Certification (CRCC) professional knowledge standards (CORE, 2017).

Meara et al. (1988) articulated the essence of the scientist-practitioner model of counselor education:

> The scientist-practitioner model is an integrated approach to knowledge that recognizes the interdependence of theory, research, and practice. The model emphasizes systematic and thoughtful analyses of human experiences and judicious application of the knowledge and attitudes gained from such analyses. An attitude of scholarly inquiry is critical to all the activities of those educated in the scientist-practitioner model. (p. 368)

Thus, one key focus of the scientist-practitioner model is that all counselors, regardless of their professional activities, need to develop the scientific reasoning skills that are reflected in a scientific approach to knowledge. A background in research is necessary for practitioners to make informed analyses of professional counseling techniques, to critically evaluate research findings and draw appropriate implications for practice, and to sharpen analytical skills (Bolton, 1986; Remer, 1981). Training in scientific reasoning skills refers to a controlled method of inquiry and reasoning, beginning with a research question or hypothesis, collecting data for the purpose of confirming or disconfirming the hypothesis, interpreting the data, and revising the knowledge claim based on the findings. The scientist-practitioner model is rooted in the application of the self-corrective nature of the scientific method of thinking to counseling practice (Bellini & Rumrill, 1999b; Spengler, Stromer, Dixon, & Shivy, 1995).

Training in scientific reasoning skills allows rehabilitation counselors to view their assumptions as tentative, problematic, and subject to revision when they fail to conform to observations and other empirical data. The practice of developing alternate, rival hypotheses for client data can provide a "check" on the counselor's initial (or subsequent) impressions that may be inaccurate and negatively influence counseling practice (Roessler et al., 2017). Thus, an important advantage of approaching practice in a scientific manner is that it is easier to correct misperceptions and biases (Spengler et al., 1995; Tracey, 1991). If counselors learn to regard their initial judgments as tentative hypotheses and evaluate these on the basis of empirical observations, they can identify, examine, and change their assumptions because these are explicit and operationalized rather than implicit and unexamined. The scientific approach to actively testing alternate assumptions (i.e., hypotheses) against observations is a critical feature that distinguishes professional counselors from lay counselors, in large part because of the self-corrective features of the scientific method (Spengler et al., 1995).

A second focus of the scientist-practitioner model is that the research process closely parallels the procedures that skilled counselors use in their work with individual clients (Heppner et al., 2015; Strohmer & Newman, 1983). As Figure 1.1 indicates, the various stages of rehabilitation service provision parallel specific research activities. Hence, the first stage in service provision is assessment of relevant personal, social, and environmental characteristics of an individual with a disability. Assessment is fundamentally an effort to observe and accurately describe the pertinent aspects of the situation in which the individual is embedded. As effective service provision is founded on detailed assessment, the scientific/research enterprise is founded on accurate observation and description. From the data gathered in the assessment phase, counselors begin to conceptualize the goals, issues, assets, and challenges of the individual. In this phase of the service process, the counselor integrates these elements into a congruent "theory" of the case, and from this theory/case conceptualization, the counselor begins to develop specific hypotheses related to the case. Service planning is the next stage of the service process. Service planning often implies a prediction of probable outcomes based on the provision of a specific sequence of services. Prediction studies in rehabilitation may inform service planning by providing group data that may assist the counselor and client in making informed choices about likely consequences of different courses of action. Service provision is the next phase of the process, and services are the specific interventions in rehabilitation. In the research process, the development and testing of interventions closely parallels the phase of service provision. Finally, case reporting is the final phase in service provision. Case reporting provides a record of all relevant data gathered during the previous four phases of service provision, and these data are essential for an evaluation of the benefits derived from participation in the process. Program evaluation serves a similar capstone function and is a concrete application of scientific principles to evaluation of human service programs. Thus, scientific methods contribute directly to more effective practice in every phase of service provision.

The Crux Model (Roessler et al., 2017) is an example of an explicit application of scientific thinking (i.e., hypothesis testing) to vocational assessment and service planning. In the Crux Model rehabilitation counselors apply the skills of generating and testing hypotheses relative to the task of identifying appropriate vocational objectives for individuals with disabilities. Information on clients' past, current, and potential physical, psychosocial, and educational functioning are analyzed in relation to available medical, psychological, educational-vocational, placement, and financial support services in order to develop hypotheses regarding the vocational alternatives that are both attainable and consistent with the clients' vocational goals. The counselor treats these hypotheses as tentative conclusions to be tested against observations and modifies them when the data fail to confirm them. The coun-

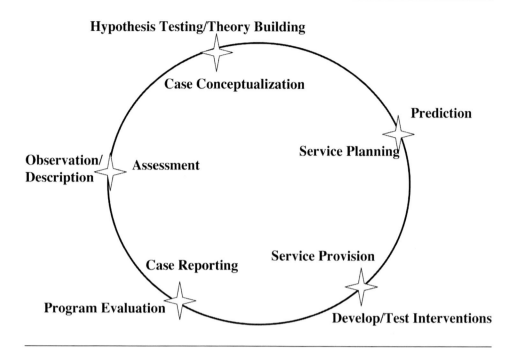

Figure 1.1. Research Activities in the Rehabilitation Counseling Process.

selor is then prepared to facilitate a parallel analysis by the client, leading to enhanced client/counselor agreement on the client's vocational goals, intermediate objectives, and associated services needed to facilitate the client's achievement of these goals. The Crux Model is an example of how rehabilitation counselors can use hypothesis generation and testing to identify vocational options and enhance counselor/client agreement and client success in the rehabilitation process.

In the past, research training in graduate rehabilitation counseling programs focused primarily on developing the analytical skills and scholarly habits needed for students to become informed consumers of research findings. Research competencies that are necessary for informed practitioners include the ability to read, understand, and evaluate research publications, distill the important ideas from these, and translate research-based knowledge to their own counseling practice (Bolton, 1986). The implication is that rehabilitation counselors who are literate in research principles and methods, and who approach their practice with an attitude of scholarly inquiry, apply this knowledge to differentiate and utilize rehabilitation research findings to improve their practice (Bolton, 1986; Dellario, 1996; Rubin & Rice, 1986).

Dellario (1996) suggested that the purpose of research education at the masters' level should not be restricted to developing research utilization skills and scholarly attitudes that are relevant to practitioners. Rather, as a result of the changing demands of the rehabilitation marketplace, the research component of graduate education should also prepare students for *doing* research. Crystal and Espinosa (2012) noted that the forces of health care cost containment (e.g., managed care) are shaping the future of how medical and rehabilitation services are delivered. Programs are expected to be more accountable, more productive, and more capable of demonstrating successful outcomes. Programs are also expected to be more efficient, have better understanding of what works and does not work with clients, and produce documentation based on empirical evidence of successful outcomes.

Outcome assessment, quality assurance and improvement, and program evaluation are examples of areas that are stressed in the managed care environment and where research skills are needed (Brodwin, 2016). "Individuals are needed who have a clinical understanding of the needs and potentials of persons with disabilities so that data can be interpreted relative to these needs and potentials. The ability to work with data, to perform research procedures, and to interact with computer technology are essential in the data-driven decision-making systems such as managed care" (Dellario, 1996, p. 229). Thus, Dellario's perspective is that masters' level rehabilitation counselors need the skills to conduct and utilize research in order to ensure that they continue to have a legitimate role in the changing rehabilitation marketplace.

The need for rehabilitation counselors to have research and program evaluation skills is not restricted to the proprietary rehabilitation systems that are most strongly influenced by managed care. Increasingly, these skills are needed in not-for-profit community rehabilitation agencies that are also under pressure to increase the efficiency of their service provision to people with disabilities. Agencies that demonstrate their efficiency in producing measurable, successful outcomes will likely be rewarded with greater funding in future years, whereas agencies that cannot demonstrate successful performance will likely see their funding reduced (Rubin et al., 2016). Thus, there is increased need for masters' level counselors in the not-for-profit service sector who can (a) utilize research findings to improve agency practice, and (b) plan and conduct research, particularly program evaluation research, for their home agencies.

Dellario (1996) advocated that rehabilitation counselor education be built more solidly on the scientist-practitioner model. A stronger focus on training in utilizing research findings in practice and conducting field-oriented research "sends a clear signal that graduates of rehabilitation counselor education programs have both the clinical base and the quantitative sophistication that is essential for the provision of quality clinical services and the documentation of the effectiveness of those services" (Dellario, 1996, p. 230). We share the still-timely opinion of Dellario that contemporary master's level rehabilitation counselors need the skills to conduct and utilize research to ensure that they maintain their professional roles in the rapidly changing rehabilitation marketplace.

Spengler et al. (1995) noted that scientific reasoning skills should be infused into all phases of the counseling curriculum, rather than being confined to a single class on research methods. We agree and have provided some examples of how research activities can be integrated into various classes in the rehabilitation curriculum (see Bellini & Rumrill, 1999b). The benefits of training in the scientist-practitioner model are not only skill based, they are also directed to the development of positive attitudes toward science and application of scientific reasoning skills to counseling practice. To improve their clinical judgment it is vital for counselors to maintain an attitude of curiosity and openness to new or alternative explanations for individual clients' experiences. "A scientific attitude is humane and is characterized by curiosity and caution in judgments. These qualities comprise the prerequisites of a scientific attitude in counseling because they reflect a complex, open, informed, and tentative approach to the study and treatment of human challenges" (Spengler et al., 1995, p. 521).

THE POLITICS OF REHABILITATION COUNSELING RESEARCH

Rehabilitation research does not take place in a vacuum and should not be regarded as a simplistic search for scientific "truth." Rather, rehabilitation research, like science in general, takes place within particular social, historical, and political contexts and is strongly influenced by these factors. It is important for graduate students in rehabilitation counseling to understand the political dimensions of rehabilitation counseling research. Most research in rehabilitation is funded by the Federal government through the National Institute on Disability, Independent Living, and Rehabilitation Research (NIDILRR), the National Institutes of Health (NIH), or the Centers for Disease Control (CDC). Public policy and political mandates substantially influence both the specific priorities in rehabilitation counseling research and the money available to researchers to implement research projects.

Disability and rehabilitation research have been substantially politicized over the past five decades. Beginning with early advocates in the independent living movement, disability activists, both academic and laypersons, have argued successfully that disability is inherently a political phenomenon, pertaining to *whom* social resources are allocated to, *what* resources are allocated (typically public benefits such as services, income replacement, and health care), and *how* social benefits are allocated (e.g., by what processes or mechanisms; Hartley, 2012; Toriello & Keferl, 2012). With the passage of the Americans with Disabilities Act (ADA) in 1990 and the ADA Amendments Act in 2008, people with disabilities have established themselves as an empowered political constituency to protect their civil rights and ensure equal access to the same goods, services, and resources that all citizens should enjoy. A primary goal of the contemporary disability rights movement, "nothing about us without us" (Charlton, 1998; Rubin et al., 2016; Smart, 2009), has become a central focus of disability and rehabilitation researchers and impacts all phases of the research process from establishing priorities at the Federal level to conducting research in community settings.

Thus, one of the most significant influences on the process and content of contemporary rehabilitation research is the increased involvement of people with disabilities as valued partners in the research enterprise (Graves, 1991; Seelman, 1998; NIDILRR, 2017). Rehabilitation research for many years was something done "to" people with disabilities. Although it has been mandated by the Rehabilitation Act since 1973, consumer involvement did not substantially impact the rehabilitation research agenda or enterprise for many years (Seelman, 1998). Current Federal policy emphasizes the reform of disability and rehabilitation research in the context of the principles articulated by the ADA (NIDILRR, 2017). These principles challenge the research community to involve people with disabilities in all phases of the research process, including:

> increasing the involvement of people with disabilities in all aspects of research, including setting the research agenda, developing research questions, participating in decision making about what projects are funded by government agencies, participating in carrying out research as researchers, advisors, and consultants, testing research ideas and providing feedback to researchers and meaningfully analyzing research findings. (Seelman, 1997, p. 8)

The increased participation of people with disabilities in all aspects of rehabilitation research has two important consequences. First, the research agenda is broadened to include aspects of the environment that impede the participation of people with disabilities, rather than focusing on individual deviance and the central role of the professional. Secondly, by responding to issues of importance to people with disabilities (who are the ultimate beneficiaries of rehabilitation research), research can potentially have greater relevance for and impact in their daily lives (Seelman, 1997). Current Federal policy emphasizes that the central goal for federally funded research is to enhance the participation of persons with disabilities in their communities (NIDILRR, 2017).

A second, major influence on the knowledge base and research agenda in rehabilitation counseling is the development of the new model of disability, which maintains that the limitations associated with disability are largely due to non-accommodating environments and discriminatory attitudes of persons without disabilities rather than functional deficits associated with having disabilities (Livneh, 2016; Seelman, 1998; World Health Organization, 2001). The new model of disability serves as the organizing structure for all research projects funded by NIDILRR and emphasizes the role of the environment as a causal factor related to rehabilitation outcomes (NIDILRR, 2017). Consistent with this new model and emphasis on participation outcomes, there is a great need for programs of research to examine the role of architectural and attitudinal barriers that inhibit participation as well as accommodations and supports that facilitate participation for persons with various types of functional impairments and disabilities. There is also a great need to better understand what participation means to persons with various disabilities. The new model of disability also challenges rehabilitation practitioners to (a) establish partnerships with people with disabilities in the delivery of rehabilitation services, and (b) examine the present and future roles of the professional in the delivery of rehabilitation counseling services and develop new competencies (e.g., advocacy) to better fulfill these roles and serve the needs of people with disabilities (Seelman, 1998).

A third vital area for contemporary and future rehabilitation counseling research, also associated with social, cultural, and political developments–in this case, the changing demographics of America–is the need to improve the quality of services and outcomes for persons with disabilities from racial and ethnic minority backgrounds. Given the increasingly multicultural demography of the United States, the economic disadvantages of persons from racial and ethnic minorities, and the intersection of gender, race, disability and economics, it is likely that multicultural issues will continue to be a primary focus of rehabilitation counseling research and practice for many decades.

Because the pursuit of scientific knowledge takes place within the context of broader historical, cultural, and political processes, there is likely to be spirited disagreement among various stakeholders regarding the fundamental agenda or purposes of rehabilitation counseling research. One area of contentious discussion concerns the research agenda devoted to validating enhanced professionalization of rehabilitation counselors. For example, Thomas (1990) criticized the rehabilitation counseling profession for devoting too much research time and effort to empirically validate the superior service outcomes associated with rehabilitation graduate education rather than dedicating more effort to promoting the welfare of people with disabilities on humanistic grounds. Others view empirical validation of rehabilitation counseling graduate education as essential for establishing public confidence in the profession of rehabilitation counseling and promoting quality assurance in the services that people with disabilities receive (Bolton, 1979; Leahy et al., 2013; Leahy & Szymanski, 1995). The lack of agreement among experts in rehabilitation counseling is a sign of the essential health of the profession that reflects a diversity of informed opinions in a time when the tentativeness of scientific knowledge in all areas, particularly in the social sciences, is the rule rather than the exception.

SUMMARY

The goal of the social sciences is to develop valid knowledge about human realities. The fundamental aims of rehabilitation research are to understand the consequences of disability on psychological and social functioning, and identify effective practices that facilitate the successful adjustment and participation of persons with disabilities in environments of their choice. Research methods are tools for establishing and verifying knowledge. Two distinct approaches to developing knowledge are qualitative and quantitative methods. Qualitative research methods are oriented toward identifying thematic, conceptual categories and developing theoretical propositions based on interviews with informants and in-depth personal observation.

Quantitative research methods involve the transcription of words and observations into numbers for the purpose of summarization, classification, analysis, interpretation, and generalization. The complexity of the subject matter of the social sciences—human motivation, volition, and behavior—requires that multiple methods of research inquiry be utilized.

Knowledge comes from a variety of sources, including personal experience, intuition, tradition, and authority. Scientific knowledge claims, like claims that ensue from other sources, are rooted in social and historical processes of consensus building. However, science (ideally) represents an ongoing, self-correcting method of generating and verifying knowledge claims, and it differs from more mundane sources of knowledge in that it is based on adherence to a specific set of norms that govern the research enterprise. These norms are common to both qualitative and quantitative research methods, and include universal standards for knowledge claims, common ownership of information, cultivated disinterestedness, and organized skepticism.

Science has two fundamental goals, to provide answers to practical problems and to develop theoretical propositions or models that explain empirical observations. Theory building and testing proceed through an interplay of inductive and deductive logic. Scientific research has contributed to the rehabilitation counseling profession in three essential ways: (a) build the professional knowledge base, (b) develop and test theories to guide practice, and (c) identify effective practices. Ultimately, the contributions of research to the rehabilitation counseling profession are defined by the answers that research provides to resolve the practical issues facing people with disabilities and the professionals who work with them, and the development of explanatory theories that provide a framework for organizing and understanding the professional knowledge base.

The purpose of the scientist-practitioner model of rehabilitation graduate education is to develop master's level practitioners who can successfully apply the self-corrective methods of scientific thinking to their professional practice as rehabilitation counselors. Master's level training in rehabilitation research methods is predicated on the assumption that counselors who are literate in scientific methods of investigation and who approach their practice with an attitude of scholarly inquiry will utilize research findings to improve their practice. Also, master's level rehabilitation counselors who have the ability to apply scientific principles and conduct research will be more competitive in the changing rehabilitation marketplace.

Rehabilitation research, like science in general, is strongly influenced by social, historical, and political contexts, and has been substantially politicized over the past several decades. Three important influences on the process and content of rehabilitation research emerging from the contemporary political context are (a) the involvement of people with disabilities in all phases of research, (b) the development of the new model of disability that emphasizes the role of the environment, and (c) the focus on multicultural issues that affect the rehabilitation process. Each of these issues influences the contemporary agenda of rehabilitation research and challenges both researchers and practitioners to embrace new attitudes, learn new skills, and adopt new professional roles. Given the political context of research, there is likely to be considerable disagreement among various stakeholders regarding the future rehabilitation research agenda.

Chapter 2

BEGINNING THE RESEARCH PROCESS: RESEARCH QUESTIONS, VARIABLES, AND SAMPLING ISSUES

INTRODUCTION

Research is rooted in conceptual frameworks or theories; that is, every research investigation begins with an idea or hypothesis. Both qualitative and quantitative research methods are characterized by the careful collection and analysis of data. Indeed, making careful observations to confirm or disconfirm a hypothesis is the sine qua non of scientific investigation. However, between the identification of a fruitful idea for research and the collection and analysis of data are several intermediate, but vital, steps in the research process. This chapter will address issues that are preparatory to designing and evaluating rehabilitation research. It includes sections on phases of the research process, sources of ideas for research, identifying and operationalizing research questions, statistical hypotheses, types of variables, and sampling issues in research.

THE RESEARCH PROCESS

The research process is best understood as a series of interrelated decisions or steps that begins with formulating a research question to be investigated and concludes with an evaluation of the status of the research question based on the empirical findings that have been reported. Figure 2.1 presents the research process as a series of nine phases:

1. Formulate the research question.
2. Define the constructs of interest.

3. Determine the data to be gathered.
4. Determine the appropriate sample.
5. Determine additional research procedures.
6. Gather data.
7. Analyze data.
8. Interpret data.
9. Determine the status of the research question.

It is important to emphasize that most empirical research in the social sciences, including qualitative and quantitative research methodologies, adheres relatively closely to this model, although within these different traditions there are differences in how the steps are accomplished. For example, given the standard, deductive approach to hypothesis testing in the quantitative methodologies, the investigator using these methods typically establishes formal research questions and definitions of the constructs of interest early in the research process. In the qualitative tradition, the investigator may engage in a less formal, open-ended inquiry into the target phenomenon. In all cases, empirical research involves formulating a research question, gathering data from an appropriate sample of individuals or groups, analyzing and interpreting the data, then determining the status of the original questions or hypotheses.

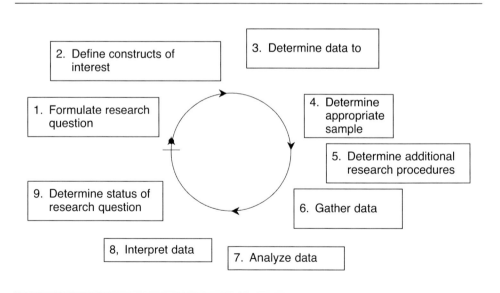

Figure 2.1. The Research Process.

One important consequence of conceptualizing the research process in this fashion is that these decisions are appropriately viewed as being interrelated rather than independent. Decisions made at one stage of the process have implications for subsequent decisions made at later stages, and the strength of the knowledge claim that can be made at the conclusion of the study depends on the coherence or consistency of this series of decisions. Tracey and Glidden-Tracey (1999) have argued for a reasoned approach to research that involves the integration of theory, research design, measurement, and statistical analysis. As they noted, it is far more common for the different components of the research process to be viewed as discrete entities. To promote a reasoned approach to designing and implementing research, Tracey and Glidden-Tracey recommended a shift in conceptualizing research from common questions such as "How should I test this?" What measure should I use?" and/or "What is the best design for my question?" to the more global question "What do I wish to be able to say?" As Tracey and Glidden-Tracey noted, their recommended question requires researchers to approach research conceptualization as a reasoned argument. In this approach, and beginning with the research question that is posed, researchers are encouraged to logically examine the entire research process to consider the assumptions that underlie particular decisions related to theory, design, measurement, and analysis, as well as the likely impacts of decisions made during one phase on subsequent phases. In this way, the overall consistency of the research plan in relation to the research goal is enhanced. When researchers are explicit about their assumptions and decisions, they are better able to evaluate the consequences of particular decisions on the process as a whole, and each decision will make a positive contribution to the knowledge claim that can be made at the conclusion of the study.

SOURCES OF RESEARCH IDEAS

Ideas for research can come from a number of different sources. Simple curiosity, personal interests, past and current rehabilitation counseling practice, service work with community agencies, and ongoing contact with rehabilitation practitioners and/or people with disabilities may provide inspiration for a rehabilitation research project.

Theory is a particularly rich source of research ideas. In an effort to understand phenomena, scholars propose concepts, models, and theories to synthesize ideas, variables, and processes in an orderly fashion and explain how they relate to each other. Often research is undertaken to test specific hypotheses suggested by theories or models. Moreover, there is an ongoing, reciprocal dynamic between theory and research. Theory suggests possible fruitful avenues of research. The theory or model may specify the nature of the relations among its concepts, elements, or processes that can be tested directly, or the researcher may deduce other hypotheses from theory. Research is then implemented to test the predicted relations among the elements of the theory or model. If the researcher's hypothesis is supported by the data analysis, the validity of the theory is strengthened. If the hypothesis is not supported, proponents of the theory need to critically examine the propositions of the theory that failed the empirical test. This process may lead to revision of the theory, new hypotheses, and subsequent tests of these revised hypotheses.

Research efforts are often stimulated by the need to measure or operationalize various constructs. For example, in the early years of rehabilitation, counselors recognized that attitudes toward people with disabilities were key to promoting the gainful employment and acceptance of people with disabilities in society. These observations spawned theories to explain the phenomenon (e.g., Siller's psychodynamic theory of attitudes toward disability) and numerous research efforts to measure the construct "attitudes toward persons with disabilities" (Smart, 2009). In the process of developing and validating measures of attitudes toward disability, a large body of empirical data was generated concerning personality characteristics associated with positive and negative attitudes toward disability, efficacy of various attitude change strategies, and possible distortions (e.g., social desirability, halo effect) to which attitude measures are subject. The development of measurement instruments is both a precondition of quantitative research in the social sciences and a consequence of it.

Most importantly, research is often stimulated by previous efforts in a given area. A substantial proportion of the published research in rehabilitation counseling is directed to building upon or expanding the results of previous studies. It is vital for researchers to have a thorough knowledge of the literature in their area of research interest. This permits them to select a topic for research that is capable of yielding significant new knowledge and that builds on the previous efforts of others. In the discussion section of a research paper, the author will often include suggestions for future research efforts in the given area that are intended to build upon the findings discussed in the paper, address ambiguities in the research findings, or illuminate areas not addressed directly in the paper. These suggestions provide valuable direction for subsequent researchers.

IDENTIFYING AND OPERATIONALIZING RESEARCH QUESTIONS

Constructs and Indicators

Stated most simply, "research explores or examines the relationships among constructs" (Heppner et al., 1999, p. 36). A *construct* is a concept that has no direct physical referent (e.g., intelligence, self-esteem, role, joy, sorrow). Constructs refer to such characteristics as a person's mental state, capacities, or motivations as well as valued social outcomes such as independence, empowerment, and community integration. Constructs are also known as *latent variables* (Loehlin, 1992) because they cannot be directly sensed or perfectly measured. Rather, we must infer their presence from behaviors and other consequences of their existence (Krathwohl, 1993). These manifest variables are known as *indicators* of the construct of interest. Research questions in the social sciences are questions about the relationships between or among constructs, but the research study is an empirical evaluation of the relationships among the indicators of the construct.

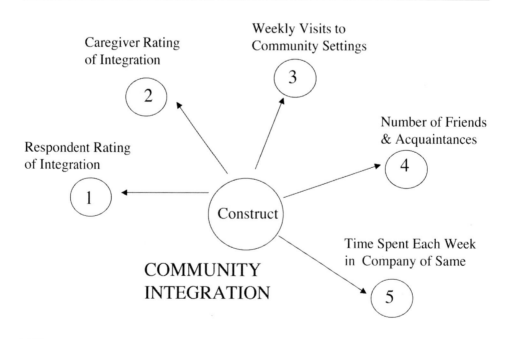

Figure 2.2. Latent Variables (Constructs) and Indicators.

Figure 2.2 is an illustration of a construct—community integration—that has been the focus of considerable attention in rehabilitation research. Grouped around the source construct are five distinct indicators of community integration: self-reported integration, caregiver-reported (observer-rated) integration, weekly visits to community settings, number of friends and acquaintances, and time spent in the company of friends or acquaintances each week. Each indicator has been used to represent the construct of community integration in a published research study, and each indicator is flawed in its own way. For example, self-reported rating of community integration reflects the respondent's own evaluation, but may be distorted, particularly if the research sample includes persons with significant cognitive disabilities. Observer-rating (or caregiver rating) of community integration may remove this particular distortion, but may be inaccurate if the caregiver is not aware of the full range of opportunities and experiences of the subject of the research in regard to community involvement.

The example of community integration illustrates the difficulties present in designing any research. Indicators vary in how well they represent their target construct, and all indicators are flawed in some way or other. Measurement in the social sciences often involves the use of indicators that reflect people's opinions, preferences, or perceptions about a phenomenon. In choosing appropriate indicators, a researcher must often make a determination of whose opinion has the greatest credibility with regard to the phenomenon or construct of interest (Tracey & Glidden-Tracey, 1999).

Research Questions

Researchers generate ideas for their investigations from a number of sources, including personal experience and casual observation, existing theory, and previous investigations of phenomena of interest. Whatever the original idea that provides the impetus for research, it must be described concretely so that it can be tested. The research question is stated in very broad, abstract terms. On occasion the research question that motivates a given study is not stated explicitly in the research article, but it can usually be deduced from a careful reading of the title, the abstract, and the purpose statement that concludes the introductory section of the article (American Psychological Association, 2013). The following is a sampling of research questions drawn from the *Rehabilitation Counseling Bulletin* over the past two decades:

A. What major job functions are perceived by Certified Rehabilitation Counselors (CRC) as important for effective rehabilitation counseling practice? (Leahy, Chan, & Saunders, 2003)

B. What are the effects of extent of disability disclosure in an employment interview and type of disability presented (i.e., physical, psychiatric) on the employability of persons with invisible disabilities? (Dalgin & Bellini, 2008)

C. What are the relationships among client functional capacities and limitations, services provided, and VR outcomes achieved? (Bolton, Bellini, & Brookings, 2000)

Drew (1980) identified three categories of research questions: descriptive, difference, and relationship. Descriptive questions ask what some phenomenon is like. Example A is a descriptive research question because the study sought to describe the job functions that rehabilitation counselors perceive to be important for rehabilitation practice. Difference questions ask if there are differences between groups of people as a function of one or more identified variables. Example B asks a difference question. The research question that motivated the Dalgin and Bellini study was: Are there different consequences for employers' ratings of employability and hiring decisions based on job applicant disability status and the extent of disability disclosure in an employment interview? Example C is a relationship question. The study examined whether and to what degree clients' functional capacities, limitations, and VR services are related to VR employment outcomes.

Operational Definitions

Each of the research questions cited previously represents the fundamental research idea that motivated the given study. However, considerable work is needed to translate these research ideas into an empirical research project that can be executed. The concepts inherent in the broad research question must be operationalized, that is, formulated into operational definitions. Operational definitions refer to defining constructs on the basis of the specific activities and operations used to measure them in the investigation (Heppner, Wampold, Owen, Thompson, & Wang, 2015). Particular measurement instruments are often used to operationalize the constructs inherent in the broad research question. For a knowledge claim to have merit, the manner in which the broad research question is translated into the specific operations of the investigation must make sense to others in the research community.

Operational definitions link the constructs that motivate the study to the specific, measurable events that constitute the data for the empirical test of the research question (Heppner et al., 2015; Kazdin, 2003). The linkage between a construct and its operational definition is a key element in the chain of reasoning leading from formulating a research question to making a warranted knowledge claim based on the results of a study. A weak link between research questions and research operations will reduce the credibility of the knowledge claim no matter how exemplary the investigation may be along other important dimensions (Goodwin & Goodwin, 2012). A second function of the operational definition is to permit replication of the research procedure by other researchers on similar and different samples (Cronbach, 1988).

In example A cited in the previous section on research questions, "major job functions of rehabilitation counselors" represents the construct of interest to the investigators. In the study, job functions were operationalized using the Rehabilitation Skills Inventory-Revised, a 120-item survey instrument that was developed for the study and was administered by mail survey (Leahy et al., 2003).

In example B, "type of job applicant disability," "extent of disability disclosure," and "applicant employability" were the constructs of interest. Applicant disability and disability disclosure were each operationalized as distinct conditions. Applicant disability was operationalized by having the applicant disclose and request an accommodation for an invisible physical disability (i.e., insulin-dependent diabetes), an invisible psychiatric disability (i.e., bipolar disorder), or no disability (the control condition) during a staged employment interview. Extent of disability disclosure consisted of opposing conditions in which the job applicant disclosed and requested an accommodation for an invisible disability briefly or in detail. Employability was operationalized using two measures: (a) the Candidate Employability Scale (CES; Krefting & Brief, 1976), a 10-item scale designed to measure employability along a number of relevant dimensions; and (b) hiring decision, a single 4-point item that assessed the likelihood of hiring the candidate. It should also be noted that the Dalgin and Bellini study used real employers as research participants, and the research stimuli were operationalized as a series of employment interviews in which the job applicant and interviewer were played by actors. In order to control for possible differences in employer responses that could result from contextual features that were not the focus of this investigation, the researchers (a) chose two invisible disabilities that plausibly required the same job accommodation, and (b) held the content of each script constant across all experimental conditions except for the type of disability disclosed and the extent of disclosure.

In example C, the construct of "functional capacities and limitations" was operationalized as counselors' ratings of clients using the Functional Assessment Inventory (FAI; Crewe & Athelstan, 1984), VR services were operationalized as the specific services documented in counselors' case files, and employment outcomes were operationalized using two outcomes: employment status at closure and weekly salary at closure.

Although the previous examples represent quantitative research studies, it is important to note that the operationalization of variables is not exclusive to quantitative investigations only. Qualitative studies also translate key abstract concepts into specific research operations for the purpose of generating knowledge. For example, Mullins et al. (1997) utilized a qualitative methodology (i.e., in depth interviews) to investigate the strategies that exemplary counselors used to achieve successful outcomes for persons with severe disabilities. Clearly, how "exemplary" was defined in the context of rehabilitation counseling and the methods the researchers used to identify these counselors were key to the credibility and usefulness of the study findings. If the approach to operationalizing this key concept was not plausible, it would limit the strength of the knowledge claim that is based on this approach. Mullins et al. used a dual strategy for identifying exemplary counselors: (a) a peer-nomination approach, whereby those counselors who received the most votes from their peers as "exemplary" were included in the study sample; and (b) an empirical approach, in which counselors who had the highest competitive employment outcome rate with persons with severe disabilities were also interviewed. This dual strategy for identifying exemplary counselors resulted in the inclusion of 11 counselors in the study (Mullins et al., 1997).

Limitations of Operational Definitions

Operational definitions (i.e., indicators) of constructs are essential for quantitative investigations of phenomena and serve to link the abstract conceptual foundation for a study to its concrete procedures. However, there are several limitations of operational definitions to keep in mind (Kazdin, 2003):

1. An operational definition may be incomplete, may greatly simplify, or may bear little resemblance to the abstract construct of interest. As noted previously, the construct community integration may be operationalized for the purpose of an investigation as respondents' self-reported level of integration in the community. However, respondents' perceptions of their level of integration may be affected by mood, recent events, or other factors. An alternative indicator, number of times per week or month that an individual goes into "the community" for an activity, is a measure of quantity rather than quality of integration. It is an objective rather than a subjective evaluation of the status of the construct and may serve as an indicator of physical integration in the community, but it may not accurately reflect the individual's actual level of community involvement and it bears little relation to what is commonly understood as community integration. A caregivers' rating of the individual's level of integration depends on the observer's objec-

tive knowledge of the person's actual activities and/or may not accurately reflect the individual's subjective perception. Thus, each of these distinct operational definitions for the construct "community integration" leaves out dimensions related to common sense notions of what it means to be integrated into a community. Despite the difficulty in measuring "community integration," its importance as a policy and service goal for persons with disabilities has spawned a number of different approaches to operationalizing this construct for the purpose of investigating the phenomenon.

2. Operational definitions may include features that are irrelevant or not central to the original concept (Kazdin, 2003). Consider the variable "number of friends and acquaintances" as an indicator of community integration. Most people would likely agree that individuals with a larger number of friends and acquaintances probably experience a higher level of community integration. However, an individual may list a great number of friends and acquaintances, yet spend little time with any of them. In this case, the construct of community integration may be conflated with sociability, extraversion, or social desirability (it is socially desirable to report more rather than fewer friends). To remove these irrelevant features in the operationalization of community integration, a researcher may choose to use a more objective measure: time spent each week in the company of friends or acquaintances. It is reasonable that a person who spends more time each week in the company of friends and acquaintances is more likely to experience a higher level of community integration, and on this basis the indicator seems like a good proxy for the target construct. However, an individual may spend most of his or her time with friends who reside together in a residential group home, or some other setting that would not accurately represent physical presence in one's community of choice. Also, an individual may have a large network of friends and acquaintances and numerous opportunities to spend time with them, but may choose to spend time alone. Thus, this indicator contains potentially irrelevant features that may distort the measurement of the construct of interest. Unless the investigator thoroughly explores the implications of selecting one or another indicator to represent a construct, there is a concern that the methods used to define the concept of interest may include components that are not related to the original concept but that influence the study findings in ways the researcher has not anticipated (Tracey & Glidden-Tracey, 1999).

3. It is very common in the social sciences for different researchers to employ different operational definitions for the same target construct across their respective studies. Particularly in the case of a complex social phenomenon like community integration, each available single indicator measures a somewhat different facet of the target construct (e.g., subjective perception of

integration, physical presence in the community). Researchers may differ from one another on the formal definition for the construct, on which facets are central and which are less relevant, and on which measuring instruments are most valid for their purpose. It is likely that two studies that use different operational definitions of the same target construct will also yield different empirical findings, making it difficult to compare these studies to each other or to evaluate the credibility of findings as a whole in the area of research. Thus, findings that are based on a particular operational definition of a construct may or may not be generalizable to other studies that use different indicators of the same phenomenon. The reader must use his or her own informed judgment–informed by knowledge of relevant theory and research literature in a given area–to decide when caution in generalizing findings is warranted and whether or not the results of an investigation should be restricted to the specific operational definitions used in that study.

Fortunately, researchers and practitioners are not restricted to single studies in evaluating the status of knowledge in a given area. As research within a topic advances and becomes more complex, subsequent researchers are wise to incorporate the lessons of previous studies in that area, and a consensus may develop over time in the research community in regard to the most appropriate indicators of key constructs. In this way, operational definitions may acquire greater specification as knowledge accumulates in a research area (Heppner et al., 2015).

The concept of a latent variable underscores the notion that it is not possible to measure any construct in a "pure" form that is separable from the method of measurement. The scores on an indicator or measured variable are a mixture of two component parts: that portion of the measured variable that reflects the trait or construct of interest and the portion that is associated with the specific method of measurement. In other words, scores are trait-method units (Campbell & Fiske, 1959). The linkage between constructs and operational definition underscores the fact that measurement is essential for quantitative studies, but it also implies that the method of measurement presents a potentially confounding influence. When only one indicator is used to represent a construct in a study, there is no way to sort out the confounding influence of measurement method from the construct of interest. However, when a construct is measured using at least two distinct methods in a single study, it is possible to statistically separate the effects due to the construct from the effects due to the measurement method so as to estimate the amount of trait-related component that is shared by the two indicators (Campbell & Fiske, 1959; Kazdin, 2003). Moreover, the use of multiple indicators of key constructs in an investigation permits researchers to more accurately represent the multiple facets or dimensions of complex social phenomena.

It is the (sometimes) weak connections between constructs and operational definitions (i.e., between latent variables and indicators) that may underlie the common perception of social sciences as "soft sciences," that is, less amenable to clear and convincing confirmation and disconfirmation by empirical tests than the "harder" physical sciences. However, Kazdin (1998) noted that "clinical research is not in any way soft science: indeed, the processes involved in clinical research reflect science at its best precisely because of the thinking and ingenuity required to force nature to reveal its secrets" (p. 8).

Research Hypotheses and Statistical Hypotheses

Whereas research questions are stated in abstract, conceptual terms, research hypotheses are typically stated in terms of the expected relationships among the constructs. They may also be stated in an if/then format that expresses the presumed causal relationship: If these specific conditions are met, then the following result is expected. For example, one research hypothesis tested in the Dalgin and Bellini (2008) study could be stated as: "Employers will perceive an applicant who discloses an invisible disability in greater detail to be more employable than an applicant who discloses a disability more briefly."

Statistical hypotheses refer to the specific operational definitions used to measure the variables of interest and the specific statistical approach used in the given study. Typically, the statistical hypothesis is stated in its "null" form; in other words, it posits no significant differences on the variables of interest. This is because the logic of statistical tests, based on probability theory, is oriented toward *disconfirming* the hypothesis of no differences between experimental (the group that receives a treatment or intervention) and control (the group that receives no intervention or an intervention that is not relevant to the study purpose) groups (see Chapter 6). For example, the previously cited research hypothesis may be stated in the following null form: "There will be no statistically significant differences in employers' perceptions of employability for job applicants who disclose an invisible disability in greater or lesser detail."

Research Questions, Research Operations, and Knowledge Claims

Research questions are developed from a variety of sources. In order to test particular hypothesized relationships developed from observation, existing theory, or previous research, it is necessary to operationalize these abstract concepts, that is, make them concrete through specific procedures and measurement operations. In this way, the hypothesis is tested using empirical data. After the experiment is concluded and the results are analyzed, the researcher typically wishes to make statements about the more abstract level of concepts that inform the particulars of the research situation. In other words, science seeks generalized knowledge rather than knowledge that is limited to a particular experimental situation. However, the inferences that the researcher wishes to draw from the study findings may be delimited by the particular definitions and measures used to operationalize the constructs of interest and the specific conditions in which the constructs were investigated. The strength of a knowledge claim of a given study depends on the quality and coherence of each decision made in the course of implementing the study and the global research context. These considerations include decisions regarding theory, operational definitions, measurement instruments, research design and implementation, and appropriate statistical analyses, as well as the clarity or non-ambiguity of the findings, and how the results of a particular study contribute to the weight of empirical evidence in a given research area.

IDENTIFYING RESEARCH VARIABLES

The term variable refers to "characteristics of persons or things that can take on two or more values" (Bolton & Parker, 1998, p. 444). Variables may be directly observable (e.g., eye color) or non-observable (e.g., self-esteem). In the social sciences in general, and rehabilitation research in particular, many key variables of interest are non-observable (e.g., constructs such as attitudes toward disability, psychosocial adjustment)–these must be inferred from indirect sources of measurement, such as self-report questionnaires.

Variables are also distinguished by their measurement characteristics. *Categorical* variables are variables whose values may include a limited number of discrete categories. Examples of categorical variables include marital status (e.g., married, single, divorced, never married) and occupational classification (e.g., sales, manufacturing, service). Categorical variables may take on only one of a limited range of possible values for each person in a sample. When the categorical variable contains only two categories, it is called a dichotomous variable (e.g., gender, employment status). Continuous variables are variables that may take any value along a continuum of scores. For example, age (for human beings) may take any value ranging from 0 to approximately 110 years.

Independent and Dependent Variables and the Logic of Experimentation

Variables are also distinguished by their role in the research process. *Independent variables* are the variables that the researcher manipulates in an experiment. Other synonyms for independent variables include: input, cause, antecedent, predictor, process, and treatment variable (Bolton & Parker, 1998). In the logic of experimentation, the independent variable causes or produces changes in the dependent variable. Synonyms for the dependent variable include: measured, consequent, criterion, outcome, and response (Bolton & Parker, 1998). In the Dalgin and Bellini (2008) study, the dependent variables are the indicators of employability—CES total score and hiring decision score—that the researchers hypothesized would be impacted by varying the experimental conditions of type of applicant invisible disability and extent of applicant disclosure.

The purpose of experimentation is to examine causal relationships among variables. In the logic of experimentation, a researcher attempts to examine causality by "systematically varying or altering one variable or set of variables and examining the resultant changes in or consequences for another variable or set of variables" (Heppner et al., 2015, p. 49). The variable that is varied, altered, or manipulated in the study is the independent variable. Often the independent variable is an intervention that is provided to one group but not to other groups. When the independent variable is an intervention or treatment package it is called a treatment or situational variable (Kazdin, 2003).

In experimentation, the term *manipulation* refers to the deliberate process of examining the effects on the dependent (outcome) variable when the value or level of an independent variable is systematically varied. In the simplest experiment, this manipulation of the independent variable is accomplished by using two groups, a group that receives an intervention and a group that does not receive the intervention. If all other preexisting differences between the two groups are minimized except for the difference in the value or level of the independent variable (an extremely difficult proposition to actualize), then the logic of the experimental design permits the researcher to conclude that the measured differences between the two groups on the dependent variable (measured after the intervention is concluded) are the result of the independent variable.

In many examples of rehabilitation research it is not possible, due to ethical constraints or logical impossibility, to manipulate the independent variable. For example, it is not possible in the real world to randomly assign study participants to a disability status, or to racial/ethnic groups. Also, in "field" research it is often impossible to ensure that all preexisting differences between experimental and control groups are identified and controlled in the investigation. In these cases, it is more difficult to infer causal relationships between independent and dependent variables based on the study findings (Goodwin & Goodwin, 2012). It is the research design of a study rather than the specific statistical analyses used in the study that determines the inferential status, or strength of the causal inferences that can be made on the basis of a study's findings (Kazdin, 2003). In its traditional meaning, independent variable refers to a variable that is amenable to experimental manipulation for the purpose of inferring causal connections to an outcome or dependent variable.

Status or Individual Difference Variables

Variables that are related to subjects but cannot be assigned or manipulated by the researcher are known as *status* or *individual difference variables* (Kazdin, 2003). These variables may be aspects of personality (e.g., self-esteem, locus of control, intelligence), aspects of a person's socioeconomic situation (e.g., education level, marital status, family income), or aspects of group membership (e.g., gender, race/ethnicity, sexual orientation). Characteristics of counselors, such as level and type of education, years of experience, and disability status are also examples of status or individual difference variables that have been studied in rehabilitation counseling research.

Often status variables are labeled independent variables in the research literature and perform the same role as predictors in a statistical analysis. In these cases, making causal inferences based on study results is problematic because the status variable has not been manipulated. The purpose of using status or individual difference variables in a statistical analysis is to detect *association* between the status and dependent variable, rather than to establish causal explanations. Also, we do not mean to suggest that causal explanation is impossible when the study does not include an experimental manipulation of independent variables. Causality can be inferred from the association between variables on the basis of logic, such as when the status variable is logically prior to the "effect," when the status variable covaries with the effect (that is, changes in the status variable are associated with changes in the dependent variable), and when there is a mechanism of explanation that rationally links the variation of the status variable to its consequences (Cook & Campbell, 1979; Kazdin, 2003). As we noted in Chapter 1, causality may also be inferred on the basis of the total evidence gathered from a series of investigations.

Moderator Variables

Moderator variables are status variables that alter "the direction or strength of the relationship between a predictor and an outcome" (Frazier, Tix, & Barron, 2004, p. 116). Moderator variables are used to address questions regarding "for whom" or "when" a variable most strongly predicts or causes an outcome variable. Research hypotheses pertaining to moderators are typically introduced in a research study when the investigator suspects that the relationship between a predictor and an outcome is modified in the presence of the moderator variable. A classic example of a hypothesized moderated relationship is provided in the resiliency research program. Numerous researchers have theorized that resiliency, conceived as a combination of personal attributes (e.g., optimism) and person-environment interaction strategies (e.g., engaging social support), moderates the relationship between challenge and psychosocial outcome. More specifically, it is hypothesized that highly resilient individuals are able to achieve positive outcomes despite the presence of significant challenges or risks. In other words, the relationship between challenge and psychosocial outcome may be different in direction or strength, depending on the level or value of the individual's resiliency.

In the rehabilitation literature, Bellini (2003) examined the separate effects of counselor ethnicity, client ethnicity, and counselor multicultural competencies on the vocational outcomes of vocational rehabilitation (VR) clients in one state agency. He also examined whether the relationship between client ethnicity and VR outcome was moderated by counselor ethnicity and counselor multicultural competency. In other words, the author hypothesized that (a) counselors achieve different VR outcomes with clients depending on the ethnicity of the client, and (b) counselors achieve different outcomes with clients depending on the counselors' self-reported multicultural competency. Both moderation hypotheses were confirmed for each of two VR outcomes: provision of vocational training services and employment status following service provision. Bellini reported that European American counselors were more likely than non-European American counselors to achieve successful employment outcomes with African American and European American VR clients; however, Hispanic clients were equally likely to achieve a successful employment outcome regardless of the ethnicity of the counselor. Similarly, he reported that European American counselors with higher self-reported multicultural competencies were more likely to provide vocational training services to African American and Hispanic clients than were European American counselors with lower reported multicultural competencies.

In statistical analyses, the test of a moderator variable involves creating a new variable that reflects the interaction of the predictor and moderating variables. The new variable is called an interaction term and is computed by multiplying the value of the predictor variable by the value of the moderator variable for each subject in the data file. The interaction term can then be included in any subsequent descriptive or inferential analysis. Most commonly, moderator variables are employed within studies that use analysis of variance and/or multiple regression analytic strategies.

The inclusion of moderator variables in a research design should be based on relevant theory or an explicit rationale. The testing of hypotheses related to moderator variables permits researchers to more precisely model the nature of complex relationships among predictor and dependent variables. As Frazier et al. (2004) noted, "the identification of important moderators of relations between predictors and outcomes indicates the maturity and sophistication of a field of inquiry and is at the heart of theory in social science" (p. 116).

Mediator Variables

Whereas moderator variables address questions pertaining to "for whom" or "when" a variable predicts an outcome, mediator variables are key to establishing "why" or "how" a predictor variable influences an outcome. A mediator is formally defined as "a variable that explains the relation between a predictor and an outcome" (Frazier et al., 2004, p. 116). In other words, the mediator is the mechanism through which a predictor influences an outcome variable. In the context of evaluating the efficacy of rehabilitation interventions and models, it is essential to understand what causal relations and/or change mechanisms are critical for influencing outcomes. This information can enable us to focus on the effective components of treatments and remove the ineffectual elements as well as build and test theory related to the causal mechanisms responsible for change (Frazier et al., 2004).

Establishing that a variable serves as a mechanism by which a predictor influences an outcome requires that the investigator hypothesize and demonstrate the following variable relationships: (a) the predictor variable is significantly correlated with the outcome variable; (b) the predictor variable is significantly correlated with the mediator; and (c) the mediator is significantly correlated with the outcome. If these conditions are established, then mediation is demonstrated if the predictor variable fails to explain significant variation in the outcome variable when the variation in the outcome explained by the mediator is taken into account (Frazier et al., 2004). If the relationship between the predictor and the outcome drops to zero (i.e., statistical non-significance) in the presence of the mediator, then a fully mediated relationship is demonstrated. If the relationship between the predictor and the outcome is significantly reduced in the presence of the mediator but remains statistically significant, then a partially mediated relationship is demonstrated. In the case of the fully mediated variable relationship, the predictor has only an indirect effect on the outcome (i.e., through the mediator), whereas, in the case of partial mediation, the predictor has both direct and indirect effects on the outcome.

An example of several discrete tests of mediated variable relationships within a model of quality of life for persons with epilepsy was provided by Bishop, Berven, Hermann, and Chan (2002). Within their model, Bishop et al. theorized that, for persons with epilepsy, the relationship between physical function and perceived quality of life would be mediated by the respondents' perceptions of general health and mental health. In other words, the authors posited that physical functioning had no direct impact on respondents' quality of life. Rather, physical functioning would influence quality of life through its effects on perceptions of general health and mental health. The analysis confirmed the authors' hypotheses. The findings suggest that improvement or deterioration in physical functioning impacts individuals' quality of life because change in physical functioning influences their perceptions of general health and mental health, which in turn affects quality of life.

It is important to note that mediated variable relationships are demonstrated using statistical procedures, but their logic depends on a sound and relevant theoretical foundation. The anticipated mediated effect must be deduced a priori, based in reason or logic, rather than based on statistical operations only. It is the theoretical basis for the anticipated variable relationships that helps to distinguish between spurious variable effects and mediated effects. Mediation may be tested through statistical procedures that "partial out" or assign proportions of variation in a dependent variable to different variable sources. Several different analytic strategies can accomplish tests of mediated variable relationships, including multiple regression, path analysis, and structural equation modeling (Tacq, 1997). As Frazier et al. (2004) noted in their discussion of mediator variables, "it is a sign of a maturing discipline when, after direct relations have been demonstrated, we have turned to explanation and theory testing regarding these relations" (p. 116).

SAMPLING ISSUES IN RESEARCH

In conducting a study, researchers ideally would investigate all persons to whom they wish to generalize their findings. These persons constitute a *population,* meaning that they make up the entire group of persons having the characteristic or characteristics that interest the researchers. For example, researchers who are interested in how persons adjust to an acquired severe spinal cord injury (SCI) in American society would ideally include all individuals with an acquired SCI in the United States. However, the time and expense needed to include all members of a population would make the research infeasible. Therefore, researchers must content themselves with studying a *sample* of persons who presumably represent the population of interest. A sample is a given number of subjects who are selected from a defined population and who are presumed to be representative of the population (Goodwin & Goodwin, 2012; Heppner et al., 2015).

In using a smaller sample to conduct research, the problem of feasibility is solved. However, a new problem is created for the researcher, namely, whether she can generalize the results from her sample to the population of interest. In other words, it is possible that the results of the study may only be valid for the specific sample that is studied. The representativeness of a sample in relation to its population is a key issue in the conduct and evaluation of research findings (Fowler, 2002). The term *population validity* refers to "the degree to which the sample of individuals in the study is representative of the population from which it was selected" (Borg, Gall, & Gall, 1993, p. 99). The method of selecting a sample is vital to the whole research process. If research findings are not generalizable to some extent beyond the particular sample used in the study, the research does not provide us with new, practical knowledge. A study whose findings cannot be generalized to a population of interest may be considered a waste of time and effort.

Random and Systematic Sampling Error

Samples rarely have the exact same characteristics as the populations from which they are drawn. The differences between the characteristics of the sample and the characteristics of the population on the variables of interest are *sampling errors.* These may be of two types: random and systematic sampling error (Groves et al., 2004; Kalton, 1983).

Random sampling error refers to the "accidental" differences between sample and population characteristics that are likely to occur whenever a sample is drawn from a population of interest. The size of these errors (i.e., the magnitude of the differences between sample and population) tends to become smaller as we select a larger random sample. This is common sense. Individuals who have characteristics that are unusual for the population will, if included in the small sample, have a larger effect on the average sample values for those characteristics. On the other hand, in a larger sample, more individuals will reflect the "average" value for the population on the given characteristic, and individuals with unusual characteristics, although present in greater numbers in the larger sample, will have a smaller effect on the average values of the characteristic. For this reason, we can be more confident in generalizing results from studies that employ large random samples than studies that use smaller random samples.

An important advantage of random sampling is that the degree to which the sample differs from the population (i.e., sampling error) can be reliably estimated using mathematical procedures. The statistic most often used to describe sampling error is called the *standard error of the mean* (Fowler, 2002). When results of surveys are reported, a margin of error or confidence band, calculated from the standard error of the mean, is typically included. The confidence band is the mathematical estimation of the range of fluctuation between the sample and population values on the characteristic being measured.

Often researchers use non-random samples in conducting studies. When non-random samples are used there is always the chance that *systematic sampling error* is introduced. Systematic sampling errors result from variables that have not been taken into account by the researcher, but which nevertheless influence the results of sampling procedures in ways in which the researcher is not aware (Fowler, 2002). Systematic errors tend to be in a given direction and, unlike random sampling error, cannot be estimated by mathematical procedures. These errors are more serious because they may distort research findings in ways that cannot be estimated and therefore may lead to false conclusions.

Types of Sampling

As should be clear from the preceding discussion, random sampling is the best way of ensuring that the results of a study will generalize to the population of interest. Several distinct methods of random sampling may be used, depending on the purpose of the research and the resources available to the investigator. Four common types of random sampling are simple random, systematic, stratified, and cluster sampling. Researchers may also use non-random sampling procedures in gathering data; however, when non-random sampling is used, the results of a study are less likely to generalize to the population of interest. Convenience, or volunteer, sampling is a non-random approach to sampling that is common in quantitative research investigations, and purposeful sampling is a non-random method that has widespread application in qualitative research.

SIMPLE RANDOM SAMPLING. One of the most effective sampling procedures in conducting research is simple random sampling. In simple random sampling each member of a population has *an equal and independent chance* of being included in the sample. In this context "independent" means that the selection of one individual does not affect in any way the chances that other individuals may or may not be selected. It is an effective sampling technique because it yields research data that can be generalized to the population of interest within margins of error that can be mathematically estimated.

SYSTEMATIC SAMPLING. Systematic sampling is similar to simple random sampling except that, in the former, all individuals in the defined population are known to the researcher (e.g., are listed on a directory or registry). In systematic sampling the first name is chosen from a list in random fashion (i.e., using a random number generator, or a simple roll of dice), and then every third, eighth, or fifteenth name is selected, until the researcher has the sample size required for the study (Groves et al., 2004). Thus, after the first name is randomly chosen, all other members of the sample are automatically determined by their placement on the list. Systematic sampling is easier to accomplish than simple random sampling in cases where all members of the population are known, such as when the researcher has access to a directory of members of a professional organization. However, it is possible for systematic error to be introduced into a systematic sampling procedure if there exists some bias (unknown to the researcher) in how names are arranged on the list (Fowler, 2002).

STRATIFIED SAMPLING. Stratified sampling is a procedure for ensuring that members in the population who have certain characteristics are represented in the sample. The Federal government often uses stratified sampling to ensure that a sample is as close to the national population as possible on a number of identified characteristics, such as gender, race/ethnicity, education, or socioeconomic status. One approach to stratified sampling is to draw random samples of different sizes from identified subgroups of a specified population so that the proportion of individuals in each group is the same as their proportion in the population (Groves et al., 2004). Consider research into the roles and functions of rehabilitation counselors. Researchers may know that the role and functions of rehabilitation counselors differ on the basis of work setting and may have estimates (drawn from a registry) of the proportions of counselors in the various settings. It is therefore possible for the researcher to use a sampling technique that stratifies the sample on the basis of work setting: A specified proportion of counselors are drawn from private, proprietary rehabilitation, state vocational rehabilitation, community non-profit settings, school settings, and so on. This approach would ensure that counselors in particular work settings are not overrepresented or underrepresented in the sample so that systematic error related to a particular work setting is not introduced into the study. By ensuring that the sample reflects the population on this key characteristic, the generalizability of the study results is enhanced (Borg et al., 1993).

CLUSTER SAMPLING. Cluster sampling is a sampling procedure that is often utilized in educational research (Borg et al., 1993). Whereas in simple random, systematic, and stratified sampling the sampling unit is the individual, in cluster sampling, the cluster (or preexisting group of individuals) is the sampling unit. A classic example of a cluster sampling unit is the school district. An educational researcher who is interested in comparing the performance of students in various school districts may well choose a cluster sampling procedure to accomplish the study. The researcher would therefore randomly select the districts for inclusion in the study rather than randomly select students from all possible school districts. A key advantage of cluster sampling is that the resources needed to accomplish the study may be conserved by applying them more selectively; thus, fewer resources are needed to carry out the investigation (Fowler, 2002). A key disadvantage of cluster sampling is the possibility that, unknown to the researcher, clusters may differ on variables that influence the study findings. The educational researcher who compares the performance of students in various school districts would likely use a combination of stratified and cluster sampling procedures to take into account the well known influence of socioeconomic status of districts on school performance (Borg et al., 1993).

CONVENIENCE SAMPLING. Research is often limited by availability of funds. Drawing large random samples is very expensive and therefore infeasible in most rehabilitation research. Utilizing large samples in research is generally possible only when research makes few or minimal demands on individuals such as in public opinion or market research. Random sampling is also difficult in most social science research because researchers have the legal and ethical obligation to obtain informed consent from human subjects before involving them in a research project (see Chapter 4). Individuals can refuse to participate for any reason.

For these reasons, most research in rehabilitation is conducted using volunteer or convenience samples. The main problem with convenience samples is the possibility of introducing systematic sampling error into the selection process. When systematic error is introduced, the sample's membership will have different characteristics from the population from which it is drawn, potentially limiting the ability of the researcher to generalize the results of the study to the population of interest. In fact, research on volunteer subjects reviewed by Rosenthal and Rosnow (1969) and more recently by Goodwin & Goodwin (2012) indicated that people who volunteer for research tend to be different in a number of ways, including being better educated, of higher socioeconomic status, more intelligent, more sociable, and in greater need of social approval than non-volunteers. In evaluating the relationship between psychological findings and the typical composition of psychological research samples, Rosenthal and Rosnow remarked, "the existing science of human behavior is largely the science of the behavior of (college) sophomores who choose to volunteer" (p. 112). Student volunteer samples are far less common in rehabilitation research and most often are used appropriately, that is, when the selection of this type of sample is warranted by the specific research questions that are posed.

The likelihood that systematic sampling error affects the results of a study that employs volunteer subjects can be evaluated by checking the ratio of individuals who agree to participate to individuals who are invited to participate, known as the response rate. When using questionnaires to collect study data, it is common practice for researchers to report the percentage of participants who actually complete the questionnaire (Fowler, 2002; Kalton, 1983; Rumrill, Cook, & Wiley, 2010). It is less likely that systematic sampling error is introduced when the response rate is high. If the researcher has access to additional data on the subjects who were invited to participate, he can provide a check on systematic sampling bias by comparing participants with non-participants on selected characteristics that are presumed to be related to subjects' responses.

In evaluating the representativeness of a volunteer sample, the researcher and readers should consider the following questions: How likely is it that participants who volunteer for the study differ from the target population on selected characteristics? How relevant is this characteristic to the independent and dependent variables used in the study? And, if relevant, how would differences between the participants and the population on this characteristic be likely to influence the study results?

Because of the problems associated with volunteer subjects and differential response rates, skillful researchers work closely with personnel in the research setting, fully explain the nature of the research, solicit their ideas, and provide benefits to those who participate in order to increase the percentage of participants and reduce sampling bias.

PURPOSEFUL SAMPLING. Qualitative researchers typically study only a few cases of individuals from a specified population. Because the sample size in qualitative studies is typically small, the procedures used to select a sample in quantitative research are not applicable. For example, a qualitative researcher may select a respondent or setting to study because the individual or setting is an exemplary case of the phenomenon of interest to the researcher, or a case from which the researcher feels she will learn the most. Purposeful sampling refers to sampling decisions that are made in qualitative research based on theoretical and practical considerations relative to the research question (Bogdan & Biklen, 1998). For example, Nochi (1998) was interested in investigating the sense of loss of self that individuals with traumatic brain injury (TBI) experience when they interact with society. Ten informants were recruited from a local TBI support group. In selecting informants with TBI who were able to provide first person accounts of their experiences post-injury, Nochi used the following selection criteria: "(a) the individual understood that he or she had TBI, (b) the individual was living in the community after discharge from a hospital, (c) the individual was exhibiting observable language and intellectual abilities for in-depth interviews, and (d) the individual was interested in talking about and reflecting on his or her experience" (p. 667). These criteria for respondents were necessary to ensure that participants were representative of the population of interest (individuals with TBI living in the community) and were able to engage in the interview process.

SUMMARY

This chapter has addressed issues that are preparatory to the design and evaluation of rehabilitation research. Ideas for research come from a number of sources including curiosity about a phenomenon, personal interests, rehabilitation counseling practice, existing theory or models, and previous research efforts. The idea that motivates a research project is typically expressed in broad, abstract terms. To translate a research question into an empirical research project, the concepts inherent in the research question must be formulated into operational definitions. Operational definitions refer to defining concepts on the basis of the specific activities and operations used to measure the concept in the investigation. Statistical hypotheses are grounded in the specific operational definitions used to measure the constructs of interest and the specific statistical approach used in the given study. Typically, the statistical hypothesis is stated in the "null" form that posits no significant differences on the (dependent) variables of interest.

Variables are characteristics of persons or things that can take on two or more values. Variables can be categorized by their measurement characteristics (categorical and continuous), or by their role in the research process (independent, dependent, status, moderator, and mediator). In rehabilitation research it is typically not possible to manipulate independent variables to evaluate their causal relationships to dependent variables. Therefore, most rehabilitation research is concerned with the relationships between status variables and dependent variables.

Sampling is vital to the research process because researchers rarely have the resources to access all individuals who constitute a population of interest.

A sample is a given number of subjects who are selected from a defined population and are representative of the population. The representativeness of a sample in relation to its population is a key issue in the conduct and evaluation of research findings. In simple random sampling, each member of a population has an equal and independent chance of being included in the sample. Simple random sampling is usually the preferred sampling strategy because sampling errors can be reliably estimated using statistical methods. Stratified sampling may be used to enhance the representativeness of a sample in relation to population characteristics that are known. Convenience samples are used extensively in social science research including rehabilitation research. The key problem with using convenience samples is the possibility of introducing systematic sampling error into the selection process, which limits the ability of the researcher to generalize the results of the study to the population of interest. Purposeful sampling, typically used in qualitative research, is based on theoretical and practical issues involved in implementing the qualitative investigation.

Chapter 3

MEASUREMENT AND STATISTICAL ISSUES IN REHABILITATION RESEARCH

INTRODUCTION

The purpose of this chapter is to discuss key measurement and statistical concepts related to designing and evaluating rehabilitation research. Quantitative research in rehabilitation counseling uses standardized and nonstandardized instruments to measure observable phenomena and translate these measurements into numerical data for the purpose of analysis. Thus, in the quantitative research tradition, measurement issues are central to the operationalization of research hypotheses and the interpretation of research findings. Measurement issues also have important implications for statistical analyses of research findings, because research conclusions are only as credible as the quantitative data on which they are based.

Once a sample is identified, appropriate measurement instruments are chosen, and data are collected, analysis of the data is the next step in the research process (McMillan & Schumacher, 2009). Statistics is the branch of mathematics that pertains to analyzing numeric data. Having an adequate understanding of statistical methods and the role of statistics in interpreting research results is necessary for evaluating the contribution of particular research studies to the rehabilitation literature. In the second part of this chapter, we will address selected statistical concepts that are important for designing and evaluating rehabilitation research. We will not address the mathematical calculation of various statistical indices as would be included in a basic statistics text; instead, we will focus on conceptual explanation of key statistical concepts and various methods of analyzing quantitative data.

MEASUREMENT ISSUES

Measurement refers to the assignment of numbers to the responses of individuals, according to specific rules (Bolton & Brookings, 2001; Power, 2013). The responses of individuals may pertain to psychological attributes, behaviors of others, or the characteristics of environments or processes, depending on the purpose and target of measurement (Heppner, Wampold, Owen, Thompson, & Wang, 2015; Rubin, Roessler, & Rumrill, 2016). Most measurement instruments typically require a scoring key (or computer software program) that provides the "rules" for how to sum the separate items into a total score, which item responses need to be reverse scored, which items go together to form interpretable scales, and so forth. Other "rules" associated with measurement include standards for administering tests and inventories, for evaluating the stability of scores, and for interpreting test results.

There are literally thousands of measurement instruments that are used for the purposes of (a) rehabilitation client assessment, and (b) design and implementation of rehabilitation research. These include measures of academic aptitude and achievement, normal personality, mental health and adjustment, vocational interests and values, career choice and development, career and life planning, functional capacities and limitations, and consumer outcomes in rehabilitation (Power, 2013; Rubin et al., 2016). Most of these instruments are available from commercial test developers, but some instruments are developed to measure selected constructs in the context of particular rehabilitation research projects. The first part of this chapter addresses several measurement concepts that are important for the design and evaluation of research, including levels of measurement, standardization, reliability, and validity of measurement instruments.

Levels of Measurement

One of the most important measurement considerations pertains to the utility or meaningfulness of the scores that result from an assessment instrument. In the social sciences, four different levels of measurement are recognized, based on (a) the types of mathematical manipulations that can be performed on the numbers generated by the measurement instrument and (b) the amount of information that can be gleaned from the numbers (Stevens, 1946, 1951). Table 3.1 summarizes the hierarchy of measurement scales.

The simplest type of measurement scale is the *nominal scale*. This type of scale classifies the characteristics of a variable by assigning numbers to the values of the variable without a consideration of a logical or numeric ordering of the categories. In a study where racial/ethnic status is a variable of

Table 3.1. A Summary of the Hierarchy of Measurement Scales Used in the Social Sciences

Information Provided	Properties	Scale	Examples
One category is different from another	Classification	Nominal	Gender, Race
All information from previous level and one category is greater than another	Classification, order	Ordinal	Supervisor rankings, Letter grades
All information from previous levels and differences between classifications are equal	Classification, order equal distances between points	Interval	Standardized Tests
All information from previous levels and a true zero	Classification, order, equal distances between points, true zero	Ratio	Height, weight

interest, the researcher could assign different numbers to the different racial categories: 1 for African American, 2 for Hispanic/Latino, 3 for Asian American, 4 for Native American, and 5 for European American. However, the numbers assigned would not imply that any one category is lower, worse, or weaker than any other, and it is not meaningful to compute an "average" value for the variable as a way of describing the central tendency of its distribution. With nominal scale variables, the researcher is restricted to simply counting the number of individuals (i.e., determining the frequency of responses) who have a particular characteristic in common.

When characteristics of a variable are categorized and follow a logical or numeric order (i.e., are ranked), the variable is said to be measured on an *ordinal scale*. With ordinal-level data, it is implied that one category is less, lower, or weaker than a higher-ranked category; however, it is not possible to determine how much more or less any one value of the variable is above or below another. A good example of this characteristic of an ordinal-level scale is the measurement of academic rank. Class rank clearly indicates which student performed better or worse than another, but it does not tell us how much better or how much worse students performed academically. That is, the class valedictorian could have finished .02 points ahead or 3.5 points ahead of the second ranked student. The nature of an ordinal scale does not provide information regarding the magnitude of the difference between the values of the variable.

The third level of measurement in the hierarchy is referred to as an *interval scale*. Variables measured on an interval scale are considered to have all the properties of the previous scales (levels are categorized and follow a logical order based on the amount of the measured characteristic), plus an additional characteristic–the difference between any two points on an interval scale reflects equal differences at any point on the scale. Thus, with interval scales, it is possible to determine the magnitude of differences between values on the scale. For example, most standardized intelligence tests are measured on an interval scale. An individual with an IQ score of 115 is considered to have demonstrated both a different and a higher level of IQ than an individual with an IQ score of 105. Moreover, given that the scale has equal intervals of values along the scale, the difference between individuals who obtain IQ scores of 105 and 115 is of the same magnitude as the difference between individuals who obtain scores of 120 and 130 (i.e., a 10-point difference).

The final, and highest, level of measurement is a *ratio scale*. In addition to having all the properties of the previous scales, the ratio scale has another important property: a true zero point. Age, time, and most physical measurements such as height, weight, and length are examples of variables that are measured on a ratio scale. The advantage of having a true zero point is that ratio comparisons can be made across scale values. For example, because weight has a true zero point, it is possible to validly state that a person who weighs 250 lbs. weighs twice as much as a person who weighs 125 lbs. Conversely, because IQ is measured on an interval scale, it is not meaningful or accurate to state that the person who has an IQ score of 100 is twice as intelligent as the person who has an IQ score of 50.

As suggested earlier, the types of measurement scales used to operationalize a variable ultimately limit the mathematical operations that can appropriately be applied to the data generated from the variable, thereby setting a limit on the types of statistical tests that can also be applied to the data (Bellini, Fitzgerald, & Rumrill, 2000). A mean value can be calculated for any variable distribution that is measured at the interval or ratio level. The ability to calculate an average score for a distribution is fundamental for most commonly reported (i.e., parametric) statistics, and also permits the meaningful calculation of other essential building blocks of statistics (e.g., the variance and standard deviation). Thus, interval and ratio level data permit the full range of mathematical manipulations that are required when data are analyzed using statistics, whereas the options for statistical analysis are more limited when using variables that are measured on nominal or ordinal scales.

Most psychological instruments measure on a scale somewhere between the ordinal and interval levels; therefore, the data that are generated are appropriate for conventional statistics (Bolton & Brookings, 2001).

Standardization

A measurement instrument is said to be standardized when it has been carefully developed; its psychometric characteristics (e.g., reliability, validity) have been assessed and reported; and guidelines for administration have been provided, including minimum competency standards for those who administer, score, and interpret tests (Cronbach, 1990; Power, 2013). Test manuals specify in detail the procedures used in instrument development, as well as the steps to be used in administering, scoring, and interpreting test data. Standardization is vital for ensuring consistency in the administration and interpretation of test data. Standardized tests also provide tables of *norms,* or scores of the individuals in the standardization sample, as well as a description of the characteristics of the individuals who composed this sample. These data facilitate the application of the measurement instrument to other, similar samples of persons and provide valuable benchmarks for the interpretation of scores for individuals who complete the test or inventory at a later time. Standardized tests or inventories provide evidence that the scores are consistent over time, across different forms of the test, and/or across the items that compose the test, as well as evidence that scores are meaningfully related to other measures of the same construct, related constructs, and important social outcomes.

Altogether, these characteristics of standardized measures enhance the interpretability and therefore the practical application of test scores to the helping professions. These data are often not available for nonstandardized instruments, and the scores that these instruments generate are not as readily interpretable. Therefore, nonstandardized instruments are less credible and less useful for assessment and research. Reliability and validity are key measurement concepts for evaluating the usefulness of tests and inventories.

Reliability

Reliability refers to the consistency or precision of measurement, and the extent to which it eliminates chance and other extraneous factors in resulting scores (Power, 2013; Thorndike, 2005). Common synonyms for reliability include dependability, reproducibility, and stability. In classical test theory, the score that an individual obtains on a test or inventory on a given occasion can be partitioned into two parts, a true score and an error component. A *true score* is a hypothetical concept that refers to the score that the person would obtain under perfect testing conditions that eliminated all sources of error. To grasp what is meant by a true score, suppose that an individual is administered a standardized intelligence test each day for one hundred days. The individual would likely obtain a number of different scores over these 100 occasions from which an average score could be computed. This hypothetical average score approximates the person's true score, around which (depending on the magnitude of the error component on each occasion) the scores for all the testing occasions would vary. Thus, in classical test theory, the person's true score remains the same on each testing occasion, but the observed (i.e., actual) score varies from occasion to occasion as a function of the magnitude of the error component for that occasion (Thorndike, 2005). Reliability of a measurement instrument refers to the approximate proportion of true score that is present in a person's observed (i.e., actual) score. Fortunately, the conventional procedures used for estimating reliability render it unnecessary to subject a person to multiple administrations of the same test.

Where does error come from? Major sources of error in psychological measurement include non-representativeness of the instrument items; fluctuation in individual traits over time; lack of standardization in testing conditions; and subjective factors related to test performance such as stress, anxiety, depression, fatigue, or annoyance. These are designated as errors because they influence observed scores yet are irrelevant to the purpose for which the test was designed (Hood & Johnson, 2002; Thorndike, 2005). One of the most important reasons for standardizing testing conditions is to reduce the incidence of extraneous errors and enhance the reliability or dependability of test scores.

Reliability, as applied to psychological measures, is also a function of the relative stability of the personality trait being measured (Thorndike, 2005). All psychological traits are developed and expressed within specific contextual frameworks (e.g., family, friends, neighborhoods, religious communities, etc.)–we all tend to act somewhat differently depending on the demands of the context. Yet, once adulthood is reached, many psychological traits are relatively stable (e.g., extroversion, independence, tough-mindedness). Some traits, however, are more stable than others. For example, for most people, there is considerable stability in the scores they obtain on intelligence tests at different times in their lives, but there is likely to be considerably less stability in scores obtained on measures of depression, anxiety, or stress. Thus, the relative stability or instability of the source trait that the test or inventory purports to measure sets an upper limit for the stability of scores on a particular instrument.

Although it is common in the literature to see references to the reliability of tests, reliability is actually a property of the test scores (i.e., data) for a particular group on which the test was administered–not a characteristic of the test itself (American Psychological Association [APA], 2013). The current *Standards for Educational and Psychological Testing* (American Educational Research Association [AERA], APA, & National Council on Measurement in Education [NCME], 2015) emphasize that test developers should provide test users with substantial information on test reliability, including details about the populations used to obtain reliability estimates, the methods used, and the time interval between retests.

Reliability of a measure is reported in the form of a correlation coefficient. Reliability coefficients range from 0 to +1.0. A rule of thumb for acceptable reliability in a measurement instrument is the range .80 to .95; however, what is considered to be acceptable reliability also depends on the purpose of measurement, the constructs being assessed, and the type of reliability. Reliability for tests used in national testing programs (e.g., Graduate Record Examination, Stanford Achievement Tests) are typically above .90, whereas for personality, interest, and attitudinal measures reliability is often in the .70 to .90 range (Hood & Johnson, 2002). If reliability is below .70, it is a cause for concern because it suggests that scores on an instrument contain a large proportion of error.

Types of Reliability

Reliability can be estimated in a number of ways, including test-retest, alternate forms of a test, internal consistency, and inter-rater reliability. Each of these approaches to reliability represents an estimate of the stability, consistency, or dependability of scores.

TEST-RETEST RELIABILITY. Test-retest reliability is a measure of the stability of individuals' scores on a test or inventory over time. The basic procedure is as follows: A sample of individuals completes a measure at a given time and then returns at a future time to retake the same measure. The test-retest coefficient is an estimate of the magnitude of the relationship between the scores for test occasion 1 and test occasion 2, averaged across all the individuals who compose the test-retest sample. The magnitude of the relationship between individuals' scores on the two occasions is related to at least two factors that are independent of the test itself: (a) the stability of the trait being assessed, and (b) the time interval between the two testing occasions. One would not expect a high test-retest reliability coefficient for a measure of depression, mood, stress, or other constructs that typically fluctuate over time. If the time interval between testing occasions is short and the test is performance-oriented, the reliability estimate may be inflated by memory and practice effects. If the time interval between testing occasions is long (e.g., one year or more), a lower reliability estimate is expected. Test-retest is generally regarded as a conservative estimate (i.e., a baseline figure) of the true reliability of the test (Cronbach, 1990).

ALTERNATE FORM RELIABILITY. Alternate or parallel form reliability is assessed by comparing the consistency of scores for the same individuals on different forms of the same test. Alternate form reliability is common in educational testing (e.g., Scholastic Aptitude Test, Graduate Record Examination, Stanford Achievement Tests) as a method of eliminating the influence of memory and practice effects on performance, but it is less common in other testing venues (McMillan & Schumacher, 2009). Alternate form reliability is a measure of the consistency of scores across comparable forms of a test.

INTERNAL CONSISTENCY RELIABILITY. Internal consistency reliability is a measure of the stability of scores across the items that compose a test or a scale within a test. Internal consistency reliability is by far the most frequent method of estimating reliability used by researchers in the social sciences because these estimates can be obtained from a single administration of a test (Hood & Johnson, 2002; Onwuegbuzie & Daniels, 2002; Power, 2013). Split-half and inter-item reliability are common approaches to estimating the consistency of responses across the test items. Split-half reliability is computed by dividing a test or inventory into two comparable halves (typically odd and even items), and then assessing the magnitude of relationship (i.e., correlation) between scores on the two halves for individuals in a sample. Dividing the test into odd and even items is the most common approach to ensuring comparability of the two halves because it eliminates possible effects of fatigue and practice that are likely to vary from the beginning to the end of the test. The general weakness of split-half reliability estimation is related to a principle of sampling, which is that, all other things being equal (e.g., adequate item coverage, elimination of errors related to the conditions of test administration), the more items that comprise a test, the more stable or reliable are the scores. Thus, splitting a test into halves has the consequence of decreasing the reliability estimate. The Spearman-Brown prophecy formula may be used to correct for the shortened length of each half of the test and provide an estimate of reliability for the full test (Thorndike, 2005).

Like split-half, inter-item reliability is obtained from a single administration of a test. Inter-item reliability differs from split-half in that it is computed by averaging all of the intercorrelations among the items that compose the test or scale. Thus, inter-item reliability measures the extent to which all items are related to each other, and it indicates the stability of scores across all items rather than across two halves. The Kuder-Richardson Formula 20 is used to estimate inter-item reliability when the test items require two-response answers (e.g., yes/no, true/false), and Cronbach's alpha coefficient is used when test items call for more than two response categories (Thorndike, 2005). Inter-item reliability for most tests is often higher than estimates using other methods (e.g., test-retest); hence, it should be considered to be a liberal (i.e., a ceiling figure) estimate of reliability.

INTER-RATER RELIABILITY. Inter-rater reliability is used when the items that comprise a test or scale consist of ratings of individuals' behaviors that are made by an observer (e.g., teacher, counselor, supervisor; Goodwin & Goodwin, 2012; Rumrill, Cook, & Wiley, 2010). In these instances, it is important to have an estimate of the consistency of scores across several observers or raters. Inter-rater reliability is computed by assessing the relationship (i.e., correlation) between ratings of two or more observers of the same individuals' behaviors. The consistency of observers' ratings can be improved by training the raters in the use of the test and by providing clear guidelines for assessment of the target behaviors prior to the estimation of reliability.

Standard Error of Measurement

Reliability coefficients are estimates of the proportion of true score that is present in observed scores. Because we know that an individual's score on a test is composed of both true and error score components, it is useful to translate this knowledge to the interpretation of the observed score so as to compute a range of scores within which the person's true score likely falls. The *standard error of measurement* (SEM) is an index of the estimated reliability of a test that is applied to an individual's test score (Hood & Johnson, 2002). The SEM for an individual's score equals the standard deviation (for the standardization sample) times the square root of one minus the reliability of the test. The SEM allows one to calculate from the observed (i.e., actual) score the approximate range of scores (i.e., confidence interval) within which the person's true score probably falls. Test users can be confident that, approximately 68 percent of the time, the person's true score is within the range of scores defined by the interval minus one to plus one SEM, and approximately 95 percent of the time, the person's true score falls within the interval defined by minus two to plus two SEMs. Based on the formula for computing SEM, tests with higher reliability estimates and with lower average deviation around the mean score for the standardization sample will have a smaller SEM and therefore a narrower range within which the true score likely falls. Thus, the SEM is useful in facilitating the interpretation of individuals' scores on measurement instruments as a probable range rather than as an absolute number (Anastasi, 1992).

Validity

In the context of psychometric assessment, validity pertains to whether a test measures what it purports to measure, or "the soundness and relevance of a proposed interpretation" (Cronbach, 1990, p. 150). The term validity shares a common root with value, and validity is a judgment of the value of the test. Whereas reliability is an estimate of the consistency or stability of scores, the issue of validity in measurement addresses questions such as: "What does the test measure?" "What do the test scores mean?" and "What types of decisions are appropriate to make on the basis of the test scores?"

The Standards for Educational and Psychological Testing (AERA, APA, & NCME, 2015) states: "Validity is the most important consideration in test evaluation. The concept refers to the appropriateness, meaningfulness, and usefulness of the specific inferences made from test scores" (p. 11). Thus, validity concerns the appropriate uses of tests, the interpretability of test scores, and the social consequences associated with their uses (Parker & Patterson, 2012; Zunker, 2015).

Validity is always a matter of degree. Tests may be useful and defensible for some purposes and populations but less useful or defensible for other purposes or populations (Hartung, 2013). No test is 100 percent valid for every purpose and every population of potential users. Moreover, use of a test for a population on which it has not been normed, or for a purpose whose consequences have not been investigated, may constitute misuse of the test data (APA, 2013; Hood & Johnson, 2002). Validation of a measurement instrument is a process of inquiry into the meaning of test scores and its uses and consequences for specific purposes (Betz & Weiss, 2001). For example, an important question for the validity of the GRE is whether and to what degree GRE scores predict performance in graduate school.

Types of Validity

Establishing the validity of a test involves three separate but interrelated lines of investigation: content, criterion, and construct validity. All three aspects of validity are important for identifying the meaning and usefulness of a test. However, in evaluating the strengths and limitations of particular measurement instruments, the type of validity that is emphasized depends on the purposes and consequences of measurement.

CONTENT VALIDITY. Content validity inquires into the content of the items of a test. The fundamental question in content validity is: "Do the items adequately sample the content domain of the construct or constructs that the test purports to measure?" Content validity is usually established by a careful examination of items by a panel of experts in a given field. For example, establishing the content validity of a measure of work adjustment would likely involve soliciting the judgment of experts regarding whether the items on the proposed measure adequately sample the content domain of work adjustment.

CRITERION VALIDITY. Criterion validity inquires into the relationship (i.e., correlation) between scores on a test or inventory and other, external criteria. Criterion validity is an inquiry into the empirical basis for particular interpretations of test data. For example, because the GRE was developed for use in selecting applicants for graduate schools, an important question related to this purpose is, "Do GRE scores actually predict (and to what extent) academic performance in graduate school?" Criterion validity assesses the empirical (i.e., observed) relationship between test scores and other criteria that are conceptually related to the construct in question.

Two types of criterion validity are concurrent and predictive validity. *Concurrent validity* pertains to the relationship between test scores and an external criterion that is measured at approximately the same time. For example, concurrent validation of a self-report measure of depression might involve clients who complete this measure and counselors who independently rate the depressive symptoms of those clients. The counselors' ratings of depressive symptoms would be the external criterion against which the validity of the self-report measure of depression is assessed. The strength of the correlation between the two measures of depression would indicate their degree of relationship, and it would therefore provide substantiation for the meaning and interpretability of the scores on the self-report measure. *Predictive validity* refers to the relationship between test scores and an external criterion that is measured some time later. For example, one approach to investigating the predictive validity of the Strong Interest Inventory (SII) has involved assessing whether and to what degree individuals' scores on the SII predict future career decisions. Several studies that assessed the relationships between individuals' scores on the SII and their subsequent career placements five to twenty years later have indicated that 55 to 70 percent of these individuals became employed in occupations congruent with their high scores on the SII Occupational Scales (Hood & Johnson, 2002; Zunker, 2015).

Overall, validity coefficients are nearly always lower than reliability coefficients. Whereas reliability coefficients for common assessment instruments are typically in the .70 to .90 range, validity coefficients are rarely above .60 and are often as low as .10 (Hood & Johnson, 2002). However, this does not mean that test scores that have low correlations with external criteria are invalid. Whenever the relationship between a test score and an external criterion is assessed, the degree of relationship that is observed is a function of the measurement characteristics (e.g., range of scores, reliability) of both variables, the sources of error that enter into the measurement of each variable, the similarities or differences in the methods used to measure the variables, and many other factors. Thus, measuring a criterion variable for the purpose of evaluating the validity of a measurement instrument introduces additional sources of error that usually serve to reduce the magnitude of the observed relationship between the test score and the criterion.

CONSTRUCT VALIDITY. Construct validation studies are concerned with understanding the underlying constructs, dimensions, or attributes being measured by means of a test or measurement instrument (Cronbach & Meehl, 1955; Messick, 1980). Construct validity pertains to the linkages between the theoretical construct and its measurement. For example, consider a measure of introversion that, by definition, would claim to describe a particular cognitive, social, or behavioral orientation. To evaluate whether the instrument accurately measures what it purports to measure, it is first necessary to understand the meaning of the construct. How do introverts act in this or that situation? What incentives do they respond to? How do they handle stress? For what activities do they exhibit preferences? The meanings of the construct need to be spelled out. Articulating the construct domain takes place during the process of instrument development, and evaluating the degree to which the appropriate content is covered by the items that comprise the instrument is an issue of content validity. However, in inquiring about the validity of the measure, it is also necessary to evaluate whether the intended construct meanings are reflected in the patterns observed in empirical data, that is, whether persons who are introverted in ways specified by the theory underlying the test actually score high on the introversion scale. In the absence of explanatory theory and empirical evidence, there is no way to judge the appropriateness, meaningfulness, and usefulness of test scores (Messick, 1988).

Constructs are the building blocks of theories, and theories specify how particular constructs are related (Betz & Weiss, 2001; Cronbach, 1990). Thus, construct validity involves a back and forth movement between scores observed on a test and the implicit or explicit theory within which the construct is embedded. What is sought in construct validity is the mutual verification of the measurement instrument and the theory of the construct the instrument is intended to measure. The theoretical conception of the construct dictates the nature of the data used to verify the specific inferences that are warranted from scores on an instrument. In turn, the scores on a test are used to validate, refute, or revise the theory itself. In this way, all the data (both conceptual and empirical) that flow from a theory and its application are useful in the process of construct validation (Angoff, 1988; Cronbach & Meehl, 1955). The emphasis placed on construct validity in contemporary approaches to test validation reflects the renewed focus on and appreciation for the role of explanatory theories, particularly testable theories, in the development of scientific knowledge (Betz & Weiss, 2001; Zunker, 2015).

For the reasons specified above, Messick (1980, 1988) stated that construct validity is the unifying form of validity that integrates content and criterion considerations into a common framework for testing specific hypothetical relationships between the construct in question, other indicators of the construct, and distinct constructs. Construct validity is the bridge that integrates content and criterion validity issues. The construct meaning provides a rational basis for hypothesizing the concurrent and predictive relationships with other variables, and for judging content relevance and representativeness. For an instrument to be construct valid, appropriate content is essential. Concurrent and predictive studies are also needed to demonstrate the empirical bases for construct meaning, which, in turn, provide the foundation for the interpretation of test scores. As Cronbach (1990) stated, "all validation is one, and in a sense, all is construct validity" (p. 99).

As demonstrated in the previously cited introversion example, establishing the construct validity of a measurement instrument typically follows a deductive process of investigation, the practical goal of which is to provide an empirical foundation for the interpretation of test scores. A test developer makes a claim that an instrument reflects a particular construct. From the construct meaning and the network of theoretical constructs and relationships within which the construct is embedded, the test developer deduces specific testable hypotheses and then tests these hypotheses against empirical data. If the hypotheses are confirmed, it enhances the credibility of a particular interpretation of the test scores (and the theory that underlies the interpretation). Thus, construct validity is a process of testing the theoretical meanings of a construct against empirical data as a means of verifying specific interpretations and uses of test scores. Construct validity is fundamentally an empirical issue that is not demonstrated by the results of one or a small number of studies. Rather, it is a judgment based on the integration of findings from a large number of sources.

Relationship Between Reliability and Validity

Based on the previous discussion, it should be clear that measurement instruments that are used for assessing rehabilitation clients and conducting rehabilitation research should have high reliability and validity. However, it is possible for a measurement instrument to have high reliability (i.e., scores are dependable, consistent, stable) yet not be valid for specific purposes. For example, a thermometer that yields the same temperature reading no matter what the air temperature happens to be would have perfect reliability because the measure is completely dependable. However, the thermometer would have no validity because the reading is inaccurate on all but a very few occasions (i.e., the reading does not correspond to the actual air temperature).

This analogy reflects the relationship between the reliability and validity of measurement instruments. Measurements must be reliable in order to be valid, but they can be reliable without being valid. Thus, reliability is a necessary but not sufficient condition for validity. Reliability forms the upper limit for the validity of a test, because measurement must be dependable for it to be useful. However, validity is the single most important consideration in test use (Cronbach, 1990).

Reliability is a general characteristic of test or inventory scores, but validity is specific to a particular purpose or use. For what purpose can the test be used and what are the consequences that flow from its use are the fundamental questions of validity. Thus, technically speaking, one does not validate a test, or even the scores yielded by a test. Rather, one validates the inferences that the user draws from the test scores and the decisions and actions that flow from these inferences. The emphasis on inferences and uses of test data firmly places the responsibility for validity on the test user (Angoff, 1988). Conversely, responsibility for the reliability of test scores belongs to the test developer (AERA, APA, & NCME, 2015).

Sources of Information on Instruments

The vast majority of the tests and inventories that are available in the United States are published by a few large publishers such as Consulting Psychologists Press, the Psychological Corporation, and Pro-Ed. Test publishers distribute catalogs each year from which manuals, scoring keys, and the tests themselves can be ordered. Often these companies offer "specimen kits" that include a copy of the item booklet, the test manual, and a scoring key. The test manual should include information regarding the construction of the test; scores (i.e., norms) and characteristics of the standardization sample; directions for administering, scoring, and interpreting the test; reliability and standard error of measurement estimates; and validity studies.

The single best source of information about tests is the *Mental Measurements Yearbooks* (MMY) series, published by the Buros Institute of Mental Measurements at the University of Nebraska-Lincoln (Hood & Johnson, 2002; Rubin et al., 2016). The MMY series contains descriptive information about tests, including publishers, prices, and appropriate uses, as well as critical reviews of tests by one or more experts. Also, a complete list of published references pertaining to each test is included and updated with each new edition. The annual Buros Institute *Mental Measurements Yearbook* contains information on more than 300 new or recently revised tests and inventories.

Tests in Print is also published by the Buros Institute and serves as a comprehensive bibliography to all known tests that are currently in the English language. This annual compendium includes information on test purpose, test publisher, intended test population, test authors, and publication dates for more than 4,000 testing instruments.

Tests and *Test Critiques* are published by Pro-Ed. *Tests* contains the latest information on more than 2,000 assessment instruments, organized into separate sections related to psychology, education, and business. The 14 volumes of *Test Critiques* provide in-depth evaluative reviews of more than 1,000 of the most widely used assessment instruments and include information on both technical aspects and practical applications of tests (Pro-Ed, 2015).

Rehabilitation counselors may also find information on assessment instruments, especially reports about the development and use of particular instruments in research, in professional journals including the *Rehabilitation Counseling Bulletin; Journal of Applied Rehabilitation Counseling; Rehabilitation Psychology; Journal of Rehabilitation; Rehabilitation Research, Policy, and Education; Journal of Rehabilitation Administration; Journal of Vocational Rehabilitation; Work; Journal of Counseling and Development; Journal of Counseling Psychology;* and *Measurement and Evaluation in Counseling and Development.* Additionally, published research studies that use measurement instruments to operationally define constructs should document in the Methods section of the manuscript the reliability and validity evidence for these instruments (APA, 2013).

STATISTICAL METHODS

Statistical methods consist of two types: (a) descriptive statistics, which include methods of organizing, summarizing, and presenting data; and (b) inferential statistics, which include procedures for reaching tentative conclusions, based on probability theory, about population values from data that are derived from samples. This section of the chapter describes commonly used descriptive and inferential statistics.

Descriptive Statistics

Descriptive statistics include concepts and tools that are useful in studying distributions of variables. As defined in Chapter 2, variables are "characteristics of persons or things that can take on two or more values" (Bolton

& Parker, 1998, p. 444). A distribution is the total set of values or scores for any variable. Thus, whenever quantitative data are obtained in the course of a research investigation, these numeric data are understood and described in terms of the characteristics of their distributions. Also, distributions are a natural starting point for understanding quantitative measurement and statistics because both descriptive and inferential statistical procedures are based on the distributions of variables.

DISTRIBUTIONS. Whenever a continuous variable is measured, the total set of values obtained takes the form of a distribution of scores. For example, if a measure of weight is taken for a sample of male and female adults, the distribution of scores is likely to range between the values of 100 and 250 pounds, although more extreme values may also occur. A number of concepts are useful in describing the characteristics of distributions including shape, central tendency, variability, and relationship.

A frequency distribution is a distribution of the frequency of scores' occurrence within a particular sample. Frequency distributions are graphic displays of scores. The familiar bar graph, or histogram, is a graphic display of a distribution of scores for a sample along horizontal (score or variable value) and vertical (frequency of scores' occurrence) dimensions. In a bar graph, the length of each bar reflects the frequency of the associated score in the sample. In a frequency polygon, the frequency of each score is plotted as a single point rather than a bar, and these points are then connected to achieve a simple representation of the shape of the distribution.

SHAPE. When a large sample of individuals is measured on a continuous variable (e.g., weight, height, intelligence, age), it is likely that the distribution of scores will approximate a normal distribution. A *normal distribution* looks like the familiar bell-shaped curve, with one high point in the center where the majority of scores are clustered and tapering "tails" at either end where fewer scores are distributed. Although many physical and mental characteristics tend to be normally distributed, it is important to understand that no measurable characteristic is precisely normally distributed. The bell-shaped curve is a mathematical concept that appears to closely approximate the distribution of many variables in nature, but it is not a fact of nature. Non-normal distributions may have two or more "humps" (bimodal or multimodal distributions) rather than the familiar one, or the single hump may be off center rather than in the middle of the distribution of scores (asymmetrical distribution). A distribution is said to be skewed when the majority of scores occur at the low or high end of the score value range rather than in the center of the range as in a symmetrical, normal curve.

The normal distribution is the foundation for descriptive and inferential statistics. Most inferential statistical tests require an assumption that the variables to be analyzed are distributed normally, known as the normality assumption (Miles & Shevlin, 2001). Notable exceptions can be found in the form of non-parametric statistics, which are used to analyze data that are not normally distributed (see Non-Parametric Statistics subsection later in this chapter). Fortunately, many statistical tests are not severely influenced by violations of the normality assumption and, hence, can be applied with reasonable confidence to distributions that are non-normal. Most textbooks on statistical methods (Cohen, Cohen, West, & Aiken, 2003; Keith, 2006; Stevens, 1996) provide thorough discussions of the theoretical assumptions that underlie particular statistical procedures and the various ways that violations of the normality assumption may affect the interpretation of statistical significance tests.

MEASURES OF CENTRAL TENDENCY. Measures of central tendency are used to describe the typical or average performance of a group on a measured characteristic. The *mode* is the numerical value or score that occurs most frequently in a distribution. As noted in the previous paragraph, sometimes a distribution of scores has two or more scores that may occur most frequently. These are known as bimodal or multimodal distributions. The mode is an appropriate measure of central tendency for both categorical (e.g., eye color) and continuous variables. The *median* is the middle-most score, or the score that divides the distribution in half, with 50 percent of scores falling below the median and 50 percent above the median. The *mean* score is the arithmetic average score. It is the most common measure of central tendency, is used to describe the distributions of continuous variables, and is the basis for most inferential statistics. However, the mean score of a distribution may be strongly influenced by extreme scores. A few extremely low scores will move the mean score downward, whereas a few extremely high scores will move the mean higher. Because the distribution of income in the United States indicates a small percentage of individuals with extremely high incomes, government agencies and the media report national income in terms of the median income rather than the mean. In distributions with extreme values the median is a more accurate measure of central tendency when a distribution is skewed because it is not as strongly influenced by the presence of extreme scores as the mean is. When a distribution is precisely normal, the mean, median, and mode are identical.

MEASURES OF VARIABILITY. Measures of variability provide information about the dispersion or spread of scores in a distribution. The *range* is a rough measure of how compact or extended a distribution of scores is. It is computed by subtracting the lowest score from the highest score and adding 1 to the difference. For example, a distribution of IQ scores wherein the low score is 66 and the high score is 140 would have a range of 75 (140-66+1).

Although the range is easy to compute, it is not particularly useful in describing the variability of scores in a distribution because a single extreme score at the lower or higher end inflates the range yet may not accurately reflect the pattern of variability in the distribution.

Variance is a statistic that provides more accurate information than the range regarding how widely spread scores are from the mean score. The variance is a single index that indicates the amount of deviation (or distance) of scores from the mean score in a distribution. The variance of a distribution of scores is calculated by computing the deviation between each observation or score (X) and the mean value (M), squaring the deviation, adding together these squared deviations from the mean (1), then dividing by the number of observations (N), as indicated in the following equation:

$$\text{Variance} = I\,(X - M)^2 \div N.$$

In any distribution there will be observations that are below and above the mean. Squaring the deviations from the mean removes the negative signs associated with observations that are below the mean, so that the variance indexes the total amount of variation from the mean value rather than the direction of each deviation.

The *standard deviation* is the most useful and most commonly reported measure of the variability of a distribution. The standard deviation is calculated by taking the square root of the variance and, like variance, it reflects the average deviation of scores from the mean score. The utility of the standard deviation as a measure of variability is that it is expressed in the same units as the mean score. When a mean and standard deviation for a variable are reported, it permits the reader to understand both the average value of scores and the average variability of scores around the mean value for the total distribution.

Variance and standard deviation also provide additional understanding of the characteristics of a normal distribution. By definition, when a variable is normally distributed, 68 percent of scores will fall within one standard deviation of (i.e., above and below) the mean value, 95 percent of scores will fall within two standard deviations of the mean, and 99.9 percent of scores will fall within three standard deviations of the mean. The characteristic variability of scores in a normal distribution is the foundation for most inferential statistics.

MEASURES OF RELATIONSHIP. The correlation statistic is a measure of the linear relationship of two distributions of variables, or whether they covary. The correlation statistic contains information about both the *magnitude* (or strength) and *direction* of the relationship between two variables. A correlation coefficient can range from +1.0 to −1.0. A correlation of +1.0 means that there is a perfect, positive relationship between two variables. As the values of one variable increase, the values of the second variable also increase in perfect proportion. However, there is rarely such perfect correspondence between two variables. In fact, a perfect correlation may be said to represent a tautology; that is, two ways of expressing the same phenomenon. An example of a perfect correlation is the correspondence between height in inches and height in centimeters.

Indeed, correlation coefficients are most informative when they are not perfect; that is, when they provide meaningful information about the relationship between two distinct variables. Consider measurements of height and weight. Most of the time, individuals who are taller are also heavier. However, some tall individuals are thin and weigh less than expected, and some short individuals weigh more than expected. The observed correlation between height and weight is approximately .80, a less than perfect but quite strong linear relationship. A zero correlation between two variables means that they are not related in linear fashion: As one variable increases, the other may increase, decrease, or remain constant with no identifiable order to the relationship. A negative correlation means that as the value of one variable increases, the value of the second variable decreases.

The *coefficient of determination* is the square of the correlation coefficient, and it represents the amount of variance shared by the two variables. In the example given above, a .80 means that height and weight share 64 percent of their variation, or alternately that 64 percent of the variability in weight is predicted by variability in height. In statistical terms, the coefficient of determination is an index of the amount of covariation of two variables as a proportion of the total (summed) variation of the variables.

The Pearson product moment correlation coefficient is the most commonly reported correlation statistic and is appropriate as a measure of linear relationship when the two variables are continuous. Other types of correlation statistics may be employed when different combinations of continuous, dichotomous, categorical, or ranked variables are the focus of analysis, although these statistics are rarely observed in the rehabilitation literature. A table of different correlation statistics and their appropriate application to variables with given measurement characteristics is found in Gay and Airasian (2003, p. 318).

Inferential Statistics

As Drummond (2004) stated, "One of the major roles of statistics is to provide an inferential measuring tool, to state our degree of confidence in the accuracy (for a population) of certain measurements (of a sample) (p. 52).

Inferential statistical methods consist of a family of techniques for translating empirical data into probability statements that are used as the primary basis for reaching decisions about research hypotheses. The purpose of inferential statistics is to make warranted *inferences,* based on probability theory, about the nature of the relationships between variables *in a population of interest based on the relationships between these variables that are observed in the sample.* In other words, the purpose of statistical significance tests is to determine the likelihood that the findings obtained in the sample are also reflected in the population from which the sample is drawn. The statistical significance test is used to determine whether the statistical hypothesis, stated in its null form (see Chapter 2), is likely to be true in the population.

It is important to understand that significance tests focus on the confirmation or disconfirmation of the null hypothesis, not the confirmation or disconfirmation of the research question or hypothesis. In other words, the strategy of statistical significance testing is to nullify the null hypothesis and thereby provisionally support the research hypothesis (Cohen, 1990). If the null hypothesis is rejected, based on the significance test, it means that it is unlikely, at a specified level of probability, that the results obtained could be due to chance alone. Tentative confirmation of a research hypothesis by disconfirming, at a specified level of probability, its null inverse is the most that statistical significance tests can accomplish. The test does not confirm that the positive research hypothesis is true. Nor does a statistically significant result in a given sample ensure that a similar result will be obtained if the study is replicated with a different sample (Cohen, 1990). These caveats underscore the tentative nature of all research conclusions based on statistical significance tests and the tentative connection between results obtained in a particular research investigation and the actual state of affairs that exists in the population.

STATISTICAL SIGNIFICANCE AND PROBABILITY VALUES. What is the basis for determining that a statistically significant result exists in the population based on the sample data? The behavioral sciences (including rehabilitation counseling) have adopted *by convention* a benchmark (or decision rule) for determining when a result is statistically significant. The conventional benchmark is the probability value, or *p-value, $p \leq .05$.* When a p-value less than or equal to .05 is obtained in hypothesis testing, it is interpreted to mean that there is likely to be a statistically significant relationship between the variables in the population of interest. When a p-value greater than .05 is obtained, it is interpreted to mean that it is likely that there is no statistically significant relationship between the variables in the population.

In the logic of statistics, a statistically significant result in a sample at the *$p \leq .05$* level means that there is a 95 percent probability that the decision of statistical significance obtained in the sample data accurately reflects a true, significant relationship between the variables in the population. It also means that 5 percent of the time it is likely that a decision of statistical significance may be obtained in the sample when no actual significant relationship between the variables exists in the population. In other words, when a $p \leq .05$ is adopted as the benchmark of statistical significance, the researcher is willing to have the significance test be wrong approximately 5 percent of the time. As noted previously, the $p \leq .05$ benchmark is only a convention that has been adopted among social scientists. Other benchmarks could be adopted by individual researchers which provide a more or less stringent decision rule for the statistical test, such as $p \leq .01$ for a more stringent test, or $p \leq .10$ for a less stringent test. A more stringent benchmark enables the researcher to be more confident that the results obtained in a sample are true for the population, but the more stringent decision rule also requires a stronger relationship among variables to infer statistical significance. Conversely, a less stringent benchmark provides less confidence that the results for the sample are true for the population, but the relationship among variables need not be as strong to infer statistical significance.

The value of the statistical significance tests is that it provides the researcher with a decision rule for identifying potentially non-chance results at a specified level of confidence. Statistical significance does not guarantee that results are meaningful, but it can identify results that are likely due to chance factors rather than the factors under investigation.

TYPE I AND TYPE II ERRORS. Two types of "errors" or false conclusions—when the statistical hypothesis test provides conclusions that do not correspond to the actual state of affairs in the population—are possible in hypothesis testing. The first type of error—*Type I error*—occurs when the researcher finds a statistically significant relationship between variables in the sample, but no actual significant relationship between these variables exists in the population of interest. It means that the null hypothesis (i.e., no significant differences between the variables in the population) is rejected, based on the statistical significance test, when the null hypothesis is actually true for the population. The Type I error rate that the researcher is willing to accept is expressed as the Alpha level (a) that is selected prior to conducting the statistical analysis. As noted previously, by convention most researchers in the social sciences set the Alpha level at .05.

The second type of error—*Type II error*—occurs when the researcher finds that there is no significant relationship between the variables in the sample, but a significant relationship between the variables exists in the population. A Type II error means that the null hypothesis is accepted, based on the statistical significance test, when the null hypothesis is actually false in the population. Type I errors occur when the statistical test is overly sensitive to statistical differences, and it picks up statistical "noise" that is misinterpreted as a significant effect (or "signal"). Type II errors result when the statistical test is not sensitive enough to accurately detect true differences between the variables, hence, the researcher concludes erroneously that no significant differences exist in the population. In other words, a Type I error represents a "false positive" conclusion, and a Type II error represents a "false negative" conclusion. The Type II error rate for an investigation is known as Beta I.

It is important to reiterate that the basis for statistical significance tests is probability theory. Statistical significance tests yield only probability statements about the nature of a relationship between variables in a population based on the observed relationship in a sample. The only way to know for certain the actual nature of the relationship between these variables in the population of interest is to sample every member of the population, an impossible task in nearly every instance of research. Therefore, it is effectively impossible to know for certain when a Type I or Type II error has occurred in a statistical analysis. However, some conditions of the research situation and statistical analysis have been identified that make it more or less likely that a Type I or Type II error is responsible for the obtained results.

CONDITIONS THAT MAKE TYPE I AND TYPE II ERRORS MORE LIKELY. Using a higher (less stringent) benchmark for the statistical significance test– $p \leq .10$ or $p \leq .20$–makes it more likely that a researcher will find a statistically significant result in the sample when no true significant relationship between the variables exists in the population. Also, Type I errors are more likely when the researcher performs a large number of separate and independent statistical significance tests within a research study.

The principal condition that makes Type II errors more likely is when statistical significance tests are based on a small sample of subjects. The actual size of the sample needed to reduce the likelihood of Type II errors depends on the type of statistical analysis performed. The reason that quantitative analyses of small samples are more likely to result in Type II errors is that statistical significance tests are known to be highly sensitive to sample size: The larger the sample, the more sensitive the statistical test is for identifying significant relationships between variables (Cohen, 1990; Keith, 2006). As an example, consider two investigations, one using a sample of $N=10$ and the other using a sample of $N=100$. Analyses of these two data sets obtain the same magnitude of correlation between two variables, $r=.25$. In the case of the smaller sample, the correlation is found to not be statistically significant ($p>.05$), whereas in the second case the correlation is found to be statistically significant ($p<.05$). However, the magnitude of the correlation ($r=.25$) between the two variables is the same! Because the first study is based on a very small sample, and statistical tests are highly sensitive to sample size, it is likely that in this study the test was not sufficiently sensitive, or powerful enough, to detect a true significant relationship that exists between the variables in the population. The concept of power (Cohen, 1988) refers to the sensitivity of a statistical test to detect true relationships or differences. Given the different results of statistical significance testing in the two studies, it is likely that a Type II error occurred in the former study. In the second study ($N=100$), the test was sufficiently powerful and a statistically significant result was obtained. Low statistical power has been found to be a pervasive problem in social science research, including rehabilitation counseling research (Bellini & Rumrill, 2009; Cohen, 1990). We will return to the issue of power in Chapter 5 when we address the statistical conclusion validity of research investigations.

LIMITATIONS OF STATISTICAL SIGNIFICANCE TESTING. Statistical significance tests are useful tools for identifying when results based on sample data are probably due to chance, or when the variable relationships indicated in a study likely reflect true variable relationships in the population of interest. The statistical significance test provides a dichotomous decision rule within specified levels of probability: yes, the variables are probably related, or no, the variables are probably not related. However, the goals of science are not limited to providing insight into whether or not variables are related. A more ambitious goal of science is to provide an understanding of causality, that is, the nature, magnitude, and mechanisms of variable relationships. Statistical significance testing yields information about whether variables are related, but not about the magnitude of the variable relationships that are identified. Statistical significance tests play an important but limited role in the advancement of human knowledge. As Cohen (1994) observed, the significance test "does not tell us what we want to know, and we want so much to know that, out of desperation, we nevertheless believe that it does" (p. 997).

As a practical matter, statistical significance tests are known to be highly sensitive to sample size, such that very small correlations between two variables or very small differences in the mean values for two groups are likely to be statistically significant (i.e., not likely due to chance) given a large enough sample. This characteristic of statistical significance tests has contributed to considerable confusion and some inaccurate conclusions about the veracity of numerous findings in social science research (Cohen, 1990; Heppner et al., 2015).

Most standard statistical significance tests also require that certain assumptions about the data are met. One key assumption is that the measured variables approximate a normal distribution (i.e., the normality assumption). A second key assumption is that the variance of the dependent variable is consistent across the different values of the variable distribution, known as the homogeneity of variance assumption (Cohen et al., 2003; Miles & Shevlin, 2001). Finally, it is assumed that the measurement of the dependent variable is interval-level or higher. When these assumptions of the data are not met, the statistical analysis that is based on the data will not be as valid or credible.

EFFECT SIZE. The limitations of using statistical significance tests as the primary benchmark for determining when research results are important has led to a focus on alternate measures of experimental effects, known as effect size measures, to complement statistical tests. *Effect size* is the proportion of variance in one variable or a set of variables that is accounted for by another variable or set of variables (Cohen, 1988). Consistent with the consensus in the social sciences on the importance of effect size measures in reporting research findings, the 2013 *APA Publication Manual* emphasized that:

> It is almost always necessary to include some index of effect size or strength of relationship. . . . The general principle to be followed . . . is to provide the reader not only with information about statistical significance tests but also with enough information to assess the magnitude of the observed effect or relationship. (APA, 2013, pp. 28–29)

Guidelines of most major journals in the social sciences also require that authors report effect sizes associated with statistical analyses in published research, so that readers can assess the magnitude and practical value of the variable relationships identified. Readers should also keep in mind that, like the mean and standard deviation, effect size is a summary statistic, that is, an average value for the data set as a whole. This means that, within a given data set, there are likely to be subsets of participants for whom the effect size will be larger and subsets for whom the effect size will be smaller.

There are three major classes of effect size measures that may be reported based on the type of research design and statistical analysis used in a study: standardized difference effect sizes, variance accounted for effect sizes, and corrected effect sizes (Vacha-Haase & Thompson, 2004).

Standardized difference effect sizes are computed for statistical analyses that involve testing mean differences on a relevant outcome variable across two groups. Standardized differences are computed by the generic formula:

$$(MT - MC) \div SD$$

Where MT is the posttest sample mean of the experimental or treatment group, MC is the posttest mean of the control group, and SD is some estimate of the population standard deviation (Vacha-Haase & Thompson, 2004). As the formula indicates, standardized difference effect sizes express the differences in mean values for two groups in standard deviation units. Hence, an effect size of .5 indicates that the experimental group mean for an outcome variable is one-half of a standard deviation higher than the mean for the control group, whereas an effect size of −1 indicates that the control group mean is one standard deviation unit higher on the outcome variable than the experimental group.

In practice, the standard deviation that is used to calculate effect size can be estimated in different ways, depending on the assumptions of the researcher. Glass (1976) proposed *delta* as a measure of standardized differences, which divides the sample mean difference by the sample standard deviation of the control group. This approach is preferred when the researcher suspects that the intervention that is being tested may increase (or decrease) both the mean level of the outcome variable and the variance of the distribution. In these cases, the standard deviation of the control group is likely to more accurately reflect the population variance and, hence, lead to a more accurate estimate of the effect size. Alternately, Cohen (1969) proposed *d*, which uses a standard deviation estimate that is averaged (pooled) across the intervention and control groups. In most cases these different approaches to estimating mean difference effect sizes will yield similar results.

Variance accounted for indices are effect size measures that indicate the amount variation in a dependent variable or set of dependent variables that is explained by a predictor variable or set of predictor variables, as a ratio of the total variation of the dependent variable(s). The square of the correlation coefficient (r^2) and multiple correlation coefficient (R^2) are the most common effect size measures used in published research. If the correlation between a predictor and an outcome variable is .7, then $r^2 = .49$, indicating that 49 percent of the variation of the outcome variable is shared with the predictor variable.

The most commonly used statistical analyses are part of a single analytic family, known as the general linear model (GLM; Cohen, 1969; Miles & Shevlin, 2001; Tacq, 1997). All GLM analyses (e.g., t-tests, analysis of variance [ANOVA] and covariance [ANCOVA], multiple regression, factor analysis) are essentially correlational methods. An r^2-type effect size can be computed from any of these statistical methods, though the manner of computation may differ. In all cases, the computed variance accounted for index represents the amount of variation of the dependent variable that is explained by the "model" (i.e., the independent or predictor variable or set of variables) as a ratio of the total variation of the dependent variable(s). In the context of ANOVA/ANCOVA, this index is known as the *correlation ratio* or *eta squared* (n^2) (Vacha-Haase & Thompson, 2004).

Corrected effect size measures are estimated population effect indices that adjust the sample effect size by removing the influence of sampling error variance (Vacha-Haase & Thompson, 2004). Every sample that is drawn from a population of interest has its own uniqueness or personality (i.e., sampling error variance), and some samples have more sampling error variance than others. Also, GLM procedures utilize mathematical procedures that maximize the effect size for the sample data. Therefore, the effect size for a sample tends to overestimate the effect size in the population and in future samples. Corrected effect size measures are generally more accurate estimates of population effects (Snyder & Lawson, 1993). Adjusted R^2 is a commonly reported corrected effect size index in the context of multiple regression, and *omega squared* (~ 2) is used in the context of ANOVA/ANCOVA. Correction formulae are also available for most multivariate analyses (Vacha-Haase & Thompson, 2004).

A key advantage of computing and reporting effect size in published research is that it allows a direct evaluation of various investigations within a research domain that use samples of different size and different outcome measures. In particular, standardized difference measures of effect size (i.e., *delta* or *d*) are used extensively in meta-analysis (see Chapter 6) for analyzing, summarizing, and interpreting findings from large research programs so that global conclusions are accurate and cumulative.

Methods of Statistical Analysis

This section introduces a number of techniques of statistical analysis by which data are analyzed and which are relatively common in rehabilitation counseling research. Methods are tools, and the methods of statistical analysis are meaningful only when they are applied within an appropriately designed study and interpreted within the theoretical context of the research question. As Pedhazur (1982) stated, "Data do not speak for themselves but through the medium of the analytic techniques applied to them. Analytical techniques not only set limits to the scope and nature of the answers one may obtain from data, but also affect the type of questions a researcher asks and the manner in which the questions are formulated" (p. 4).

THE T-TEST. A number of different inferential statistical tests are used to analyze quantitative data in the social sciences. One of the simplest statistical tests is known as the t-test, or test of mean differences between two samples, typically a treatment group and a comparison group. Consider the following example:

A researcher has developed a psychosocial intervention designed to enhance the adjustment of persons with physical disabilities. She wishes to know whether the intervention is effective. She identifies a sample of persons with disabilities in a local agency and negotiates the support of the agency (and consent of the participants) in implementing the investigation. She randomly assigns the participants to two groups, a group that receives the intervention and a group that does not receive the intervention. Then she implements the intervention. After the intervention is concluded, she administers a self-report measure of psychosocial adjustment to both groups. She expects that the mean scores on adjustment for the intervention group will be greater than the mean scores on adjustment for the comparison group; this will signify that the intervention was effective in enhancing psychosocial adjustment.

But how can the researcher determine whether a mean difference is large enough to be noteworthy or indicative of a treatment effect, rather than the spurious result of chance sampling fluctuations? The t-test is used in this case to make warranted inferences about treatment effects (i.e., receipt or non-receipt of an intervention) for a population (i.e., people with physical disabilities) based on the differences in the distributions of variables (i.e., performance on a measure of psychosocial adjustment) in a randomly drawn sample. The researcher anticipates that, as a function of the psychosocial intervention, the mean score on the measure of adjustment for the treatment group will be larger than the mean score for the comparison group. Thus, the effect of the intervention is indicated by *between-group differences,* or the difference between the two group means on the adjustment variable. The researcher also knows, however, that individuals within each group will obtain different scores from each other on the adjustment measure. The differences between the individuals within each group are known as *within-group differences* and reflect the variability of individuals within a sample or sub-sample on the measured variable.

The t-test is a ratio of between-group differences to within-group differences on an outcome variable. The t-ratio is then compared to a theoretical distribution of t-ratios, and a probability value is computed that indicates the likelihood that the sample t-ratio is the result of chance. Roughly stated, the purpose of the t-test is to determine whether the ratio of between-group differences to within-group differences is large enough to make it unlikely that the observed between-group differences are due to chance variation. In the case of the example provided above, a statistically significant probability value ($p<.05$) associated with the t-ratio indicates that the two groups differ significantly on the adjustment outcome variable.

In the language of inferential statistics, the treatment effect is known as systematic variance or variance in scores that result from a known condition, intervention, or other predictor variable (Kazdin, 2003). Variation that is due to other, unmeasured factors on which the two groups may differ and that affect scores on the dependent variable is known as residual or error variance. The residual variance is actually the variation in the sample data that is due to individual differences (i.e., within group differences). Residual or error variance may also reflect random sampling fluctuations (i.e., sampling error) that occur whenever a sample is drawn from a population. The t-test is one statistical method for partitioning the variation of scores into systematic and error variance and is the appropriate inferential test when comparing the mean scores of two groups on an outcome variable that is measured on a continuous scale.

Statistical significance is a function of four factors: the potency of the treatment (the between-groups difference on the outcome variable) or effect, the amount of variability within each group (individual or within group difference), the size of the sample, and the benchmark (i.e., Alpha level) that is established a priori by the investigator. Thus, the researcher is likely to be rewarded with a statistically significant result when the treatment effect is relatively large (i.e., the intervention results in substantial differences between groups on adjustment scores), when the variability of individuals' adjustment scores within each group is relatively small, and when a large sample is used.

ANALYSIS OF VARIANCE. Analysis of Variance (ANOVA) is the appropriate statistical strategy when more than two groups are compared on an outcome variable that is measured on a continuous scale. For example, a researcher may wish to compare the effectiveness of two distinct interventions to enhance adjustment and compare both of these to a group that did not receive an intervention. In this case, the independent variable is a categorical variable that has three values that represent the three groups. Like the t-test, ANOVA partitions the variation of the dependent variable in the three groups into systematic and error variance. In ANOVA the ratio of systematic to error variance is known as an F-ratio. The F-ratio is then compared to the theoretical distribution of F-ratios and a probability value is computed to determine whether an F-ratio of this magnitude is likely to be the result of chance.

The statistical test for an ANOVA (i.e., F-test) provides the information that the means on the outcome variable are or are not significantly different across the three groups. However, the F-test does not provide information about which among the three or more group means are significantly different from the others. If the goal of the researcher was to compare the efficacy of two different interventions with a non-intervention group, the statistically significant F-test should be followed with post hoc, pair-wise comparison tests to evaluate which group means significantly differ. The post hoc tests provide information about whether one intervention is more effective than another, and whether each intervention is more effective than no intervention.

Factorial Analysis of Variance permits researchers to examine the separate and interactive effects of two or more categorical variables on an outcome variable. For example, Leierer et al. (1996) examined the separate and interactive effects of counselor disability, attending skills, and salience of client problem relative to disability on ratings of counselors' credibility. Leierer et al. hypothesized that the relationship between counselors' disability status (i.e., independent variable) and their credibility with clients (i.e., outcome variable) may be moderated by whether the client was addressing a disability-salient counseling issue or not (i.e., second independent variable). They anticipated that clients with disabilities may prefer to have a counselor with a disability when the issue addressed in counseling is salient to disability, whereas, when the issue is not salient to disability, counselor disability status may be irrelevant to the client. The separate effects of the independent and status variables on the outcome variable are known as main effects, and the moderating effects of combinations of independent and status variables are known as interactive effects. Factorial ANOVA provides a technique for partitioning the variation in the outcome variable into variance due to the separate main effects, variance due to interactive effects, and residual or error variance (i.e., individual differences within each distribution).

Repeated-measures ANOVA is a special case of factorial ANOVA in which one of the independent variables is the repeated measurement of the dependent variable over time (e.g., at pretest, posttest, and follow-up). In these cases, the test of the independent variable "time" assesses whether the scores of the groups differ across the times of measurement, and the interaction term (i.e., treatment x time) assesses whether there are differential effects between treatment groups and the outcome variable depending on the time of measurement (e.g., the treatment and control groups are equivalent on the outcome variable measured at pretest, but are significantly different at posttest and/or follow-up).

Analysis of Covariance (ANCOVA) represents another variation of ANOVA. The basic framework is identical to ANOVA; however, in ANCOVA one or more covariates are included in the analysis. Typically covariates are variables on which the treatment groups may differ, that may impact the outcome variable, and that represent plausible rival explanations for the findings. Thus, incorporating covariates in an ANOVA is a method of controlling for the influence of these variables in the statistical analysis.

Covariates must be measured on a continuous scale. For example, when a pretest-posttest strategy of measurement is used in an investigation, the researcher may wish to include participants' pretest scores on the outcome variable as a covariate as a way of controlling for the influence of the pretest on the posttest scores for the outcome.

MULTIPLE REGRESSION. Multiple regression analysis is a method of analyzing "the collective and separate effects of two or more independent or predictor variables on a dependent (or outcome) variable" (Pedhazur, 1982, p. 6). Akin to the factorial ANOVA technique, multiple regression provides a way to (a) assess the collective contribution of two or more variables to the variation in the dependent variable, and (b) partition the variation in the dependent variable into variance explained by each separate predictor variable as well as error variance (Keith, 2006). Akin to ANCOVA, multiple regression permits the evaluation of the impact of an independent variable on an outcome while simultaneously controlling for the influences of other predictor variables on the outcome.

Multiple regression analysis has two primary purposes: prediction and causal explanation (Miles & Shevlin, 2001). These different purposes are distinguished not by different statistical procedures, but rather, by the role of theory in guiding the decisions of the researcher and the interpretation of the data. Multiple regression is a highly flexible analytic technique. It can be used with multiple continuous independent or status variables or a mixed set of dichotomous, categorical, and continuous independent or status variables. Typically, the dependent variable in a multiple regression analysis is a continuous variable, but variations of regression (e.g., logistic regression) are used to predict dichotomous dependent variables (Keith, 2006).

Multiple regression is an extension of simple correlation. Whereas correlation assesses the relationship between two variables, multiple regression assesses the relationship, or multiple correlation, between a *set* of predictor variables and one dependent variable. The regression analysis results in an equation that represents a composite variable that is composed of the observed predictor values and specific weights (i.e., multipliers) that are assigned to each predictor variable to predict as well as possible the observed values of the outcome variable. How well the predicted values for the outcome, generated by the regression equation, correspond to the actual values of the outcome variable observed in the sample is indicated in the variance accounted for statistic (i.e., R^2). Output statistics from a regression analysis include (a) measures of effect size (i.e., multiple R for the multiple correlation and R^2 for the variance explained in the dependent variable by the set of independent variables) and (b) statistical significance tests to assess the contribution of each independent variable to the prediction of the dependent variable. Output statistics also include two types of regression coefficients: *unstandardized regression coefficients* or *B-weights* that indicate the amount of change in the outcome variables that can be expected based on a one-unit change in the value of each predictor variable, and *standardized regression coefficients* or *Beta-weights* that indicate the relative influence of each variable in predicting the outcome variable (Keith, 2006).

Multiple regression has been widely used in rehabilitation counseling research to predict a variety of rehabilitation outcomes. For example, Bellini, Bolton, and Neath (1998) used multiple regression to assess the collective contribution of counselors' ratings of vocational rehabilitation (VR) clients' functional limitation to the prediction of services that clients subsequently received. This is an example of a model-driven approach to multiple regression analysis because, as the authors noted, Rehabilitation Services Administration (RSA) guidelines stipulate that clients' functional limitations are indicators of service needs, and rehabilitation services are provided to address service needs identified in the assessment process (RSA, 1992). The Bellini et al. study was an examination of the validity of rehabilitation counselors' assessments of clients in relation to the services clients received, a key theoretical proposition for vocational rehabilitation.

Logistic regression has many of the same advantages as ordinary multiple regression and is the preferred data analytic method when the outcome variable is dichotomous (e.g., employed/not employed). Like ordinary regression, logistic regression (a) results in a prediction equation that is composed of the observed predictor values and coefficients that best predict the outcome variable, and (b) permits the researcher to assess the separate and combined effects of the set of predictors on the outcome. However, logistic regression uses the criterion of maximum likelihood rather than least-squares to estimate population parameters from the sample data (Keith, 2006). Whereas in ordinary multiple regression the unstandardized regression coefficients reflect the amount of change in the outcome associated with a one-unit change in the value of each predictor, in logistic regression the *odds ratio* represents the predicted change in the odds of occurrence for the dichotomous outcome associated with a one-unit change in the predictor variable. It is common for rehabilitation research to examine outcome variables that are dichotomous in nature (e.g., rehabilitated/not rehabilitated, employed/not employed); hence it is not surprising that logistic regression analysis is increasingly common in rehabilitation research (Huang et al., 2016; Kaya et al., 2016).

MULTIVARIATE ANALYSIS. Multivariate analysis consists of a family of statistical techniques that are used to examine the effects of one or a set of independent or status variables on a *set* of continuous dependent variables (Spicer,

2005; Tacq, 1997). The term multivariate analysis is typically reserved for statistical analyses that use multiple, correlated outcome variables. Similar to multiple regression, the different multivariate approaches generate one or more equations that combine the set of predictor variables to best predict the outcome variables. These equations include different weights assigned to each predictor variable to maximize the prediction of the outcomes for the sample data, although the weights or multipliers are given different names in the different types of analysis (e.g., discriminant function coefficients in multiple discriminant analysis, path coefficients in path analysis). Multivariate analysis was relatively rare prior to the era of the personal computer (when the complex and time-consuming calculations were done by hand), but it is much more common in rehabilitation counseling research since user-friendly statistical programs have become available.

There are also substantive reasons why multivariate analysis is preferred to other, less sophisticated approaches to data analysis. Bolton (1986) advocated for a multivariate approach to research design and analysis to enhance causal explanation of key processes (a primary goal of science) given the impossibility of randomly assigning treatment conditions to assess the effects of independent variables in most rehabilitation counseling research. Also, these more complex approaches to modeling social or psychological processes or outcomes better reflect the nature of the phenomena that are the focus of research in the social sciences. In this view, social reality is multivariate, and most social science is research "in which the researcher cares about multiple outcomes, in which most outcomes have multiple causes, and in which most causes have multiple effects" (Thompson, 1986, p. 9). Parker (1990) advanced a more cautious view of the appropriateness of multivariate procedures for rehabilitation research, stating that sophisticated statistical analyses are no substitute for attention to the quality of the data and well-conceived and executed research designs.

Selected multivariate techniques include multivariate analysis of variance (MANOVA) and covariance (MANCOVA), multivariate multiple regression, multiple discriminant analysis (MDA), path analysis, canonical correlation analysis, multilevel modeling (MLM), factor analysis, and structural equation modeling. MANOVA and MANCOVA are extensions of ANOVA and ANCOVA, respectively, and they permit the evaluation of a set of predictor variables on a set of correlated outcome variables. Similarly, multivariate multiple regression is an extension of multiple regression in which a set of predictor variables is used to predict a set of correlated outcome variables. MDA is similar to multiple regression in that multiple predictor variables are included; however, in MDA the criterion is a categorical variable with at least three levels, and the purpose of the analysis is to predict group separation (Tacq, 1997). Path analysis is an extension of multiple regression that permits the evaluation of models of social phenomena, wherein a variable may be an outcome in one phase of a process model and a predictor variable in subsequent phases (Klem, 1995). Canonical correlation analysis is used to evaluate the degree of covariation or overlap between two theoretically related sets of variables, without consideration of priority or causality. MLM permits the analysis of data that are "nested" or hierarchically-ordered to include more than one level (e.g., counselor characteristics and client characteristics when both are relevant to explaining client outcomes, or student-level, teacher-level, and school-level data when all three levels of data are relevant to explaining student achievement). MLM is used to assess the separate and combined effects of these different "levels" of data on selected outcomes.

Factor analysis is utilized extensively in the development and validation of psychometric instruments (Floyd & Widaman, 1995). Factor analysis differs from the other techniques discussed to this point in that the goal of factor analysis is to identify sources of covariation that are *internal* to a set of variables or items, rather than to identify the sources of covariation in an outcome variable or set of outcome variables using one or more independent or predictor variables (Floyd & Widaman, 1995; Tacq, 1997). In other words, the purpose of factor analysis is to identify the latent (i.e., underlying) structure of a set of correlated variables. Although these variables are most often items of a test or inventory, factor analysis may also be used to operationalize a construct using multiple indicators (see Figure 2.1). Finally, structural equation modeling is an advanced multivariate technique that permits investigators to use sample data to evaluate both how *well* selected indicators (i.e., measured variables) of constructs represent their source latent variables *and* the nature of the relationships among the latent variables (Fassinger, 1987; Merchant, Li, Karpinski, & Rumrill, 2013).

These different multivariate strategies differ in purpose and in the methods used to calculate composite variables. However, these techniques are not qualitatively different from the simpler analytic strategies such as the t-test or ANOVA. Rather, all of these statistical strategies are fundamentally similar in that they (a) assess the linear relationships among variables, and (b) provide methods for partitioning the variation of dependent variables into systematic (i.e., covariance) and residual variation. The systematic variance of the dependent variables is further partitioned into its different sources, that is, the unique contribution of each predictor variable to the observed variation in the dependent variable(s).

Nonparametric Statistics

As noted previously, parametric (i.e., conventional) statistical procedures require that the sample data reasonably approximate the assumptions for these tests (e.g., normal distribution, homogeneity of variance, interval-level data). When substantial violations of these assumptions occur, it is more appropriate to use non-parametric statistical tests (Gay & Airasian, 2003; Bellini et al., 2000). Non-parametric tests require no assumptions about the shape of the variable distributions and are usually employed when the data are measured on a nominal or ordinal scale. In general, non-parametric tests are less powerful than parametric tests; therefore, these tests usually require larger sample sizes to reach the same level of statistical significance as a parametric test (Gay & Airasian, 2003). Hence, unless the assumptions for the statistical test are greatly violated, parametric tests are preferred.

Non-parametric analogies have been developed for most classical (i.e., parametric) statistical tests (Tacq, 1997). However, these are rarely observed in contemporary rehabilitation research. The most common non-parametric test is the *chi-square* test of association, symbolized as $x2$. Chi-square is an appropriate test when the data are in the form of frequency counts or proportions that can be converted to frequencies (i.e., nominal or ordinal-level data). Two or more exclusive categories are required. A chi-square test compares the variable frequencies or proportions actually observed in a data set to the proportions expected (the null hypothesis typically posits equal proportions, although occasionally expected frequencies may be based on previous findings). The chi-square value increases as the difference between the observed and expected frequencies increases. As with parametric tests, the chi-square value is compared to the theoretical distribution of chi-square to determine whether differences of the given magnitude can be expected as a function of chance.

Table 3.2 lists the variety of statistical techniques discussed in this and earlier sections, the measurement characteristics of variables that are most appropriate for each procedure, and the research purpose for each technique. A number of sources are available for readers who are interested in learning more about multivariate analysis in the social sciences. Textbooks by Spicer (2005) and Grim and Yarnold (1995) explain the different multivariate techniques in a manner that is accessible to persons who have a limited background in statistics. For students who have the requisite advanced knowledge of statistics, Stevens (1996) and Tacq (1997) present detailed discussions of multivariate techniques and examples using sample data sets.

Table 3.2. Types of Statistical Analyses

Type of Analysis	Variables	Purpose of Analysis
Chi-Square	two categorical	assesses the association between two variables
Correlation	two (may be any combination of continuous, dichotomous, or categorical)	assess the linear relationship of two variables
t-test	one categorical independent, one continuous dependent	tests mean differences between two groups
ANOVA	one or more categorical independent and/or status, one continuous dependent	tests mean differences for more than two groups
ANCOVA	one or more categorical independent and/or status, one or more continuous covariate, one continuous dependent	tests mean differences for two or more groups while holding moderator variable constant across groups
Multiple Regression	two or more categorical and/or continuous independent and/or status, one continuous dependent	assesses collective and separate correlation of multiple predictor variables to single outcome
Multiple Discriminant Analysis	one categorical independent or status, set of continuous dependent	assesses the differences among two or more groups on a set of dependent variables
Logistic Regression	two or more categorical and/or continuous independent and/or status, one dichotomous outcome	assesses collective and separate correlation of multiple predictor variables to a single dichotomous dependent variable
Multivariate Multiple Regression	two or more categorical and/or continuous independent and/or status, two or more continuous dependent	assesses collective and separate correlation of multiple predictor variables to two or more outcome variables
MANOVA	at least one categorical independent and status variables, two or more continuous at least two correlated dependent	tests mean differences on two or more outcomes for two or more groups

Table 3.2–*Continued*

Type of Analysis	Variables	Purpose of Analysis
Canonical Correlation	two or more sets of continuous variables	assesses the relationships among two or more latent constructs
Factor Analysis	set of continuous variables	assesses the dimensionality of a set of continuous variables
Cluster Analysis	set of continuous variables	assesses the dimensionality of a set of continuous variables
Path Analysis	set of continuous variables	assesses the degree to which variable relationships are consistent with a specified theoretical model
Structural Equation Modeling	set of continuous variables; ideally, at least two indicators representing each construct	same as path analysis but at the level of latent constructs; also assesses how well measured variables represent the source constructs
Multilevel Modeling	independent variables that are hierarchically ordered, or that operate at different "levels" within a research context; one continuous dependent variable	assesses collective and separate correlation of multiple predictor variables; apportions variation of dependent variable to different "levels" in the analysis

Note on Theory, Hypothesis Testing, and Professional Practice

As noted previously, the purpose of inferential statistics is to make warranted inferences, based on probability theory, about the nature of the relationships between variables in a population of interest based on the relationships between these variables that are observed in the sample. Once an inference about specific variable relationships in a population is made, a second inferential step—from the population of interest to the general hypothesis that was tested—is necessary to ensure the meaningfulness and generality of research propositions (Serlin, 1987). Whereas the inferential leap from sample to population is based on statistical procedures, the inferential leap from the population to the research hypothesis is based on the plausibility of the theory that provides an explanation of the results. It is the plausibility of theory that is supported by particular research findings and that substantiates the contribution of research findings within an area of inquiry. As applied to statistical procedures, the linkages among sample, population, and hypothesis imply that theoretical considerations should guide the design, analysis, and interpretation of empirical results (Tracey & Glidden-Tracey, 1999). As Serlin (1987) stated:

> Statistical analysis is not separate from but rather is part of the whole piece of theoretical confirmation and disconfirmation. Statistics and theory inform each other. In terms of scientific progress, any statistical analysis whose purpose is not determined by theory, whose hypotheses and methods are not theoretically specified, or whose results are not related back to theory must be considered, like atheoretical fishing and model building, to be hobbies. (p. 371)

It is important to underscore that research consumers (i.e., readers) should always attend to the actual differences among means (when group comparisons are made) or other indicators of the magnitude of relationship that are independent of sample size (e.g., d, R^2) in order to assess the practical significance of a research finding. Evaluating the practical significance of research findings also involves reassessing the status of the theoretical proposition following the empirical test, as well as the heuristic and practical value of the theoretical proposition relative to the goals, activities, and procedures of the particular agency, program, or other entity. As Serlin (1987) and Tracey (1991) noted, research conclusions rarely apply directly to practice. Instead, research findings confirm or disconfirm particular theoretical propositions or models. When theoretical propositions survive repeated attempts at disconfirmation, their credibility and usefulness for professional practice is enhanced.

Dembo and Wright's theory of value changes associated with adjustment to physical disability, known as the acceptance of loss theory (Dembo, Leviton, & Wright, 1975; Wright, 1983), is a good example of the connections among theory, empirical research, and professional practice. Dembo et al. and Wright developed their propositions about value changes from a creative mix of social psychological theory, research, and clinical observation. They tested the validity of these propositions against empirical data in a series of investigations and found that the propositions were relatively robust (Wright, 1983). Over time, other researchers and scholars explored the applicability of the theory of value changes to adjustment to psychiatric disabilities, invisible disabilities, and substance abuse disabilities (Alston, 1992; Butts & Shontz, 1962; Keany & Glueckauf, 1999). When Wright's propositions were not consistent with all of the empirical evidence gathered, the theory was revised to be more inclusive (Keany & Glueckauf, 1999). Thus, acceptance of loss theory provided a basis for developing research hypotheses, and empirical findings that result from research enhance the credibility of the theory or force changes to the theory.

As Keany and Glueckauf (1999) noted, the work of Dembo et al. and Wright have guided the thinking and practice of rehabilitation psychologists for four decades. Despite its importance to the rehabilitation profession, however, the major premises of acceptance of loss theory have not been adequately tested in empirical research. It is the theory, confirmed by research findings, that provides rehabilitation practitioners with tools for understanding the relationships among personal values, beliefs about disability, and subsequent adjustment of persons with disabilities. To be sure, there is nothing so practical as good theory.

SUMMARY

In quantitative research, measurement issues are central to the operationalization of research hypotheses and the interpretation of findings. Three important characteristics by which to evaluate tests are standardization, reliability, and validity. Standardized tests provide evidence that scores are both consistent and meaningfully related to other important social outcomes. Reliability refers to the stability of scores, the extent to which measurement eliminates chance and other extraneous factors, or the approximate proportion of true score that is present in an obtained score. Several different strategies may be used to estimate the stability of scores, including test-retest, alternate forms, internal consistency, and inter-rater reliability. These methods refer to the stability of scores over time, across comparable forms of a test, across items of a test, and across different raters, respectively.

Validity is a judgment of the value of a test, or the appropriateness, interpretability, and social consequences of particular uses of a test. Three types of validity investigations are content, criterion, and construct validity. Content validity refers to whether the items of a test adequately sample the appropriate content domain. Criterion validity pertains to the relationships between test scores and other, external criteria. Construct validity has to do with understanding the underlying constructs, dimensions, or attributes being measured by a test. Validity is the single most important consideration in test evaluation. Reliability is a necessary but insufficient condition for test validity.

Statistical methods of data analysis are utilized in quantitative research. Descriptive statistics are methods of organizing, summarizing, and presenting data. A number of concepts are useful in describing distributions of variables, including shape, measures of central tendency (mean, median, and mode), measures of variability (range, variance, and standard deviation), and measures of relationship (correlation). The normal distribution is the basis for both descriptive and inferential statistical methods. Measures of central tendency describe the typical performance of a group on a measured variable. Measures of variability provide information about the spread of scores in a distribution. Measures of relationship furnish information about the magnitude and direction of the linear association of two variables.

Inferential statistics provide a basis for making inferences about the relationships among variables in a population based on the relationships that are observed in a sample. The probability value, $p \leq .05$, is the conventional benchmark for determining whether a research finding is statistically significant. However, two types of errors, referred to as Type I and Type II errors, are possible in hypothesis testing. A Type I error occurs when the null hypothesis (i.e., no significant differences on the outcome variable) is rejected but is actually true in the population. A Type II error occurs when the null hypothesis is accepted but is actually false in the population. It is impossible to know for certain when these errors have occurred in a data analysis; however, several conditions that make these errors more likely were identified. Given that statistical significance tests are highly sensitive to sample size, it is also important to evaluate research findings on the basis of effect size. Standardized differences, variance accounted for measures, and corrected indices are three types of effect size measures that permit a direct evaluation of research findings across different studies.

A number of different inferential statistical techniques are used in rehabilitation research, including the t-test, analysis of variance and covariance, multiple regression, and multivariate analysis. These statistical techniques were presented in an order of increasing sophistication; however, all are part of a single analytic family, known as the *general linear model.* Table 3.1 presents the types of variables and research purposes associated with different statistical approaches. Practical significance of findings is a central issue in the evaluation of a research study. In assessing the practical significance of a study, the research consumer should attend to the actual differences among means when group comparisons are made, or other measures of the magnitude of relationships that are independent of sample size (e.g., d, R^2). Evaluating the practical significance of research findings also involves assessing the pragmatic value of the theoretical proposition that was tested relative to the goals, activities, and methods of the agency or program to which the consumer seeks to generalize. It is the practical value of the theoretical proposition, confirmed by the empirical test, which substantiates the contribution of research to rehabilitation practice.

Chapter 4

ETHICAL ISSUES AND GUIDELINES FOR REHABILITATION RESEARCH

With Contributions by Aundrea Gee Cormier

INTRODUCTION

Ethics can be defined as a set of rules or guidelines concerning what is "right" or appropriate conduct (Corey, Corey, & Callanan, 2011). Although we all maintain our own core set of ethics that guides us in our daily lives, most professions set forth ethical guidelines, or codes, that specify how we should conduct ourselves as representatives of those professions. For example, the *Code of Professional Ethics for Rehabilitation Counselors,* which was last revised in 2017 (Commission on Rehabilitation Counselor Certification [CRCC], 2017) provides a lengthy (41 single-spaced pages) structure for professional conduct with respect to such issues as the counselor-client relationship, confidentiality, advocacy and accessibility, professional responsibility, relationships with other professionals, evaluation and assessment, intervention, teaching, training and supervision, research, electronic communication, business practices, and resolving ethical issues.

Given the applied emphasis of research in rehabilitation counseling, as described in Chapter 1 of this text, and considering the close contact that rehabilitation researchers have with people with disabilities, ethical issues are of paramount importance in the design, implementation, and dissemination of research in our field. To be sure, the rehabilitation researcher has obligations to several constituency groups that have vested interests in ensuring that empirical studies are carried out under the highest ethical standards and circumstances. Specifically, rehabilitation researchers have ethical obligations to participants in their research, to other researchers collaborating on investigations, to their employers, to the agencies that support research projects, to professional consumers (i.e., readers) of research results, and to professional organizations with which they are affiliated.

The purpose of this chapter is to describe the considerations and standards that shape ethical or appropriate conduct in scientific inquiry as they apply to rehabilitation counseling. We begin with an overview of ethical principles that underlie all aspects of rehabilitation counseling, then follow with standards concerning the treatment of human subjects in rehabilitation and social science research. We conclude the chapter with a discussion of ethics as they apply to the process of reporting and publishing rehabilitation research.

ETHICAL PRINCIPLES OF REHABILITATION COUNSELING

Before the rehabilitation researcher begins to conceptualize and design a study, he or she must become familiar with the abiding ethical provisions that guide all interactions with clients or consumers in counseling relationships. Borrowed from the medical paradigm (Beauchamp & Childress, 1989) and specified to clinical applications of counseling and psychology by the American Counseling Association and the American Psychological Association (Goodwin & Goodwin, 2012; Heppner, Wampold, Owen, Thompson, & Wang, 2015; Kazdin, 2003), the concepts of *non-maleficence, beneficence, autonomy, justice,* and *fidelity* have been identified as hallmarks of ethical conduct by professional rehabilitation counselors (Rubin, Roessler, & Rumrill, 2016). The following paragraphs define and explain these concepts as they apply to all aspects of rehabilitation counseling and research. For more detailed information regarding the specific rules of ethical conduct in rehabilitation counseling practice, readers should consult the *Code of Professional Ethics for Rehabilitation Counselors* (CRCC, 2017).

Non-Maleficence

"First, do no harm." Known as non-maleficence, the "do no harm" maxim in applied counseling and psychology means that researchers must take every precaution to ensure that participants are not subject to danger or negative consequences (Heppner et al., 2015). Most social science ethicists agree that non-maleficence is the most basic and important guideline for the conduct of researchers and practitioners (Diener & Crandall, 1978).

Doing no harm requires the rehabilitation researcher to do more than simply avoid inflicting intentional harm. Researchers must minimize unintended risks to every extent possible, inform participants of any risks that cannot be controlled, and maintain vigilance in assessing any potential harmful situations that may arise during the implementation of a study (CRCC, 2017). Moreover, non-maleficence is seen as even more important than the ideal of providing benefit to (i.e., helping) the client, consumer, or research participant. In other words, when a rehabilitation researcher is considering an intervention or other research approach that could benefit one participant while potentially harming another, ethical standards dictate that he or she should not apply that approach until the potential risks have been minimized and explained to the participant who may be subject to harm.

Beneficence

If non-maleficence constitutes the most basic ethical obligation of the rehabilitation researcher, then beneficence (i.e., acting in a manner that promotes the well-being of others) must be viewed as the core principle that defines the purpose of any rehabilitation counseling relationship (Rubin et al., 2016). Heppner et al. (2015) aptly noted that professional counselors exist to help people solve problems that they are not able to solve on their own. In that regard, research to demonstrate or evaluate clinical practices has an obvious and important role in shaping the facilitative problem-solving process that is rehabilitation counseling.

For example, the applied rehabilitation researcher who demonstrates an intervention to assist people with disabilities in obtaining jobs (Strauser, 2013) upholds the principle of beneficence in two ways. Not only is a direct benefit provided to participants in the investigation (especially to those who successfully enter or re-enter the workforce), but readers of the research report or published article who incorporate the researchers' placement strategies into their own practices stand to enhance their clients' prospects for successful rehabilitation outcomes. In other words, beneficence in rehabilitation research can be observed in terms of both direct benefits to participants in particular studies and the contributions that published research makes to the professional knowledge base.

Implicit in the principle of beneficence is the notion of competence. Rehabilitation counselors have an ethical obligation to ensure that they have had appropriate training and possess sufficient skills to help people with disabilities achieve their career and life goals (CRCC, 2017). This also means that counselors must realistically appraise the limitations of their training and experience and not attempt to exceed their qualifications by providing services that would be the more appropriate purview of another professional. This self-assessment process is equally important for the beneficent rehabilitation researcher. When applying the designs and techniques described in subsequent chapters of this book, researchers must ensure that their methods and analyses are compatible with their current levels of proficiency. For example, the researcher conducting an investigation of the factors that influence quality of life among people with chronic illnesses (Bishop, 2012) must be thoroughly familiar with existing research in that subject area, possess skills in designing studies that test relationships among multiple variables, and understand the statistical analyses that will enable him or her to answer the research questions. Thus, in the research context, beneficence includes not only the desire or intention to contribute to the well-being of people with disabilities via rehabilitation research but also the ability to carry out a responsible and scientifically sound investigation.

Autonomy

The concept of autonomy, defined by Kitchener (1984, p. 46) as "respect for the freedoms of choice and action of the individual to the extent that those freedoms do not conflict with similar freedoms of others," is a cornerstone of American laws, politics, and culture. The freedom to choose and act in accordance with our own values, interests, and ambitions is among our most precious liberties, and ethical standards in medical and social science research are imbued with the rights of subjects to participate (or not participate) of their own volition and without negative consequences.

Since the Nuremberg trials following World War II and the World Medical Association 1964 *Declaration of Helsinki,* the principle of autonomy has received steadily increasing attention from research ethicists (Heppner et al., 2015; Kazdin, 2003). Anyone who has conducted a research investigation at a college, university, or hospital during the past 40 years is well familiar with the notion of informed consent, a mainstay requirement of ethical research practice mandating that potential participants in studies must be informed about the nature and purpose of the research prior to their voluntary enrollment in any investigation.

As it applies to rehabilitation research, autonomy encompasses more than soliciting and securing informed consent from potential participants. The researcher must ensure that delivering an intervention or collecting data does not intrude any more than is absolutely necessary upon participants' other pursuits (Bellini & Rumrill, 2009). In the event that an investigation requires or is intended to result in a particular course of action, participants must be granted assurances that the ultimate locus of control for their choices rests with them. Even if the study involves activities that appear to be inherently helpful as per the principle of beneficence (e.g., substance abuse treatment [Atherton & Toriello, 2012]; a psychiatric vocational rehabilitation intervention [Koch & Rumrill, 2016], assistive technology to combat the effects of traumatic brain injury [Hendricks et al., 2015]), participants must retain absolute prerogative concerning whether, when, and to what extent they engage in the investigation.

Justice

In any field or sector of society wherein finite resources do not allow decisionmakers to meet all of the needs of all people, difficult choices must be made regarding "who gets what and why" (Howie et al., 1992, p. 49). Such is certainly the case in rehabilitation. The Rehabilitation Services Administration requires states that cannot serve all eligible applicants in the Vocational Rehabilitation program to institute Order of Selection procedures whereby services are prioritized for people with the most significant disabilities (Rubin et al., 2016). In making decisions concerning who gets what and why, the principle of justice often serves as the ethical benchmark (Corey et al., 2011; Heppner et al., 2015; Szymanski & Parker, 2010).

In rehabilitation and other areas of counseling, justice implies that resources and services are disbursed fairly and not on the basis of advantaging or disadvantaging characteristics (Howie et al., 1992). In other words, just distribution of resources means that people who occupy a status of privilege do not receive a disproportionate share of goods or services. It also means that people whose status is one of disadvantage are not disproportionately excluded from accessing benefits or resources. Toriello & Keferl (2012) noted that justice in disability policy is not simply a matter of dividing resources evenly among all people who have a need or claim; rather, they asserted the wel-laccepted notion that the purpose of social services is to equalize opportunities for people to access certain benefits or amenities of society. In that regard, however, Bellini (1998) noted that justice or equity for one person often results in injustice or inequity for another. For example, a medical researcher conducting a study with an experimental drug to treat fibromyalgia limits her investigation to 15 participants because of modest funding for the project. The 16th and subsequent participants are not provided with the treatment; rather, they form a "standard practice" comparison group. The treatment turns out to be highly successful, which is, of course, beneficial to the participants who received the intervention. One could make the point, however, that the comparison group incurred an injustice, albeit an unavoidable one given the fiscal constraints of the study, by not having the opportunity to receive the experimental medication. As a means of more justly allocating the benefits of the intervention, the researcher might decide to administer the experimental drug to the comparison group sometime after the study has concluded.

Justice is a key principle in the delivery of rehabilitation counseling services, and it poses essential considerations for rehabilitation researchers as they design investigations, select participants, and apply consistent standards in determining who gets what and why. By establishing a clear scheme and rationale for determining how research studies are justly and fairly carried out, rehabilitation researchers can add to the knowledge base in a manner that reflects the full spirit of ethical conduct in all social science disciplines.

Fidelity

The principle of fidelity is another core element of any helping relationship. Fidelity means faithfulness, keeping promises, honoring agreements, and loyalty (Heppner et al., 2015). Being honest, not engaging in undue deception, and maintaining confidentiality are commonly accepted ways of ensuring fidelity in such relationships as supervisor/worker, teacher/student, counselor/client, and researcher/participant (CRCC, 2017). Being viewed as trustworthy, credible, and honest provides a foundation upon which rehabilitation researchers design and implement investigations that are imbued with the ideals of non-maleficence, beneficence, autonomy, and justice. Therefore, in a fundamental sense, the principle of fidelity serves as a building block of ethical practice and effective relationships in all aspects of scientific inquiry in our field.

TREATMENT OF HUMAN SUBJECTS IN REHABILITATION AND SOCIAL SCIENCE RESEARCH

As is exemplified in the ethical precepts described in the preceding section of this chapter, protecting the welfare of research participants is an absolute guiding mission for all social scientists. The *Code of Professional Ethics for Rehabilitation Counselors* (CRCC, 2017) requires rehabilitation researchers to "plan, design, conduct, and report research in a manner that reflects cultural sensitivity . . . and is consistent with pertinent ethical principles, applicable laws, host institutional regulations, and organizational and scientific standards governing research with human subjects" (p. 27). Implicit in any investigation wherein researchers collect data from human subjects is the assurance that participants have not been coerced and that they have made informed choices based upon the risks and benefits associated with participation. The following paragraphs address such key ethical issues related to the treatment of human subjects as protecting participants from harm, institutional review procedures, informed consent, privacy and confidentiality, deception and debriefing, considerations related to applying and withholding treatment, minimal intrusiveness, and diversity.

Protecting Participants from Harm

Although the principle of autonomy implies that research participants should have the freedom to choose whether and to what extent they will be involved in a study—even in one where some measure of risk can be foreseen—the superseding non-maleficence maxim dictates that researchers take precautions to ensure that potential risks have been minimized before inviting participants to join an investigation. Indeed, the *Code of Professional Ethics for Rehabilitation Counselors* dictates that "rehabilitation counselors who conduct research with human subjects are responsible for the welfare of participants throughout the research process and take reasonable precautions to avoid causing psychological, emotional, physical, or social harm to participants" (CRCC, 2017, p. 28). The *Code* goes on to state: "The ultimate responsibility for ethical research practice lies with the principal researcher(s). All others involved in the research activities share ethical obligations and responsibility for their own actions" (p. 28).

Ary, Jacobs, and Razavieh (1985, p. 382) delineated the following guidelines for researchers to use in developing studies wherein participants may be subject to risks:

1. Only when a problem is of scientific significance and it is not practical to investigate it in any other way is the psychologist (researcher) justified in exposing research subjects, whether children or adults, to physical or emotional stress as part of an investigation.
2. When a reasonable possibility of injurious after-effects exists, research is conducted only when the subjects or their reasonable agents are fully informed of this possibility and agree to participate nevertheless.
3. The psychologist (researcher) seriously considers the possibility of harmful after-effects and avoids them, or removes them as soon as permitted by the design of the experiment.

It should be noted that harm can take many forms in rehabilitation research, and that it cannot always be reasonably foreseen. Harm includes such obvious effects as physical injury and death, but it may also include embarrassment, irritation, anger, physical and emotional stress, loss of self-esteem, delay of treatment, sleep deprivation, loss of respect from others, negative labeling, invasion of privacy, damage to personal dignity, loss of employment, and civil or criminal liabilities (Heppner et al., 2015). Harm can also emerge as either a direct consequence or an indirect result of participation in a research study. Direct harm is often seen in medical research in the form of unintended side effects of medication or treatments, but more subtle, indirect harmful consequences of research can be just as serious. For example, Rumrill (1999) demonstrated a self-advocacy training program in which employed participants who were blind or visually impaired received instruction regarding how to request reasonable accommodations from their employers under Title I of the Americans with Disabilities Act. A number of trainees actually made accommodation requests with their employers following the intervention, a result which, at first glance, might seem to justify itself. However, requesting a reasonable accommodation to overcome a disability-related work limitation is legally tantamount to conceding that one cannot perform the job task in question without the accommodation (Rubin et al., 2016). Therefore, in the event that the employer deems the requested accommodation unreasonable, the worker may be in jeopardy of losing his or her job because of that inability to perform the job. To reconcile the risks versus benefits dilemma, the researcher included a module in the training that delineated possible risks associated with disclosing one's disability status and/or accommodation needs to an employer.

Institutional Review Procedures

The National Research Act of 1974 requires institutions receiving Federal funds (e.g., colleges and universities, research centers, hospitals, state Vocational Rehabilitation agencies, public schools) to review the ethical and legal soundness of proposals for research that is to be conducted at those institutions. The primary target of this statute is research that involves human subjects. To proactively protect such rights of participants as privacy, dignity, freedom from harm, choice, consensual participation, and withdrawal without consequence, most institutions covered by the National Research Act convene Institutional Review Boards (IRBs) to evaluate research proposals and to monitor the execution of those studies. Typically, these institutions do not allow the researcher to initiate a study without first receiving official clearance from the IRB. An example of the form that is used to consider research proposals involving human subjects is provided in Table 4.1. Many institutions also require researchers to submit progress reports to the IRB at specified points throughout studies, and to develop final reports following the conclusion of investigations carried out under institutional auspices.

IRB proposals to conduct research on human subjects may be assigned to different statuses or categories for review based on the level and type of involvement with different types of research participants in the proposed investigations. For example, the *exempt status* is reserved for those studies that involve no direct contact with participants and requires only that the IRB certify that the study is exempt from further review. Proposals that have expedited status are those that involve contact with human subjects, but the focus of the study and the data gathered in the course of investigation are determined to carry minimal risk of harm to participants. Full IRB review is typically reserved for investigations that are determined to involve greater than minimal risk of harm to participants or involve participants who are perceived to occupy a more vulnerable position in society. Studies that focus on children and persons with disabilities typically require a full IRB review.

Table 4.1. Sample Institutional Review Board Document

APPLICATION TO THE INSTITUTIONAL REVIEW BOARD FOR THE PROTECTION OF HUMAN RESEARCH SUBJECTS

ANSWERS **MUST** BE TYPED

DATE SUBMITTED:_____ IRB#_____
(The above to be completed by IRB Secretary)

SUBMITTED BY: (**NOTE**: If this application is submitted by a student, it must also have the name of the faculty member who will assume responsibility for seeing that the research is carried out in accordance with regulations.)

_____   Dept._____Phone_____
(Faculty Member)

_____   Dept._____Phone_____
(Student)

Undergraduate_____Graduate_____Program of Study_____

TITLE OF
PROPOSAL:_____

CHECK APPROPRIATE REPLY:

A. Will the research be submitted as a grant or contract proposal? Yes____No____

Table 4.1–*Continued*

If the answer is Yes, who is the proposed sponsor?_____

Submission Deadline_____

B. Is the research currently being funded, in part or in whole? Yes___No___

State_____Federal_____University_____Other (specify)_____

C. Has the research been reviewed before the IRB? Yes_____No_____

If yes, please give the date of the review_____and the IRB# (if known)_____.

D. Is this research to be performed for a master's thesis? Yes___No___

Is this research to be performed for a doctoral dissertation? Yes___No___

is this research to be performed as part of a course requirement? Yes___No___

Is this research to be performed as an honor's thesis? Yes___No___

Other (explain)_____

PLEASE READ INSTRUCTIONS BEFORE COMPLETING THIS FORM

To avoid delays, all questions must be answered. Incomplete forms will be returned to the investigator for additional information.

1. **Summary of proposal.** In concise, non-technical language, describe the rationale and methods (experimental tests and procedures) to be used. (**DO NOT USE JARGON**) State clearly what the subjects will be required to do or be subjected to in the experiment. Use the space below. **Applications without a summary in the space allotted will not be considered by the Board.**

A. Rationale

B. Methods
(The source of questionnaires and surveys should be indicated, whether published, adapted, or newly formulated.)

Table 4.1–*Continued*

2. Who will have direct contact with the subjects? Who will administer tests, conduct interviews, etc.? State their qualifications specifically with regard to the procedures to be used in this study.

3. Characteristics of subjects.

A. Sex M____ F____ Both____

B. Age_____ *Any* subjects under age 18? Yes____ No____

C. Special ethnic group_____

D. Institutionalized Yes____ No____ (See item #4 below.)

E. General state of health_____ ("unknown" unless you will obtain health data on subjects prior to beginning the study.)

F. Source of subjects_____

G. How will subjects be identified and Recruited_____

_____

NOTE: *If the research is conducted at an off-campus institution (e.g., a school, hospital, etc.), attach a statement signed by an appropriate official authorizing access to subjects (e.g., school district superintendent), or current approval from that institution's review committee. Full approval cannot be given without this authorization.*

4. Special groups - If subjects are either (1) **children**, (2) **mentally incompetent**, or (3) **legally restricted** (i.e., institutionalized), please explain the necessity for using this particular group. *Proposals using subjects from any of these groups cannot be given expedited review, but must go to the full Board.*

Yes____ No____ If yes, please attach memo explaining who and why.

5. Type of consent to be obtained. Informed consent requires that subjects be informed of and understand, by oral or written form, the procedures to be used in the research, and that they may refuse to participate or withdraw from the investigation at any time without

Table 4.1–*Continued*

prejudice. If oral consent is used, the investigator must explain to the subjects all of the points as required on a written consent form. A written version of what will be said when requesting oral consent must be attached to this application. **If written consent is used, the procedures must be clearly stated on the form signed by the subject. A copy of the written consent must be included as the last page of this application. All consent forms must be on university letterhead unless exempted by the IRB. APPROVAL WILL NOT BE GRANTED WITHOUT A COPY OF THE CONSENT FORM!**

A. Oral___Written___Obtained and explained by whom_____

B. From whom will consent be obtained and by what means for minors(minors or children aged 7 and older must be asked for ASSENT) or the mentally incompetent?

6. Confidentiality

A. What precautions will be taken to insure the privacy an anonymity of the subjects, and the confidentiality of the data, both in your possession and in reports and publications?

B. Will audio, video or film recording be used? Yes___ No___ Specify which _____. If yes, what will be the description of the records when the research is complete? (All tapes, audio or video, MUST BE DESTROYED.)

7. Risk to Subjects
NOTE: *Investigators should complete this portion as succinctly as possible. If the Board has to request additional clarification or explanation, approval may be delayed a full month until the next meeting.*

A. Describe in detail <u>any possible</u> physical, social, political, legal, economic, or other risks to the subjects, either immediate or long range. Estimate the seriousness and extent of the risk. *Risk may be minimal but never totally absent. Do not say "No Risk."*

Table 4.1–*Continued*

B. Describe what procedures will be used to minimize the risk you have stated above.

8. **Benefits**
Assess the benefits of research to:

A. The subjects
B. Society at large

C. Explain how the benefits outweigh the risks involved.

9. **Signatures**

A. Faculty

This is to certify that the procedures involved in this study are appropriate for minimizing risks to the subjects and acknowledges that I take full responsibility for the conduct of the research.

Signed_____ Date
                (Faculty member)
Name typed
Campus phone_____ Campus address

B. Student**

Signed_____ Date
Graduate_____ Undergraduate _____

Name typed

Campus phone_____ Campus address

**Please note: *If this study is being conducted by a student, a faculty member must sign in the space provided. A form without a faculty member's approval will be returned for signature.*

Informed Consent

One of the most important ethical and procedural issues that IRBs consider is informed consent. Informed consent is typically achieved by providing potential participants with a description of the purposes of the investigation, a statement of possible risks and benefits, an option not to participate without penalty or consequence, and the opportunity to withdraw from the study at any time and for any reason. The *Code of Professional Ethics for Rehabilitation Counselors* (CRCC, 2017) states:

> In seeking consent, rehabilitation counselors use language that: (1) accurately explains the purpose and procedures to be followed; (2) identifies any procedures that are experimental or relatively untried; (3) describes any attendant discomforts and risks; (4) describes any benefits or changes in individuals or organizations that might be reasonably expected; (5) discloses appropriate alternative procedures that would be advantageous for participants; (6) offers to answer any inquiries concerning the procedures; (7) describes any limitations on confidentiality; (8) describes formats and potential target audiences for the dissemination of research findings; and (9) instructs participants that they are free to withdraw their consent and to discontinue participation in the project at any time without penalty. (p. 28)

Informed consent consists of three major elements or conditions: *competence, knowledge,* and *volition* (Kazdin, 2003). To give meaningful consent to participate in a study, the individual must be capable of making a well-reasoned decision (i.e., be competent). Any characteristic of the person (e.g., significant intellectual disability, neurological impairment that impedes cognitive functioning) that interferes with his/her ability to make thoughtful, deliberative decisions would present a threat to informed consent. Meaningful consent also requires that participants have sufficient knowledge and understanding of the nature of the study, its potential risks, and its potential benefits. Finally, meaningful consent must be given willingly, that is, free from duress, constraint, or penalty. Volition also requires that participants be free to revoke their consent to participate at any time.

Consent is secured by asking participants (or parents of minors) to sign a form indicating that they understand their rights as human subjects, are aware of the potential risks and benefits of participation, and agree to participate voluntarily and without coercion. Table 4.2 presents an example of an informed consent document.

It should be noted that obtaining informed consent from participants is not necessary in all research investigations involving human subjects. Studies that examine extant data (i.e., data that have already been collected for an-

Table 4.2. Sample Informed Consent Form

Purpose

The Center for Disability Studies conducts research on the employment and other life experiences of people with disabilities. This research is conducted to learn more about how to improve vocational rehabilitation and employment outcomes for people with disabilities. Information from participants is maintained by the Center and will be used for research purposes only.

Agreement

By signing this form, I agree to participate in research conducted by the Center as described below:

A Study of Accommodation Needs and Activities

I agree to participate in a study of my experiences in requesting and using reasonable accommodations in the workplace. The study will involve no more than two personal visits of less than one hour each with a trained interviewer. The interviewer will request information on my perceptions of barriers in the workplace and possible reasonable accommodations. I will also provide information regarding my background and personal views of my current life and situation in no more than two telephone contacts with the interviewer.

I understand that the Center may provide research data to qualified persons and/or other research centers subject to ethical restrictions. If such information is shared with qualified persons or organizations, I understand that it will not be possible to connect my name with the information that I provide. Information from this investigation may be published in an anonymous case study format. I have the right to approve any information developed for publication.

I also understand that I have the option of withdrawing this consent and release of information and withdrawing my participation in this research project at any time. Should I withdraw, I understand that this will not affect my participation in any service program.

_____
Signature of Participant   Date

Participant Mailing Address_____

_____Daytime Phone #_____

other purpose), provide only summary data to the researcher(s) without linking individual participants' information with their names, and/or ask participants to provide anonymous information may not require the researcher(s) to secure informed consent from each participant. An exception to the informed consent rule is also commonly invoked in legal research that interprets information that is a matter of public record.

For example, Cichy, Li, McMahon, & Rumrill (2015) conducted an analysis of complaints received by the Federal Equal Employment Opportunity Commission (EEOC) during 2009-2011 alleging employment discrimination under Title I of the Americans with Disabilities Act Amendments Act. Because the data that Cichy et al. received from the EEOC were in summary form, did not include complainants' names, and were considered public information, it was not necessary for them to obtain informed consent from the thousands of individuals who had filed Title I complaints during the period under study.

Privacy and Confidentiality

As can be seen in the informed consent document presented in Table 4.2, research participants also have the right to privacy with respect to information that they provide in a study. Researchers who hold the Certified Rehabilitation Counselor credential must ensure that "Confidential information obtained about research participants during the course of research remains confidential. When the possibility exists that others may obtain access to such information, ethical research practice requires the possibility, together with the plans for protecting confidentiality, be explained to participants as part of the procedures for obtaining informed consent" (CRCC, 2017, p. 29). McMillan and Schumacher (2009) identified several ways of safeguarding research participants' rights to privacy, including (1) collecting and coding data anonymously without ever knowing the participants' names; (2) using numeric or alphabetic coding systems to link data to participants' names, then destroying the system at the end of the investigation; (3) retaining a third party who links names and data and then provides the researcher with anonymous results; (4) using aliases or code numbers (e.g., a portion of one's Social Security number) in linking personally identifying information; and (5) reporting only summary or aggregate results for the entire sample or particular groups, rather than reporting information garnered from individual participants' responses.

Another level of safeguarding participants' rights to privacy is often employed in investigations that involve case studies (Nardone et al., 2015). A common design in epidemiological medical research and in qualitative investigations in various fields, the case study approach involves gathering in-depth information about a relatively small number of individuals. Although aliases are almost always used in these studies, the level of specificity in the information reported is such that participants may be recognizable to some readers. To minimize the prospects of unwanted recognition, researchers often send copies of the manuscript or research report for participants' review before the paper is submitted for publication. This measure gives the research participant an opportunity to check the report for accuracy and to change any representations of his or her personal experiences that are objectionable.

Deception and Debriefing

The principle of fidelity implies honesty and trustworthiness, as noted in a previous section of this chapter. Fidelity does not, however, mean that a rehabilitation researcher must fully disclose all aspects of an investigation to participants at the inception of the study. In fact, to fully disclose all aspects of a particular study often biases the results or outcomes. The researcher should inform participants of the general purposes of the study, but degrees of deception are seen as necessary aspects of many, if not most, investigations. Deception can include withholding specific details of a study, not informing members of a control or comparison group what intervention or stimulus to which other participants will be exposed, collecting data under some auspice other than a research study, and overtly lying to participants (Heppner et al., 2015; Kazdin, 2003).

Of course, how much deception is too much from an ethical standpoint is always a judgment call. Institutional Review Boards examine the level of deception that a researcher intends to use, with the primary consideration being how necessary deception is to the conduct of the study. McMillan and Schumacher (2009) asserted that deception should only be used in cases where (1) the importance of potential results is greater than the effects of lying; (2) employing deception is the only practical way to conduct the study; and (3) the researcher utilizes appropriate debriefing, in which the researcher tells the participant about the nature of and reasons for the deception following the completion of the study. The CRCC Ethical Code states:

> Rehabilitation counselors do not conduct research involving deception unless alternative procedures are not feasible. If such deception has the potential to cause physical or emotional harm to research participants, the research is not conducted, regardless of prospective value. When the methodological requirements of a study necessitate concealment or deception, the investigator explains the reasons for this action as soon as possible during the debriefing. (CRCC, 2017, p. 28)

Indeed, most research ethicists agree that, regardless of whether or how much deception was used in executing a study, participants have the right to a full disclosure of the purpose, methods, and findings of an investigation after it is completed. Some researchers provide a summary report of the study to all participants as a matter of routine, whereas others prefer to hold in-person debriefing meetings with participants. Whichever the forum, the 2010 *Code of Professional Ethics for Rehabilitation Counselors* (CRCC, 2010) included the following debriefing requirement: "After data are collected, rehabilitation counselors provide participants with full clarification of the nature of the study to remove any misconceptions. . . . Where scientific or human values justify delaying or withholding information, rehabilitation counselors take reasonable measures to avoid causing harm" (p. 25). Curiously, CRCC removed the preceding debriefing requirement from the 2017 version of the Code.

Applying and Withholding Treatment

In studies that involve the application of a treatment or intervention, the principle of beneficence is often contravened by limitations associated with resources, time, and scientific controls. Researchers are often faced with the thorny issue of choosing who will participate in an intervention and who will be excluded. These issues are among the most controversial in contemporary research ethics (Rumrill, Cook, & Wiley, 2010).

The ethics of applying and/or withholding treatment are almost always complicated, and they interact with and sometimes contradict some of the foundational principles of scientific inquiry. In general, based on the principle of beneficence, it would seem that any ethical researcher would want as many people as possible to benefit from a successful intervention. This aspiration is often contravened by limitations in time, funding, and other resources. Also, the strongest warrants for knowledge claims in experimental designs (Heppner et al., 2015) derive from the use of randomly assigned treatment and control groups. By definition, a control group does not receive the intervention or the benefit that derives from it. To compound this issue, the most recent Amendments to the *Declaration of Helsinki* state explicitly that new treatments should be compared to standard treatments rather than to no-treatment or to a placebo or "inert" treatment (World Medical Association, 2000, cited in Kazdin, 2003). Strict adherence to the Declaration of Helsinki would make true no-treatment control groups extremely rare in experimental research and would likely reduce the research validity of these designs. Alternatively, an ethical researcher may wish to implement an intervention for individuals who are in the greatest need, have the most severe symptoms, or the most significant involvement. The fact that some participants with clear need have to wait for an efficacious treatment may constitute an ethical concern for the researcher (Falvo & Parker, 2000). Yet, the inclusion of persons in treatment groups based on severity may bias any planned comparison to a group that is not equivalent on these dimensions. Thus, in the latter case, what appears to be the most ethical decision (e.g., to treat those individuals in the greatest need prior to treating other individuals) may weaken research validity by introducing a variable that represents a rival, plausible explanation for the study findings.

The issue of providing and/or withholding treatments often resurrects the question of "who gets what and why" as per the principle of justice. To address some of these concerns, many researchers provide abbreviated versions (e.g., written informational packets, self-help brochures) of interventions to participants who, for one reason or another, were not assigned to an experimental condition (Rumrill, Roessler, & Cook, 1998). Other researchers place such participants on a waiting list and provide the treatment or training to them at a later date. For example, Palmer (1998) demonstrated an effective model for training college students with disabilities to request classroom accommodations from their instructors. Social scientific protocol dictated that he withhold the intervention from a number of interested participants who formed a comparison group. However, the Palmer study, as initially designed, would have effectively excluded half of the sample, and the comparison group would not have benefited from the intervention. Noting the inherent potential for injustice in his original design, the researcher decided to provide training to the comparison group after he had gathered baseline data from them concerning the hypothesized effects of the intervention.

Minimal Interference

Rehabilitation researchers are ethically bound to avoid intruding any more than is absolutely necessary upon the lives of research participants. The CRCC (2017) requires researchers holding the Certified Rehabilitation Counselor credential to take precautions that minimize the disruptiveness of research activities to participants or to the setting in which the research is conducted. These precautions may include gathering only data that are central to the purpose of the investigation, making contacts over the telephone and via e-mail as an alternative to time-consuming and often inconvenient in-person contacts, and honoring participants' scheduling preferences.

Diversity

The CRCC Code of Ethics requires covered researchers to "plan, design, conduct, and report research in a manner that reflects cultural sensitivity..." (CRCC, 2017, p. 27). CRCC also requires rehabilitation researchers to seek consultation on research matters related to cultural diversity when appropriate. Perhaps the best way to meet the ethical requirement of diversity in rehabilitation research is to ensure that the samples involved in particular studies are as representative as possible of the broader populations from which they were drawn. Some researchers use stratification and/or case weighting procedures to make certain that people from traditionally underrepresented groups are included in empirical investigations.

ETHICS INVOLVED IN REPORTING AND PUBLISHING REHABILITATION RESEARCH

The role of ethics in rehabilitation research clearly and rightfully centers on the treatment of subjects or participants. Not only is the rehabilitation researcher responsible for upholding the fundamental ethical principles that underlie the profession and practice of rehabilitation counseling (i.e., nonmaleficence, beneficence, autonomy, justice, and fidelity), he or she must ensure that defined ethical standards related to scientific inquiry and the treatment of human subjects (e.g., confidentiality, informed consent, institutional review) are followed. However, the ethical rehabilitation researcher's obligation is not completely fulfilled by virtue of right conduct in the execution of a study. There are also ethical considerations to be made in the process of reporting and publishing research results (CRCC, 2017). Synthesizing ethical provisions promulgated by the American Counseling Association, the American Psychological Association, and the American Rehabilitation Counseling Association, Parker and Szymanski (1996) distilled 10 standards for ethical practice in publishing rehabilitation research that have proven to stand the test of time. The following paragraphs summarize; discuss; and, in some cases, amplify on those standards within the context of such key issues as authorship credit, the roles of editors and peer reviewers, acknowledgement of contributions, plagiarism, and copyright laws.

1. PROTECTION OF RESEARCH PARTICIPANTS. As described in an earlier section of this chapter, rehabilitation researchers must adhere to the ethical standards of their home institutions. They must document how informed consent was obtained, and the Method section of a published research article should include a description of the manner in which participants were recruited for the study. The article should also include only information that cannot be

linked to a participant's name or other identifying characteristics. Whenever possible, participants should be given the option to review the final manuscript before it is submitted for publication. It should also be noted here that research participants who are considered to be at greater risk for harm, owing to other disadvantaging characteristics (e.g., children, people with disabilities, prisoners), are afforded a higher degree of protection under the National Research Act than are participants who are considered to be at less risk.

2. ACCURAY AND INTEGRITY OF DATA. Rehabilitation researchers must report data as collected. Tampering with, fabricating, and exaggerating results are considered unethical conduct. Also, the norm of common ownership of information (Merton, 1968; see Chapter 1) implies that all data presented in a research article are essential to the full and accurate reporting of the results of an investigation. Extraneous information may serve to distract the reader from the true meaning of the study and, therefore, should not be reported. Conversely, providing too little information in a research report or article makes it difficult for other researchers to replicate the investigation.

Procedures that were used to analyze data must not mislead the reader, distort findings, or artificially amplify the impact or meaning of research results. Many authors include a description of the scientific limitations of their studies in the Discussion sections of published articles. This measure serves as a means of accurately characterizing the overall contributions of their research.

3. CORRECTION OR RETRACTION OF ERRORS. If the author notices an error of fact or omission in a published article, he or she should make reasonable effort to notify readers by printing a correction or retraction in the next issue of the journal. To prevent foreseeable errors from appearing in print, many journals provide authors with galley page proofs just prior to the finalized publication of each issue.

4. CITATION AND ACKNOWLEDGMENT CREDIT. When citing facts, findings, or ideas that are not their own, authors must afford credit to the originator(s) of previously published work. Short direct quotes should be attributed to the page number of their original published source. Longer direct quotes or reprinting of an entire article may require the permission of the author(s) and/or publisher of the original work. Failure to obtain an original author's consent or offer appropriate acknowledgement may be viewed as plagiarism and a violation of copyright law. Most journals in rehabilitation adhere to the American Psychological Association's (APA, 2013) guidelines for citing and acknowledging the work of another author.

Of course, avoiding plagiarism is much more complicated than simply citing the work of others in accordance with a professional association's style manual. Plagiarism can range from unintentional omissions of necessary citations to willful theft of another author's words in an attempt to make them one's own. Where the "give credit where credit is due" issue becomes murky is in circumstances related to the origination of ideas. Given that a discipline's knowledge base is built in small increments with each advance serving as an extension of the one before it (Heppner et al., 2015), it is sometimes confusing to authors (and readers) who originated a particular concept and who served to extend or amplify on it. How much one must revise or extend an existing theory or model before claiming a new one is not provided in current ethical guidelines, nor is any allowance given for the possibility that two or more authors could independently arrive upon similar ideas at approximately the same time. Given that plagiarism almost always amounts to a judgment call, the best advice for rehabilitation researchers is to take every step possible to credit others for the work that others have done and be sure that claims of original ideas are qualified by acknowledging authors whose works contributed to the development of new knowledge.

5. AUTHORSHIP CREDIT. To be granted authorship credit for a published article, an individual must have made an appropriate, substantive contribution to the work. Unfortunately, there are no agreed-upon guidelines as to what constitutes a substantive contribution (Kazdin, 2003). Scholarly contributions to a research article that typically merit publication credit include conceptualizing and refining research ideas, literature search, developing a research design, instrument selection, designing instruments or measures, selection of statistical analyses, collection and preparation of data, performing statistical analyses, interpreting statistical analyses, preparing selected sections of manuscripts, and editing the manuscript (Falvo & Parker, 2000; Heppner et al., 2015; Kazdin, 2003). Individuals who do not warrant authorship credit but who contributed to an article in a minor way are credited in an Acknowledgements or Author Note section at the end of the article. Minor contributions to research articles have been identified by Heppner et al. (2015) as including giving editorial feedback, consulting on design or statistical questions, serving as raters or judges, administering an intervention, and providing extensive clerical services.

In our opinion, authorship also implies that the person has not had a role in the editorial process or peer review of that article. In the event that an editor of a journal submits a paper for publication consideration by that journal, he or she should defer all editorial decisions to a coeditor or editorial board member. Author credits should also list each author's institutional affiliation at the time work on the article was completed. If an author changes his or her institutional affiliation during the editorial or publication processes, he or she may elect to add the new affiliation to the former one. In that event, the author credits would bear both institutional affiliations.

6. ORDERING OF MULTIPLE AUTHORS. If an article features two or more authors (which is the case in the vast majority of articles published in rehabilitation journals), the first author listed should be the one who has made the most significant contributions to the development of the article. Secondary authors' names should be listed in descending order of their contributions.

7. WORK RESULTING FROM DISSERTATIONS OR THESES. If an article with more than one author is the result of a student's dissertation or thesis, the student should be listed as the first author (Kazdin, 2003). Regardless of the student's institutional affiliation at the time of the article's publication, the institution that sponsored his or her study (where he or she earned the degree that was culminated by the dissertation or thesis) should also be included in the author credits.

Most experts agree that the student should be the first author in articles resulting from his or her dissertation, but how and whether the student's dissertation supervisor is accorded authorship credit remains a source of some debate among research ethicists. The APA (2013) issued guidelines indicating that only secondary authorship is acceptable for the dissertation supervisor and that secondary authorship may be considered obligatory if the supervisor designates the variables or makes major interpretive contributions to the study. The APA noted that secondary authorship is a courtesy if the supervisor helps to identify the topic for the student's dissertation or is substantially involved in designing the study. Authorship is not acceptable according to the APA if the supervisor provides only encouragement, facilities, financial support, critiques, or editorial contributions.

8. DUAL SUBMISSION AND PUBLICATION OF THE SAME ARTICLE. Authors must submit manuscripts to one journal at a time; submitting a paper for review by a professional journal implies that the paper is not under current consideration by any other journal. Authors may not publish the same article in two different journals without tacit agreement from the editors of both journals that a reprint is warranted and permissible. Authors also must not publish multiple articles from the same data or within the same content area unless they have (a) secured necessary releases from the publishers of previous work, and/or (b) included (in the article) an explanation of how the new study differs in terms of purpose, research questions, or hypotheses.

9. REANALYSIS AND/OR VERIFICATION OF REPORTED DATA. To every extent possible, authors should make their data available to other researchers who wish to reanalyze and/or verify the results of a published study. Parker and Szymanski (1996) noted that: "It is recognized, however, that other issues such as confidentiality of participants, legal rights concerning proprietary data, or the competence of the requesting professional may preclude sharing of data" (p. 163).

10. INTEGRITY OF RESEARCH QUESTIONS AND/OR HYPOTHESES. It is imperative that researchers report all findings that are relevant to the research questions and hypotheses posed, not only those that are statistically significant or that support a particular point of view. Amplifying some results while ignoring others as a means of supporting a particular point of view or prediction is ethically unacceptable and should be avoided at all times.

11. ETHICAL CONSIDERATIONS FOR EDITORS AND PEER REVIEWERS. Rehabilitation professionals who serve as journal editors, editorial board members, or reviewers for grant competitions must protect the confidentiality of authors who submit their work for peer review (Falvo & Parker, 2002; Parker & Szymanski, 1996). Moreover, editors and reviewers may not use information contained in prepublished work without expressed consent from the originating author(s). We also believe that an editor or reviewer should not be added to a list of authors if he or she did not appear in the original manuscript's author credits—even if he or she makes substantial contributions in an editorial role.

SUMMARY

The rehabilitation researcher is subject to a number of ethical considerations in the design, implementation, evaluation, and reporting of empirical investigations. First, the researcher must conform to the rules of right conduct as they apply to the ethical principles that underlie the field of rehabilitation counseling. Non-maleficence, perhaps the most basic tenet of any helping profession, sets a priority on doing no harm to clients or participants in research projects. Beneficence, a concept that serves to define the ultimate purpose of rehabilitation counseling, implies that counselors and researchers should strive to help people in a way that improves their quality of life. Autonomy provides a basis for absolute deference to individuals' rights to choose whether and to what extent they will participate in a service program or research investigation. Justice connotes fair and equal treatment of all participants without offering undue advantages to one participant or disadvantaging another. Fidelity in rehabilitation research means that the researcher is honest, trustworthy, and credible. The *Code of Professional Ethics for Rehabilitation Counselors* provides authoritative guidance for implementing the ethical principles that underlie our field.

In addition to the macro-level ethical considerations that rehabilitation researchers must make as representatives of their primary profession, it is important to abide by current ethical standards regarding the treatment of human subjects. Institutions that receive Federal funds are required by law to convene and maintain permanent Institutional Review Boards on Human Subjects to ensure affiliated researchers' compliance with contemporary ethical standards in the treatment of research participants. Issues of informed consent, the use of deception, applying or withholding treatments, confidentiality, minimal interference, and diversity are paramount concerns for ethical rehabilitation researchers, and ethical guidelines for doing social scientific research may not always support best practice from a research validity standpoint.

Finally, as the rehabilitation researcher seeks to disseminate his or her findings via articles in professional journals, he or she is subject to ethical standards associated with the publication process as set forth by the CRCC (2017) and the APA (2013). In this chapter, we discussed such ethical concerns as biased outcomes, the accuracy of results, unfavorable results, privacy of participants, recognition of contributors, student research, duplicate submission, and professional review.

Given the breadth and depth of ethical issues that rehabilitation researchers face as they design, implement, evaluate, and disseminate their studies, it is essential to become familiar with the standards set forth by host institutions and professional associations. By maintaining vigilance in applying the highest benchmarks for ethical conduct in all interactions with human subjects, one another, and those who review their work, researchers can continue a long tradition of safe and responsible research practices in the field of rehabilitation counseling.

Chapter 5

RESEARCH VALIDITY

INTRODUCTION

In this chapter, we discuss the criteria by which quantitative research designs are evaluated. We apply the concept of research validity to the methods that researchers use to make warranted knowledge claims. Throughout this chapter, it is important to remember that the designs researchers employ to ensure validity (e.g., experimental, small-n, survey, correlational) are determined primarily by the research question or problem being addressed. In that regard, no approach is inherently better than any other, but each contributes in different ways to the development of scientific knowledge.

Validity and Knowledge Claims

The purpose of all research is to generate warranted (valid) conclusions about the relationships among variables (Kazdin, 2003). A warranted knowledge claim is one whose credibility is based on the total available empirical evidence rather than on findings from a single investigation. Whereas test validity (as discussed in Chapter 3) refers to knowledge claims related to measurements or observations, the terms validity and invalidity as applied to research design refer to "the best available approximation of the truth or falsity of propositions, including propositions about cause" (Cook & Campbell, 1979, p. 37). Thus, validity in research pertains to the warrant for a knowledge claim based on the characteristics of the entire study, including the quality of sampling procedures, measurement, research design, statistical analysis, and conclusions drawn from the findings (Heppner, Wampold, Owen, Thompson, & Wang, 2015).

A research investigation may result in a weak knowledge claim if the types of inferences that the investigator wishes to draw are not substantiated adequately in the design and implementation of the study. From the standpoint of methodology, the better the design and implementation of an investigation, the more implausible it makes alternative explanations for the results, and the stronger the knowledge claim of the investigator becomes (Cook & Campbell, 1979; Goodwin & Goodwin, 2012). Thus, an exemplary research design is one in which the researcher's explanation for the findings is buttressed by the elimination, or falsification, of rival, alternative explanations (Popper, 1959). The falsificationist approach to evaluating knowledge claims underlies quantitative hypothesis testing and stresses the ambiguity of definitively confirming causal hypotheses. Moreover, it encourages a modest, incremental approach to the development of scientific knowledge (Creswell, 2014; Goodwin & Goodwin, 2012).

Validity and Causality

The ultimate goal of scientific inquiry is causal explanation, which involves identifying what variables are related, how they are related, the nature of the specific mechanisms or processes that are involved, and the extent to which relationships can be generalized across populations, settings, and conditions. Research designs differ in their ability to illuminate causal mechanisms and substantiate causal explanations. Experimental research designs are particularly well-suited to examining the causal relationships among variables. All experiments involve a treatment (i.e., identification, isolation, and manipulation of an independent variable), an outcome measure, units of assignment, and some comparison by which change can be inferred and hopefully attributed to the treatment (McMillan & Schumacher, 2009; Rumrill, Cook, & Wiley, 2010). One of the key aspects of experimental research is that the experimental context provides a simplified situation from what would be the case in an analysis of variable relationships as they exist in nature (Manicas & Secord, 1983). Thus, experimental research design serves to highlight specific, targeted variable relationships while attempting to limit or control the influence of other factors. It is the identification, isolation, simplification, control, and manipulation of the independent variable, and subsequent analysis of its effects through a comparison of treatment and control groups, that form the essential bases for ascribing causality to the independent variable (Creswell, 2014).

As will be discussed in greater depth in Chapter 6, non-manipulation and descriptive quantitative designs are categories of non-experimental research that involve the analysis of relationships among variables that are not manipulated, or analysis of variable relationships as they exist in the real world. Non-experimental research designs serve to identify what variables are related, how they are related, and the magnitude of their relationships, but they afford a weaker basis for inferring causality than experimental designs. Nonexperimental research designs establish the necessary foundation for examining specific causal relationships among variables and typically predominate during the early stages of inquiry into a knowledge domain (Bellini & Rumrill, 2009). Also, these designs are key to assessing the generalizability of identified variable relationships.

TYPES OF RESEARCH VALIDITY

The four types of research validity to be discussed in this chapter are internal, external, construct, and statistical conclusion validity. Each type of validity addresses the empirical status of a given knowledge claim in different ways, but each is important. Together, internal, external, construct, and statistical conclusion validity convey the multiple considerations that researchers attempt to address when they design a research investigation (Heppner et al., 2015; Kazdin, 2003). Awareness of the various threats to valid inference and the methods of eliminating these so as to strengthen the warrant for a scientific knowledge claim is central to designing and evaluating rehabilitation research.

Internal Validity

Internal validity is the approximate certainty with which we infer that a relationship between two variables is causal (McMillan & Schumacher, 2009), or the extent to which an investigation rules out alternative explanations for the results (Kazdin, 2003). Possible causal factors other than the independent variable(s) that are not accounted for in the research design but that may also explain the results are called threats to internal validity. Overall, random assignment of research participants to experimental and control groups provides the best protection against threats to causal inference, because random assignment reduces the possibility of systematic group differences that may influence scores on the dependent measures. We will discuss the major threats to internal validity, including history, maturation, instrumentation, selection, attrition, and ambiguity about the direction of causal influence. Readers interested in a more comprehensive discussion of these issues should consult texts authored by Cook and Campbell (1979) or Kazdin (2003).

HISTORY. History as a threat to valid causal inference refers to historical events that are common to all subjects in their everyday lives or unplanned events occurring during the process of implementing an experimental procedure that may plausibly represent rival, competing explanations for the results (Kazdin, 2003). For history to be a threat, the event must impinge on the experimental situation in some fashion and influence scores on the dependent variable. Consider the example of a researcher who uses a post-test only experimental design (see Chapter 6) to test whether an intervention improves the attitudes of participants toward persons with disabilities. The researcher implements a number of activities to enhance the sensitivity of treatment group members to disability issues. The comparison group receives a lecture on a topic unrelated to disability. Following these separate activities, the participants in both groups complete a standardized measure of attitudes toward persons with disabilities. The researcher hopes to demonstrate that the intervention is effective in improving the attitudes of treatment group members as indicated by higher scores on the attitude measure. However, participants in intervention and control groups may differ in their sensitivity to disability issues as a function of their life experiences, and their scores on the dependent measure may be a reflection of these differences in personal history rather than differences associated with the intervention. Thus, history represents a rival, competing explanation for the results of the investigation.

History can also become an issue in experimental research when events such as political elections, military action, or natural disasters occur during the course of an investigation. These historical events can affect participants' interest, attention, and ability to participate in research projects and they may affect performance on outcome measures over and above any relationship that can be ascribed between the independent and dependent variables.

MATURATION. Maturation is a threat to internal validity when an observed effect may be due to respondents growing older, wiser, stronger, or better adjusted between the pretest and posttest when this maturational process is not the target of the investigation (Kazdin, 2003; Rumrill et al., 2010). Maturation is most likely to represent a rival, competing explanation for results when there is a long interim period between pretest and posttest. For example, consider a hypothetical intervention designed to enhance psychosocial adjustment to disability for adolescents that is implemented over a several month period. In this case, posttest adjustment scores, which are intended to measure the effect of the intervention, may instead reflect normal, adolescent maturational processes. Thus, the researcher's conclusion that the psychosocial intervention caused increased adjustment scores may be challenged by the rival explanation.

INSTRUMENTATION. Instrumentation is a threat to valid inference when an effect, as measured on the dependent variable, is due to systematic changes in the measuring instrument from pretest to posttest. It is most likely to occur when the dependent variable consists of observers' ratings of others' behaviors (e.g., sociability, aggression) and the raters (a) become more experienced, more stringent, or more lenient over the course of the data collection efforts, or (b) otherwise apply ratings criteria inconsistently from pretest to posttest. Thus, observed changes in ratings from pretest to posttest may be due to changes in raters' performances rather than the treatment or intervention that is the focus of the research. Instrumentation can also threaten internal validity when different forms of the same test, or different tests measuring the same construct, are used at pretest and posttest.

SELECTION. Selection is a threat to internal validity when the effect of an intervention may be the result of the different types of people who choose and choose not to participate in research investigations. The effect of an intervention can only be unambiguously attributed to the independent variable when the researcher is assured that treatment and control groups do not systematically differ on other variables that may influence the dependent measure. Random assignment to treatment and control groups provides the best protection against selection biases. The threat of selection as an alternate explanation for results often occurs in rehabilitation research when intact groups (reflecting unknown and possibly systematic biases) are used rather than groups composed of randomly assigned individuals. Selection may also be an issue when participants are selected for treatment and control groups on the basis of severity of presenting issues, because severity may systematically influence group means on the outcome variable (Heppner et al., 2015; Kazdin, 2003).

ATTRITION. Attrition (also termed Mortality) is a potential threat to valid inference when the effect of an intervention (that is, differences between treatment and control groups on an outcome measure) may be due to systematic differences associated with the characteristics of individuals who withdrew during the course of the experiment. Longitudinal research is more vulnerable to this validity threat than other types of studies because of the long timeline needed to complete these investigations. Attrition may result in a selection bias even when groups are initially chosen by random assignment, when, as a function of differential mortality, the experimental groups at posttest consist of different kinds of people. Faced with this circumstance, a researcher may make post hoc comparisons of the initial and reduced samples on key variables in order to demonstrate that attrition did not result in a selection bias. It is important to note that this post hoc strategy can effectively reduce but not totally eliminate the possibility of this threat to causal inference (Kazdin, 2003).

AMBIGUITY ABOUT THE DIRECTION OF CAUSAL INFERENCE. This threat to causal inference is salient when it is not possible to determine with certainty whether variable A causes variable B or variable B causes variable A. For example, a researcher may hypothesize that the increased stress associated with living with a disability causes reduced adjustment to disability. The data analysis reveals a significant relationship (correlation) between stress and adjustment. Also, the researcher has ruled out other threats to internal validity on the basis of research design features or logic, which strengthens the warrant for the claim that the relationship between the variables is causal.

However, the possibility remains that the direction of causal influence is reversed, that having a poorer adjustment to disability results in experiencing greater stress. Ambiguity with regard to the direction of causality is not usually a problem when the order of precedence of variables is clear, or when variables are collected at different time intervals, because in those cases the researcher can specify which variable comes first (the causal agent) and which variable follows (the effect). Lack of certainty with respect to the direction of causal influence is most likely to be a problem in correlational studies where the conceptual foundation of the investigation is ambiguous or provides insufficient direction.

External Validity

A fundamental purpose of research is to establish valid knowledge that transcends the particular context of a given investigation. External validity addresses this issue of generalization, and it refers to the extent to which an observed relationship among variables can be generalized beyond the conditions of the investigation to other populations, settings, and conditions (Goodwin & Goodwin, 2012; McMillan & Schumacher, 2009). It is a particularly cogent issue for practitioners who wish to utilize research findings in clinical practice and, therefore, need to evaluate whether the findings associated with a particular sample, procedure, and research setting will generalize to their service context. Whereas random assignment to experimental groups provides the best protection against threats to the internal validity of findings, *random selection* of research participants from the population of interest affords the strongest warrant that results will generalize to other individuals in that population. However, random selection does not ensure that findings will generalize to different populations, settings, or conditions. The most persuasive demonstration of generalization (i.e., external validity) is when empirical findings of several studies are consistent across various types of subjects (e.g., college students, rehabilitation clients, families), settings (e.g., laboratory and diverse community settings), and other conditions (e.g., different researchers, diverse cultures).

Potential threats to the generalization of research findings include those specific features of the design that are associated with the sample, stimulus, context, and assessment procedures used (Kazdin, 2003). Many of these threats can be excluded based on common sense considerations. It is important for consumers of research to consider the context and findings of an investigation, as well as how a particular threat may plausibly restrict the study results. If a particular threat does plausibly apply, caution in generalizing findings should be exercised.

SAMPLE CHARACTERISTICS. One vital question in assessing generalization is the extent to which findings may apply to persons who vary in age, race, ethnic background, education, or other salient characteristics from those who composed the research sample. For example, a program developer for a psychiatric rehabilitation agency has read an article on social skills training found to be highly effective for a sample of adults with autism spectrum disorders. How generalizable are the findings for adults with psychiatric disabilities? External validity may be undermined as a direct function of the differences between the study sample (people with autism) and the population to which findings are sought to be generalized (adults with psychiatric disabilities). The two groups in this example are likely to be quite different, suggesting that findings reported for one group may not generalize to the other.

STIMULUS CHARACTERISTICS. Stimulus characteristics refer to the specific features of a given intervention that may restrict generalization of experimental findings. These features include the characteristics of the setting, the characteristics of the researcher(s), and how the stimuli are presented in an experiment. The external validity concern is that the specific stimulus conditions of an experiment may restrict the validity of findings to those conditions only. Examples of experimental features that could limit external validity include employing only one experimenter to implement an intervention, showing only one videotaped vignette to illustrate the experimental condition, and using a specific setting that may have different characteristics and conditions than are found in other settings. For example, Leierer et al. (1998) used an experimental analogue strategy to investigate the relationships among counselor characteristics (disability status and reputation) and clients' perceptions of counselor expertness, trustworthiness, and genuineness. The analogue approach involves examining the relationships among variables in an artificial, experimental situation that is analogous to actual counseling, often by using videotaped counseling vignettes (scripted counseling sessions performed by actors) and samples of graduate students (as the experimental "clients"). The carefully scripted counseling session used by Leierer et al. permitted greater experimental control over both the targeted independent variables and other, extraneous variables than would have been possible in the context of real counseling sessions. Thus, the analogue approach potentially enhances the internal validity of findings. However, the ultimate purpose of these investigations is to generate knowledge that generalizes to real world counseling. Therefore, the issue of external validity—whether the stimulus conditions of the experimental situation are similar enough to actual counseling to permit generalization to the real world—is particularly relevant to practitioners who wish to utilize findings from analogue studies.

CONTEXTUAL CHARACTERISTICS. The specific conditions in which an intervention is embedded or the experimental arrangements that are key to implementing an experiment may restrict findings to those conditions or arrangements only. The responses of participants who are aware of the fact that they are participating in an experiment or correctly guess the purpose of the experiment may be influenced by this knowledge. In other words, study participants may react to the specific experimental arrangements in ways that influence their responses. Participants who correctly guess the purpose of the experiment may also seek to please investigators by (a) avoiding responses that they believe will result in negative evaluation, or (b) providing "correct" responses. The external validity concern is: Would these same results be obtained if the subjects did not know they were being studied or did not correctly guess the purpose of the investigation? If it is plausible that subjects' responses were affected by their knowledge of the study purpose, then results may be restricted to these conditions only.

In some research contexts (particularly in real world settings), subjects may be exposed to several different treatments in addition to the intervention that is the target of the investigation. For example, clients with psychiatric disabilities may be receiving drug therapy and psychological counseling at the same time that they are participating in a social skills intervention program. *Multiple treatment interference* refers to the difficulty of drawing warranted conclusions about the target intervention when it is being evaluated in the context of other treatments. In these cases, the generalization of findings may be restricted to those conditions in which multiple treatments are administered.

ASSESSMENT CHARACTERISTICS. The method of assessing the dependent variable in an investigation may plausibly influence participants' responses and therefore restrict the generalization of findings to similar conditions of assessment. Many rehabilitation research investigations utilize self-report, paper and pencil measures to assess change in the dependent variable of interest. When self-report instruments are used, participants are typically aware that their performance is being evaluated, and what is being assessed is often made obvious by the nature of the specific items that comprise the instrument. These assessment characteristics can alter subjects' responses from what they would be under different conditions. When subjects are aware that they are being assessed, the evaluation is said to be *obtrusive*. When this awareness affects clients' responses, the measures are said to be *reactive* (Kazdin, 2003). Use of obtrusive and reactive methods of assessment may restrict the findings to these specific data collection conditions.

Assessment can also lead to participants becoming sensitized to the constructs that are the target of the investigation, particularly when self-report assessments are administered prior to the implementation of the experimental intervention to measure participants' baseline status. When a pretest causes subjects to become more sensitive to the construct that is the focus of the intervention, it can alter both the effect of the intervention and subjects' responses to the intervention at posttest from what would be obtained under different conditions (i.e., real world conditions in which sensitization does not take place). Sensitization is a threat to the generalization of findings because it raises the question of whether results can be extended to those situations in which prior sensitization to the construct of interest does not take place.

Construct Validity

Internal validity is an evaluation of the status of the observed relationship between independent and dependent variables, or whether change (as measured by the dependent variable) can reasonably be attributed to an intervention (the independent variable) rather than to other factors (e.g., history, maturation, selection). Construct validity of research operations focuses on the specific causal factors or mechanisms that are responsible for the observed change in the dependent variable.

As explained in Chapter 2, empirical research depends on translating key abstract concepts into specific research operations for the purpose of generating knowledge. Operational definitions form the essential linkage between the abstract, conceptual definition of a construct and the concrete procedures that comprise the study. Once data are analyzed, researchers typically wish to draw general conclusions from the specific case that was the focus of the investigation. The process of scientific investigation, then, is a circular movement from abstract constructs (research conceptualization and planning) to concrete exemplars of these constructs (implementation of procedures, data gathering, and data analysis), and back to the conceptual level (interpretation of findings). Two linkages in this circular movement are vital in the generation of valid scientific knowledge: (a) the linkage between the abstract constructs and the concrete research procedures and (b) the return linkage between concrete procedures and the conceptual interpretations that are made based on the findings. Construct validity pertains to both of these linkages. Thus, when considering the linkage between conceptual foundations and research operations, construct validity pertains to the "fit" between the operational definitions and research procedures and the hypothetical constructs that are assumed to underlie them (Kazdin, 2003). When considering the linkage between specific findings and conceptual conclusions, construct validity is the approximate validity of the generalizations about the higher-order constructs that the researcher makes on the basis of the concrete research operations (Cook & Campbell, 1979). Taking both linkages into account, construct validity of research is an evaluation of the specific nature of the causal relationships that are demonstrated within a quantitative study (Bellini & Rumrill, 2009). The threats to construct validity are confounds that call into question the researcher's interpretation regarding the specific factors that account for the study findings (Kazdin, 2003).

An example from the rehabilitation literature helps to clarify what is meant by construct validity in the research context. Decades of research on attitudes toward persons with disabilities indicate that attitude measurement is difficult because: (a) the items may serve to sensitize respondents to the issue, essentially transforming non-existent attitudes to transient attitudes that the researcher then interprets erroneously as meaningful; (b) respondents realize that attitudes are the focus of the assessment and seek to "manage" the public impression that their responses reflect; and (c) attitudes may be confounded with unrelated personality attributes, such as the desire to appear agreeable, disagreeable, or consistent (Antonak & Livneh, 1995; Smart, 2009; Wright, 1988). In particular, many items that comprise widely used measures of attitudes toward persons with disabilities are rather transparent; i.e., respondents typically know which item responses are socially desirable (or "politically correct") and which responses are less socially desirable. In regard to the construct validity of measurement, the transparency of items raises the question of what construct is actually being measured by the instrument, attitudes toward disability, social desirability, or some other personality preference? In the context of research validity, the imperfect construct validity of the measuring instrument also has important implications for the validity of research conclusions that are based on this measure as an operational definition of the construct "attitudes toward persons with disabilities."

Consider the hypothetical example of a researcher who wishes to demonstrate that counselors who have more positive attitudes toward persons with disabilities will make use of a more empowering approach in providing rehabilitation services. The investigator chooses a standard measure of attitudes toward persons with disabilities to operationalize counselor attitudes (the independent variable), and a simple scale to operationalize client perception of empowerment (the dependent variable). The investigation may be successful in demonstrating that higher scores of counselors on the attitude scale (more positive attitudes) are related to clients' perceptions of greater empowerment. However, the inadequate operationalization of the construct of interest makes it difficult for the researcher to convince readers that the specific nature of the relationship is that positive attitudes of counselors predict enhanced client empowerment. An alternate explanation–that socially desirable responses on the part of the counselor result in greater empowerment of clients–has not been ruled out.

A number of aspects of a study's design and procedures may make it difficult to accurately attribute the causal relations indicated by the results to the constructs of interest. Threats to the construct validity of research conclusions include inadequate explication and operationalization of constructs, single operations and narrow stimulus sampling, experimenter expectancies, and cues associated with the experimental situation.

INADEQUATE EXPLICATION AND OPERATIONAIZATION OF CONSTRUCTS. This construct validity issue pertains to the "fit" between the conceptual and operational definitions used by the investigator and how the construct is typically defined in the literature and operationalized in research. If there is a poor match between the commonly accepted definition and the researcher's definition, this is likely to raise questions about the warrant for specific interpretations that the researcher makes regarding the relationship between variables. For example, attitude in the psychological literature is typically defined as consistency across modes of responding (i.e., cognitive, affective, behavioral) to the attitude object and consistency in subjects' responses over time (Cook & Campbell, 1979). A measure of attitude that is taken at one time only is not likely to accurately reflect the commonly accepted definition of attitude (consistency over time). If an investigator operationalizes the construct of attitude using observations taken at only one point in time, the specific data-based interpretations of the relationships between attitudes and other variables of interest may be challenged on the basis of the poor fit between the conceptual and operational definitions.

SINGLE OPERATIONS AND NARROW STIMULUS SAMPLING. The definition of attitude cited in the previous section raises questions about the advisability of using a single measure taken at one point in time as a sole indicator of "attitudes toward persons with disabilities." The use of a single indicator to operationalize a construct is a problem because indicators underrepresent constructs and contain irrelevant variation that is mixed with the variation that is due to the construct of interest (Cook & Campbell, 1979). Method of measurement represents one major source of irrelevant variation in a measured variable (see Chapter 3). Using two or more indicators that represent different methods of measurement allows the investigator to triangulate the construct, that is, separate the variation that is due to the construct from the variation associated with the method of measurement. When a construct is confounded with a second, irrelevant construct (e.g., attitude toward persons with disabilities and social desirability), the researcher can eliminate the effect of the confounding construct on the dependent variable by (a) including a standard measure of the confounding construct in the investigation and then (b) correlating this variable with the target construct to estimate the variation that can be attributed solely to the construct of interest.

Construct validity may also be limited by the use of a single exemplar or stimulus to operationalize a treatment of interest. For example, Dalgin and Bellini (2008) used a single dyad of actors to perform the roles of employer and job applicant to examine the impact of short and detailed disclosure of an invisible disability in an employment interview. The experimental procedures employed in this analogue study may be challenged on the bases of both external validity and construct validity considerations, and this example is instructive for highlighting the different focuses of these research issues. The relevant external validity issue is: Can these findings, associated with a single, highly specific rehabilitation scenario, be generalized to rehabilitation counseling practice, or should the scope of findings be limited to the specific stimulus conditions used in the study? The relevant construct validity issue is: Does the single case scenario adequately exemplify the domain of disclosure and accommodation requests, such that the researcher can draw warranted, general conclusions about disclosure of an invisible disability from the findings of this study?

Construct validity may also be limited by the use of a single individual to implement a treatment or intervention. Even if the treatment proves effective in comparison to a non-treatment group, a critic who is conversant with construct validity issues may counter that the special character of the instructor may be responsible for the observed change in the dependent variable rather than the intervention per se. In each of these cases, both external and construct validity may be enhanced by the use of multiple scenarios, actors, or interventionists.

EXPERIMENTER EXPACTANCIES. In research situations where the principal investigator directly implements a treatment, the researcher's expectations regarding the intervention may confound the interpretation of findings (Kazdin, 2003). For example, a researcher who is enthusiastic about a given psychotherapeutic strategy may wish to contrast it with an alternate approach (e.g., Rational-Emotive Therapy versus Client-Centered Therapy). However, the experimenter's enthusiasm for the preferred strategy, coupled with her intention to demonstrate its efficacy, could lead to differences in how she implements the different interventions. The construct validity issue in this case highlights the possibility that the experimenter's expectations provide a plausible, alternate explanation for the causal mechanism responsible for the observed change in the dependent variable.

CUES ASSOCIATED WITH THE EXPERIMENTAL SITUATION. Research participants may inadvertently receive cues, such as rumors about the experiment or information provided during the recruitment phase, that are incidental to the experimental treatment but that may contribute to the study results. Hypothesis guessing by subjects–the basis of the well-known Hawthorne Effect–may lead to enhanced motivation on the part of the experimental group (and alter their performance) to "please" the researcher. Incidental contact between members of the treatment and comparison groups may also lead to: (a) compensatory rivalry, whereby comparison group members are especially motivated to perform as well as or better than the treatment group on the outcome variables; or (b) demoralization, when cues of the experimental situation result in lower than normal motivation on the part of the comparison group and adversely affect their standing on the outcome variables. Each of these situations may be a threat to construct validity because they represent plausible, alternative explanations for the causal mechanisms that are presumed to account for the experimental findings. Depending on the specific context of the investigation, these threats to construct validity can be minimized by providing fewer cues that permit subjects to guess the precise nature of the research hypotheses; reducing the incidental contact between experimental groups; and providing a "treatment" to the comparison group that is valued and, hence, is less likely to result in demoralization.

Statistical Conclusion Validity

Covariation between an independent and dependent variable is a necessary first step in establishing that their relationship is causal. Statistical conclusion validity pertains to the approximate validity of conclusions about the covariation of variables based on the specific research operations and statistical tests used in an investigation. When research conditions or statistical tests are not sufficiently rigorous, the conclusions that are based on these procedures may be erroneous. Threats to statistical conclusion validity are conditions that result in invalid statistical conclusions. Common threats include low statistical power, violated statistical assumptions, fishing and error rate problems, low reliability of dependent measures, and low reliability of treatment implementation.

LOW STATISTICAL POWER. As defined in Chapter 3, the power of a statistical test is the probability of detecting a significant relationship between two variables in a sample when the variables are related in the population. Power is a function of the interaction of three characteristics of a study: sample size, the size of the "effect" (i.e., the size of mean differences between groups on the variables of interest, or magnitude of variable relationships), and the researcher's pre-set Alpha level or benchmark of statistical significance (Cohen, 1990). Low statistical power is most likely to result when the sample size and effect size are small and the pre-set Alpha level is conservative. Low power may result in an invalid statistical decision (Type II Error), whereby the investigator concludes that two variables do not covary (e.g., a decision of no statistical significance) for the sample when, in fact, the two variables are significantly related in the population. Poor statistical conclusion validity resulting from low statistical power is a common problem in social science research in general (Cohen, 1990; Creswell, 2014; Goodwin & Goodwin, 2012) and rehabilitation counseling research in particular (Bellini & Rumrill, 2009; Ferrin, Bishop, Tansey, Swett, & Lane, 2007). However, it is a problem that researchers can minimize by (a) using larger samples in their research, (b) enhancing the size of the "effect" between groups by implementing treatments more consistently, and/or (c) choosing (prior to the statistical analysis) a less rigorous Alpha level as the benchmark of statistical significance (e.g., $p-<.10$ rather than $p-<.05$). Also, contemporary researchers are encouraged to perform a power analysis prior to their main analyses to estimate the likelihood that their statistical conclusions will be valid (Cohen, 1990; Ferrin et al., 2007).

VIOLATED STATISTICAL ASSUMPTIONS. The conclusion validity of most tests of statistical significance requires that certain statistical assumptions be met. When these assumptions are not supported for the sample data, the statistical test is less accurate and the interpretations based on the analyses are less valid. For example, a key assumption for most mean comparisons between groups (e.g., t-tests, ANOVA, MANOVA) is that these groups represent separate samples from the same population and, therefore, have roughly equal variances as indicated by the standard deviation of the dependent variable. Specific assumptions for various statistical tests can be found in most introductory statistics textbooks.

FISHING AND THE ERROR RATE PROBLEM. When multiple statistical tests are performed on a single data set, each comparison may be evaluated at a given, pre-set Alpha level (e.g., $p-<05$), but the Alpha level for the investigation as a whole (i.e., investigation-wise alpha) is the sum of all comparisons made. Thus, performing multiple statistical tests without correcting for the number of comparisons increases the probability of concluding that covariation exists in the sample when, in fact, no covariation exists in the population from which the sample was drawn. In that event, the statistical test yields a false positive result, or Type I error. The fishing and error rate problem refers to the situation in which the investigator goes "fishing" for statistically significant differences among variables in a data set and makes all possible comparisons among variables, which increases the likelihood that the statistical tests will yield false positive results. When making multiple comparisons, the researcher can reduce the likelihood of false positive results by applying a more stringent Alpha level for each separate test, known as the Bonferroni adjustment. For example, if five separate t-tests (comparing five separate dependent variables for two groups) are evaluated at the $p-<.01$ level of statistical significance, then the $p-<.05$ level of significance is maintained for the study as a whole, and the investigator can be reasonably assured that a false positive result has been avoided. The researcher can also reduce the likelihood of Type I errors by making a few, carefully planned statistical comparisons that are guided by theory rather than making all possible comparisons.

RELIABILITY OF MEASURES. Because measurement instruments with low reliability have a larger component of error score mixed with true score, they cannot be depended upon to register true changes in the dependent variable. A large error component in the measurement of the dependent variable may increase the likelihood that (a) the mean differences between treatment groups do not reflect true differences in the population or (b) the observed relationship between two variables is not a true relationship.

In the case of correlational studies, the index of the linear relationship (i.e., correlation coefficient) between two scores that are measured at less than perfect reliability will usually be lower than the true (i.e., population) correlation for the variables (Miles & Shevlin, 2001). Given that most operational variables include some error component (i.e., error variance), it follows that most correlations reported in published studies are underestimates of population values. Miles and Shevlin use the following example to illustrate the fact that unreliability of measurement has a more dramatic impact on correlations than is typically appreciated. Consider that the true correlation between two variables is .90 (a very high correlation), and the reliability of the two measures is .70 (not unusually low for psychological measures). Using the correction for attenuation formula given by Cohen and Cohen (1983), the observed correlation between the two scores in the sample will be .63, a considerable reduction from the population value of .90. Miles and Shevlin caution against the overuse of this correction formula, because in doing so we are making the assumption that all errors in the measurement of variables are random and uncorrelated, and it is rare that this assumption will be absolutely true. Despite this caveat, unreliability of measurement tends to increase the error component in a statistical analysis, and thereby reduces the power of the statistical test and increases the likelihood of making a Type II error in the statistical decision.

RELIABILITY OF TREATMENT IMPLEMENTATION. If, within a study, different persons or agencies are responsible for implementing a treatment or intervention, a lack of standardization in the execution of the intervention may result. There may also be differences from occasion to occasion when the same person implements the treatment. This lack of standardization–both within and across persons and agencies–can inflate the error variance in the measured variables associated with the treatment and decrease the accuracy of the statistical inference to the population of interest. As Rumrill et al. (2010) noted, this threat is pervasive in field research where the researcher may be unable to control the quality of implementation of the intervention. The investigator should use all available means (e.g., extensive training of individuals and agencies) for ensuring that the intervention is as standard as possible across individuals, agencies, and occasions.

The Research Process and Research Validity

In Chapter 2 we presented the nine stages of the research process as a series of decisions about how to implement an investigation (see Figure 2.1). Given the complexity of issues related to establishing a strong warrant for knowledge claims, it is very difficult for a single study to address each aspect of research validity equally well. Moreover, decisions made at different phases of the research process impact different types of research validity. For example, the decisions made at Phase 2–Defining the constructs of interest–involve determining what constructs are to be included in the study and how these constructs will be defined. These decisions establish the conceptual or theoretical basis for the study and primarily impact the construct validity of the investigation. Decisions made at Phase 3–Determining the data to be gathered–involve the operationalization of key variables and complete the linkage between the conceptual definitions and empirical indicators of these variables. Selection of instruments that are demonstrated to validly measure the constructs of interest strengthens the construct validity of the investigation. Decisions related to data gathering may also significantly impact both internal and statistical conclusion validity. Internal validity can be strengthened by the inclusion of control variables that are not the target of the investigation but that may represent alternative explanations for the results. Statistical conclusion validity can be strengthened by the use of instruments with high reliability.

Decisions made at Phase 4 of study planning–Determine the appropriate sample–have the largest impact on external validity, or the degree to which the findings can be generalized to the population of interest. Phase 5–Determine additional research procedures–will impact different types of validity depending on the procedures that are adopted. In intervention studies, this phase may involve assignment of participants to different groups prior to the provision of a treatment. If, in this phase, study participants are randomly assigned to these groups, internal validity of the investigation is strengthened. Control variables may also be used to match study participants to ensure that groups are roughly equivalent on that variable (e.g., level of education, in the event that the researcher suspects that persons with different levels of education may respond to the intervention differently). When stimulus materials are developed for use in a study, additional research procedures may include (a) manipulation checks to evaluate whether the independent variable has been manipulated effectively, or (b) a protocol to standardize the intervention for treatment groups. These procedures can strengthen the construct validity of a study by reducing the plausibility that rival causal processes are responsible for the findings. Use of more than one stimulus and/or more than one experimenter may enhance construct validity and external validity at the same time, by reducing the likelihood that the findings result from unique aspects of the stimulus or experimenter or may be limited to these circumstances only. Finally, when an intervention is implemented across multiple sites, maintaining the consistency of its implementation (i.e., reliability of treatment implementation) serves to strengthen the statistical conclusion validity of the study by reducing error variance in dependent variables caused by differences in treatment implementation.

Decisions made during Phase 6–Data gathering–are closely related to decisions made regarding what data are determined to be needed (Phase 3). However, decisions during the data gathering phase may impact both the quality and quantity of data available for analysis. For example, follow-up efforts to secure additional research participants in a survey design (by using multiple mailings, reminder cards, or incentives) may yield a larger, more representative sample for a study, which can enhance the warrant for the generalizability of the findings (i.e., external validity) and improve the sensitivity of the statistical analysis (i.e., statistical conclusion validity). When using multiple instruments in data gathering, the researcher may choose to randomize the order in which the instruments are completed to reduce the possibility that an order effect has influenced participant responses (an external validity concern).

When the research process has reached Phase 7–Data analysis–all data for a study have been gathered and entered into an appropriate data file. Data analysis has direct implications for statistical conclusion validity, or the approximate validity of conclusions about variable relationships based on the statistical tests used in the study. Many decisions made during earlier phases of the research process also impact the statistical conclusion validity of a study—for example, choosing highly reliable instruments, implementing a treatment in consistent fashion, and determining a priori the size of the sample needed in order to achieve a sensitive statistical test given the estimated size of the variable effects under investigation (i.e., power analysis). Additional decisions made at Phase 7 that also impact statistical conclusion validity include choices regarding the number and type of statistical tests to run, and whether the assumptions underlying the appropriate use of particular statistical tests (e.g., independence of observations, normal distribution of variables) are met by the data being analyzed. Any research decision that has the potential to increase Type I or Type II errors may reduce the warrant for statistical conclusion validity.

Both the Interpretation of the empirical data (Phase 8) and Determination of the status of the research question (Phase 9) pertain to the strength of the linkage between the concrete research operations that underlie the study findings and the conceptual conclusions about higher order constructs. This is primarily an issue of construct validity, and in these concluding stages of the research process, it is the totality of research assumptions, operations, and findings that must be kept in mind when considering how well the study supports the author's specific generalizations about the constructs under study. Consistent with the empirical approach to knowledge that is exemplified in the scientific method, interpretation of data should be conservative and flow directly from the findings of the investigation. In other words, interpretations and conclusions should not exceed the warrant provided by the study methodology and results. Typically, the author's conclusions regarding the study findings are also evaluated within the context of the larger body of research in the given area, and are a key aspect of the Discussion section of journal articles.

Order of Priority Among the Four Research Validities

Although each type of research validity is important, and the warrant for a knowledge claim is based, in part, on how well the researcher addresses these issues in an investigation, there is a logical order of priority (Cook & Campbell, 1979). Before it can be shown that two variables have a causal relationship, it is first necessary to establish that they covary. Thus, statistical conclusion validity, or the demonstration that two variables are statistically related, is the initial criterion by which a knowledge claim is evaluated in quantitative studies. Internal validity is the second issue in research, which is to determine (a) whether a causal relationship between two variables can be inferred, and (b) the direction of the relationship. The third issue of research, construct validity, is to determine the particular constructs or mechanisms that are involved in the demonstrated causal relationship between variables. External validity, the fourth and final issue in research, involves the question: How generalizable is the relationship and causal mechanism to other populations, settings, and conditions? Each dimension of research validity contributes to causal explanation, which is the ultimate goal of scientific inquiry.

It is important to note that no single research investigation can address each of these validity issues equally well, and that limited resources often require an investigator to make compromises in designing research. The specific procedures that strengthen the internal validity of an investigation (i.e., experimental control) may also serve to reduce the generalizability of findings to real world settings (i.e., external validity). Ideally, the types of validity that the researcher chooses to emphasize in designing a particular investigation are a function of the global research context; that is, the totality of relevant studies in the given area, the degree to which relationships among variables have been established in previous research, and the extent to which generalizability of findings has been investigated. When the specific relationships among variables are not well understood, the research validity focus should be on statistical conclusion validity and internal validity: Do the targeted variables covary, and can a causal relationship be demonstrated? Once the warrant for these conclusions has been established, the research program moves on to address issues of construct and external validity: What is the specific causal mechanism at work, and do results generalize to other populations, settings, and conditions? The variety and complexity of research validity issues cannot be addressed in a single study or even in a small group of related studies. Rather, valid scientific knowledge can only be established through multiple investigations carried out by many researchers spanning a long period of time.

SUMMARY

In this chapter, we have discussed the four types of research validity as criteria for establishing the warrant for scientific knowledge claims in the quantitative research paradigm. Each type of validity—internal, external, construct, and statistical conclusion—addresses a different aspect of the knowledge claim. Internal validity pertains to the strength of the inference that the relationship between two variables is causal. Threats to the internal validity of an investigation are rival, alternate explanations for the results that may not be adequately ruled out on the basis of the research design. External validity is the degree to which research findings can be generalized to other populations, settings, and conditions. Threats to external validity are those aspects of the study that may plausibly restrict findings to the specific circumstances of the study. Construct validity pertains to the specific causal mechanisms that are presumed to underlie the study findings. Threats to construct validity are those aspects of research design and procedures that make it difficult to accurately attribute the causal relationships indicated by the results to the constructs of interest. Statistical conclusion validity is the approximate certainty of conclusions about the covariation of variables based on the specific research operations and statistical tests used in an investigation. Threats to statistical conclusion validity are aspects of research design and implementation that may result in erroneous interpretations of observed findings.

Chapter 6

QUANTITATIVE RESEARCH DESIGNS

With Contributions by Courtney Vierstra, Mykal Leslie, Rowan Blundell and Sarah Davis

INTRODUCTION

As noted in the first chapter of this book, the research paradigm that comprises quantitative designs features the numeric expression of information for purposes of summarization, classification, interpretation, and generalization. Rooted within the quantitative paradigm are fundamental precepts of scientific inquiry including sampling and population issues, validity and scientific control, probability and statistics, power, significance, and generalizability (see Chapters 1, 2, 3, and 5). Quantitative research approaches share in common the transcription of words and observations into numbers, but there is great variance within the paradigm in terms of how researchers address their questions and hypotheses.

We have organized this chapter around three broad categories of quantitative studies: intervention/stimulus studies, non-manipulation studies, and descriptive studies. Primarily, these categories are differentiated based upon the purpose or reason for a particular investigation—not on the basis of the methodological or analytic techniques that are used in each study. The foremost consideration in determining the suitability of a particular design or set of methods is the researcher's curiosity, that is, the question or problem that his or her research is devised to address (Creswell, 2014).

INTERVENTION/STIMULUS STUDIES

One key purpose of research in all social science disciplines is to gauge the effects that interventions and stimuli have on individuals' behaviors, knowledge, attitudes, and emotions. Whether assessing the effects of self-advocacy training programs for people with disabilities, evaluating the impact of Americans with Disabilities Act consultation on employers' willingness to provide workplace accommodations, or determining the effectiveness of different teaching techniques within a graduate rehabilitation counselor education program, rehabilitation researchers have a long history of intervention/stimulus studies that attempt to answer the question, What happens when...? Including such approaches as true experiments, quasi-experimental designs, analogue studies, and small-N designs, intervention/ stimulus studies have played an important role in shaping preservice training, counseling practice, and policy initiatives in the field of rehabilitation. This section describes each design sub-category, illustrated with examples from the rehabilitation and disability studies literature.

Experimental Designs

Although relatively rarely employed in contemporary rehabilitation research, true experiments constitute the most readily apparent images that people bring to mind when they think of scientific inquiry in the social and physical sciences. Indeed, the quantitative research paradigm is deeply ingrained in experimental design, to the extent that experiments are often viewed as the highest form of investigation into new knowledge (Heppner, Kivlighan, & Wampold, 2007; Rumrill, Cook, & Wiley, 2010). We believe that researchers should not view designs in hierarchical, this one is better than that one fashion; however, true experiments provide the strongest warrant for claims to knowledge because of the systematic ways in which the effects of an intervention are isolated, other influences are controlled, and alternative causal explanations are reduced or eliminated. We have divided quantitative designs into three major categories–intervention/stimulus studies, non-manipulation studies, and descriptive studies–but many experts categorize all research as either experimental or non-experimental. This dichotomy does not permit one to fully appreciate the breadth of approaches that are used within the overarching umbrella of quantitative methodology, but it does provide a useful rubric for explaining what experimental design is and what it is not.

The logical structure for experimental research is relatively simple. One hypothesizes: If X, then Y; if therapy, then wellness, for example, or if training, then employment. Usually related to the tenets of a particular body of knowledge (theory), the researcher uses some method to manipulate or measure X (the independent variable) and then observe Y (the dependent variable) to see if concomitant variation occurs (Heppner, Wampold, Owen, Thompson, & Wang, 2015; McMillan & Schumacher, 2009). Concomitant variation is the amount of variation in Y that is attributable to (or caused by) variation in X. If sufficient concomitant variation (sufficient as determined by

(a) the magnitude of relationship between X and Y and (b) the size of the sample [i.e., a test for statistical significance]), the If X, then Y proposition is evidenced to be valid. In that scenario, the control or manipulation (variation) of X accounts for, or causes, variation in Y.

In non-experimental research, Y is observed, and an X (or a number of Xs) is also observed before, after, or at the same time as Y. No attempt is made to control or manipulate X (Creswell, 2014; Goodwin & Goodwin, 2012). This does not mean that the If X, then Y hypothesis is not tested in non-experimental research. Researchers use a number of non-experimental techniques to ascribe *logical* validity to a variety of propositions. For example, high scores on the Graduate Record Examination (GRE) are generally considered to predict academic performance in graduate school. There is a positive correlation between GRE scores and grades in advanced degree programs; as GRE scores increase, so does the likelihood that the student will do well. It follows logically, then, that Y (grades in graduate school) is a partial function of X (GRE scores), even though both X and Y were observed as they occur without any manipulation or control of X. In terms of *empirical validity*, however, the warrant for new knowledge based on the linear relationship of two variables as in the GRE example is not as strong as it would be in the event that there is a cause and effect relationship between them. The primary reason for the limited empirical validity of non-experimental research, as exemplified above, is that it does not account for alternative explanations for variation in the outcome (Y) variable. The linear relationship between GRE scores and graduate school grades does not account for other factors that might be attributable to (i.e., cause) grades in advanced degree programs (e.g., study habits, undergraduate grades, socioeconomic status, intelligence).

To make the strongest warrant for a cause and effect relationship between the independent and dependent variables, the researcher must systematically control or manipulate the independent variable *and* do so using random procedures (Heppner et al., 2015; Kazdin, 2003). In a typical true experiment, X is manipulated across groups of people who are randomly chosen to receive varying degrees of the independent variable. The simplest example is the two-group experiment, wherein one randomly constituted group of participants receives an intervention (treatment group) and one randomly constituted group does not (control group). Random assignment to the two groups ensures that the two groups are more-or-less equal along demographic, psychological, and functional dimensions (i.e., status variables), or that any preexisting differences between the groups are attributable to chance rather than systematic factors (Goodwin & Goodwin, 2012; McMillan & Schumacher, 2009). Then, sometime after the treatment group has completed the intervention, the researcher compares the two groups on whatever outcome (i.e., dependent) variables theory dictates should result from the intervention. The If X then Y proposition is supported if the treatment group performs at a higher level than the control group on outcome or dependent measures; in that event, the treatment group's superior outcome performance is viewed as the result of the intervention.

Once experimental researchers have identified their independent and dependent variables based upon existing theory, they face several key issues in designing experiments so as to highlight the causal relationships among variables. The first issue involves how to manipulate the independent variable. One approach is to compare an active intervention to a group that completes the assessments at the same time as the treatment group, but otherwise does not receive an intervention (i.e., a pure control group). Although this design provides the simplest comparison for the impact of an intervention, it does have potential problems. One problem is that control group participants, without any formal intervention, may improve on an outcome due to maturation or other natural processes (Kazdin, 2003).

It is also possible that the treatment group improves on an outcome at the conclusion of the intervention, but it may be unclear whether improvement is due to the intervention activities or the result of researcher attention, contact with participants, or expectancies for change on the part of the participants. These issues are incidental to the intervention and do not prevent the researcher from concluding that the intervention was responsible for the change. However, they may present difficulties in drawing valid conclusions about the specific aspects of the intervention that were responsible for the change (Goodwin & Goodwin, 2012; Kazdin, 2003). The power of expectancies to influence outcomes is known as the *placebo effect.* Placebo effects result from factors other than the active ingredients in the intervention itself, such as the belief of the participants, that the treatment is efficacious. To draw valid conclusions about what specific features of an intervention are responsible for the change, researchers may opt to include a non-specific treatment group in the design. A non-specific treatment group—also known as an *attention-placebo control group*—is designed to control for common factors that are associated with participation in a treatment. The inclusion of a non-specific treatment group in the experimental design permits the researcher to eliminate the plausible explanation that the results of the treatment were due to factors other than the specific ingredients of the intervention.

Researchers may also design an experimental study to assess the impact of two or more treatment conditions on an outcome variable (or set of variables), with or without the addition of a control group. *Multigroup experiments* have the benefit of comparing different treatment modalities or intervention strategies within the same study (Heppner et al., 2015). The treatment conditions may involve different levels of the same intervention (e.g., a written how-to informational packet to one group as compared to a complete training program for another group) or two or more different interventions (e.g., supported employment services delivered in an integrated community setting and vocational services delivered in a non-integrated workshop setting for young adults with developmental disabilities). This multi-group design allows the researcher to assess whether Intervention A is better (more effective) than Intervention B, and the inclusion of a control group permits an assessment of whether either Intervention A or B is better than nothing. However, it is also reasonable that the mean differences (i.e., effect size) on an outcome measure in a study that compares two active treatments will be smaller than the mean differences on an outcome in a study that compares an active treatment to no treatment. Thus, the nature of the comparisons made in a study has important implications for the various types of research validity, including statistical conclusion validity. In the event that a researcher wishes to compare two active treatments, and given that smaller effect sizes are likely in this comparison, the researcher could opt to increase statistical power to identify smaller mean differences across the groups by including more subjects or by using a more liberal Alpha value (e.g., .10 rather than .05) for the statistical benchmark.

Experimental researchers also face the issue of how outcomes will be assessed. Pretests are often used to establish a baseline for each participant's performance that is measured at some point before an intervention is begun. Then, sometime after the intervention has concluded, the researcher takes the same measures from all participants in a posttest. The established baseline gives the researcher an opportunity to gauge the degree to which participants have benefited from the intervention, as indicated by the average differences between pretest and posttest for treatment and control groups. Kazdin (2003) noted that the use of a pretest also yields statistical advantages for the data analysis. By using a pretest, within-group variability is reduced and more powerful statistical tests (e.g., analysis of covariance or repeated measures analysis of variance) may be used, potentially resulting in greater statistical power for the analysis and stronger statistical conclusion validity for the study.

Pretest-posttest experimental designs have the advantage of comparing individual participants' scores and group means at different points in time and then comparing progress on outcome measures across groups, permitting the researcher to make specific statements about change. The primary weakness in using a pretest-posttest design pertains to the possibility that administration of a pretest sensitizes the participants to the intervention, known as the *pretest sensitization effect.* A plausible pretest sensitization effect means that the results of a study can be generalized only to subjects who received a pretest. Pretest sensitization is most likely when the pretest and intervention are close together in time and in the perception of research pparticipants (Kazdin, 2003).

To eliminate this possible pretest bias, the researcher may opt for a *posttest only experimental design.* In this design, participants are randomly assigned to two or more groups, an intervention is provided, and posttest measures are taken. Given random assignment to treatment and control groups and manipulation of the independent variable, the researcher can assume that any characteristics that could influence performance on the posttest are randomly distributed across the two groups. Furthermore, given the fact that participants were assessed on the outcome measure only after the conclusion of the intervention, the researcher can eliminate pretest sensitization as a rival explanation for the findings. However, the posttest only design does not allow the researcher to establish a baseline on the outcome variable for the participants, nor assess the degree to which participants improved as a result of the intervention. The posttest-only design does enable the researcher to answer the question, "Did individuals who received the treatment have higher (or lower) scores on the outcome variable than participants who did not receive the intervention?" The lack of a pretest also raises the discomforting possibility that the group differences on the outcome variable assessed at the conclusion of the intervention may actually be the result of preexisting group differences. Although the use of random assignment in the posttest only design allows for the assumption that all preexisting differences are randomized across the groups, in practice this is more likely to be true when the study includes a large number of subjects. Hence, selection may be a plausible threat to internal validity in the case of posttest only experimental designs that use smaller numbers of subjects.

A number of studies in the existing rehabilitation literature have used different variations of experimental designs. For example, Palmer (1998) employed a two-group, posttest only experimental design to assess the impact of an intervention to enhance self-advoc-acy behaviors of college students with disabilities. He randomly assigned students with disabilities to a treatment group ($n=24$) and a wait-list control group ($n=26$). The treatment group participated in a small-group self-advocacy training program that focused on (a) requesting classroom accommodations from professors, and (b) conflict resolution strategies in the event that the students' desired accommodations were not acceptable to the professor. The control group did not participate in the intervention until after the investigation had concluded. Palmer's independent variable was the self-advocacy training, which was provided for one group and withheld from the other. His dependent variables were target behaviors related to requesting classroom accommodations and to resolving conflicts, as identified in previous research. Palmer engaged the treatment group in role plays after they participated in the training to determine their level of acquisition of such behaviors as disclosing one's disability status and related accommodation needs, negotiating an acceptable accommodation plan, identifying disagreements, mediating conflicts, and formulating a mutually acceptable arrangement. He engaged the control group in the role plays at the inception of the project to establish a baseline regarding self-advocacy and conflict resolution behavior that was not subject to the intervention.

Palmer hypothesized that the treatment group's receipt of the training program would result in (i.e., cause) higher scores than the control group on the behavioral measures: If participants engage in the training, then their proficiency in requesting accommodations and in resolving conflicts will be higher on average than the control group's proficiency. Results upheld Palmer's hypotheses, which, given the manipulation of the independent variable and random assignment to groups, provided the researcher with a strong warrant for a cause-and-effect relationship between receipt of self-advocacy training and acquisition of accommodation request and conflict resolution skills.

Using a pretest posttest experimental design, Rogers, Anthony, Lyass, and Penk (2006) examined the effectiveness of two vocational rehabilitation interventions in improving employment, educational, clinical, and quality of life outcomes for people with psychiatric disabilities. Participants ($N=135$) were randomly assigned to receive either a psychiatric vocational rehabilitation (PVR; $n=70$) intervention or enhanced state vocational rehabilitation services (ESVR; $n=65$). The PVR intervention was based on the Choose-Get-Keep model of psychiatric rehabilitation wherein practitioners diagnose, plan, and intervene to assist individuals with psychiatric disabilities in developing the skills and supports required to be successful and satisfied in their employment environments. PVR also included attendance three times per week for classroom instruction in career planning and individual meetings with a vocational specialist. The ESVR treatment was considered the control condition in this study. ESVR participants received standard vocational rehabilitation services, with the addition of a research assistant (hence the designation of "enhanced" VR services) who advocated on behalf of and intervened with participants to ensure that they engaged in the service process and stayed in the EVRS intervention. The length of the intervention for EVRS participants varied according to their individual rehabilitation plans.

Assessments on all outcome measures were taken at baseline, and again at nine, 18, and 24 month follow-ups. Given that there was attrition from the study sample over the two years of the study, missing data at 18 and 24 months were imputed using a last post-baseline value carried forward method (i.e., called an "intent to treat" analysis). Results indicated that the two groups did not differ on educational outcomes across the assessment periods and did not differ on employment outcomes 9 months post-baseline or 24 months post-baseline. The only employment outcome difference between the groups was observed at 18 months post-baseline on the measure "involved in any productive activity;" unexpectedly, a significantly greater proportion of EVRS group members endorsed this item as compared to the PVR group. There were no significant differences across the PVR and EVRS groups on clinical or quality of life outcomes for the 9, 18, and 24 month post-baseline assessments, except for a small difference on quality of life satisfaction with friends, which advantaged the EVRS group. Moreover, both groups improved on the overall set of outcomes across the time of the study. Rogers et al. (2006) noted that the failure to find significant differences between the groups was unexpected given the oft-cited difficulties of the state VR system in effectively serving people with psychiatric disabilities. The authors speculated that the positive outcomes experienced by the EVRS participants may be the result of the enhancements to state VR services introduced during the investigation. In other words, these enhancement strategies may have attenuated the differences in intervention impact between the two groups. In addition, attrition of participants over the 24 months of the investigation and imputing of missing data for these individuals at 9, 18, and 24 months post-baseline may have reduced the differences in effects between the two interventions, leading to mostly non-significant findings for the study as a whole.

Wusthoff, Waal, and Grawe (2014) used a two group, pretest-posttest experimental design to examine the effects of an integrated treatment approach for reducing substance use, reducing mental health symptoms, and increasing motivation for treatment among individuals with dual diagnoses of substance use disorders and mental illness. The independent variable in the study was the treatment received, with participants being randomly assigned to either the integrated treatment group ($n=55$) or a treatment as usual control group ($n=21$). The dependent variables, which were measured at baseline and after 12 months, included substance and alcohol use, psychiatric symptoms, and motivational levels. The researchers found that, although both groups significantly reduced substance use from baseline to the 12-month follow-up, there was not a significant difference in substance use reduction between the integrated treatment group and the control group. No change in psychiatric symptoms was seen for either group. Both groups increased their levels of motivation for treatment, with the integrated treatment group increasing motivation significantly more on average than the control group. The researchers concluded that the integrated treatment approach is an effective means for increasing motivation for consumers with dual diagnoses in outpatient clinics.

Quasi-Experimental Designs

The protocol and logical structure of the true experiment is what permits the researcher to limit the effects of extraneous variables and ascribe causation to the independent variable (Rumrill et al., 2010). True experiments are characterized by random assignment of subjects to groups. Sometimes, however, it is not possible to gather all potential participants at the inception of an intervention study and randomly assign them to experimental conditions. When researchers test If X, then Y hypotheses by comparing two or more groups that are not randomly constituted, they do so using quasi-experimental methods.

As in experimental studies, quasi-experiments involve one or more treatment groups and a comparison (the non-random correlate for control) group who are subjected to varying levels of the independent variable. The same issues related to how the independent variable will be manipulated and how to assess outcomes that apply to experimental design also pertain to quasi-experiments. However, non-random assignment to groups affords less protection against the various threats to causal inference (i.e., internal validity; see Chapter 5). This means that alternate explanations for results (e.g., history, maturation, selection) cannot be ruled out as readily in quasi-experimental designs.

For example, Schaller and Parker (1997) conducted a quasi-experiment to determine the effects of graduate-level research instruction on perceived research anxiety, perceived utility of research for professional practice, and confidence in research skills of a sample ($N=23$) of masters-level students in rehabilitation counseling and special education. Fifteen (15) participants signed up for a semester-long course entitled, Applied Research in Special Education and Rehabilitation Counseling. The remaining 8 students were enrolled in Instructional Designs Using Assistive Technology, a course that did not focus on research methods and utilization. Having gathered pretest data on the three dependent measures from all 23 participants, Schaller and Parker hypothesized that the course in applied research would result in lower levels of research anxiety, higher levels of perceived research utility, and greater confidence in using research skills among the 15 enrollees in comparison to the 8 enrollees in the assistive technology course. Given that small sample sizes require larger between-group differences (i.e., larger treatment effects) for the researcher to infer statistical significance (see Chapter 3), it is not surprising that there were non-significant differences between the two groups on two of Schaller and Parker's three outcome measures (perceived utility and research confidence). Only research anxiety was significantly impacted by the applied research course; students in that course reported significantly lower levels of anxiety at posttest than did students who had taken the assistive technology course.

More recently, Zimmerman, Kowalski, Niggemeier-Groben, Sauer, Leonhardt, and Strohle (2015) used a two-group pretest posttest quasi-experimental design to examine the effects of a 3-week preventative treatment program on posttraumatic stress as experienced by soldiers returning from deployment in Iraq and Afghanistan. The independent variable in the study was the 3-week preventative treatment program, which was given to one group of soldiers returning from deployment ($n=200$). The comparison group of returning soldiers ($n=60$) received no therapeutic intervention. The dependent variable was stress, as measured by the Posttraumatic Stress Scale 10 (PTSS-10). The PTSS-10 was administered to both groups before and after the first group received the preventative treatment. Results indicated that participating soldiers in both groups had a significant reduction in posttraumatic stress symptoms. An analysis of covariance showed, however, that this therapeutic effect depended on participants' military rank and their initial stress level at pretest rather than on their assignment to the preventative treatment and comparison groups.

Analogue Studies

Researchers in rehabilitation counseling and other social science fields have a long history of applying experimental and quasi-experimental techniques in what have come to be known as analogue studies (Heppner et al., 2015). The key distinguishing feature of analogue studies is that they approximate or mirror the processes involved in the counselor-client relationship or in the employment-related interactions between people with disabilities and other individuals (e.g., coworkers, employers). Analogue studies involve laboratory or clinical simulations of particular counseling techniques, screenings of fictitious case files to gauge counselors clinical judgments, and research to assess attitudes toward people with disabilities on the part of various rehabilitation stakeholders. Typically, analogue studies involve exposing one group to a stimulus or intervention while withholding treatment (or providing a different stimulus/intervention) to another group. Analogue studies almost always fall into experimental or quasi-experimental classifications, depending upon whether groups are constituted using random assignment.

Gouvier, Systma-Jordan, and Maryville (2003) designed an experimental analogue study to investigate the effect of disability type, job complexity, and public contact on hiring preferences regarding job applicants with disabilities. In this study, 295 undergraduate students taking upper division business courses at a large university (who represented potential future employers) read fictitious job descriptions and four fictitious resumes of individuals who had closed head injuries (CHI), chronic mental illness (CMI), developmental disabilities (DD), and back injuries (BI). Participants were asked to rate the desirability of each applicant for two jobs that reflected different levels of job complexity: janitor (low complexity) and telephone operator (high complexity). Participants were then randomly assigned to one of two groups. One group read job descriptions indicating that the applicant would work during the day (high public contact); the other group believed that the available positions were for night jobs (low public contact). On one of the dependent measures utilized by Gouvier et al., participants completed paired comparisons between all possible pairs of applicants for each of the two jobs. In other words, participants selected whom they would hire from the six possible pairings (CHI/CMI, CHI/DD, CHI/BI, CMI/DD, CMI/BI, and DD/BI) for each job.

Results indicated a significant main effect for disability type and a significant two-way interaction between disability type and job complexity. The applicant with a back injury was more likely to be hired as a telephone operator than were applicants with the three other disabling conditions. Likelihood of being hired for this position did not differ among the applicants with the other three disabilities. However, for the janitor position, the applicant with mental illness was significantly less likely to be hired than the other three applicants—for whom the likelihood of being hired did not significantly differ. No significant differences were found in relation to amount of contact with the public (i.e., day job versus night job). Gouvier et al. (2003) concluded that bias toward applicants with disabilities varies according to different job requirements.

Broussard and Crimando (2002) also reported the results of an analogue study utilizing an experimental design. They investigated the effects of attribution of responsibility for disability, race of consumer, and race of rehabilitation counselor on counselors' predictions of consumers' personal adjustment to disability and vocational outcomes. One hundred fifty rehabilitation counselor trainees (juniors, seniors, and graduate students) from two universities (a historically black southern university and a predominantly white Midwestern university) participated in the study. Each participant read a fabricated vocational evaluation report that contained vocational interest results, academic aptitude scores, recommendations for next steps, work history, level of education, and a brief description of a job in which the individual was interested (Broussard & Crimando, 2002). These elements of the vocational evaluation report remained constant, whereas the investigators varied attribution of responsibility and race.

The client was described as (a) exhibiting either characterological self-blame attribution (i.e., "I'm the kind of person to whom these things always seem to happen. I deserve my fate and have nobody to blame but myself . . . It's just the way it was meant to be" [p. 247]) or behavioral self-blame (i.e., "I think in the past I've taken too many chances and not considered the consequences of my actions. It seemed like this was going to happen to me eventually . . . I regret that I was not more careful" [p. 247]); and (b) being either Caucasian or African American. Thus, four conditions (behavioral attribution-Caucasian consumer, behavioral attribution-African American consumer, characterological attribution-Caucasian consumer, and characterological attribution-African American consumer) were randomly distributed to participants (Caucasian and African American preservice counselors). After reading the fabricated vocational evaluation reports, participants completed a two-part instrument on which they predicted the clients' personal adjustment to disability and vocational outcomes.

Broussard and Crimando (2002) reported a significant main effect for participants' inferences regarding client personal adjustment. Participants predicted better personal adjustment for fictitious clients who made behavioral attributions than they did for those who made characterological attributions. Therefore, the authors concluded that counseling trainees should be made aware of how their own perceptions of attribution, and the attribution self-beliefs of the consumers with whom they work, may influence the decisions they and their consumers make and ultimately affect the success of consumers in the rehabilitation process. An additional analysis was conducted to determine the effect of racial similarity or difference between the rehabilitation students and the fictitious consumer on participants' predictions. Personal adjustment scores were reported to be higher when the consumer and trainee were of the same race.

Small-N Designs

In the preceding discussions of experimental, quasi-experimental, and analogue studies, there is an underlying assumption that the effects of interventions or stimuli are best assessed by comparing groups of people. In those approaches, groups are typically differentiated based upon the level or type of treatment or information that they receive in the course of an investigation. This group comparative method is applied primarily because the results of intervention/stimulus studies are usually viewed as most compelling when they generalize to even larger groups than were involved in each study; in general, the larger the study sample and the larger the treatment group, the more representative the researcher's conclusions become with regard to the broader population from which the study sample was drawn. These are important precepts of parametric statistics and quantitative research methods, but they require the reader to infer, based on group performance, how an intervention or experience might affect a given individual.

Small-N research (also known as single subject design) applies experimental principles of intervention, control, and outcome analysis in an effort to track individual participants' progress across time and situations (Heppner et al., 2015). Whereas the between-subject experimental researcher compares a group of participants who received an intervention to a group of participants who did not, the small-N researcher compares the progress of one or a small number of participants at various points in time and across treatment or training situations. Typically, the small-N approach involves skill training initiatives in which the behavioral execution of tasks is viewed as the primary dependent or outcome variable (Rumrill et al., 2010). Applied behavioral techniques such as modeling, rehearsal, role plays, and feedback are common training strategies that are utilized in small-N designs (Kazdin, 2003).

The specific procedures used in small-N studies vary, but these designs share some unifying features. For example, all small-N research designs have a baseline phase and an intervention phase. During the baseline phase, the individual's behavior is systematically observed on multiple occasions prior to the manipulation of the independent variable, and during the intervention phase the treatment is applied. Moreover, these designs are characterized by careful observation and quantification of a target behavior, systematic data collection, and repeated observation (Lundervold & Belwood, 2000). Directly observable target behaviors (e.g., initiating a conversation) are preferred over indirect measures (e.g., empathic awareness) because observable targets reduce the level of inference needed to determine whether the target has or has not occurred. Careful definition and systematic observation of the target behavior enhances the construct validity of a small-N design (Kazdin, 2003).

Experimental control (i.e., internal validity) is exercised in these designs by careful measurement of the target behavior (dependent variable) during the baseline phase, followed by the application of a treatment (i.e., manipulation of the independent variable) during the intervention or training phase. The individual's behavior during the baseline phase is used as the standard by which the efficacy of the intervention is judged. In other words, the baseline measurement is analogous to the "no treatment control condition" used in experimental, between-groups research methods; however, in the single-subject design, each participant serves as his or her own control (Goodwin & Goodwin, 2012; Kazdin, 2003).

Data analysis takes the form of a visual inspection of graphed frequency counts of the target behavior across the baseline and intervention phases of the study to determine whether a pattern in the data exists and whether this pattern of effects conforms to expectations regarding the intervention. Five primary concepts are used in the analysis of these data: trend, slope, level, overlap, and stability (Lundervold & Belwood, 2000). A *trend* in the data indicates that the target behavior is increasing (upward trend), decreasing (downward trend), or remaining the same (stable trend). *Slope* is the magnitude or steepness of the trend. *Level* refers to the relative magnitude of change in the target behavior (e.g., the amount of increase/decrease in the frequency). *Overlap* refers to the extent to which data patterns across phases of the study overlap with each other. The less overlap that is observed from baseline through intervention phases, the stronger the argument for the functional effect of the intervention on the target behavior. *Stability* in the data is demonstrated when repeated baseline measurement yields a stable pattern in the frequency of the behavior, and repeated measurement following the intervention also yields a stable pattern (although at a higher or lower level of frequency, depending on the purpose of the study and the targeted behavior). Excessive variability in the data during baseline and intervention phases makes it more difficult to draw warranted conclusions about the effects of the intervention. Intervention effects are most obvious when there is a large and immediate change in the slope and level of the target behavior following the intervention. Moreover, a stable post-intervention data pattern provides evidence that the intervention results in a consistent expression of the target behavior over time, as distinct from one in which an effect disappears over time.

In the *multiple baseline design,* treatment effects are demonstrated by showing that behavior change accompanies or parallels the introduction of the intervention at different points in time (Kazdin, 2003). A multiple baseline design may include baselines that reflect different responses (e.g., symptoms, behaviors) for a given individual, the same response (or target behavior) for different individuals, or the same response for an individual across different situations. In the case of the multiple baseline design that includes one target behavior and different individuals, the timing of the intervention is staggered—in other words, some participants experience a longer baseline phase and a delayed start to the intervention phase. Each participant therefore serves as his or her own "control" condition (baseline measurement) and replication of the intervention across individuals is incorporated into the design. If, at the conclusion of the study, the data pattern accurately reflects the timing of the intervention across the participants, the warrant for the validity of findings (i.e., internal validity) is enhanced as a function of the logic of the design.

There are four major types of small-N designs, which are primarily differentiated based upon the order in which the intervention or treatment is applied, withdrawn, and/or modified. The simplest small-N design is known as the AB design, which is characterized by one baseline phase followed by a single treatment phase. A major limitation of the AB design is that there is no return to baseline; therefore, it is difficult to demonstrate that the intervention was responsible for any desired behavioral change.

The ABA design is an extension of the AB design whereby treatment (i.e., the B phase) is withdrawn during an additional third phase (i.e., return to baseline, or A). This approach is more powerful than the AB design because it enables the researcher to conduct a baseline assessment after the intervention has been delivered and discontinued (Tawney & Gast, 1984). If the behavior change that emerged in response to the intervention diminishes during the second baseline phase, then the researcher can conclude with greater certainty than is possible in the AB design that the level of target behavior is attributable to the application of the intervention. The researcher may also reintroduce the treatment or intervention in a fourth phase; this variant is known as the ABAB design. The ABAB design represents an improvement over ABA because it allows for two observations of each condition, namely, baseline and treatment (Tawney & Gast, 1984).

Multiple baseline designs extend the AB approach by implementing the treatment (B) phase at different times across at least two behaviors, settings, or research participants (Kazdin, 2003). This approach is typically used when it is not feasible to remove an intervention that has been implemented and return the participant to baseline (e.g., when the participant has acquired specific problem-solving skills as part of the intervention, he or she cannot unlearn those skills for purposes of the baseline assessment). According to Tawney and Gast (1984), there are three common sub-types of multiple baseline designs–multiple baseline across participants (in which two or more individuals receive baseline and treatment phases), multiple baseline across behaviors (in which the same individual receives baseline and treatment phases with regard to two or more behaviors that are observed in the same setting), and multiple baseline across settings (in which the same person receives baseline and treatment phases regarding the same behavior in two or more applied settings).

The changing criterion small-N design is used when the researcher wishes to demonstrate a change in the participants' behavior in predetermined, graduated increments over the course of an extended treatment period. This approach is especially effective in evaluating the behavioral impact of exercise regimens, weight loss programs, and smoking cessation treatments, to name a few (Kinugasa, Cerin, & Hooper, 2004).

Although small-N research is less common in rehabilitation counseling than it is in special education and school psychology, there are a number of examples of this applied approach that can be found in the contemporary rehabilitation literature. For example, White, Thomson, and Nary (1996) developed a training package to teach four consumers with various disabilities how to write effective advocacy letters to potential change agents in the community to resolve disability-related problems. Their investigation used an AB multiple-baseline design across the four participants to assess the effects of the training. Participants independently completed a self-paced letter-writing training packet. Following the completion of training, the participants were asked to write advocacy letters in response to different vignettes that involved particular disability concerns expressed within the context of a story. Then, two weeks after training was completed, participants were asked to write an actual letter in response to their own disability-related concern and addressed to a community change agent. A rating system was used to score the two letters on both form and content dimensions, based on a content analysis of what elements should be contained in an advocacy letter.

The results of the White et al. study indicated that each of the four participants experienced moderate improvement in ability to write an effective advocacy letter, with a mean increase of 29 percent in the number of advocacy letter elements included in the letters from baseline to post-training assessment. However, an error analysis indicated that the participants showed larger improvements in the mechanical elements of the letters and smaller improvements in the analytical elements of the letter (e.g., explanation of the problem, probable solution offered). Overall, White et al. demonstrated the efficacy of the self-paced advocacy letter writing intervention to enhance the self-advocacy skills of persons with disabilities.

Paterson, Hamilton, and Grant (2000) used an AB small-N design to investigate the impact of an individually adapted intervention to reduce wandering for a 79-year-old woman with Alzheimer's Disease who resided in a nursing home. The dependent variable was the number of minutes during one-hour observation periods that this lady wandered around the nursing home. The intervention included a package of environmental adaptations and behavioral interaction procedures; for example, the participant was taken on a walk for 20 minutes prior to the time during which she typically wandered away. Another preventative strategy was to escort her to activities. In addition, the following environmental adaptations were used during the intervention: she was seated with another resident during activities; soothing music was played during all activities; lighting was adjusted to a medium level;

and she was encouraged to sit in her favorite rocking chair. Results indicated that the target behavior of wandering decreased by 40 percent after the intervention was introduced.

Persel, Persel, Ashley, and Krych (1997) utilized an ABAB small-N design to investigate the efficacy of an intervention developed to reduce self-injurious behavior and physical aggression toward others for a 40-year-old man with a traumatic brain injury who resided in a long-term care facility. The intervention included non-contingent reinforcement in combination with contingent restraint. The non-contingent reinforcement consisted of spending three minutes in social conversation with the participant, which occurred every 30 minutes and was not dependent on his behavior. Contingent restraint involved three trained staff members physically restraining the participant whenever he was physically aggressive toward himself or others. In combination, the intervention was shown to be effective in reducing the incidence of self-injurious and physically aggressive behavior.

NON-MANIPULATION STUDIES

The very nature of the quantitative research paradigm continually reminds researchers that proving or demonstrating something new is a primary objective of scientific inquiry. Experimental designs exemplify the spirit of purposeful and active investigation in an effort to draw causal inferences concerning independent and dependent variables. By systematically manipulating the independent variable (usually an intervention or a stimulus) and randomly assigning participants to treatment and control groups, researchers using experimental techniques can claim the strongest warrants for new knowledge, that is, a causal link between an intervention or stimulus and realized outcomes. In many studies, however, it is not possible (or even desirable) to manipulate the independent variable in an effort to establish the warrant for causal connections. In these cases, researchers may test group differences or relationships among variables as they occur or as they have occurred. Non-manipulation studies examine the strength or magnitude of association among variables, but no attempt is made to infer causality within an individual study. In this section, we describe non-manipulation studies in two categories, correlational and causal comparative designs.

Correlational Designs

One of the most common methods of establishing a relationship between variables is the correlation. A correlation coefficient is a statistic that describes the direction and magnitude of the linear relationship between two quantitatively coded variables. The independent variables in correlational studies must be continuous in nature, meaning that scores fall along a continuum from low to high levels of the variable. The dependent variable in correlational research is usually (but not always) continuous, as well. As discussed in Chapter 1, demonstrating that two variables covary is a necessary (though insufficient) condition for establishing that a causal relationship between the variables exists. The correlation coefficient provides empirical support for the strength of this relationship, and it serves as the initial condition for establishing that the variables are causally related.

It is important to keep in mind that the correlation is, first and foremost, a method for analyzing data. The procedure is undertaken to determine how much variation in the dependent variable (also known as the criterion variable) is shared with the independent variable (also known as the predictor variable). Although individual correlational studies are typically not able to establish strong warrants for causal relationships between variables, research consumers may draw causal inferences based on the total evidence generated in a number of related studies. Also, theory-based hypotheses used in correlational studies may provide a stronger warrant for causality when the proposed temporal sequence (i.e., the cause precedes the effect in time) of the variables is reflected in the data gathering phase, as is the case in longitudinal designs. Therefore, both covariation and temporal sequence may be established if the findings support the research hypothesis.

For example, a researcher wishing to determine the relationship between income and job satisfaction among employed adults with disabilities conceptualizes income as the independent or predictor variable and job satisfaction as the dependent or criterion variable. Because income is a precursory component of job satisfaction according to the researcher's theory, income is hypothesized to predict job satisfaction rather than vice versa. Therefore, if a positive correlation between the two variables is observed (meaning that, as income increases, so does job satisfaction), it is assumed that variable X (income) predicts variable Y (job satisfaction). Even though the relationship between predictor and criterion variables cannot be considered causal (because there was no manipulation of the independent variable), a positive correlation between the variables permits readers to conclude that, in general (though not necessarily for every individual), higher income indicates a higher probability of job satisfaction than does lower income.

The example presented above describes a simple, bivariate correlation, which involves one predictor variable and one criterion variable. Rehabilitation researchers also commonly use multiple correlations, which assess the additive relationship between a set of two or more predictor variables and one criterion (Cohen et al., 2003). These studies are usually conducted using multiple regression analysis, though there are several other related multivariate statistical techniques that allow researchers to test more sophisticated theoretical hypotheses pertaining to the interrelationships of multiple predictors and multiple criterion variables (Tacq, 1997). These related techniques are subsumed under what is known as the general linear model and include multiple discriminant analysis, canonical correlation analysis, path analysis, structural equation modeling, and multilevel modeling.

Correlational studies have long played a major part in rehabilitation research. Investigators use simple, multiple, and canonical correlations to test relationships for a number of scientific purposes. These include assessing the psychometric properties (e.g., reliability and validity) of standardized measurement instruments, developing variable equations to predict important outcomes of the rehabilitation process (e.g., counselors successful case closure rates, clients post rehabilitation employment status, quality of life among people with disabilities), and evaluating the interrelationships among key constructs that may not lend themselves to precise causal (X predicts Y) hypotheses regarding their direction or sequence in time (e.g., self-efficacy, acceptance of disability, locus of control, depression).

CORRELATIONAL DESIGNS–MULTIPLE REGRESSION. Bolton, Bellini, and Brookings (2000) used hierarchical multiple regression analysis to examine the utility of several independent variables, organized into three variable sets, to predict two dependent variables: competitive employment status and weekly salary post-closure. The predictor variable sets were entered into the regression analysis in a sequence that modeled three phases of the vocational rehabilitation (VR) process: intake, diagnostic case study, and service provision. Demographic variables (e.g., age, education level) were entered first because these variables represented the characteristics that clients bring to the VR process. Counselor-rated functional capacities and limitations (e.g., adaptive behavior, mobility, communication) were entered as a second block into the analysis because these variables represent the counselor's diagnostic case study that serves as the basis for VR eligibility determination and service planning. Finally, VR services (e.g., placement, restoration) were entered in the third block to reflect the services provided to each client during the life of the case. The study included data from 4,603 VR clients in one state, and separate regression analyses were performed for each of five relatively homogeneous disability groups: orthopedic, chronic-medical, psychiatric, intellectual, and learning disability.

Bolton et al. (2000) reported that, with a few exceptions, each variable set significantly predicted the two outcomes for the five disability groups, and subsequent variable sets explained additional variation in the two outcomes over and above the variation in outcomes explained by the previous variable set(s). Overall, the three variable sets explained approximately one-third of the variability in competitive employment rate (25% to 40% depending on the disability group) and one-eighth of the variability in weekly salary (9% to 17% depending on the disability group). The Bolton et al. study is an example of a correlational design that provides a stronger warrant for the claim that the variables are causally related based on several research design features, including: (a) a large sample that permitted separate analyses for persons with different primary disabilities; (b) the selection of variable sets that comprehensively modeled the VR process; and (c) a variable entry protocol that accurately reflected the temporal sequence of intake, service planning, and service provision stages of the VR process.

Mamboleo, Kaya, Meyer, Kamnetz, Bezyak, and Chan (2015) conducted a correlational study designed to predict employment outcomes for state Vocational Rehabilitation (VR) consumers with arthritis. The authors examined the relationship between consumer demographic characteristics and VR services received (predictor variables) and the likelihood that consumers' VR cases would result in competitive employment (criterion or dependent variable). Logistic multiple regression analysis revealed that younger, Caucasian consumers with higher levels of education were more likely to achieve successful employment outcomes. Consumers with arthritis who received Social Security disability benefits and who experienced comorbid depression or other mood disorders were significantly less likely to obtain competitive employment. Receiving counseling and guidance, occupational/vocational training, job search, job placement, and on-the-job support services was positively associated with competitive employment outcomes.

Strauser and Ketz (2002) used multiple regression to test Hershenson's theory of work adjustment, examining the relationships between a set of work personality variables and each of two criterion variables—job readiness self efficacy and work locus of control—for a sample of participants ($N=104$) diagnosed with intellectual disabilities, mental illness, or substance use disorders. Work personality was defined by the authors as the person's self-concept as a worker, motivation for work, and work related needs and values. These constructs were operationalized for the study using the subscales of the Work Personality Inventory (WPI; Bolton & Roessler, 1986). The authors found that global work personality (WPI scales Acceptance of Work Role, Ability to Profit from Instruction and Correction, Work Persistence, and Work Tolerance combined) significantly predicted internal locus of control and job readiness self-efficacy. However, only work persistence provided a unique predictive contribution beyond the other subscales in the work personality inventory on locus of control, and ability to profit from instruction and correction provided a unique contribution to job readiness self-efficacy.

McDonnall, Crudden, and O'Mally (2014) investigated correlates of employer attitudes toward workers with blindness and visual impairments. A random sample of 181 employers from four states participated in telephone interviews assessing their knowledge of, experience with, and attitudes toward workers with visual impairments and blindness. The seven independent variables included in the multiple regression analysis to predict the dependent variable of attitudes toward people with blineness and visual impairments were communication with VR counselors, contact with VR counselors, hired someone who was blind or had a visual impairment, worked with someone who was blind or had a visual impairment, personal relationship with someone who was blind or had a visual impairment, designated human resources personnel within the company or agency, and knowledge of blindness and visual impairments. The overall set of predictors significantly correlated with attitudes toward people with blindness and visual impairments–with hiring someone who was blind or had a visual impairment, communication with VR counselors, and knowledge of blindness and visual impairments being the three strongest individual predictors. The authors concluded that VR counselors should increase their outreach efforts to provide employers with information about the characteristics and needs of workers with blindness and visual impairments as a means of increasing employers' familiarity with and promoting positive attitudes toward this population.

Correlational studies using multiple regression techniques are quite common in the recent rehabilitation literature, so we will cite only a few recent examples that reflect a range of research issues that are addressed using these techniques. Lydell, Grahn, Mansson, Baigi, and Marklund (2009) examined the factors associated with successful return to work outcomes among a sample of 354 individuals with work-related musculoskeletal disorders who participated in an industrial rehabilitation program in Sweden. Stepwise multiple regression and bivariate correlational analyses revealed that the number of days off work between the initial injury and the initiation of rehabilitation services, age, self-rated pain, life events, gender, physical capacity, self-rated functional capacity, educational level, and availability of light duty work significantly predicted long-term return to work outcomes. Roessler, Rumrill, Li, and Leslie (2015) utilized multinomial logistic regression analysis to determine the predictive relationship of age, level of education, severity of symptoms, and financial security to employment status among a national sample of 1,839 Americans with multiple sclerosis. Bellini (2001) used hierarchical multiple regression to examine whether and to what degree demographic variables (e.g., age, gender), multicultural experience variables (e.g., race, caseload composition), and multicultural training variables (e.g., graduate class, number of workshops attended) predicted the self-reported multicultural counseling competence of practicing VR counselors.

In addition to studies that focus on prediction of rehabilitation outcomes, researchers often use correlational procedures to evaluate the psychometric properties (e.g., reliability and validity) of measurement instruments. Gross and Francis (2015) described the development and testing of the Community Employment Scale, a measure for assessing the frequency and quality of competitive integrated employment placements for individuals with significant disabilities. Nelson, Dial, and Joyce (2002) examined the validity of the Cognitive Test for the Blind as a measure of intellectual functioning. Adkins, Youngbauer, and Mathews (2000) used correlational procedures to evaluate the psychometric properties of the Brief Instrument to Measure Independence of Persons with Head Injury as a tool for rehabilitation planning. Li, Fitzgerald, Bishop, Zhang, and Rumrill (2015) utilized correlational techniques to examine the psychometric properties and factor structure of a home functioning scale for adults with multiple sclerosis. Fabian and Waugh (2001) examined the utility of the Job Development Efficacy Scale as a tool for identifying the proficiencies of prospective and practicing rehabilitation counselors who assist people with disabilities in seeking, securing, and maintaining employment. Tansey et al. (2016) validated the Brief Resilience Scale as a Vocational Rehabilitation (VR) outcome measure with a cross-disability sample of state VR consumers.

ADVANCED CORRELATIONAL DESIGNS. As noted previously, there are several other statistical approaches to data analysis that are based on correlations and that have become more common in rehabilitation research. These related multivariate techniques are subsumed under the *general linear model* and include multiple discriminant analysis, path analysis, structural equation modeling, and multilevel modeling. These analytic approaches allow researchers to test more sophisticated theoretical hypotheses pertaining to specific variable relationships (e.g., direct, moderated, and/or indirect/mediated variable relations) as well as the interrelationships of multiple predictors and single or multiple criterion variables (Tacq, 1997).

Bellini, Bolton, and Neath (1996) used multiple discriminant analysis (MDA) to examine the relationships between client quantitative diagnostic data (i.e., demographic data and ratings of functional capacities and limitations) and subsequent rehabilitation counselors' decisions regarding eligibility for vocational rehabilitation. Similar to multiple regression, MDA is a flexible analytic strategy that permits an evaluation of the separate and combined effects of a set of predictor variables on an outcome. However, in the case of MDA, the outcome consists of two or more discrete categories rather than a continuous variable. In the Bellini et al. study, the outcome variable consisted of four categories of clients based on the counselors' eligibility decision and ordered logically by severity: Group 1 included clients closed ineligible for services for reason of no disability or no impediment to employment; Group 2 included clients accepted for services but identified as having non-severe disabilities; Group 3 clients were accepted for services and identified as having severe disabilities; and Group 4 included clients who were accepted for services but were placed into an extended evaluation status for reason of severe disability. The predictor variables included client demographic variables drawn from the intake form as well as counselor assessments of clients' functional capacities. Bellini et al. reported that the set of client demographic and functional capacity data significantly predicted eligibility group membership and explained 44 percent of the variation in group membership. Bellini et al. also reported that the counselor assessments of client functional capacities were more strongly related to counselor eligibility decisions than were client demographic variables. This study provided modest empirical support for the validity of counselor eligibility decisions in a state VR agency that was committed to serving rehabilitation clients with the most severe disabilities.

Chiu, Sharp, Pfaller, Rumrill, Cheing, Sanchez, and Chan (2015) utilized MDA to examine propensities for certain patterns of VR services among two groups of VR applicants with diabetes, those who were employed at application and those who were not. Results indicated that employed VR applicants with diabetes had higher propensities to receive assessment, diagnosis and treatment, counseling and guidance, rehabilitation technology, and on-the-job support services than did unemployed applicants with diabetes. On the other hand, unemployed applicants with diabetes had higher propensities to receive services such as occupational/vocational training, job readiness, and job placement services.

Bishop, Berven, Hermann, and Chan (2002) used path analysis to examine the impact of physical, social, and psychological factors on subjective quality of life for a sample of 107 individuals with epilepsy. In path models, variables that are hypothesized to function as predictors only are designated as *exogenous variables*. Variables that are influenced/predicted by other variables in the model are termed endogenous variables. Depending on their placement in the model, *endogenous variables* may serve as outcomes of previous variables, as predictors of subsequent variables, or as outcomes only. The path model tested by Bishop et al. included seizure frequency, physical function, and seizure interference as exogenous variables, social support, perception of general health, perception of mental health, and employment as endogenous variables, and perceived quality of life as the final (endogenous) outcome variable. Bishop et al. reported that the hypothesized model explained 78 percent of the variation in participants' quality of life scores, and most of the hypothesized variable relationships (i.e., paths) were statistically significant. Bishop et al. noted that the fit of the original theoretical model was only marginally acceptable. They used a post hoc analysis to re-specify the model based on the study data (they eliminated the non-significant paths and retained the significant paths) and reported that the re-specified model was a closer "fit" to the data. The authors appropriately noted that, due to the correlational and descriptive nature of the study, no firm causal attributions can be made regarding the variable relationships. However, the study enhances our understanding of the processes by which the functional limitations associated with epilepsy impact social support and perceptions of health, which, in combination, influence subjective quality of life.

Kosciulek (2005) used structural equation modeling (SEM) to examine the consumer-directed theory of empowerment in vocational rehabilitation (VR). SEM is similar to path analysis in that both approaches are used to test variable models that include exogenous and endogenous variables. However, SEM is an analysis of the hypothesized relationships among constructs (i.e., latent variables), whereas path analysis is an analysis of variable indicators. In other words, path analysis uses single indicators for variables, whereas SEM utilizes multiple indicators of each construct and includes an evaluation of how well the sets of indicators represent the constructs under study. Kosciulek theorized that consumer direction (represented by variables measuring consumer direction/control of services, variety of service options, information and support, and participation in policymaking) served as the initial, exogenous construct in the model. In turn, consumer direction influences community integration (represented by variables measuring integration in home and family, in social/leisure activities, and in work/other productive activity)–and both consumer direction and community integration impact empowerment (represented as internal/psychological and situational/social empowerment). In Kosciulek's initial model, consumer direction and community integration were theorized to influence quality of life only indirectly, through their combined influences on empowerment (fully mediated variable relationships), and only empowerment was hypothesized to directly influence subjective quality of life.

Kosciulek (2005) tested the model of empowerment using a nationally-representative sample of 721 VR clients who achieved a successful rehabilitation outcome. He reported that the specification of latent variables in the measurement model was adequate, but the theorized structural model of construct relationships was not an adequate fit to the data. Kosciulek then tested a re-specified construct model that added direct paths (i.e., effects) from both consumer direction and community integration to quality of life as well as the originally hypothesized indirect effects, and he reported that the re-specified model was a good fit. The SEM analysis supported the knowledge claim that providing clients with enhanced control and direction of services and greater community integration increases clients' perceptions of empowerment and subjective quality of life following a successful service outcome.

Matrone and Leahy (2005) used multilevel modeling (MLM) to examine the relationships among counselor-client racial similarity and dissimilarity, counselor multicultural competencies, and clients' vocational rehabilitation outcomes. MLM is the appropriate analytic strategy in this case because it is reasonable to anticipate that client outcomes will vary as a function of (a) the advantages and disadvantages that clients bring to the rehabilitation process, and (b) the competencies of the rehabilitation counselor, including multicultural competencies in those instances when the counselor and client have different racial/ethnic backgrounds. MLM is a variation of multiple regression that permits inclusion of these different "levels" of variables in the statistical analysis. In this case, the analysis included data at the level of the client (i.e., client race/ethnicity and client outcome) and the level of the counselor (i.e., counselor race/ethnicity and counselor self-reported multicultural competency).

Matrone and Leahy used a sample of 118 VR counselors and 5,669 clients in one state VR agency whose cases were closed in 2001–2002. They reported that counselor multicultural competency did not significantly predict client outcome, and in general counselor characteristics (e.g., age, race, multicultural training) were significantly related to client outcomes only in combination with other factors. These researchers reported that most of the explanatory variables (i.e., significantly related to client outcome) were located at the client level (age, race, receipt of Social Security benefits) and that, overall, the odds of a successful closure were significantly lower for non-white clients than for white clients, regardless of the race/ethnicity of the counselor.

Causal Comparative Studies

Causal comparative studies (also known as Case Control studies) compare differences between derived or intact groups on theory driven dependent measures. As with correlational studies, the warrant for causality in causal comparative studies is limited because the independent variable (group membership or some other nominally coded characteristic) is not systematically manipulated. Instead, the purpose of these studies is to establish that variable relationships conform to theoretically or rationally derived expectations. Researchers typically use between group statistical methods (e.g., chi-square, t tests, analyses of variance, multivariate analyses of variance, discriminant analysis) to gauge whether the observed differences between groups on selected outcome measures are statistically significant.

Although the conclusions that causal comparative researchers are able to draw are limited by the passive nature of the between group design (i.e., the independent variable is not manipulated, nor is there random assignment to groups), examining group trends as phenomena occur or have occurred provides the rehabilitation field with valuable information about the differential impact that services have on clients of different ages, races, residential circumstances, occupational types, and disability types. Causal comparative designs are commonly used to examine large, extant data sets such as those maintained by the Social Security Administration or the state federal VR program. They are also common in epidemiological (i.e., medical) research.

Capella (2002) conducted a study examining the differences in VR acceptance rates between participants of different racial backgrounds. The author examined two samples of 10,000 participants. The first sample included those diagnosed with severe disabilities, and the second included those with non-severe disabilities. Capella conducted a binary logistic regression analysis with race and gender as the independent variables, age and education level as covariates, and acceptance for VR as the dependent variable. Logistic regression was used because the acceptance for VR variable was dichotomously scored (i.e., accepted versus not accepted). The author found that African Americans were significantly less likely to be accepted for VR than European Americans within the severe disability group. However, African Americans and European Americans were equally likely to be accepted for VR in the non-severe disability group. In addition, the author conducted a similar analysis with success in obtaining employment and quality of successful closures (i.e., high versus low quality occupations) as dependent variables. Capella reported that African Americans and Native Americans were significantly less likely to successfully obtain employment than European Americans, and Hispanic Americans were more likely than European Americans to obtain high quality closures.

Nosek and Young (1997) assessed differences in the prevalence of abuse by significant others among women with and without physical disabilities. The authors hypothesized that women with disabilities would report significantly higher rates of abuse than women without disabilities. The actual rate of reported abuse was not significantly different for the two groups; however, women with physical disabilities reported abusive relationships of significantly longer duration. Nosek and Young also identified several factors that make women with physical disabilities uniquely vulnerable to abuse, namely, social stereotypes of asexuality and passivity, lack of adaptive and assistive technology, inaccessible home and community environments, increased exposure to medical and institutional settings, dependence on perpetrators for personal assistance, and lack of employment options.

Araten-Bergman, Tal-Katz, and Stein (2015) used a causal comparative method to explore the differences in psychosocial adjustment among Israeli veterans with disabilities who were employed and non-employed. The researchers compared employed veterans with disabilities ($N=101$) to non-employed veterans with disabilities ($N=111$) on self-reported levels of hope, acceptance of disability, social networks size, and social participation patterns. Results indicated that employed veterans reported significantly higher levels of psychosocial adjustment as evidenced by higher levels of hope, more acceptance of disability, and larger social networks. No differences were found with respect to social participation patterns. The researchers concluded that results demonstrated the importance of assessing psychosocial adjustment as a multidimensional construct, the importance of examining the psychological parameters of the adjustment process, and the existence of interaction between employment status and different aspects of psychosocial functioning for veterans with disabilities.

In another example of causal-comparative design, Matthews, Harris, Jaworski, Alam, and Bozdag (2014) examined the differences in health, social needs, and function for individuals with anxiety, mood, and psychotic disorders accessing VR services. The study included adult job seekers ($N=106$) who were assigned to observation groups based upon the disorders with which they had been diagnosed. Between-group differences were assessed using various self-report measures and the Executive Exit Interview. Results from the *Behavior and Symptom Identification Scale* (BASIS-32) showed that job-seekers with psychotic disorders reported significantly better social functioning than did those with anxiety or mood disorders. The study also found that job-seekers with psychotic disorders reported longer periods of unemployment than did the anxiety and mood disorder groups. The researchers concluded that researchers and practitioners should consider perceived psychosocial problems for individuals with anxiety and mood disorders as well as perceptions of poor employability for persons with psychotic disorders when developing rehabilitation interventions.

Other examples of causal comparative designs in rehabilitation research include investigations into such important phenomena as wage differentials across disability and non-disability groups (Barnartt & Altman, 1997), employer characteristics (e.g., number of employees, location, industrial classification) as differential indicators of unlawful discharge allegations under Title I of the Americans with Disabilities Act (Rumrill & Fitzgerald, 2010), the workplace discrimination experiences of Americans with multiple chemical sensitivity in comparison to people with other disabling conditions (Vierstra et al., 2007), and the influence of VR counselors education and experience on caseload management practices (Wheaton & Berven, 1994). Researchers have also used causal comparative designs to investigate self-employment opportunities for VR clients in rural and urban areas (Arnold, Seekins, & Ravesloot, 1995), ethnic differences in community expectations among women and men with physical disabilities (Westbrook, Legge, & Pennay, 1995), and gender differences in the outcomes of allegations of unfair treatment in the workplace among individuals with multiple sclerosis (Rumrill, Roessler, McMahon, Hennessey, & Neath, 2007).

Descriptive Studies

As noted in Chapter 1, an important purpose of scientific inquiry is to describe or explain observable phenomena in a manner that adds understanding or insight to a question or problem. In rehabilitation counseling, the professional literature is replete with investigations whose primary goal is to describe events, experiences, attitudes, and observations as they relate to rehabilitation counselors and people with disabilities. Although rehabilitation researchers may use a wide range of statistical approaches to analyze data, what distinguishes this category of research from those covered in previous sections is that its purpose is fundamentally descriptive.

Descriptive research involves collecting data to test hypotheses or answer questions regarding the past or current status of selected variables. Researchers in this mode describe such phenomena as achievement, attitudes, opinions, behaviors, and written documents that are collected or observed from individuals or groups of subjects. A descriptive study asks what is or what was; it reports conditions or people the way they are at a point (or several points) in time or the way they were at a given point (or points) in history. It is important to note that descriptive designs do not manipulate variables in an attempt to draw causal inferences, as is the case in intervention/stimulus studies—nor do they apply statistical tests to gauge relationships among variables or groups of participants, as is the case in the correlational and causal comparative studies discussed in the preceding section. Descriptive studies simply report what exists as it exists, which, as observational evidence concerning a particular phenomenon mounts from a number of studies, can make a valuable contribution to the knowledge base in rehabilitation counseling. Descriptive data can be collected from a variety of sources, including self-reports from research participants, reports from significant others, direct observations, and review of documents. As in other types of research, the data collection and data analytic techniques are chosen primarily based on the research questions or hypotheses that are posed by the researcher. There are a number of descriptive methodologies that fall into the quantitative realm, each of which has many possible iterations depending upon the specific research question being asked and the resources available to the investigator(s). We have divided descriptive designs into six categories: surveys, case studies, historical/archival research, longitudinal studies, empirical literature reviews, and meta-analyses. This section provides general overviews of these descriptive designs, illustrated with examples from professional journals in rehabilitation, counseling, psychology, and disability studies.

Surveys

The most common type of descriptive research in rehabilitation over the past four decades has been the survey. Utilizing self-report data that are collected in interviews with respondents (in which the researcher records data on the instrument) or via questionnaires (in which the respondent records his or her own answers on the instrument), surveys have become a part of virtually every aspect of life in American society. The primary purpose of survey research is to describe a phenomenon of interest within a sample of respondents (e.g., employer attitudes toward people with disabilities) or to draw inferences regarding the constitution of a population of people based upon the characteristics reported by a sample drawn from that population (e.g., demographic characteristics of people with traumatic brain injuries). Surveys elicit relatively brief measures from relatively large numbers of people (Babbie, 1995; Dillman, 2000), in contrast to the more in-depth case study designs that involve collecting large volumes of information from small samples.

In our comprehensive review of the recent rehabilitation literature while composing this third edition of our book, survey approaches remained the most frequently employed quantitative design in empirically-based journal articles. Contemporary survey research in rehabilitation counseling reflects the broad diversity of topics and issues facing our field, and we expect to see a continuing trend of large-sample inquiries that address key concerns in the lives of rehabilitation consumers and professionals.

For example, Siperstein, Heyman, and Stokes (2014) conducted a survey to examine the characteristics and concerns of employed adults with intellectual disabilities. The researchers received responses from a nationally representative sample ($N=1,055$) of parents/guardians of adult children (21 years of age and older) with intellectual disabilities. Respondents were contacted by the Gallup Organization and completed telephone interviews regarding their adult children's work experiences. Participating parents described each worker's employment status and history, adaptive functioning, presence or absence of behavior problems, and present living situation. Respondents most often attributed their adult childrens successful employment to early work experience, effective adaptive behavior, positive coping skills, and the availability of natural supports in the workplace. Familial and social support, availability of transportation, and effective school-to-work transition services were also seen as important factors facilitating positive vocational outcomes.

Leahy, Chan, Sung, and Kim (2013) presented findings from a national survey of the roles and functions of Certified Rehabilitation Counselors (CRCs). Using the Rehabilitation Skills Inventory–Revised, they identified several major domains and sub-domains of CRC job functions, including providing vocational counseling and consultation, conducting counseling interventions, using community-based rehabilitation services, managing cases, applying research to practice, conducting assessments, and practicing professional advocacy. Case management, vocational counseling, and client advocacy functions were viewed as most important by respondents. Practicing CRCs also identified medical and functional information on disabling conditions, knowledge of community resources to assist people with disabilities in their independent living and vocational pursuits, and proficiency with career counseling strategies and occupational information systems as particularly important future knowledge domains for preservice training and continuing education. This research provides the numerous key stakeholders in the rehabilitation profession with an accurate, detailed description of the scope and dimensions of contemporary rehabilitation counseling practice. Moreover, these findings have served as an empirical foundation for the revision and updating of standards for certification and licensing bodies for individual rehabilitation counselors and accrediting bodies for graduate programs in rehabilitation education. The Leahy et al. investigation is the most recent in a long series of role and function studies that span five decades. These studies have served to distinguish rehabilitation counseling from its sister counseling and rehabilitation professions and to validate the unique role of rehabilitation counselors in the lives of persons with disabilities.

Numerous other examples of survey research can be found in existing rehabilitation literature. Tansey, Bezyak, Chan, Leahy, and Lui (2014) utilized survey methods to examine the attitudes and readiness of state-Federal Vocational Rehabilitation counselors regarding the adoption of evidence-based counseling and job placement practices. Denson (2000) surveyed 482 individuals with disabilities to gauge their satisfaction with a public paratransit system. Riemer-Reiss and Wacker (2000) examined the patterns of assistive technology usage among 115 people with physical, sensory, and/or intellectual disabilities. Clarke and Crewe (2000) described stakeholder attitudes toward Title I of the Americans with Disabilities Act in their survey of 62 college students with disabilities, 57 rehabilitation counseling students, and 83 small business employers. Rumrill, Roessler, Li, Daly, and Leslie (2015) conducted a national survey of the employment concerns of a stratified random sample of 1,924 people with multiple sclerosis. Gilbride, Stensrud, Ehlers, Evans, and Peterson (2000) surveyed employers regarding their attitudes toward (a) hiring people with disabilities, and (b) the state-Federal VR system as a recruitment resource. Hunt and Rosenthal (2000) queried 153 practicing rehabilitation counselors regarding their experiences in dealing with the death of clients.

Case Studies

Whereas survey approaches typically involve taking relatively brief measures from relatively large numbers of respondents, case studies feature in-depth and/or prolonged examination of a small number of people (Heppner et al., 2015) using quantitative methodologies. Rooted in epidemiological research in the medical field (especially as a means of understanding low-incidence illnesses or conditions), the quantitative case study method has been applied in a number of rehabilitation counseling investigations to better understand the psychosocial, educational, and vocational aspects of disability.

Reporting data in numeric fashion with small samples of respondents, researchers use case study techniques to present a depth of information that may not be attainable using other quantitative approaches. Attempts are not made to generalize findings to the broader population from which respondents were selected, which undermines external validity and, thereby, vitiates the researchers warrant for new knowledge claims. Nonetheless, the quantitative case study often yields information that piques readers' attention to the need for more systematic inquiry or to the need for more responsive services. In that regard, this method provides important preliminary insights into key issues and problems that have not yet been systematically investigated.

A fairly common technique is to use case studies to illustrate how a program or intervention can be implemented or evaluated. Typically, this involves in-depth analysis of the experiences reported by past and present participants in the program of interest. Burgstahler (2001) presented an organizational case study of one university's innovative approach to providing career development and advocacy services for students with disabilities. Glenn, Danczyk Hawley, and Mann (2000) described one rehabilitation counselor education program's approach to doctoral-level leadership training. Lemaire, Mallik, and Stoll (2002) examined the impact of a model program designed to address the academic and vocational needs of out-of-school youth with learning and psychiatric disabilities. Hendricks et al. (2015) presented a multisite case study of a Federally-funded project designed to promote use of cognitive support technology and provide customized vocational services for civilian and veteran college students with traumatic brain injuries. Hasnain, Sotnik, and Ghiloni (2003) highlighted the positive impact of a person-centered planning approach for a group of culturally diverse individuals with disabilities being served by a state VR agency. Wickert, Dresden, and Rumrill (2013) presented case studies of several families who were in need of healthcare and independent living services for elderly loved ones with disabilities.

Other quantitative case studies describe phenomena or issues related to particular disabilities that have not been addressed in large sample empirical studies. For example, Roessler, Reed, and Brown (1998) interviewed five employees with various chronic illnesses (rheumatoid arthritis [2 participants], multiple sclerosis, lupus, and diabetes) who had participated in a job retention service. The researchers identified factors that inhibited or enhanced job maintenance for respondents who were attempting to continue their careers while coping with unpredictable diseases. Roessler and Gottcent (1994) examined the career maintenance needs of several workers with multiple sclerosis who had experienced difficulties in accommodating their disability-related work limitations. Roberts (1998) chronicled the psycholinguistic development of two deaf women. Nardone et al. (2015) presented case studies of several college students with traumatic brain injuries, describing participants' academic and career preparatory experiences.

Historical/Archival Research

In many cases, the impact of a program, policy, or intervention is not readily apparent by observing phenomena as they occur or by conducting follow-up studies at a point in time (usually shortly after the program has been completed). Historical/archival studies are retrospective in nature and involve the analysis of quantitative data that were collected over a specified period of time. These studies may use correlational methods of data analysis or may compare intact groups as in a causal-comparative study; however historical-archival studies differ from these in that they are retrospective and have the purpose of documenting program or policy outcomes for selected beneficiaries. Primarily, historical/archival studies in rehabilitation have involved examinations of disability-related laws and Federal policies and programs designed to meet the needs of Americans with disabilities.

For example, Wheaton and Hertzfeld (2002) investigated the ancestry and severity of disability among VR consumers using the Rehabilitation Services

Administrations VR database from Calendar Year 1998. The authors found that the more money spent on clients' cases, the more services clients tended to receive. Moreover, the addition of assistive technology (training and equipment) contributed positively to desirable case outcomes like successful closures.

Using the same Rehabilitation Services Administration database for consumers who received rehabilitation services between 1985 and 1995, Gilmore, Schuster, Timmons, and Butterworth (2000) analyzed service and outcome trends for people with mental retardation (now referred to as intellectual disabilities), cerebral palsy, and epilepsy. Gilmore et al. were specifically interested in examining the use of competitive labor market employment settings as preferred outcomes in vocational rehabilitation over sheltered workshop settings. Findings indicated that the proportion of clients with these disabilities who were placed into sheltered workshops was significantly reduced during the 10-year retrospective observation period, whereas the proportion of competitive labor market employment closures increased.

Fraser, McMahon, and Danczyk-Hawley (2003) conducted an historical/archival study of 201 people with multiple sclerosis who had filed claims for short-term disability insurance with one disability insurance carrier between 1994 and 1996. Specifically, the researchers sought to determine trends in what they described as progression of disability benefits: beginning with short-term disability, progressing to long-term disability, and culminating in permanent disengagement from the workforce on Social Security Disability Insurance (SSDI) rolls. They found that 35.3 percent of short-term disability applicants with multiple sclerosis progressed to SSDI benefits within two years of receiving short-term disability insurance, a proportion that vastly exceeds the 3.8 percent short-term disability-to-SSDI progression rate of claimants with all other kinds of disabling conditions who received benefits from the single insurance carrier.

Numerous other historical/archival studies have appeared in rehabilitation and disability studies journals in recent years. Some of these investigations have examined the economic well-being of SSDI and Supplemental Security Income beneficiaries (Brucker & Houtenville, 2014), the workplace discrimination experiences of Americans with disabilities over the age of 55 (Cichy, Li, McMahon, & Rumrill, 2015), patterns over time in the incidence of unlawful disability-related discharge complaints against various types of employers (Rumrill & Fitzgerald, 2010), the impact of Vocational Rehabilitation services and receipt of disability benefits on the employment outcomes of people with diabetes mellitus (Chiu et al., 2015), workplace discrimination against people with diabetes and other chronic disabling conditions (McMahon, West, Mansouri, & Belonia, 2006), written opinions from the Commission on Rehabilitation Counselor Certification regarding ethics consultation over a 17-year period (1996-2013; Cartwright & Hartley, 2016), and the long-term progression of workers with intellectual and developmental disabilities from sheltered workshops to competitive employment in integrated community settings (Cimera, 2011).

Longitudinal Studies

Whereas historical/archival investigations track participants retrospectively over an extended period of time that has already elapsed, longitudinal studies actively follow participants over extended time frames, collecting data at specified intervals (Kazdin, 2003). These studies typically involve large samples of people with a set of common characteristics, and they monitor participants' progress over time as a means of framing life activities, experiences, and outcomes in developmental contexts. The most common longitudinal approaches usually involve an initial survey at one point in time (e.g., immediately following onset of an illness), accompanied thereafter by a series of follow-up evaluations wherein the same data that were gathered initially are re-collected. This method enables the researcher to make comparisons between participants' initial responses and the experiences that they record at each checkpoint. Longitudinal techniques are frequently used in educational research to gauge children's academic and intellectual development (McMillan & Schumacher, 2009). Medical researchers also frequently employ longitudinal approaches as a means of assessing the long-term effects of chemotherapeutic and surgical interventions, calculating survival rates among people with serious chronic illnesses, and analyzing the interactions among medical conditions and maturational processes such as aging.

In recent years, the most common application of longitudinal techniques in rehabilitation research has involved the observation and monitoring of employment patterns of people with disabilities, especially those who have completed particular training, educational, or rehabilitation programs. Crewe (2000) conducted a longitudinal study of 50 people with spinal cord injuries to determine their vocational experiences 22 to 45 years after their injuries. At the time of the last interview, all except seven participants ($n=43$) had engaged in remunerative employment since the onset of disability. Fifty-eight percent of participants were working full-time at the time of the last interview, and 16 percent were working part-time, a much higher rate of labor force participation than is commonly reported for the general population of working-age Americans with disabilities.

Elliott, Kurylo, Chen, and Hicken (2002) conducted a longitudinal study of the relationship among alcohol abuse history, emotional adjustment, and pressure sore occurrence during the first three years following spinal cord injury. They collected data from 175 people with spinal cord injuries throughout the three-year observation period, and they found that people with alcohol abuse histories were more likely to experience secondary physical complications from their injuries, including pressure sores.

Wilcox et al. (2015) conducted a longitudinal study with a sample of National Guard members ($N=126$) who had returned from a one-year deployment in Iraq. The researchers examined participants' rates of psychological and behavioral problems at baseline and at three-month and six-month follow-ups. Participating National Guard members were assessed at each point in the study on post-traumatic stress disorder (PTSD) symptoms, anxiety symptoms, depression symptoms, aggression, employment status, alcohol problems, relationship satisfaction, and family reintegration challenges. Results indicated that rates of post-deployment behavioral and psychological problems were elevated upon return from deployment and remained elevated throughout the observation period. Dissatisfaction with relationships and family reintegration challenges were the two most frequently reported issues. The researchers concluded that, even with low combat exposure, returning National Guard members are at risk for a number of adjustment issues including mental health symptoms, alcohol misuse, and relationship difficulties. They also noted their intention to continue tracking respondents over the following several years.

Empirical Literature Reviews

The empirical literature review is characterized by the creation, codification, and analysis of numeric data based on the themes, topics, authors, and/or methods of existing rehabilitation literature. It is the numeric expression of data that distinguishes the empirical literature review from the narrative literature reviews described in Chapter 8. Rehabilitation researchers have used numeric expressions of data generated from the literature to answer such questions as: "What authors have made the most significant contributions to the literature?", "What institutions are most frequently represented in the professional literature?", and "What types of studies have been done in particular areas of inquiry?"

For example, Collins, Markham, Service, Reini, Wolf, and Sessoms (2015) conducted an empirical literature review to examine the use of the Computer Assisted Rehabilitation Environment (CAREN) in published rehabilitation research involving military veterans with combat-related disabilities. The authors performed a literature search with the National Center for Biotechnology search engine and entered the following search terms: CAREN, computer assisted rehabilitation, environment, and virtual rehabilitation. The researchers examined studies that were published beginning in

1999, the year that the CAREN system was developed. Findings were cross-referenced with the Motek Medical website, which includes another literature search engine. Results of this empirical literature review indicated that 29 journal articles, two book chapters, and two entries in conference proceedings had been published since 1999 on the CAREN system. The researchers noted that the vast majority of publications on the CAREN system found it to be a useful and cost-effective assessment and rehabilitation strategy.

Kelley, Sikka, and Venkatesan (1997) categorized research articles concerning parenting skills among people with disabilities on the basis of source (the journal in which the article was published), specific topic area, population examined, empirical methods used, and salient findings. Beck, Janikowski, and Stebnicki (1994, 1996) examined trends in doctoral dissertation research from 1990–1993. The authors provided comprehensive lists of all dissertations related to rehabilitation or disability studies during that time period, and listed frequencies and percentages of dissertations in particular content areas (e.g., rehabilitation outcomes, policy studies) and by type of program from which researchers had graduated (e.g., rehabilitation-specific and non-rehabilitation programs). These articles serve the dual benefit of summarizing the trends in doctoral dissertation research in our field and introducing readers to a large volume of recently published empirical research, thereby making a valuable contribution to the professional knowledge base.

In another empirical literature review, Cook, Andrew, and Faubion (1998) tallied the publication frequencies of authors at universities with graduate rehabilitation programs for three widely read rehabilitation journals (i.e., *Rehabilitation Counseling Bulletin, Rehabilitation Psychology, Journal of Rehabilitation*). Their examination rank-ordered individual authors, universities with doctoral programs in rehabilitation, and universities with stand-alone master's degree programs in rehabilitation counseling, based on the number of articles published in the three journals during the 15-year period of 1981 to 1995.

Meta-Analysis

As described in the above examples, empirical literature reviews examine broad trends in the rehabilitation literature in a way that brings new understanding to widely researched phenomena. Rather than analyzing or interpreting the data contained in articles under review, the empirical literature review creates data from aggregate themes in existing research. This approach often yields important summary information, but it can also lead to erroneous conclusions on the part of researchers and readers.

Let us suppose that a researcher conducts an empirical literature review of 50 separate studies that examined the efficacy of Intervention A (25 studies) and Intervention B (25 studies) on the job satisfaction of employed adults with spinal cord injuries. Let us also assume that each study included a no-treatment control group and compared either Intervention A or Intervention B to the control group on job satisfaction. As is standard practice, each study made use of a statistical significance test (a t-test in this instance) to evaluate whether the mean differences on the outcome variable between each intervention and control group could be attributed to chance factors. In conducting the review, the researcher finds that 20 of the 25 Intervention A studies showed a statistically significant result ($p<.05$) in favor of the intervention as compared to the control group, and 5 studies indicated no statistically significant differences between the two groups. For Intervention B, the researcher finds that only 10 studies showed a statistically significant result in favor of the intervention, whereas 15 studies revealed no statistically significant differences between the groups in job satisfaction. Based on this simple tally of findings, the researcher may conclude that Intervention A is the more effective strategy and should be adopted in field practice with these adults. However, it is very likely that the researcher's conclusion is erroneous.

Consider that the researcher reexamines the 50 studies in greater detail, and finds that the studies that evaluated Intervention A used much larger samples as the basis for statistical significance testing than the studies that evaluated Intervention B used. It is well established that statistical significance tests are highly sensitive to sample size. Two identical studies may yield contradictory conclusions simply based on the size of the samples, because sample size has a large impact on the sensitivity of statistical tests (i.e., power) to identify significant differences in the sample data when such differences exist in the population of interest. In this case, the conclusion that Intervention A is superior to Intervention B may be a function of the different sample sizes used to compute the summary statistics rather than an indication of the inherent efficacy of the intervention.

Numerous research artifacts—such as low statistical power, sampling error, and poor psychometric quality of measurement instruments—may result in an incorrect conclusion within an individual study (Kazdin, 2003). These same research artifacts may be compounded in the empirical literature review to produce inaccurate global conclusions at the level of the research program. As Glass (1976) observed, the results of a large body of research cannot be adequately evaluated using narrative or empirical literature review approaches. Much as we utilize statistical techniques for organizing, depicting, and analyzing data from a large number of individuals in a single study, we also need statistical techniques for making sense of the findings from a large body of research. Meta-analysis provides effective methods for analyzing, summarizing, and interpreting findings from large research programs so that the conclusions reached are accurate and cumulative (Glass, 1976; Hunter & Schmidt, 1990). The primary advantage of a meta-analysis is that a multitude of studies can be effectively summarized into a few relatively simple statistics.

Meta-analysis is a family of statistical techniques that have been developed over the past five decades. It involves aggregating data across numerous studies, correcting the original data to remove the influence of numerous research artifacts (e.g., sampling error, unreliability of measures), and then reanalyzing the data for the purpose of reaching a global conclusion about the research findings in a given area (Hunter & Schmidt, 1990). To aggregate data, there must be a common metric for expressing the results across numerous studies. The common metric used in most meta-analyses is Cohen's "d" or effect size measure which, in a two-group experimental study is the difference between the mean of the treatment group and the mean of the control group, divided by the pooled (i.e., average) standard deviation of the two groups. Correlational data can also be converted to effect size units (from r^2 or R^2 to Cohen's d), making it possible to aggregate data from both experimental and correlational studies in a single meta-analysis (Hunter & Schmidt, 1990; Rosenthal, 1991).

The effect size statistic, as calculated by the formula noted previously, is expressed as a positive or negative whole or decimal number, and ranges between +1 to –1 in most cases. Interpretation of the statistic is also straightforward. As applied within the meta-analysis context, interpretation of effect size refers to the summarized difference between treatment and control groups on a family of outcome variables across a body of experimental studies, or to the summarized relationships between two or more variables across a body of correlational studies.

In the process of doing a meta-analysis, a researcher may also choose to code individual studies according to key methodological variables (e.g., type of research design used) and relevant substantive variables (e.g., length of training program, complexity of skills taught) for the given area of study (Hunter & Schmidt, 1990). The inclusion of these newly-coded variables permits the researcher to evaluate the impact of key moderating influences on the research program, and to partial out the total observed effect size into the sources of variability in effects across the program as a whole. In this way, meta-analysis is far more than simply a family of techniques for summarizing existing research: It may also contribute new knowledge by clarifying the sources of variation in research outcomes within a body of research. By illuminating these relations, which are the building blocks of theory, meta-analysis has an important role in the development of theory in the social sciences (Glass, 1976; Hunter & Schmidt, 1990).

Important considerations in the conduct and evaluation of meta-analytic studies include (a) the degree of similarity (and dissimilarity) of studies that are included, (b) the different approaches used by the original researchers to implement their studies and analyze their data, and (c) the criteria used by the meta-analyst in selecting studies for inclusion (Hunter & Schmidt, 1990). These criteria must be made explicit and the original studies must contain quantitative or quantifiable data. Studies may be considered similar enough if they share commonalities in target population (e.g., studies involving persons with severe disability), intervention strategies (e.g., career counseling interventions), and/or similar outcome variables (e.g., measures of psychosocial adjustment).

There have been numerous meta-analyses conducted to date in the areas of rehabilitation and counseling. In rehabilitation, these have included meta-analyses of the effectiveness of attention rehabilitation after acquired brain injury (Park & Ingles, 2001), psychoeducational interventions for adults with chronic obstructive pulmonary disease (Devine & Pearcy, 1996), and cognitive rehabilitation in schizophrenia (Krabbendam & Aleman, 2003). In counseling, these have included meta-analyses of psychotherapy outcomes (Smith & Glass, 1977), microcounseling training (Baker & Daniels, 1989) and career counseling interventions (Oliver & Spokane, 1988).

In rehabilitation counseling, Bolton and Akridge (1995) conducted a meta-analysis of 10 skills training interventions for VR clients across 15 experimental evaluations reported in 12 refereed journal articles. Across the 15 investigations, Bolton and Akridge calculated effect sizes and variances for 61 outcome measures, which had been gathered using such methods as videotaping, standardized assessment, self-reports, and observational judgments of rehabilitation professionals and researchers. The 15 studies included a total of 220 rehabilitation consumers who underwent 6,420 hours of skills training in the areas of independent living, socialization, career planning, stress management, and self-care. Bolton and Akridge reported a weighted mean effect size (weighted by number of effects per study) of +.82 standard deviation units for the 15 investigations, and an estimated true population effect size of +.93 for the type of skills intervention described in the studies. A straightforward interpretation of this outcome is that the average participant (i.e., 50th percentile) in the training programs exceeded 82 percent of the non-participants on the outcome measures.

Bolton and Akridge also coded the 15 studies according to the type of outcome measure used. They reported that the weighted mean effect size estimates were +1.35 for behavioral measures, +.77 for self-report measures, and +.12 for observer-rated measures. These ancillary findings suggest that the type of outcome measure used accounts for some of the variation in effect size across the 15 studies.

Finally, Bolton and Akridge (1995) identified several common characteristics of the participants in these 15 investigations, including predominantly male, young adults; with primary or secondary disabilities of mental illness, behavior disorders, or mental retardation. Moreover, the participants reported high rates of failure in previous educational and vocational activities, had high rates of severe or multiple disabilities, had been characterized as difficult or high risk, and had been enrolled in a comprehensive residential rehabilitation facility. Based on the results, Bolton and Akridge identified several themes that characterize successful rehabilitation training interventions, including active participation by trainees, focus on behavioral outcomes, mastery-and-maintenance emphasis in behavioral training, reliance on established learning principles, establishment of clear goals, careful monitoring of individual progress, and a dual emphasis on didactic and experiential activities.

SUMMARY

Rehabilitation researchers apply quantitative techniques to answer a vast array of scientific questions in a myriad of ways. Ranging from attempts to gauge the impact that interventions and stimuli have on human behavior (as described in experimental, quasi-experimental, analogue, and small-N approaches) to non-manipulation studies (e.g., correlational, causal comparative) and descriptive approaches (e.g., surveys, case studies, program evaluation, historical/archival research, longitudinal studies, empirical literature reviews, meta-analyses)—quantitative research has provided the foundation of scientific inquiry in the field of rehabilitation counseling. Each type of study described in this chapter is distinct from the others in terms of methods, analytic techniques, the use (or non-use) of inferential statistics, the level and type of control or manipulation that is exercised upon the independent variable, and the strength of the warrant for new knowledge that is yielded. For all of the features that differentiate categories of quantitative designs, they share in common the translation of observations into numbers and a focus on summarizing or aggregating findings as a way of bringing meaning to research results.

As readers move from this chapter into an examination of qualitative research and its applicability to rehabilitation counseling, we caution against subscription to the artificial dichotomy that is often imposed between quantitative and qualitative methodologies. Although quantitative and qualitative modes of inquiry originated from different, sometimes competing schools of thought, we believe that the researcher's questions, not his or her ideological identity as a scientist, should be the primary determinant of the scientific methods that he or she selects. Only by viewing quantitative and qualitative research side-by-side and considering each corresponding set of techniques within the context of particular scientific objectives can rehabilitation researchers derive maximal benefit from the tools left by those who preceded us in pursuit of a theory-based and knowledge-generating profession.

Chapter 7

QUALITATIVE RESEARCH DESIGNS

Lynn Koch, Tricia Niesz, and Melissa Jones Wilkins

INTRODUCTION

The focus of qualitative research is on the perspectives, experiences, practices, and meanings of those individuals who are most directly affected by the phenomena under study. Qualitative inquiry, unlike quantitative inquiry, is used to analyze data sources that include text and imagery rather that numerical data. Qualitative inquiry consists of a wide variety of research designs (e.g., case study, ethnography, grounded theory, phenomenology, consensual qualitative research) used to investigate phenomena not previously studied or for which there is sparse information available (Creswell, 2007; Hagner & Helm, 1994). It is also used, regardless of how much quantitative research has been conducted on a specific topic, to acquire an understanding of participants' own views, perspectives, thoughts, feelings and experiences with these topics. In this sense qualitative research elaborates on the findings in quantitative research. Data are collected in the field, the everyday environments of the participants, rather than in laboratories through direct interactions between the researcher and the research participant (Conrad, Neumann, Haworth, & Scott, 1993). Research participants guide the direction of the study, and researchers follow their lead.

As with quantitative research, the selection of a methodological approach for a specific qualitative study is guided by the nature of the problem, the existing literature on the subject of interest, the worldview and psychological attributes of the researcher, and, most importantly, the research question(s) (Creswell, 2007). With these considerations in mind, the researcher explores the various research methodologies in pursuit of the best match for the research project.

Each qualitative research design has its own set of specific procedures for sampling, data collection, analysis, and interpretation. However, there are some general considerations that span designs. Data collection is comprised of procedures such as in-depth interviews and extended observations that enable the researcher to acquire "rich" or "thick" descriptions of the meanings that research participants ascribe to their experiences (Bogdan & Biklen, 1992; Denzin & Lincoln, 2000; Strauss & Corbin, 1990). Qualitative research findings are pursued inductively using non-mathematical analytical procedures. Linguistic structures are used to ascribe meaning to the phenomena under study (Polkinghorne, 1991). Thus, the units of analysis in qualitative research are words, sentences, and phrases rather than numbers.

With its roots in anthropology and sociology, qualitative research is conducted in social and behavioral science disciplines such as education, counseling, psychology, nursing, health care, and organizational management to garner a greater understanding of discipline-specific phenomena (Conrad et al., 1993; Hagner & Helm, 1994; Niesz, Koch, & Rumrill, 2008; Polkinghorne, 1991). Over the past few decades, the rehabilitation counseling profession has witnessed a considerable increase in the publication of qualitative research articles in its scholarly journals, and the designs and procedures used by qualitative rehabilitation researchers continue to evolve. An increase in the rate of qualitative articles in refereed rehabilitation journals is partially in response to requests by people with disabilities for greater accountability and input regarding investigations that may directly impact their lives (Agan, Koch, & Rumrill, 2008; White, 2002). Qualitative research readily lends itself to participatory action research (PAR) strategies that promote cooperation and collaboration between researchers and research participants in all phases of the research endeavor (Niesz et al., 2008; Whyte, 1991). Furthermore, as Niesz et al. (2008, p. 120) noted, "participants contribute to making public their understandings and experiences in ways that can lead to powerful changes in their worlds–through both greater public or professional understanding of their lives and even, perhaps, through their own greater interpersonal understandings." Because qualitative strategies enable researchers to acquire an "insider's understanding" of the phenomenon of interest (Miles & Huberman, 1994), it is anticipated that we will continue to see a proliferation of qualitative investigations as a means to better understand the lived experiences of people with disabilities as well as other key stakeholders in the rehabilitation process.

The three lines of inquiry that appear to have received the most attention from qualitative rehabilitation researchers include (a) psychosocial adaptation to disability, (b) career development and employment of people with disabilities, and (c) roles and functions of rehabilitation counselors. Although the rehabilitation literature is replete with quantitative research that identifies factors associated with coping and psychosocial adaptation, these constructs are surrounded by definitional ambiguity. Definitional ambiguities make it difficult to measure these constructs (Hill, Noonan, Sakakibara, & Miller, 2010). Secondly, many of the subjective aspects of psychosocial adaptation may remain uncovered if researchers rely solely on quantitative methods to examine these aspects (Shek & Lee, 2007).

One solution that researchers have found to address the dilemma of definitional ambiguity is to directly question people with disabilities about the process of psychosocial adaptation, their ways of coping with chronic illness and disability, their personal definitions of quality of life (QOL), and their individual perceptions regarding how rehabilitation service providers can assist them to enhance their adaptation, coping, and QOL. Because psychosocial adaptation is intrinsically linked to life roles, qualitative rehabilitation research is often carried out to acquire a better understanding of how individuals with disabilities perform in these roles, the problems that they encounter in their attempts to do so, and the impact of rehabilitation interventions on their ability to function in different life arenas. Once again, qualitative methods are instrumental in helping rehabilitation researchers and service providers to learn from the perspectives of people with disabilities about the life roles that are important to them, what their experiences are in assuming these life roles, and how rehabilitation services can be designed to assist them in addressing the difficulties they encounter in these life roles.

Examining the factors that influence the career development of people with disabilities as well as factors that impede and promote successful employment continue to be critical lines of inquiry among rehabilitation researchers. Qualitative research is a useful tool for gaining a better understanding of both the self-perceived barriers encountered by people with disabilities in career development and employment as well as the internal and external resources that contribute to their success. This understanding can lead to the development and evaluation of rehabilitation interventions to eradicate employment barriers and maximize success.

Because of the increasing complexity of the responsibilities that must be assumed by rehabilitation counselors as well as the expanding number of settings in which they are now employed, researchers are reexamining the roles and functions of rehabilitation counselors as well as the efficacy of rehabilitation interventions. Although the majority of role and function studies are quantitative in design, we are beginning to see a number of qualitative studies emerge in this area. Qualitative investigators interested in this line of inquiry seek input from consumers, employers, and practicing rehabilitation counselors regarding their perceptions of characteristics of exemplary rehabilitation counselors and best practices. A growing focus in this line of inquiry has been on the experiences and insights of underrepresented populations in rehabilitation counseling. The purpose of this chapter is to provide an overview of qualitative research methods and to discuss their application to rehabilitation research. In the following sections, we examine (a) the researcher's role in qualitative inquiry, (b) characteristics of qualitative research, (c) methodological issues, and (d) types of qualitative designs along with examples from the rehabilitation literature.

RESEARCHER'S ROLE

The qualitative researcher functions as a "learner" or "facilitator," and the research participants function as "teachers" or "coresearchers," making qualitative research a valuable tool for both understanding and empowering people with disabilities. Another distinguishing characteristic of researchers' roles is that they serve as the "instruments of data collection" (Polkinghorne, 1991). As the instruments of data collection, the meanings that participants' make of their experiences are shaped by their interactions with the researcher.

The quality and credibility of the research findings are dependent upon the researcher's expertise in the qualitative design being used, skills, experience, and rigor. A skillful qualitative researcher is an expert on the topic of interest and can make quick decisions about what information to seek, what questions to ask, and what observations to make. He or she knows how to approach the problem in a manner that will yield the greatest detail and depth of information (Kvale, 1996). The qualitative researcher is skilled in listening, interviewing, observing, and writing. In addition to these skills, the researcher must possess a keen understanding of human interactions as well as the ability to communicate effectively. Experiences with the phenomena under study can serve to enlighten and sensitize the researcher to the complexity of issues being explored. In fact, qualitative researchers sometimes include their own experiences as part of the database (Polkinghorne, 1991).

Because qualitative researchers interact directly with their data sources (the research participants), they must also be aware of their own experiences and personal characteristics and how these shape their interactions as well as the data collected, analyzed, and interpreted. As Corbin and Strauss (2008, p. 11) described, qualitative researchers "don't separate who we are as persons from the research and data analysis that we do. Therefore, we must be self-reflective about how we influence the research process, and, in turn, how it influences us." Contemporary qualitative researchers often include a section of their research reports devoted to their role as the instruments of data collection; how their professional and personal understanding or experiences with the phenomenon being studied may either bias or enhance their data collection and analysis; and strategies they used to suspend their biases and ensure that they follow the research participants' lead in exploring issues, concerns, and feelings about the phenomenon, rather than ignoring what is not viewed as important to the researcher. Raising awareness of one's subjectivity and its potential influence on the study is referred to as reflexivity. We discuss the importance of researcher reflexivity as a means to engage in ongoing reflection throughout the research process in greater detail in the research methodological issues section of this chapter.

CHARACTERISTICS OF QUALITATIVE RESEARCH

In addition to the researcher being the primary instrument of data collection, qualitative research has other unique characteristics that distinguish it from quantitative research. The following is a list of major characteristics (which are discussed in greater detail in subsequent sections of this chapter) about qualitative research (Creswell, 2007; Hagner & Helm, 1994; Lincoln & Guba, 1985):

1. Qualitative research is conducted in natural settings where people live, work, and play.
2. Analytic categories emerge from the data as opposed to being "overlaid like a template on the participants or their situation" (Hagner & Helm, 1994, p. 291).
3. The research data that emerge from a qualitative study are reported in words or pictures rather than in numbers.
4. Data analysis occurs through induction rather than deduction; theory or hypotheses are not established a priori.
5. Understanding occurs as a result of engaging in an in-depth study of the phenomena of interest; researchers are as interested in the process that is occurring as they are in the outcome.
6. Qualitative researchers make ideographic interpretations of the research findings; they are more interested in understanding the particulars than they are in making generalizations.
7. Meanings and interpretations of research findings are negotiated with the research participants because it is their perceptions or realities that the researcher seeks to understand and reconstruct.

8. The criteria for judging the empirical soundness of qualitative studies emphasize coherence, insight, instrumental utility, and trustworthiness rather than reliability and validity.

METHODOLOGICAL ISSUES

The methods in qualitative research consist of a variety of practices used in the collection, analysis, interpretation, and reporting of qualitative research data (Creswell, 2007). Although precise agreement among all qualitative writers and researchers regarding specific procedures does not exist, there is reasonable consensus that consideration of the following is important in designing qualitative studies: (a) the literature review and use of theories, (b) research purpose and questions, (c) sampling, (d) data collection procedures, (e) data management–recording procedures, (f) data analysis and interpretation procedures, (g) trustworthiness of qualitative findings, (h) researcher reflexivity, (i) research coherence, (j) ethical considerations, and (k) limitations of qualitative research.

The Literature Review and Use of Theories in Qualitative Research

In general, the literature review conducted for qualitative research is considered of secondary importance to the research participants' experiences, views, and meanings connected with the phenomena being investigated. Unlike literature reviews in quantitative research that establish a foundation for research questions and hypotheses, literature reviews in qualitative research are conducted to (a) identify gaps in the literature and limitations in methodological procedures used to investigate the phenomenon, (b) provide a basis for how qualitative research will close those gaps, and (c) fine-tune the research procedures being used by investigators (Glesne & Peshkin, 1992; Polkinghorne, 1991). Also, in qualitative research, the literature review continues beyond the outset of the project into the data collection and analysis phases of the study (Glesne & Peshkin, 1992; Strauss & Corbin, 1990). This continuous return to the literature occurs because emerging themes in data collection and analysis often require a review of previously unexamined literature (Creswell, 2007; Polkinghorne, 1991).

Because qualitative studies are exploratory, explanatory, descriptive or emancipatory in nature, the literature on the topic of interest is used inductively so that it does not direct the researcher's questions or suppress the development of new theoretical formulations (Creswell, 2007; Strauss & Corbin, 1990). The amount of literature reviewed varies depending on the qualitative design. For example, in theoretically-oriented qualitative studies such as ethnographies, the literature review may be quite extensive; however, in grounded theory, case studies, and phenomenological studies, the literature review may be much more restricted (Creswell, 2007).

The literature review in both quantitative and qualitative research informs readers about the results of related studies, relates the findings from the current study to prior studies, and provides a rationale for the current study (Creswell, 2007; Strauss & Corbin, 1990). In some written qualitative reports, a brief literature review is included in the introduction to the study to frame the problem of interest. In others, a more extensive literature review is provided in a separate section. In most studies, the literature is also compared and contrasted with the researcher's findings in the discussion section of their written reports (Creswell, 2007).

The use of theories in qualitative research is also more varied than it is in quantitative research, and how or whether theory is used as a part of the investigation depends on the specific qualitative design being used by the researchers (Creswell, 2007). For example, theory may be used as a conceptual framework as occurs when researchers use critical disability theory in critical ethnography. It may be a theoretical endpoint such as in the development of a grounded theory. It may be used as a guiding philosophy of knowledge and meaning-making such as in constructivist grounded theory or some types of phenomenology. Some qualitative studies engage with prior theory, using their findings to contest, extend, or further contribute to theory. Finally, theory may not be used at all such as in other types of phenomenology. When theory is used, its purpose is to provide the researcher and research participants with a lens to promote understanding rather than to make propositions to confirm or disconfirm (Koch, Niesz, & McCarthy, 2014).

Research Purpose and Questions

Qualitative research questions are broad, usually limited to one to three questions, and open-ended. Research questions are designed to capture rich, vivid descriptions of the participants' experiences with the phenomena of study. In qualitative investigations, purpose statements and corresponding research questions can be classified as exploratory, explanatory, descriptive, or emancipatory (Marshall & Rossman, 2011). Exploratory questions are posed to study phenomena that are not well-understood or to generate hypotheses for future inquiry. Explanatory questions are posed for the purpose of discerning patterns underlying the phenomena being investigated or for identifying relationships that shape the phenomena. Descriptive questions document and detail social processes and participants' experiences, views, practices, and meanings. Finally, emancipatory questions are posed when researchers want to actively engage participants, who are typically members of marginalized populations, in collaborative inquiry, social critique, and action.

Initial research questions are formulated to provide a framework within which to focus the research topic and guide the selection of a qualitative research design with corresponding sampling, data collection, analysis, and interpretation procedures (Glesne & Peshkin, 1992). Research questions are not static, nor do they lead to hypotheses to be tested as in quantitative research (Strauss & Corbin, 1990). Rather, they are continuously refined throughout the data collection and analysis processes to reflect the researcher's increasing understanding of the phenomena and the social context. This flexibility enables the researcher to follow the lead of the research participants rather than impose his or her perspective on those individuals engaged with the phenomena under study. As qualitative researchers engage in data collection, it is not unusual for them to discover that their original research question(s) fail to uncover what the participants view as important to understand. In these cases, researchers will revise their research questions and may reengage with the research participants.

Sampling

Sampling techniques in qualitative research are quite different from those used in quantitative research. The most important considerations in qualitative sampling decisions are determining the research settings, appropriate sampling times, and who will serve as the research participants. Decisions regarding these issues will have a significant impact on answering the research questions (Maxwell, 1996) and must be carefully examined prior to the initiation of the inquiry. Because it is generally impossible to interview everyone or to observe everything, a sampling strategy is employed to determine which sites, times, and participants to include (Glesne & Peshkin, 1992). The sampling strategy used in qualitative research is referred to as "purposeful" (Maxwell, 1996, p. 70) and is defined differently than "purposeful" sampling in quantitative research.

In qualitative research, purposeful sampling is used to identify participants who are best able to provide detailed information to answer the research questions. Purposeful sampling in qualitative research, also referred to as "criterion-based selection" (LeCompte & Preissle, 1993, p. 69), involves the deliberate selection of participants, settings, events, or units, not for their representativeness, but for their relevance to the research questions (Schwandt, 2001). The goals of purposeful sampling include (a) identifying homogeneity or heterogeneity in the population being studied and (b) selecting participants on the basis of their experiences with the phenomena of interest and their ability to help researchers answer their research questions.

In some qualitative research, access to research participants may be difficult to achieve (e.g., accessing individuals who are willing to discuss the effects of HIV/AIDS on their employment). Because of the potential stigma and discrimination that could occur as well as other risks involved with participants revealing their HIV/AIDS status, researchers may use a sampling technique known as snowball sampling (Patton, 2002) to access participants who otherwise would not be discovered. Snowball sampling involves asking persons interviewed or other individuals (e.g., colleagues, rehabilitation counselors, other service providers, personal contacts) to recommend additional potential participants.

SITES. According to Marshall and Rossman (1989, p. 54), the following four issues require consideration in selecting the appropriate sampling site(s): "(a) physical access to the site; (b) variety of data sources; (c) access to the site, participants, and data will be granted for as long as is necessary; and (d) quality and credibility of the data can be reasonably assured." Some research questions/problems do not require an actual site or setting, but are more global in nature. Therefore, data can be collected within geographically d-etermined boundaries. Other research questions/problems will require determination of the specific site.

TIMING. Timing of the research project includes addressing site availability and access, the approximate length of time required to access entry to data collection sites and recruit research participants, and the approximate amount of time during which data collection will take place. The researcher will need to consider each decision regarding timing by asking questions like: "What will be the effect of this particular decision?" "What will be gained?" "What could be missed?" The more aware the researcher is about the potential ramifications of each of these decisions, the wiser the final decisions will be (Bogdan & Biklen, 1998).

PARTICIPANTS. The selection of participants in qualitative research "rests on the multiple purposes of illuminating, interpreting, and understanding" (Glesne & Peshkin, 1992, p. 27) their perspectives. In most qualitative research endeavors, the researcher is unable to interview all potential participants or observe everything. Therefore, participants are selected on the basis of the *type* of information they can provide in answering the research questions. If the researcher is more interested in developing an in-depth understanding of the participants' situation, extended periods of time will be spent with a small number of participants. However, if the researcher wants to gather a broader perspective, a larger number of participants are interviewed in a less intensive manner (Creswell, 2007).

Qualitative researchers often spend substantial time in the settings they plan to study or with potential participants before data collection begins. For example, they may attend conferences sponsored by disability advocacy groups and organizations, provide presentations to disability self-help groups, and meet with gatekeepers to discuss their research. Spending this time in settings and with potential research participants enables individuals to get to know the researcher and helps to establish the researcher's credibility and trustworthiness, thus, increasing the likelihood that individuals will consent to participate in the investigation.

Each qualitative research design poses guidelines regarding the ideal number of participants or research sites, and these can range from one (e.g., case study, autoethnography) to hundreds (e.g., large grounded theory investigations). However, as noted by Hunt (2011), the primary consideration in sampling is not number of participants but the detail and insight into the phenomena that participants are able to provide.

Data Sources and Data Collection

In qualitative research, the data emerge from the interactions of researchers with their data sources (Polkinghorne, 1991). The selection of data sources is based upon theoretical grounds rather than probability theory. The data collected in qualitative research are often described as "thick" because they consist of vivid and rich descriptions of the phenomena under study.

Qualitative data collection efforts can generate hundreds of pages of information. Typical sources of data include field notes (e.g., observational notes, reflexive memos) transcripts from audio-recorded interviews, documents (personal and official), archival records, physical artifacts, photographs, video, and descriptive statistics (quantitative data). Personal documents may include diaries, journals, personal letters, poems, and autobiographies. Official documents include newsletters, policy documents, codes of ethics, statements of philosophy, minutes from meetings, client medical or school records, and personnel files.

Prior to the initiation of data collection, the researcher considers what data will be generated and how they will be documented. A protocol form is sometimes used to document observations in the field (e.g., accounts of particular events and activities, a reconstruction of the dialogue, characteristics of the research participants), reflective notes (e.g., personal thoughts, impressions, ideas, problems, biases), and demographic information (Bogdan & Biklen, 1992; Creswell, 2007). In addition, mechanical recording devices (e.g., audio or videorecorders) are often used in qualitative research. However, such devices must be used as unobtrusively as possible to minimize any possible interference with the data collection process (Marshall & Rossman, 1989).

During the data collection process, the qualitative researcher must consider methods to ensure accuracy of the information being obtained (see Trustworthiness section). Some qualitative approaches (e.g., grounded theory, most phenomenological approaches) rely solely on interviews as data sources. However, in other approaches, using multiple sources of data (e.g., interviews, medical records, school records, employer performance evaluations, diaries, journals, observational data) is considered a good strategy for building a more thorough and trustworthy account of the participants' experiences (Schwandt, 2001).

INTERVIEWS

The most widely used form of data collection in qualitative research is the interview (Creswell, 2007). The qualitative research interview explores the views, experiences, beliefs and motivations of participants. In-depth interviews provide the latitude necessary to probe for specific details based on the information offered by the participants (Bogdan & Biklen, 1992; Glesne & Peshkin, 1992; Marshall & Rossman, 1989). Research participants are encouraged to reflect upon and elaborate the details of their experiences. Interviews are conducted over a period of anywhere from thirty minutes to several hours, and in some studies, participants are interviewed more than once. Qualitative researchers are careful to avoid narrow, closed-ended questions that lead the participants in a direction that supports the researchers' assumptions about the phenomenon (Koch, Niesz, & McCarthy, 2014). In fact, asking one broad, open-ended prompt or question (e.g., "Tell me what it is like to live with chronic pain?") is often all that is required to collect rich, nuanced data from the participants. Researchers can then use probes and follow-up questions to clarify participants' responses, acquire specific examples of their experiences, and elaborate on participants' statements. This approach ensures that the researcher follows the participants' lead rather than steering responses in the direction of what the researcher assumes is relevant.

In many qualitative investigations, interview protocols or guides are developed to initiate the data collection process. These protocols may be structured, semi-structured, or unstructured. Protocols are designed to be flexible enough to incorporate modifications and changes as the data collection process continues (Denzin & Lincoln, 2000; Glesne & Peshkin, 1992). Ensuring that protocols are designed to uncover issues important to the research participants is often addressed by having focus groups or expert panels review the questions and make specific recommendations for changes or additional questions. Members of these focus groups or expert panels typically consist of individuals with characteristics similar to those of targeted research participants and experts in qualitative research design and the phenomena being investigated. In other cases, protocols may be developed on the basis of literature reviews, consultation with others who have investigated the topic being explored, the researchers' own (professional or personal) experiences with the phenomena, or using a combination of techniques. Interview protocols are often revised once researchers begin collecting data and find that the questions they are asking do not uncover what is important to the research participants.

Focus groups are used to interview several participants or informants at one time (Frey & Fontana, 1991) when the researcher wants to develop an understanding of the shared meaning of a phenomenon (Camic, Rhodes, & Yardley, 2003). "The hallmark of focus groups is the explicit use of the group interaction to produce data and insights that would be less accessible without the interaction found in a group" (Morgan, 1988, p. 12). As with any approach to research, focus groups are not without their limitations. The most specific of which is the difficulty of identifying which participant or informant provided what specific data during the course of the discussion, particularly when parallel positions are being voiced (Flick, 2002). This problem may be reduced by use of video or audio recording equipment. Another problem occurs when dominant group members do most of the talking or when individuals feel intimidated by the group process. This problem can be addressed by conducting both individual and focus group interviews or by providing members with an opportunity to respond to interview questions in writing. Confidentiality may also be an issue, especially when focus group members are discussing sensitive topics. Therefore, it is critical that at the outset of focus group meetings, researchers instruct participants that all information shared in these groups is to remain confidential.

With the vast options of research methods and the rise of technology over the last 50 years, there are now more possibilities than ever to gather interview data. Some contemporary approaches to interviewing include reciprocal peer interviews, Photovoice, and use of technology such as Skype. As an alternative to individual interviews and focus groups, Porter, Neysmith, Reitsma-Street, and Collins (2009) introduced reciprocal peer interviewing as a means to remove power inequities between the researcher and research participant by enabling participants to coconstruct their own meanings of the phenomenon being studied without influence of the researcher. In traditional interview modes, the researcher/interviewer engages the participant/interviewee in an interrogatory dialogue. This places the interviewer in a position of control and power over the interview process. Reciprocal peer interviewing attempts to reduce this power differential by allowing participant pairs to perform both the roles of interviewer and interviewee. This allows the researcher to take on a secondary role as facilitator and observer. The resulting conversation is then one of shared authority. In reciprocal peer interviewing, participants undergo a brief training session on interviewing and then pair up with another research participant to alternate roles in interviewing each other. This approach to data collection gives participants greater freedom in their verbal expressions without the influence of the researcher.

Photovoice is a participatory action research method in which individuals photograph their everyday life experiences. Photovoice can be used as an alternative method to enhance the understanding of experiences that are difficult to capture through other qualitative methods. Wang and Burris first introduced Photo novella in 1994. Since that time, Photovoice has become a vital tool for community-based participatory research (CBPR) because of its accuracy in gathering information (Graziano, 2004). The Boston University Center for Psychiatric Rehabilitation has demonstrated using Photovoice as a way to combat the stigma experienced by people with psychiatric disabilities. By using a camera as the data collection tool, people with psychiatric disabilities are able to use a powerful mode of communication that enables them to educate others about their experiences and empowers them to be active participants in creating knowledge and taking the lead in reducing stigma (Gagne, Bowers, Russinova, Bloch, & McNamara, 2010). In addition to taking photographs that represent their experiences, research participants write descriptions of the photographs' meanings. They also discuss the meanings they ascribe to their photos in interviews with the researchers. Researchers then identify both unique and common themes across participants and present these for confirmation to the research participants. In line with emancipatory research, they then use their photographs to educate others about the impact that stigma has on their lives through art exhibitions for the general public and presentations to policymakers and service providers.

Throughout history, developments in technology and changes in communication have gone hand-in-hand. These changes in communication have also influenced interview techniques in qualitative research. Online interviewing using technology such as Skype can now facilitate access to global research respondents who are geographically dispersed. Skype is a popular voice communication application that specializes in providing video chat and voice calls. Of course there are some benefits and drawbacks to the utility of Skype. For instance, using this platform helps with problems experienced with doing face-to-face interviews such as time and financial limits, geographical dispersion, and physical mobility limitations of research populations (Cater, 2011). By using a webcam, researchers are still able to see the presence of nonverbal and social cues (Stewart & Williams, 2005; Sullivan, 2012). However, seeing only a limited "head shot" provided by webcam can create obstacles in observing all of the individual's body language (Cater, 2011).

Data Management Procedures

As previously mentioned, a great deal of data is generated during a qualitative research project. Because data management and analysis are integrally linked throughout the research process, the data must be organized to facilitate easy retrieval. Therefore, an effective and efficient method of data management is required. Levine (1985) outlined five main principles in the management of qualitative data:

1. *Formatting.* Include consistent information in the field notes (i.e., name of the researcher, the site, pseudonyms or other identifiers of the participant(s), and the date). Maintain the notes in a notebook, file folder, encrypted electronic database, or other like manner.
2. *Cross-referral.* Referencing information from one file to another to permit ease of data retrieval.
3. *Coding.* Because qualitative research is inductive, the coding system evolves during the research project. It includes identifying and organizing categories as they emerge from the data. (See Data Analysis section for more detailed explanation).
4. *Abstracting.* Condensing lengthy material into summaries while retaining a clear link back to the original field notations.
5. *Locators.* The use of unique numbers/letters to serve as identification markers for specific material in field notes (see Levine, 1985 for more in-depth discussion).

Qualitative data management can be a daunting task. However, advances in technology have added great efficiency to the management of qualitative data. Computer-assisted qualitative data analysis software (CAQDAS) systems are increasingly being used by qualitative researchers as technical tools to organize or index their data (Salmona, & Kaczynski, 2016). A continually growing number of CAQDAS systems are available for Windows and Macintosh computers (Fielding, 2001) and are divided into three broad types of programs: text search, text code-and retrieve, and code-based theory-builder programs. A few examples of commonly used CAQDAS software packages include NVivo, Atlas.ti, MAXQDA, and HyperResearcher (Drisko, 2013). Some computer software companies have websites that offer a trial use of their software programs, and some CAQDAS are available at no cost to the researcher.

Although CAQDAS programs can be very efficient tools for storing and organizing data, they do not make analytic decisions for researchers (Drisko, 2013). Likewise, they are generic and are not tied to any specific qualitative approach. Finally, they do not increase the rigor of the analysis of data. The rigor of data analysis is based upon the researcher's sophistication, knowledge, and skills in qualitative inquiry rather than the approach they use (i.e., hand sorting and coding versus CAQDAS) to manage their data. Readers can refer to Silver and Lewins' (2014), *Using Software in Qualitative Research: A Step by Step Guide* (2nd Ed.) for a more detailed discussion of how QDAS software is used in qualitative data management.

Data Analysis Procedures

Qualitative data analysis involves making sense of volumes of data, determining what data to include in the analysis, and deciding on what data to exclude. Although each qualitative research design specifies its own procedures for data analysis, all designs either involve strategies for (a) organizing the data by category or code, coding the data and looking for broader themes within and across codes, and preparing a narrative for summarizing the findings, or (b) analyzing the data by looking contextually or connectedly across data sources in a chronological manner (Creswell, 2007; Maxwell, 2012). Data collection, analysis, and report writing are done simultaneously rather than sequentially.

Because interviews are the most common data sources in qualitative research, researchers often begin the data analysis process by first listening to or watching each interview and reading transcribed interviews (often several times) in their entirety to acquire a sense of the data before breaking it apart for the purpose of analysis and interpretation (Creswell, 2007). In this initial stage of analysis, researchers often write down key ideas, topics that keep coming up, or short phrases in the margins of transcripts, under photos, or on other documents collected. Qualitative researchers also take notes (i.e., memos) regarding their initial impressions, common topics that recur within and across data sources, insights about the data, and emerging patterns and themes. Data are reviewed at the micro-level (i.e., each participant interview) and at the macro level (i.e., across data sources) throughout data collection. From here, researchers may identify initial categories, codes, or structures for organizing the data. They identify variations and examples and then make comparisons of the data across codes, categories, or structures. Initially, they may develop a large number of categorical codes or structures; however, through the process of constant comparison of the codes and structures, these are often condensed into larger meaning units. Broader themes within the data are then identified through contrasting and comparing meaning units. These broader themes and their interconnections are then illustrated in a narrative, table, matrix, or set of propositions.

When multiple researchers are involved in the investigation, they discuss with each other their preliminary observations and thoughts and share their memos to obtain a broader picture of the data. After this is completed, the next steps are to (a) prepare and organize the data for analysis; (b) reduce the data into themes through the process of coding, labeling, and categorizing the data; (c) collapse and combine the initial analytic units into larger meaning units; and (d) represent the data in diagrams, tables, or a narrative discussion (Creswell, 2007).

Qualitative designs are built on an iterative process (i.e., back-and-forth movement from data gathering to analysis back to more data gathering). Thus, data collection and analysis go hand-in-hand. Researchers begin their analyses while still collecting data rather than waiting until data collection is completed. In this manner, preliminary analyses may inform future data collection (i.e., going back to previously interviewed participants to ask them new interview questions), and ongoing data collection informs data analysis (i.e., returning to preliminary analyses and modifying or expanding on these analyses based on new data collected in the field).

One aim of qualitative data analysis is thick description. Thick description, a term introduced in ethnography by Geertz (1973) refers to acquiring an understanding of the participants' experiences with the phenomenon that goes beyond surface explanations to understand the participants' experiences in as much depth as possible. Thick description requires researchers to make explicit the patterns of cultural and social dynamics that shape the participants' experiences with the phenomenon. It also requires precision and depth in documenting and representing the participants' worlds (Koch, Niesz, & McCarthy, 2014). In qualitative research, data collection and analysis typically continue until the point of saturation. Saturation occurs when no new findings are emerging in the process of data collection and analysis.

After the data are analyzed, the next step is to interpret the data. Data interpretation answers the "so what?" question (Chang et al., 2013). It involves making meaning of the data in terms of how the findings advance understanding of the phenomena that was investigated, determining new insights or understandings gained from the study that add to the researchers' professional literature base, and comparing the findings with related literature on the phenomena to identify commonalities and discrepancies across studies.

Data analyses and interpretations are sometimes shared with the research participants to ensure that these are truly representative of their experience (see Trustworthiness section). In written reports, participant quotations, vignettes, and descriptions from observations are included as evidence of the concepts and themes that emerged in the data analysis (Creswell, 2008). Quotations are written verbatim in qualitative reports and are judiciously interwoven throughout the report to support the analyses. Use of in vivo codes (i.e., assigning a label to a code using the participants' words) and participant quotes support researchers' analyses and provide evidence that their findings represent the participants' perspectives.

Trustworthiness

Because the intent of qualitative research is to "uncover meaning" rather than verify causal relationships between variables or generalize the research findings to other settings and populations, the terms "reliability" and "validity" are not usually considered applicable to the evaluation of the rigor of qualitative research studies. Rigor and quality have a different meaning in qualitative research than they do in quantitative research (Creswell, 2007; Glesne & Peshkin, 1992; Lincoln & Guba, 1985; Maxwell, 1996). In fact, many qualitative researchers use terms such as "credibility," "trustworthiness," and "authenticity" in lieu of the terms "reliability" and "validity." Established techniques used to ensure the trustworthiness of qualitative research findings are discussed in the following paragraphs.

AUDIT TRAIL. The audit trail provides a mechanism for subsequent reviews of the process of the study by other researchers and has been termed the "single most important trustworthiness technique" (Lincoln & Guba, 1985, p. 283). An audit trail consists of (a) raw data, including audiotapes, interview notes, and memos; (b) products of data reduction and analysis, including coding procedures; (c) products of data reconstruction and synthesis; and (d) process notes, including notes on trustworthiness (Lincoln & Guba, 1985).

MEMOS AND FIELD JOURNALS. Memos and researcher journals are used throughout the research process to document the researcher's reflections, perspectives, intuitions, and preliminary ideas regarding the ongoing investigation (Bogdan & Biklen, 1992). Memos and journals are also used to identify and record personal biases, assumptions, and feelings that may arise in the process of data gathering, analysis, and interpretation. Recording the researcher's preliminary ideas safeguards against the loss of important ideas during the research process (Glesne & Peshkin, 1992). Finally, memos may be used by peer reviewers to gain additional perspectives on the data.

TRIANGULATION. Triangulation is conceptualized as the comparison of information collected from different sources and settings, and, especially using different data collection methods (Denzin, 1970). Most often, this means that researchers are comparing what they learn through both interviews and observations or documents to ensure that their findings hold up to close scrutiny. Multiple sources of data serve to protect the rigor and quality of data analysis (Denzin & Lincoln, 2000). Triangulation provides a means of cross-referencing interpretations arrived at during data analysis. It minimizes the possibility of arriving at erroneous interpretations and conclusions.

MULTIPLE RESEARCHERS. The active participation of multiple researchers in qualitative research projects provides several advantages. The first is the ability to evaluate multiple sites during the same timeframe. In addition, multiple researchers bring different skills, attributes, and perspectives to the evaluation process (Cassell, 1978; Wax, 1979). Such differences further serve to reduce the possibility of personal biases or preconceptions influencing the findings (Hagner & Helm, 1994). In situations where a researcher is working alone, alternative methods are available to ensure the quality of findings (e.g., peer debriefers).

DISCREPANT CASE ANALYSIS. Another practice qualitative researchers use to ensure the trustworthiness of their analysis is to deliberately search for data that do not support the preliminary conclusions. Discrepant data must be rigorously examined, along with supporting data, to determine whether the research findings (i.e., categories/themes) are to be retained or modified. The qualitative researcher must be diligent in the search for discrepant data to avoid prematurely dismissing relevant data that do not fit with existing conclusions (Maxwell, 1996).

MEMBER CHECKS. Participant feedback is considered critically important in establishing the accuracy of data interpretations (Creswell, 2003; Denzin & Lincoln, 2000). Through a process called member checking, research participants are given the opportunity to review interview transcripts and research findings and interpretations in order to provide feedback on the data generated and the conclusions reached by the researchers (Fielding & Fielding, 1986). Member checks provide an additional level of credibility by providing opportunities for participants to clarify their views or experiences and contest any faulty interpretations of the researcher. Member checks also provide a checkpoint in protecting any confidential information or the identities of research participants.

PEER DEBRIEFING. Peer debriefing is used as a means of testing the researcher's ideas against those of a peer or peers who have not been involved in the research project. The use of peer debriefers provides an opportunity to obtain alternative perspectives regarding the interpretation of the data. Peer debriefers also serve to raise awareness of biases associated with the researcher's views, which might adversely affect the study (Lincoln & Guba, 1985). Peer debriefers may be used throughout all phases of the research process as a means for researchers to check their insights and interpretations with someone who has expertise regarding the research topic and qualitative inquiry but who is not personally invested in the project or its outcomes.

TRANSPARENCY. Transparency requires qualitative researchers to make the essential components of their investigations obvious to readers of their qualitative reports (Moravcsik, 2014). It requires qualitative researchers to provide readers with specific details regarding the choices they made in terms of research strategies, participant selection, data sources, data collection, analysis and interpretation of their findings. Enough detail should be provided so that other researchers can replicate their investigations. Moravcsik (2014) describes three kinds of transparency: data transparency, analytic transparency, and production transparency. Data transparency allows readers access to the data used by the researchers to make their analyses and interpretations. Analytic transparency requires researchers to precisely describe the interpretive process the used to draw their conclusions. Production transparency involves explaining to readers why they chose to use specific theories and methods in their investigations and demonstrating methodological coherence throughout their investigations. Moravcsik (2014, p. 48) underscored the importance of transparency, stating that "academic discourse rests on the obligation of scholars to reveal to their colleagues the data, theory, and methodology on which their conclusions rest."

RESEARCHER REFLEXIVITY. Researcher reflexivity refers to the researcher's aim "to explore the ways in which [the] researcher's involvement with a particular study influences, acts upon and informs such research" (Nightingale, & Cromby, 1999, p. 228). Reflexivity is "an attitude of attending systematically to the context of knowledge construction, especially to the effect of the researcher, at every step of the research process" (Malterud, 2001, p. 484). Reflexivity requires researchers to critically reflect on both the knowledge being generated in their investigations as well as how it is generated (Guillemin & Gillam, 2004). Reflexivity also requires continuous scrutiny of one's role and practices and a change in practices that are not respectful and representative of research participants' perspectives and experiences.

Researcher reactivity and bias can be minimized through the use of a variety of strategies, some of which have already been discussed. For example, during an interview, the researcher's use of reflective statements, open-ended questions, avoidance of leading questions, and restatement of the participant's comments are effective tools in managing reactivity (Maxwell, 1996). During data analysis, the researcher must deliberately reflect upon his or her subjective views and reactions to the data, and ensure that they are not coloring the analysis and interpretation. Bracketing, a term that originates from the phenomenological tradition, can also be used to minimize researcher bias (Schwandt, 2001; Moustakas, 1994). This technique requires researchers to "bracket," set aside, or suspend their assumptions about social reality and focus on the research participant's experience of the world. Arguing that subjectivity is inevitable in any research, Peshkin (1988) recommends that qualitative researchers conduct a subjectivity audit whereby they systematically seek out their biases and preconceptions while their research is actively in progress. This ongoing audit enables researchers to bring their subjectivity into conscious awareness so that they understand how it may be shaping their research and can employ strategies to manage it.

Other reflexivity practices include keeping a self-reflective journal during the research process to record thoughts and feelings about what is happening in order to provide the researcher some distance in the research process (Niesz, Koch, & Rumrill, 2008). Depending on the type of research study, these reflections and self-understandings can then be examined and either set aside or incorporated into the analysis (Morrow, 2005). Researchers may also ask a peer debriefer to interview them using the same or similar questions that will be asked of participants. The self-interview helps to initiate the data collection process, to clarify their research, to understand their perspectives and experiences with the phenomenon being investigated, and to alert themselves to possible biases that may interfere with their ability to accurately represent the research participants' perspectives (Polkinghorne, 1991). Beyond being aware of their subjectivity, qualitative researchers are responsible for explicitly stating their biases in reporting research results (Creswell, 2003). Safeguards such as triangulation and multiple researchers can also be built into the design and methodology of qualitative projects to minimize researcher bias and to enhance the trustworthiness of the findings. Bracketing (Epoche)—suspending judgment and setting aside assumptions, as much as possible, about social reality—is a strategy used in phenomenology to understand how it is that the participants experience their world as real, concrete, factual, and objective. Ongoing critical self-reflection, self-dialogue, meditation, journaling, and peer debriefing are strategies used by researchers to bracket their preconceived notions and subjective views. Researchers write about their own experiences with the phenomenon and the context and situations that have influenced their perspectives. Often, these personal statements are included in the methods sections describing the role of the researchers.

Methodological Coherence

In addition to considering and addressing issues of trustworthiness, qualitative researchers must also attend to issues related to the rigor of their investigations. Of utmost importance to the rigor of a qualitative investigation is methodological coherence. Methodological coherence means that "the entire research project (including the purpose and research question, interview questions, data collection methods, analysis and presentation of results) utilizes a consistent epistemological perspective" (Kline, 2008, p. 212). Drawing upon examples provided by Kline (2008), if a qualitative researcher is interested in developing a better understanding, based on the personal accounts of individuals with disabilities, of the shared experience of being discriminated against, a phenomenological design would be appropriate to develop an appreciation of the "essence" of that experience (i.e., its influence on participants' feelings, thoughts, and behaviors). Methodological coherence would be demonstrated by using data collection, analysis, interpretation, and trustworthiness procedures as established in the phenomenological research literature. Methodological coherence is demonstrated when researchers describing their research procedures in written reports using terminology from the phenomenological literature; citing authoritative sources to back up their methodological decisions; and reporting their findings as phenomenology. If however, the researchers concluded their investigation with the development of a theory grounded in their data, their investigation would be methodologically incoherent and, thus, lack rigor.

Ethical Issues in Qualitative Research

While ethical standards are inherent to all research, qualitative research poses unique ethical challenges that are not present in quantitative research. The most important consideration for qualitative researchers in their role as the instrument of data collection is the "ethical obligations a researcher has toward a research participant in terms of interacting with him or her in a humane, nonexploitive way while at the same time being mindful of one's role as a researcher" (Guillemin & Gillam, 2004, p. 264). Ethical qualitative researchers must interact with participants in a manner that is respectful of participants' autonomy, dignity, and privacy. In designing their research studies, qualitative researchers proactively anticipate potential ethical dilemmas that may arise and how to respond to these dilemmas. However, because ethical issues in qualitative research tend to be subtle and context-driven, it is not always possible to anticipate potential dilemmas that may arise (Guillemin & Gillam, 2004; Orb, Eisenhauer, & Wynaden, 2001).

To ensure privacy and confidentiality, qualitative researchers have an ethical obligation to protect their participants' confidentiality by maintaining data in a secure place and by excluding names and any other information that could lead to the identification of the participants (Guillemin & Gillam, 2004; Orb et al., 2001). However, even when using pseudonyms and leaving out other potential identifying information, confidentiality may still be unintentionally violated (Orb et al., 2001). For example, lengthy quotations included in written reports could potentially lead others to identify participants. Even demographic data (e.g., race, age, disability type, educational level), especially in small populations, could lead to the identification of participants. This potential ethical violation underscores the importance of negotiating with participants what information to include and exclude from written reports.

Because qualitative researchers directly interact with the research participants, several ethical issues can arise as a result of the partnership that is formed with research participants. For example, the practice of in-depth interviewing and prolonged engagement with the research participants may lead participants to view the researcher as a confidante and feel betrayed when the relationship is ended and the information shared with the researcher is made public (Guillemin & Gillam, 2004). Participants may find the interactions with the researcher to be therapeutic. Thus, researchers have a responsibility to ensure that participants understand that the relationship is time-limited and that the purpose of interactions is to conduct research and not to provide therapy. Potential harm may result when conducting in-depth interviews, particularly when the focus of the interview is on sensitive topics (e.g., trauma, psychosocial adaptation to disability, workplace mistreatment, stigma, discrimination). Participants may experience emotional distress when discussing these issues or may later regret personal information they revealed to the researcher (Orb et al., 2001).

Several strategies can be implemented by qualitative researchers in an attempt to address these potential sources of harm. First, the potential for emotional distress must be included as a risk of participation in consent forms. Additionally, researchers must make decisions about how far to probe a participant who reveals information about distressing experiences (Orb et al., 2001). In these instances, researchers must make ethical decisions about whether to continue the interview or to stop and make referrals for treatment or counseling. They can then follow up with the participants to check on their well-being. Researchers can also make provisions in their investigations for counseling referrals or other forms of support if emotional distress arises such as including contact information for counseling referrals on consent forms. Member checks to review transcripts provide an opportunity for participants to remove information they do not want included in the data pool.

Researchers can unintentionally cause harm to participants when they probe too far in asking questions that participants feel uncomfortable answering or, conversely, when they do not show enough interest in participants' responses (Guillemin & Gillam, 2004). These experiences with the researcher can lead the participants to feel vulnerable, rejected, ignored, or invalidated. Such feelings are especially likely to arise when interviewing members of marginalized populations who have a lifetime of experiences of being silenced, invalidated, and who lack support from others in their lives. Feelings of invalidation can also arise when researchers fail to let participants discuss what is important to them and instead focus queries on what is important to the researcher. To avoid these potential sources of harm, qualitative researchers must be adequately trained and skilled in appropriate attending and interviewing techniques.

When sharing interpretations and written reports with research participants to obtain their feedback on the accuracy of the interpretations, participants may feel too intimidated to challenge the researchers' interpretations because of perceived power imbalances (Guillemin & Gillam, 2004). Also, when data are framed in a larger context, participants may think that what they shared has been left out, and this could lead to feelings of being used or betrayed. The potential for these ethical issues to arise can be minimized by continually emphasizing to the research participants that they are the experts and the researcher's role is to learn from them. Re-emphasizing the participants' and researchers' roles increases the likelihood that participants will feel empowered to challenge the researchers' interpretations and to confront the researchers when they think their voices have been excluded in final reports.

Additional ethical issues arise when individuals report instances such as child or elder abuse (Orb et al., 2001). Participants should be clearly informed at the outset that such information would be excluded from confidentiality and anonymity, and researchers may be required by law to report these instances.

Finally, qualitative researchers have an ethical obligation to conduct rigorous qualitative research that is methodologically coherent (Oberle, 2002). If they use methodological approaches that are not coherent with their selected design, their findings may be inaccurate and fail to represent the participants' perspectives and experiences. In conclusion, although unintentional ethical violations may still occur, qualitative researchers can minimize this risk by being well-informed of their professional codes of ethics as they pertain to research, anticipating potential violations that may occur in the design of their studies, and consulting with peer debriefers and other qualitative researchers when dilemmas arise.

QUALITATIVE RESEARCH DESIGNS

As we have previously stated, qualitative research is conducted for purposes of (a) *exploring,* (b) *explaining,* or (c) *describing* certain phenomena, or for (d) *emancipatory* purposes. From this framework, the researcher considers various qualitative research designs in pursuit of the best match for the research question or problem being addressed, selecting the research strategy most appropriate to answer the research questions.

Exploratory studies are initiated when the researcher is investigating phenomena that are not well understood, when variables need to be identified or discovered, or to generate hypotheses for further quantitative research (Marshall & Rossman, 2011). Sample research questions are as follows: What is happening in this particular setting? What are the salient themes, patterns, or categories that the participants view as important? How are certain patterns linked together? The case study, phenomenological, and grounded theory designs (see below for discussion) are appropriate for exploratory studies.

Explanatory studies are conducted when an explanation is needed with respect to defining the impetus behind the phenomenon being studied or to identify plausible factors (Marshall & Rossman, 2011). Sample research questions are: What circumstances are shaping this particular phenomenon (i.e., attitudes, beliefs, and events)? How do these forces lead to this phenomenon? Multisite study and ethnography designs are applicable to explanatory research studies.

A study is *descriptive* in nature if the researcher is interested in documenting the phenomenon of interest. The driving question for descriptive research is: What are the salient features of this phenomenon (i.e., behaviors, events, processes, attitudes, beliefs)? Case study and ethnography designs typically constitute descriptive qualitative studies (Marshall & Rossman, 2011).

Finally, qualitative research is *emancipatory* when its purpose is to engage participants in social critique and action (Marshall & Rossman, 2011). The driving question for emancipatory qualitative research is: What are the sociocultural beliefs, contexts, and processes that marginalize particular populations and how do marginalized populations take action to change these beliefs and processes? Critical ethnography and community-based participatory designs exemplify emancipatory research.

The research design is selected after the purpose of the study has been determined. Within qualitative inquiry lie a number of potential research designs. For the purpose of this chapter, discussion will focus on the following designs: (a) ethnography, (b) case study, (c) phenomenology, (d) grounded theory, (e) consensual qualitative research, (f) generic designs, and (g) qualitative meta-syntheses.

Ethnography

The term ethnography is used to capture the study of culture and cultural processes through long-term participant observation. Ethnography has been a powerful tool for anthropologists and sociologists for generations (Bogdan & Biklen, 1998; Crowson, 1993), and has more recently been adopted and adapted by other disciplines and professional fields. Ethnography provides an approach to understand people and their cultural meanings and practices in natural, "everyday" settings. The approach entails exploring the complex phenomena that make up human culture. Like other qualitative researchers, ethnographers place emphasis on understanding cultural processes, practices, and meanings through the perspectives of the participants themselves. At the same time, an ethnographer's outsider view helps to analyze ethnographic data and convey cultural descriptions to wide audiences.

Ethnographic data are obtained through participant observation; ethnographers spend extensive amounts of time in a community and learn through talking, listening, observing, and participating in everyday life in the community (Guba, 1978). In addition to informal conversations at the field site, ethnographers usually engage in formal interviews with participants as well. Ethnographic data gathered through these means provide a mechanism for learning cultural symbols, meanings, practices, and processes. Bogdan and Biklen (1992) provided the following description of ethnography:

> When culture is examined from this perspective, the ethnographer is faced with a series of interpretations of life, common-sense understandings that are complex and difficult to separate from each other. The ethnographer's goals are to share in the meanings that the cultural participants take for granted and then to depict the new understanding for the reader and for outsiders. (p. 39)

Data analysis in ethnographic research focuses on understanding and building descriptions of cultural practices and cultural meanings. Research questions guiding analysis are addressed through a sociocultural lens. Because the focus is often on cultural description and the primary method of data collection is participant observation, ethnographers work with months if not years of field notes documenting what they saw and heard at the field site. Findings are supported with vignettes that relate particular observations from the site of the study. Ethnographers seek to describe cultural processes, practices, and meanings in a way that brings their reader into the cultural context at the center of the study.

Ethnographers use different methods to conduct ethnographic analysis. For many, analysis resembles that of other kinds of qualitative research in that coding and categorizing are initially used to fracture hundreds of pages of field notes and interview transcripts into manageable categories for further study. In fact, many ethnographers use methods adopted and adapted from grounded theorists (discussed below) to analyze their data (Emerson, Fretz, & Shaw, 2011; Hammersley & Atkinson, 2007). Other ethnographers, however, engage in different types of analyses to develop cultural descriptions and interpretations (e.g., Agar, 1996; Spradley, 1979). Memos, which are used in data analysis for most approaches to qualitative inquiry, are especially important in ethnography, as they provide spaces for researchers to reflect on what they are learning through cultural immersion and, later, through the data analysis process.

What is important about ethnographic analysis is the focus on working to understand the phenomena at the center of the study from the cultural insiders' point of view. Ethnographers compare what is called an emic understanding (or a cultural insider's understanding) with their own etic or outsider's understanding in order to learn about the cultural scene and relate findings to broader audiences. Most ethnographers are also engaged with theory throughout their study and, especially, during data analysis. Ethnographic findings are often used to contest, extend, or further develop social theory. Critical ethnography and feminist ethnography use theory to understand how local cultural practice and meaning is situated in larger frameworks of power, such as patriarchy, institutional racism, social class hierarchies, and so forth.

As an example from the rehabilitation literature, Prodinger, Shaw, Laliberte-Rudman, and Stamm (2014) conducted an institutional ethnographic study of the doings of seven Austrian women with rheumatoid arthritis and how their doings were shaped by their social context and disability policies. Institutional ethnographers begin inquiry with what individuals actually do in their daily lives, and then turn the gaze from the individual to social relations to understand how the individuals' experiences and perspectives become shaped by, and contribute to the perpetuation of organizational processes and social structures (Prodinger et al., 2014, p. 498). In conducting their organizational ethnographic investigation, the primary researcher accompanied the participants in carrying out their daily activities (e.g., shopping, going to medical appointments, caring for children) and kept field journals to record observations. Other data sources included interviews and academic literature about disability policy development. The researchers analyzed the data by inductively reading it to develop a broad understanding of the participants' experiences, grouped together similar doings, and explored with coresearchers how these doings were shaped by the social context and disability policies.

Their findings revealed two groups of doing that were shaped by the historical development of disability policy: (a) keeping the disability invisible to avoid consequences such as breach of confidentiality, stigmatization, and negative impacts on employment; and (b) avoiding getting a disability pass (i.e., Austrian benefits and policies related to disability) to prevent becoming a member of a marginalized group. The researchers recommended that, in providing rehabilitation services to individuals with disabilities, their cultural and political environments must be factored into decisions about interventions to use. The researchers also recommended that Austrian policies must be changed from their deficit view of people with disabilities to a focus on how to institute greater inclusion of people with disabilities in all aspects of life.

Variations of Ethnography

Variations of ethnography include autoethnography and collective autoethnograpy. Autoethnography has been referred to as "action research for the individual" (Ellis & Bochner, 2000, p. 754). It is a form of self-reflection and writing that strives to explain and examine an individual's experiences with investigated phenomena in the context of cultural norms, beliefs, and values (Ellis, 2004; Holman Jones, 2005). This qualitative research approach is not simply storytelling; rather it is a form of critical enquiry embedded in theory and practice (McIlveen, 2008). Autoethnography uses both self-reference and reference to culture as a method to combine features of life history and ethnography. Autoethnographic research findings may be reported in "short stories, poetry, fiction, novels, photographic essays, personal essays, journals, fragmented and layered writing, and social science prose" (Ellis & Bochner, 2000, p. 739). Muncey (2005, p. 10) suggested the use of snapshots, artifacts/documents, metaphor, and literal expressions as techniques for reflecting and conveying a "patchwork of feelings, experiences, emotions, and behaviors that portray a more complete view of . . . life."

While autoethnography is defined as an individual or personal account, collective or collaborative autoethnography (CAE) is the means by which two or more people explore autoethnography as a team. Chang, Wambura-Ngunjiri, and Hernandez (2013, p. 17) noted that CAE is "a qualitative research method that is simultaneously collaborative, autobiographical, and ethnographic." According to Chang, Ngunjiri, Hernandez (2012), many CAE's form from preexisting collegial relationships, often because of common interests. Collaboration with colleagues saves time in establishing rapport and can allow research to begin more quickly. However, this familiarity could also inhibit the participants from seeing new perspectives about each other. In contrast, collaborating with new research partners may allow for a new perspective on a research topic by seeing through the eyes of a stranger.

There is no set number of participants for a CAE team. Previous studies have involved as few as two and as many as 11 researchers. Deciding on a research focus will likely depend on if the CAE group is already formed from existing colleagues or needs to be made from new participants. If a group has already been formed the members must collaborate to find a common topic. However, if a group is new the initiator has the freedom to shape the focus of the research. Despite whatever is the initial focus of the study, it is important to remain open-minded about the direction of the study as collaboration can often lead to new ideas.

Data collection and analysis in CAE involve "a group of researchers pooling their stories to find some commonalities and differences and then wrestling with these stories to discover the meanings of the stories in relation to their sociocultural contexts" (Chang et al., 2013, p. 7). Specific data analytic procedures are decided upon by the research team members, may be borrowed from other qualitative designs, and evolve and change as data collection proceeds. CAE requires both solo and team approaches to data collection and analysis. For example, research team members may independently collect data (e.g., diaries, journals, personal records), engage in solo writing about their experiences, and then come together in team meetings to share their data and written narratives with coresearchers, probe each other to delve deeper into describing their experiences, and identify commonalities and discrepancies in their experiences. Team meetings are also used to identify additional topical areas for each member to write about. Through this process, a collaborative narrative is eventually developed to describe the researchers' collective experiences with the phenomena within a cultural context.

Although autoethnograpy and CAE are not commonly used qualitative approaches by rehabilitation researchers, they are used by disability studies scholars. Birk's (2013) autoethnography illustrates how greater usage of this qualitative approach could enhance our understanding of the experiences of individuals with disabilities in the context of sociopolitical constraints. Birk used personal journals and "voluminous" medical records to reconstruct her story of living with chronic pain for almost three decades. The purpose of her autoethnography was to illuminate the political and public issues inherent in the chronic pain experience. Birk's (2013) autoethnography sheds light on the stigma associated with chronic pain as well as the negative impact of being robbed of one's credibility by physicians who cannot find an "objective" reason for patients' reported pain. She describes the all-too-common experience of being told that one's symptoms are medically unexplainable or psychiatric in nature. She also explores the performative nature (i.e., relying on continual impression management and strategic self-disclosure) taken on in an all-too-often failed attempt to be perceived as credible. She elucidates through the telling of her own story how these "public issues" exacerbate chronic pain, cause intrapersonal damage, and can create the very symptoms of depression and anxiety with which individuals are often initially misdiagnosed. Moreover, Birk uses her experiences to illustrate how both the excruciating effects of severe chronic pain and the biomedical model of disability rob individuals of their voices. Birk (2013, p. 398) concludes her autoethnography by calling for more firsthand narratives and the joining together of individuals with chronic pain to create a common language through which to resist shame and stigma and "embody more empowered narratives of endurance and strength."

Case Study

Qualitative case studies are used to explore an issue or problem using a specific case or multiple cases as exemplifiers (Creswell, 2007). Cases may comprise a single individual, several individuals, a group, a program or organization, or multiple programs and organizations. Cases may be studied because of their uniqueness (i.e., intrinsic case study), to illustrate an issue or problem (i.e., instrumental cases study), or to illustrate an issue or problem through the study of multiple cases (i.e., multisite designs).

Researchers collect extensive data from multiple sources in qualitative case studies. Data sources may include interviews of various stakeholders, archival records, direct observations, participant-observations, archival records, and physical artifacts. In data analysis, case study researchers first provide a detailed description of the case including its history, chronology of events, and daily depictions of the activities of the case. Then researchers identify key issues or themes to illustrate the complexity of the case. When multiple cases are studied, researchers provide detailed descriptions of each case and then proceed to identifying both within- and across-case themes. Data analysis and interpretation conclude with lessons learned by studying the case(s).

Guba and Lincoln (1981, p. 371) further described the qualitative case study design as providing a means of exploring, characterizing, or chronicling events for the purpose of "reveal[ing] the properties of the class to which the instance being studied belongs." Bogdan and Biklen (1992) classified case studies as historical, organizational, and observational.

HISTORICAL ORGANIZATIONAL. Historical organizational case studies focus on a specific organization, examining its development over a certain period of time. Sources of information may include interviewing people who were involved in the organization since its inception, reviewing written records and other types of documentation, and observing the present organization.

OBSERVATIONAL. Observational case studies focus on the current status of a phenomenon within a small group of participants or an organization. Participant observation serves as the main technique employed for data collection. This design concentrates on a specific aspect of the organization (i.e., a particular place, a specific group of people, or a distinct activity) framed in present-tense terms (Bogdan & Biklen, 1992).

As an example of a qualitative case study conducted by rehabilitation researchers, Lindstrom, Flannery, Benz, Olszewski, and Slovic (2009) used a multisite case study design to develop an in-depth understanding of a partnership developed between four community colleges and a state vocational rehabilitation (VR) agency to offer short-term skills training to VR consumers. Because this partnership led to positive employment outcomes for VR consumers, the researchers' purpose was to understand how the partnership was implemented and developed, program characteristics and services that contributed to positive VR outcomes, and changes in the VR agency and community college system that resulted from this partnership. The researchers collected and analyzed multiple data sources including semistructured, in-depth interviews with key stakeholders; group interviews, a written survey, and document reviews. The researchers discovered that the key characteristic of the partnership that contributed to positive outcomes was the collaborative pattern used by the community colleges and VR program that allowed for changes in both systems to occur to improve access and outcomes. Key services that led to positive outcomes included screening and orientation, career exploration and planning, individualized curriculum training plans, additional community college programs and services, progress monitoring, and exit and job placement assistance. Changes that resulted from the partnership included (a) increased awareness of and access to community college programs, and (b) improved abilities for VR consumers to navigate and succeed within community colleges.

Phenomenology

Phenomenology is as much a philosophy as it is a method of research (Creswell, 2007). Guided by phenomenological philosophy, which focuses on how phenomena are perceived in human consciousness, the goal of phenomenological research is to understand the subjective world of the research participants. A phenomenological researcher strives to understand the meanings that individuals confer upon objects, people, situations, and events (Bogdan & Biklen, 1992). Phenomenologists seek to gain an interpretive understanding of the interactions between the person(s) and the environment while suspending their own assumptions (Douglas, 1976). In other words, phenomenologists do not ascribe their own meanings to events and circumstances in the research participant's life. Rather, they endeavor to learn about the conceptual and perceptual world of the people being studied (Geertz, 1973). The perceptual lens through which people view *their* world serves to define their reality. It is *this* reality that phenomenologists attempt to understand. As a method, phenomenology involves extensive interviewing to draw out narratives of experience among a small number of research participants (Creswell, 2003). Most often, research questions are stated broadly without specific reference to the literature. Findings are expressed through a descriptive narrative generated by a synthesis of participants' descriptions of the meanings they make of the phenomena being studied.

Phenomenologists are interested in what all participants have in common as they experience a phenomenon (e.g., being discriminated against, coping with chronic pain, adjusting to civilian life as a female military service member with an amputation). Researchers collect data from persons who have experienced the phenomenon and develop a composite description of the universal essence of the experience for all the individuals (i.e., what they experienced and how they make meaning of their experiences).

Data collection consists of in-depth interviews with 5-25 individuals who have all experienced the phenomenon. Other data sources sometimes include observations, journals, art, poetry, and music. Although phenomenological approaches vary in terms of how data are analyzed, Moustakas (1994) has recommended using the data analysis procedures of horizontalization, identifying clusters of meaning, developing textural and structural descriptions, and creating a composite description of the essence of participants' experiences with the phenomenon under investigation.

In the process of horizontalization, researchers go through the data and highlight significant statements— sentences or quotes that provide an understanding of how the participants experienced the phenomenon. They then develop clusters of meaning, or themes, from the significant statements. Significant statements and themes are used to write a textural description of <u>what</u> the participants experienced and a structural description of the <u>context</u> or <u>setting</u> that influenced how the participants experienced the phenomenon. From the structural and textural descriptions, the researcher writes a composite description that focuses on the essence of the common experiences shared by the participants.

As part of a larger investigation, Hunt, Milsom, and Matthews (2009) used a phenomenological design to understand the perceptions of 25 lesbians with disabilities about how their partners are treated by rehabilitation, counseling, and medical professionals. Using phenomenological data analysis procedures as specified by Moustakas (1994), two overarching themes that emerged from the analysis were how the disability affected the partnership and the varying ways that lesbian partners were treated by professionals.

At the core of their experiences, their disability status required participants and their partners to navigate and negotiate changes in their relationship, and partners played a central role in providing emotional and physical support as well as accessing needed rehabilitation services. However, partners needed more support in adapting to the participants' disability-related needs. Unfortunately, participants were not always recognized as sources of support, and the participants constantly struggled with making decisions about disclosing their partnership status to rehabilitation professionals, which they feared could negatively affect the way they were treated by rehabilitation professionals as well as the type and quality of services they received.

Based on these findings, Hunt et al. (2009) recommended a number of ways that rehabilitation counselors could proactively recognize, and support lesbian couples. These included acting as an information and referral source; helping clients find lesbian-affirming counselors, support groups, and counseling groups; increasing their knowledge about the impact of disability on lesbian sexuality; assisting lesbian couples to learn about legal and financial matters (e.g., domestic partner rights, power of attorney, medical insurance coverage); acting as advocates in accessing needed medical, mental health, and social services; educating other helping professionals about the importance of involving lesbian partners in treatment processes; and educating medical and health care professionals about verbal and written language that contributes to creating a safe and accepting environment for these partners.

Grounded Theory

The grounded theory approach was initially developed by Glaser and Strauss (1967) as a means of "closing the embarrassing gap between theory and empirical research" (p. vii) with a purpose of building a theory that manifests a faithfulness to the phenomenon being studied (Strauss & Corbin, 1990). A systematic set of procedures is used to inductively develop a grounded theory based on research findings related to a specific phenomenon. Concepts and the relationships among concepts are generated and then conditionally tested throughout the data analysis process (Denzin & Lincoln, 2000).

In the use of a grounded theory approach, the researcher does not begin with a specific theory and seek to prove it. Rather, the researcher begins with an area of interest and through the process of gathering data, analyzing the data, and forming concepts and themes, the researcher develops a theoretical formulation from which a framework for action emerges (Strauss & Corbin, 1990). Grounded theory evolves throughout the course of data collection and analysis (Denzin & Lincoln, 2000). As a scientific method, grounded theory is rigorous in data analysis, interpretation, and validation (Creswell, 2014; Denzin & Lincoln, 2000; Glaser & Strauss, 1967; Strauss & Corbin, 1990).

Data analysis is comprised of the identification of words and phrases in a series of coding processes known as open, axial, and selective coding (Strauss & Corbin, 1990).

Open coding involves a process of breaking down data for the purpose of examining, comparing, conceptualizing, and categorizing the data. Conceptual labels (i.e., themes) are constructed for specific happenings, events, or other types of phenomena. As similarities are discovered within the various concepts, they are grouped together in a new, more abstract collective called a category (Strauss & Corbin, 1990).

Axial coding is used to integrate the data, or emerging themes, in new ways by making connections between categories. Causal conditions such as events, incidents, and happenings that lead to the occurrence or development of a specific type of situation or phenomenon are explored as they lead to an emerging theory (Haworth & Conrad, 1997). This process is a necessary step in building the concepts from the open coding step previously discussed.

Selective coding provides a means of integrating information and produces a higher level of systematic analysis through a series of steps that are not necessarily linear. The first step involves the conceptualization of the "story line" (i.e., the core or primary category) identified in the previous stages of coding (open and axial). The next steps consist of relating similar categories to the core/primary category and validating those relationships by referring back to the data for corroboration (Strauss & Corbin, 1990).

Emerging relationships among categories are tested by deliberately searching for contradictory evidence. If contradictory evidence is discovered, the initial categories are revised to incorporate the new evidence. This process is repeated until categories are sufficient to account for all of the various pieces of evidence; at such point, data collection is ceased. This point is referred to as theoretical saturation. Theoretical saturation occurs when new data emerging from interviews or other data sources no longer require a revision of the theory, when the categories have been well developed, and when the relationships among categories have been clearly established (Strauss & Corbin, 1990).Glaser and Strauss (1967) identified the following criteria for determining the applicability of a grounded theory of a central phenomenon: fit, understanding, and generality. Fit is accomplished if the theory is considered to reflect the everyday reality of the area being studied. If the theory is carefully induced from diverse data, then the theory should be "understandable" to the individuals who participated in the research project and to others (Strauss & Corbin, 1990). In achieving generality, the interpretations must be conceptual in nature, broad enough to yield an abstractable quality, and include the various contexts related to the phenomenon being studied.

Grounded theory is a qualitative approach often used by rehabilitation researchers. For example, Conyers (2004) used grounded theory to explore the employment concerns of individuals with HIV/AIDS diagnoses. Participants in her study included 46 individuals from diverse backgrounds reflective of the emerging demographics of the disease. Using five focus groups to collect data, Conyers queried participants about the impact of HIV/AIDS on employment considerations, motivating factors influencing employment considerations, and barriers to employment.

Three thematic categories emerged from Conyers' data analysis: (a) the impact of HIV/AIDs on employment considerations, (b) motivation to work, and (c) barriers to employment. Subthemes of the impact of HIV/AIDS on employment considerations included changes in medical and societal beliefs about HIV/AIDS and attempts to integrate these changed beliefs into the participants' own self-concepts and employment efficacy; vulnerabilities in their physical, emotional, and financial statuses and their influence on employment considerations; expectations of others about participants' capacities to work; personal adjustment to HIV/AIDS diagnoses; and substance abuse. Factors influencing motivation to work included limited financial resources, gaining or regaining a vocational identity, mental health, the negative effects of unemployment on family relationships and responsibilities, and the threat of loss of medical, social, and financial benefits and services. Barriers to employment included fears regarding loss of medical and financial benefits, worries about how the unpredictability of HIV/AIDS would affect employment, concerns about how working would impact their ability to attend medical appointments, and doubts about their employability.

The themes that emerged in Conyers' data analysis and interpretation supported constructs and processes in Szymanski's and Hershenson's (1998) ecological model of career development. However, Conyers suggested that the model needs to be expanded to be more applicable to understanding the experiences of individuals with HIV/AIDS. This expansion should increase the model's emphases on (a) the role of mediating factors (e.g., vocational identity, self-efficacy, societal attitudes, family support, stigma, access to resources, disability benefits policies) in understanding the employment concerns of people with HIV/AIDS, and (b) how the developmental process is interpreted in relation to emergent disabilities.

Dispenza et al. (2016) used a modified grounded theory design to investigate specific strategies that rehabilitation counselors used when working with sexual minorities with chronic illnesses and disabilities (CIDs). The researchers used a semi-structured protocol to interview 12 certified rehabilitation counselors about the phenomena being investigated. Using a constant comparative analysis with open, axial, and selective coding, a model of affirmative intersectional rehabilitation counseling emerged from the data analysis.

The researchers defined affirmative intersectional rehabilitation counseling as "a dynamic means of delivering rehabilitation counseling services to sexual minorities living with CIDs. As a core construct, it considers the various forms of oppression that are associated with possessing both a sexual minority identity and a CID, while supporting and encouraging a sense of pride for possessing both identities simultaneously" (Dispenza et al., 2016, p. 148). Within this model, the researchers included professional attributes, alliance, intersectional sensitivity, and intersectional interventions as categories of affirmative intersectionality.

CONSENSUAL QUALITATIVE RESEARCH

Hill, Thompson, and Williams (1997) developed consensual qualitative research (CQR) in response to frustrations of vague descriptions of qualitative research approaches that were difficult to comprehend and implement. Consensus, being an integral part of this method "relies on mutual respect, equal involvement, and shared power" (Hill et al., 1997, p. 523). The five essential components of CQR are: (a) the use of open-ended questions in semistructured interviews; (b) the involvement of several judges throughout the data analysis process to bring about multiple perspectives; (c) eventual consensus between judges about the meaning of the data; (d) the use of at least one auditor to minimize the effects of groupthink and to check the work of judges; and (e) data analysis that involves the development of domains, core ideas, and cross-analyses.

Consensual qualitative research (CQR), like all qualitative research, is an inductive method that incorporates elements from phenomenology, grounded theory, and comprehensive process analysis. An emphasis in CQR is placed on consensus among judges in the construction of research findings. This constructivist approach to understanding reality recognizes that there are multiple realities or versions of what constitutes truth and all are equally valid. In data analysis, CQR researchers search for commonalities among research participants in their experiences and construction of meanings of their experiences.

CQR sampling involves random selection from a homogeneous population of research participants who are experts on the phenomenon under investigation. The recommended sample size in CQR is 8–15 participants. The primary source of data is collected from semi-structured interview protocols with questions developed from the literature on the phenomena of study. The role of the interviewer in CQR is usually as a "trustworthy reporter trying to uncover what the participant truly believes" (Hill et al., 2005, p. 197). Hill et al. have recommended conducting at least two interviews with each participant to ensure that researchers are able to obtain a rich understanding of the participants' experiences. Researchers follow three steps when conducting CQR data analysis: developing and coding domains, constructing core ideas, and developing categories to describe consistencies across cases (Hill et al., 1997).

In response to the growing need of state-federal vocational rehabilitation (VR) programs to demonstrate the effectiveness of VR services, Del Valle et al. (2014) used a modified CQR approach within a multiple case study design to identify organizational elements and service delivery practices of four high-performing state VR agencies. The primary sources of data that were collected and analyzed were administrative reports and semi-structured interviews (both individual and focus group) with administrators, midlevel managers, and VR counselors.

The results of the researchers' analyses revealed both systematic agency changes that promoted innovative VR service delivery practices and promising service delivery practices (Del Valle et al., 2014). Examples of systematic agency changes included encouragement from high-level administrators to "think outside the box," creation of specialized VR units to pilot new service delivery practices, the use of SharePoint for VR counselors to post-innovative ideas and best practices, implementation of a dual service delivery approach that views both individuals with disabilities and employers as consumers, use of a rapid delivery approach to service provision, and the development of specialized caseloads.

Promising service delivery practices included the outsourcing of the nonessential functions of VR counselors; training and certification for the staff of community rehabilitation programs; use of web-based cloud technology to bring together job-ready consumers with potential employers; provision of soft skills training to consumers, provision of work incentive planning and benefits counseling to consumers; formation of partnerships with other agencies and programs to share funding and develop seamless, better coordinated services; and a shift of focus from obtaining a single job to career counseling. The researchers concluded that the culture of an organization is an imperative factor in developing and sustaining innovative practices. VR agencies need to reconsider traditional rehabilitation counselor roles and offer new methods for delivering services if they are to remain viable.

GENERIC QUALITATIVE RESEARCH

Many researchers whose articles are published in rehabilitation journals either (a) draw on various qualitative methods to answer their research questions, or (b) do not identify the use of any specific qualitative design. Caelli, Ray, and Mill (2003) refer to these types of studies as generic qualitative designs. Generic qualitative research studies are described by Caelli et al (2003, p. 2) as:

> Those that exhibit some or all of the characteristics of qualitative endeavor but rather than focusing the study through the lens of a known methodology they seek to do one of two things: either they combine several methodologies or approaches, or claim no particular methodological viewpoint at all.

In generic qualitative research, the purpose is to simply understand and describe a phenomenon or process from the perspectives of research participants rather than to, for example, generate a theory based on the data as is the purpose of grounded theory research or to understand culture as is the purpose of ethnography (Caelli, et al., 2003). In generic qualitative research, the lenses used by researchers to analyze and interpret data are typically derived from the theories, models, and concepts in their disciplinary literature. Data analysis and interpretation involve the identification of recurring patterns, categories, or themes as well as clinical applications that help to further illuminate the disciplinary literature.

Some research questions may indeed be unanswerable using established designs. However, in using generic designs, researchers must still adhere to standards of methodological coherence (to be discussed in the methods section of this chapter). Establishing methodological coherence is more difficult when using generic designs than it is in using established designs. To address this problem, Caelli et al. (2003) recommended that researchers using generic approaches (a) explicitly address the theoretical positioning of the researchers, (b) the coherence of their methodological decisions with the research questions, methods, and conclusions drawn from their investigations, and (c) strategies used to ensure rigor of their investigations, and (d) the analytic lens through which they made sense of and interpreted the meaning of the data.

Roessler, Rumrill, and Timblin (in press) used a generic approach to conduct focus groups to elicit perspectives on the highest-priority employment barriers facing Americans with MS (i.e., barriers related to the Affordable Care Act, workplace accommodations and the ADAAA, job reassignment, and disclosure of disability) that were identified by participants in a previous study conducted by the researchers (Rumrill et al., 2015). Six focus groups of people with MS ($n=20$) and MS service providers ($n=27$) were conducted in three states and Washington, DC to identify the meaning that stakeholders ascribed to these barriers and strategies to remediate barriers.

The researchers used purposeful sampling to recruit participants for the focus groups. Each focus group was conducted by one of the researchers who presented the high-priority employment concerns to the focus group participants and elicited their perspectives regarding these concerns and their suggestions about how to address the concerns. Personnel of participating NMSS chapters took field notes during the focus groups, using the participants' words to describe their perspectives and offer potential solutions.

Data analysis involved an initial individual reading of all field notes resulting from the focus groups. Without consulting with other members of the research team, each researcher listed the employment problem under discussion and all strategies mentioned by consumers and service providers in their words as closely as possible. Then investigators met to review their lists of strategies, discuss differences in perceptions, review transcripts when necessary, and reach consensus about how to phrase the strategies consistent with group member input. Because members of the research team conducting the analysis had each participated in two or more focus group sessions, they were familiar with the way in which participants discussed employment problems and strategies to reduce or resolve those problems. The findings were further validated by asking two of the note takers to verify that the consensual strategy statements developed by the research team were consistent with their understanding of focus group input.

Focus group participants agreed that the high-priority concerns identified in the quantitative survey were relevant to their own experiences and discussed strategies that focused primarily on education and advocacy to remove or reduce the previously identified barriers. Their recommendations included increasing access for people with MS to information regarding Federal laws such as the Affordable Care Act and the ADAAA, more responsive services from health care providers regarding employment issues, self-advocacy training for people with MS to more effectively assert their rights in the workplace, and clearer procedures for disclosing disability and requesting needed on-the-job accommodations.

As another example, Cartwright, Washington, and McConnell (2009) used a generic qualitative approach to study the experiences of microaggressions among African American faculty members in CORE-accredited rehabilitation counselor education programs. Extending on prior research on the incidence of microaggressions against African American faculty members in counselor education and counseling psychology programs, the researchers conducted semi-structured telephone interviews with 15 participants. Data were analyzed for common themes, and interrater agreement was calculated to verify the themes.

Seven themes were identified in the data analysis: (a) feelings of being invisible and marginalized alternating with feelings of being hypervisible; (b) having colleagues, staff members, and students challenge their qualifications and credentials; (c) lack of access to adequate mentoring; (d) being expected to perform service-oriented roles that are perceived by institutions as being of low value; (e) difficulties determining if microaggressions were based on race, gender, or both; (f) coping strategies used to deal with microaggressions; and (g) experiences of unequal or different treatment by their institutions. The impact of these microaggressions on the participants included increased anxiety regarding tenure, personal diminishment, discouragement, frustration, and exhaustion resulting from constant scrutinization.

Based on these findings, Cartwright et al. (2009) recommended (a) ongoing professional training, research, and dialogue to increase awareness of and sensitivity to the effects of microaggressions on faculty of color and (b) the development of more effective approaches to modify behaviors, improve work environments, and retain faculty of color in CORE-accredited programs. The researchers also recommended strategies that can be used by junior faculty of color to cope with microaggressions such as becoming more determined to succeed, choosing their battles, and extending their support networks beyond the institutions within which they are employed.

QUALITATIVE META-SYNTHESES

Qualitative meta-syntheses are used to summarize, synthesize, and interpret the findings from a number of qualitative investigations into a specific phenomenon (Finfgeld-Connett, 2016). Hammel (2007) described the five phases of meta-syntheses as (a) determining the focus of the meta-synthesis,

(b) identifying papers relevant to the focus, (c) evaluating the rigor and quality of identified papers, (d) identifying and summarizing key themes from each paper, and (e) comparing and synthesizing themes across studies into new concepts.

Meta-syntheses require researchers to carefully select a collection of articles that address the purpose of the meta-synthesis. Analytic techniques vary and are borrowed from techniques used in other qualitative research designs. Meta-syntheses enable researchers to develop new concepts, frameworks, and theories as well as to expand those that already exist. They offer an empirical foundation for guiding evidence-based practices and fine-tuning these practices to the realities of the research participants. Meta-syntheses also are also used to generate research hypotheses and to inform policy and practice guidelines.

Hammel (2007) conducted a meta-synthesis of qualitative research for the purpose of identifying, comparing, and synthesizing the factors found to contribute to or detract from experiencing high levels of quality of life following the onset of spinal cord injury. The researcher identified published articles from Medline, CINAHL, and Sociological Abstracts databases. This search was supplemented by a hand search through relevant journals published since 1990 and identification of papers in reference lists. Hammel located 64 papers and four books, of which seven papers met criteria for relevance to the focus of the review and research rigor and quality. From these seven papers, 10 main concepts that impacted perceptions of QOL were identified, including: body problems, loss, relationships, responsibility for, and control of one's life, occupation, and ability to contribute, environmental context, new values/perspective, transformation, good and bad days, self-worth, and self-continuity.

Limitations of Qualitative Research

In judging the empirical soundness of qualitative research studies, one must keep in mind that the objective of qualitative research is fundamentally different from that of quantitative research. In qualitative research, the emphasis is placed upon understanding the subjective meaning that people give to their world, not to make broad generalizations and verify causal relationships between variables (Maxwell, 1996). Thus, the notion of empirical soundness (reliability and validity) takes on a different meaning in qualitative research. Scientific rigor and credibility are no less of a concern to qualitative researchers than they are to quantitative researchers. In fact, qualitative researchers adhere to well-established procedures (detailed in the preceding section of this chapter) to ensure the accuracy and trustworthiness of their findings.

Qualitative research (like all research) is not without its limitations. The data collected in qualitative studies, for example, are often in the form of self-reports. Self-reports can introduce error to a study because they require individuals to reconstruct their experiences with the phenomena of interest (Polkinghorne, 1991). To accomplish this, research participants often have to rely on their memories. As we know, our memories are not always 100 percent accurate, and how we remember our past experiences is often heavily influenced by our current experiences and perceptions.

Qualitative researchers as the "instruments of data collection" can introduce additional limitations to a study. They must be cognizant of how their role is perceived by research participants and how they influence the manner in which participants communicate with the researcher (e.g., what information is shared and what information is withheld). In addition, as previously mentioned, the researcher's own biases may lead to misinterpretations of meaning (Creswell, 2003). Therefore, researchers must be aware of the potential influence of their preconceptions on the selection and interpretation of observations (Murphy & Salomone, 1983). Additional limitations of qualitative research may include problems that occurred in data collection, unanswered questions by research participants, unexplored topics during data collection, or the need for better sampling of participants or sites for inclusion in the study (Creswell, 2012).

Finally, the intent of qualitative research is for the researchers to develop a unique interpretation rather than generalize findings, as is done in quantitative research. However, transferability (the extent to which findings are applicable to other contexts and settings) can be a limitation if the researcher does not provide sufficient descriptive details that can be used by readers to determine if findings can be applied to their settings. The researcher can supersede this limitation by addressing the central assumptions, the selection of participants, and biases; thereby, enhancing the possibility of replicating the study in another setting or applying the findings to other contexts (Creswell, 2003).

SUMMARY

Qualitative research is conducted with the purpose of exploring, explaining, or describing phenomena from the perspectives of research participants or engaging participants in emancipatory processes of social critique and action. The strength of qualitative approaches, as applied in rehabilitation research, resides in giving voice to the lived experiences of people with disabilities and in developing detailed descriptions of these experiences. Qualitative studies often formulate a basis for additional research, including studies that use quantitative methods. Qualitative methods can also provide illumination on the data collected in large-scale quantitative research (i.e., use of consumer focus groups to interpret the meaning of survey results and make policy recommendations).

Qualitative research provides a mechanism for conveying information through the use of "rich" and "thick" descriptions, thereby permitting a deeper understanding of the research participant's experiences and points of view. In asking individuals to describe their worlds and their experiences with phenomena such as QOL, coping, stigma, employment concerns, discrimination, and rehabilitation policies and practices, rehabilitation researchers can gain a deeper understanding of the perspectives of people with disabilities. Practitioners can incorporate what they have learned from research participants into improving their practices and advocating for policy changes to better meet their needs. Finally, qualitative research empowers people with disabilities by going beyond giving voice to involving them in making changes to policy and service delivery mechanisms to better address their rehabilitation needs.

The authors of this chapter and the previous chapter have endeavored to provide readers with an overview of quantitative and qualitative research designs with the hope that the merits of each will be given due consideration. The field of rehabilitation stands to gain immensely from the appropriate application of research designs in the study of the effects of disability on the lives of individuals with whom we work.

Chapter 8

NARRATIVE LITERATURE REVIEWS

INTRODUCTION

The preceding two chapters on quantitative and qualitative research designs present the methods by which researchers conduct investigations involving original or extant data. Indeed, much of this book is devoted to the design, execution, analysis, and reporting of empirically-based research as those activities apply to the lives of people with disabilities and the practice of rehabilitation counseling. However, a discussion of empirical research designs in rehabilitation research does not fully capture the range of techniques that scholars use in building the professional literature. A considerable proportion (more than half in some journals) of articles that appear in the rehabilitation counseling literature is comprised of works whose purpose is to synthesize existing information in a way that contributes new knowledge to the profession.

Broadly defined by Fitzgerald, Rumrill, and Merchant (2015) and Harris, Gould, and Fujiura (2013) as narrative literature reviews, sometimes referred to as scoping literature reviews, these articles make an important contribution to our field. They serve to postulate or advance theories and models, examine important and/or controversial topics in the lives of rehabilitation professionals and consumers, present "how to" strategies to improve field practices, and explain new developments in rehabilitation and disability policy (e.g., laws and their effects, administrative regulations). In so doing, narrative literature reviews frame current issues that must be addressed in future services and research. They describe the current state of both art (i.e., practice) and science (i.e., research) in focused areas of inquiry, add dimensions of insight or application that are not available in existing literature, and provide critical analyses of standing works. Thus, the concept of scholarship encompasses much more than the numerous empirical designs described to this point in the book; it also includes thoughtful, systematic examinations of the impact, implications, and applications that researchers derive from reading the work of others.

We have organized our discussion of narrative literature reviews around broad categories reflecting the overarching purposes of selected articles. We do not categorize them by topic area, although the works that we summarize and review in this chapter were purposively chosen to represent the wide range of subject matter that is embodied in the rehabilitation literature. With that in mind, this chapter describes narrative literature reviews of four types: Theory or Model-Building Articles, Treatises on Complicated or Controversial Issues, Informational Reports and How-To Strategies to Enhance Professional Practice, and Explanations of Emerging and Important Issues.

THEORY/MODEL-BUILDING

One of the recurring and most important themes of this book is that theory both prompts and results from scientific inquiry. Theory provides the conceptual basis from which investigators deduce the specific relationships among variables or propositions that are evaluated using empirical observations drawn from particular samples. In many cases, the results of scientific efforts to test theory-based propositions lead researchers to suggest modifications in existing theories, thereby adding new knowledge that transcends the findings of a particular investigation. Theory also serves to bridge the qualitative versus quantitative dichotomy; theory is, by definition, grounded in a qualitative understanding of human phenomena. It is dynamic, subjective, and based in the theorist's individual reality—but its evaluation is dependent upon objective (quantitative, if you will) and replicable methods that are used to test propositions under the most stringent knowledge-generating warrants.

The field of rehabilitation counseling, like the social sciences in general, lacks a unifying theoretical base upon which client services, counselors' professional identities, and preservice training are founded. It is our impression that the many social scientific theories that have been posited and tested over the past 100 years provide a menu of sorts from which rehabilitation professionals choose in applying their individual practices to broader explanations of human behavior. Indeed, we believe that there is no need for rehabilitation counseling to develop a single, overarching explanatory framework for the profession. We do believe that it is imperative for our field to become more aware of the utility and relevance of theory as it applies to both practice and research. Hence, we will highlight several recent articles that have advanced theories or models to explain phenomena that have bearing on the lives of people with disabilities and on the rehabilitation process. These will include recent works that present broader disability-related and/or developmental theories that frame the experience of disability in societal or developmental contexts. We will then review recent works that present theories or models related to the rehabilitation process, including counselor and client roles in the process.

Theories or Models Related to the Disability Experience

Lustig and Strauser (2007) presented a Poverty Disability Model to explain the processes through which individuals who live in poverty are more likely to acquire a disability. Although there is considerable research to explain why disability causes poverty, why poverty may cause disability is not well understood (Hartley, 2012; Koch & Rumrill, 2016; Strauser, 2013). Synthesizing literature and empirical work in various areas of study, Lustig and Strauser noted that poverty is associated with four groups of effects: (a) social role devaluation, (b) environmental risk factors, (c) negative group influences, and (d) weakened sense of coherence. Overall, poverty causes a reduction in access to resources that impact whether an individual acquires a chronic health problem or disability, and the confluence of the four risk factors places individuals at greater risk for acquiring a significant disability. Their model is a promising theoretical framework of construct relations that helps to explain the reciprocal relationships among poverty and disability. The specific construct relations posited by Lustig and Strauser may be tested either as a whole or in part in future empirical studies. The model also has numerous implications for disability policy and rehabilitation practice.

The World Health Organization (WHO) issued the revised *International Classification of Functioning, Disability and Health (ICF)* in 2001 following years of preparation by task forces representing various professional and academic disciplines (WHO, 2001). The ICF employs an ecological framework of health and disability to describe impairments, activities and activity limitations, and participation and participation limitations in the context of personal and environmental characteristics that moderate the progression from impairments to social outcomes. The ICF model closely reflects the purposes, policy, and practice of the state-Federal Vocational Rehabilitation (VR) program (Rubin, Roessler, & Rumrill, 2016) and also reflects current Federal policies and goals as indicated in the Workforce Innovation and Opportunity Act of 2014 (Rumrill & Koch, 2014). The ICF model has generated considerable interest among rehabilitation researchers. Frain et al. (2015) applied the ICF model in their scoping review of literature related to labor force participation among people with multiple sclerosis. Strauser (2013) presented the ICF as an explanatory framework for understanding the impact that cancer and other chronic illnesses have on the career development of young adults. We anticipate that the ICF will continue to be a useful model for rehabilitation counseling research in the next decades.

Hershenson (1996) presented a systems reformulation of his developmental model of work adjustment for people with disabilities. Hershenson's model casts the worker in a social-political-economic context wherein he or she interacts with a number of systems and environments, including the rehabilitation services system, the independent living environment, the working environment, and the family environment. Hershenson posited an ecological model in which reciprocal interactions among environmental and personal characteristics take place over time and result in the unique work personality, work competencies, and work goals that reflect a person's orientation to vocational activities. These reciprocal influences result in manifest work adjustment, which Hershenson operationalized in terms of work role behaviors, task performance, and work satisfaction.

Arguably, Hershenson's ecological model is the most comprehensive conceptual framework in existence that explains the dynamics of vocational adjustment for people with disabilities. Not only does it delineate and then integrate personal and environmental influences as they apply to work; it also frames this developmental process in the context of rehabilitation counselors' roles and functions. As the chief representative of the rehabilitation services system, the counselor must continually gauge the interaction of the individual client in his or her family, independent living, and work environments. Hence, along with providing a structure for conceptualizing the work adjustment process for rehabilitation clients, Hershenson's model serves to explain the role of ecologically-minded rehabilitation counselors in a holistic service milieu.

In the context of career development, Roessler (2002) advanced a Three M model of job acquisition and retention for people with disabilities. The three Ms emphasize the *match* between the person and the demands of particular jobs, career *maturity* as it enables people to make informed occupational choices, and career *mastery* as the ultimate end goal of vocational rehabilitation. Also in keeping with the dynamic, developmental conception of career choice and advancement, the INCOME framework initiated by Beveridge, Craddock, Liesener, Stapleton, and Hershenson (2002) and refined by Hershenson (2005, 2010) explicates a sometimes sequential, sometimes cyclical process involving key career development activities such as imagining, informing, choosing, obtaining, maintaining, and exiting. Hershenson (2015) extended the INCOME model to include the plans and choices people make as they exit the labor force and pursue their retirement goals.

Perhaps most importantly, the conceptual frameworks described by Roessler (2002), Beveridge et al. (2002), and Hershenson (2005, 2010, 2015) are not disability-specific. Rather, they are conceived to reflect the career development experiences of individuals regardless of disability status, although the unique and disability-specific needs of people with disabilities may affect the ways that rehabilitation counselors implement those models in their practices.

Finally, a number of theories and models have been advanced to explain the process of adjustment or adaptation to chronic illness and disability, one of the most widely researched subjects in our field. Given the large number of recent contributions in this area, we will note only a small sample of these. Livneh's (2001) integrative framework of adaptation to chronic illness unifies three sets of variables that have been found to influence psychosocial adjustment: antecedents or triggering events (including causes of disability), dynamic adaptive responses (internally and externally expressed), and psychosocial outcomes that serve as indicators of healthy and unhealthy adaptation. Livneh (2016) expanded his theory of adaptation to chronic illness and disability, emphasizing the importance of personal-level and community-level interventions to promote active coping and improve people's prospects for long-term quality of life. Bishop (2012) presented an update on the Disability Centrality model to integrate subjective quality of life with adaptation to chronic illness and acquired disability (CIAD). In this model, centrality refers to the importance that an individual attributes to an area of life that is altered by the onset of CIAD. Bishop posited that people respond to this reduction in domain quality of life by making adaptive changes in either domain importance or domain control. Livneh and Parker (2002) utilized concepts from chaos and complexity theory to better explain psychological adaptation to disability. They noted that dynamic systems (i.e., living systems) are non-linear (i.e., neither fully random nor fully deterministic) and exhibit characteristics of self-organization and self-similarity. Chaos is a necessary transitional phase before dynamic systems reorganize themselves and achieve a new, more adaptive pattern. Livneh and Parker observed that concepts drawn from chaos and complexity theory are helpful in understanding the challenges and processes associated with adjustment to acquired disability or chronic illness and in developing interventions to facilitate more optimal adjustment.

Theoretical Models of Rehabilitation Processes and/or Counselor and Client Roles

Kosciulek (2004) presented the model of rehabilitation service provision developed and utilized by the Longitudinal Study of the Vocational Rehabilitation Services Program (LSVRSP; RTI International, 2002). The LSVRSP model posits that rehabilitation outcomes are the result of the interactions among several sets of variables: applicant characteristics, services and service costs, organizational culture and resources, and local economic conditions and population characteristics. Kosciulek noted that the LSVRSP model and database are important resources for rehabilitation research, enabling basic research (particularly the testing of complex theoretical models of service provision and a set of reporting outcomes agreed upon by various stakeholders), rehabilitation counseling practice, rehabilitation counselor education, and policy evaluation and development.

A number of scholars have developed conceptual frameworks for the rehabilitation process or for specific aspects of clients' and counselors' respective roles in the rehabilitation process. For example, Kosciulek (1999) advanced the Consumer-Directed Theory of Empowerment (CDTE) to guide the development of a disability services model that incorporates an orientation of consumer direction, whereby informed consumers have control over the policies and practices that directly affect their lives. The major tenet of the CDTE is that increased consumer direction in disability policy formulation and rehabilitation service delivery will lead to increased community integration, empowerment, and quality of life for people with disabilities. Toriello and Keferl (2012) applied similar principles in their "renaissance of consumer autonomy" model, suggesting that empowerment and self-determination are the ultimate end goals of the rehabilitation process rather than factors that merely make the process easier for counselors to manage (p. 17).

Hershenson (1998, 2010) cast rehabilitation counseling practice within an ecological, macrosystemic framework, underscoring the interactions that rehabilitation counselors have with families, clients' peers and reference groups, educational and learning environments, employers, other service providers, and the structure within which rehabilitation services are delivered. Hershenson (2000, 2010) also presented a model of disability and rehabilitation, rooted in cultural anthropology, that places strong emphasis on environmental and contextual factors in explaining how rehabilitation clients and counselors interact in planning, implementing, and evaluating services. Bishop, Chou, Chan, Rahimi, Chan, and Rubin (2000) applied a wellness promotion framework to case management practices in private-sector rehabilitation. Kampfe and Dennis (2000) proposed a social stress model to explain variations in behavior and outcomes among people from similar cultural backgrounds. Chapin (2012) applied positive psychology principles to the counselor-client relationship in a variety of rehabilitation settings, resulting in a model of counselor-client interactions based on accentuating the client's assets and virtues rather than reducing his or her disability-related deficits.

TREATISES ON COMPLICATED OR CONTROVERSIAL TOPICS

Another important role of the narrative literature review in rehabilitation research is to identify, explain, and provide persuasive perspectives on complicated or controversial issues in the lives of people with disabilities and rehabilitation professionals. Typically, these treatises begin by tracing the history of the issue, then proceed with a description of its current status and implications for policy and practice. Finally, the author concludes with recommendations regarding how to best address the issue, often accompanied by a "call to action" for policymakers, practitioners, and/or people with disabilities. We categorize these treatises on complicated or controversial topics into four broad areas: professional identity issues, professional ethics, multicultural competencies and related training issues, and miscellaneous topics.

Professionals Identity Issues

One of the most controversial topics in our field over the past several years has centered on the identity of the rehabilitation counselor in today's academic and professional marketplace. Arguing that rehabilitation counseling has its theoretical and clinical roots in the well-established disciplines of counseling and psychology, Mpofu (2000) recommended that rehabilitation counseling be reconceptualized as a specialty sub-field within either or both of those more established disciplines. Mpofu's article prompted opposing reactions by Havraneck (2000), Hennessey (2001), and Hershenson (2000b), all of whom underscored the status of rehabilitation counseling as a freestanding helping profession with such distinctive features as its own accrediting body, a well-developed knowledge base, clearly delineated standards of practice, and a defined clientele.

In regard to professional identity, debate continues in the professional community as to whether training, educational, placement, and marketing efforts of Rehabilitation Counselor Education (RCE) programs should be directed toward expanding the roles and client bases of rehabilitation counselors or toward deepening the specialized skills that rehabilitation counselors bring to the American systems of human services and workforce development. Jenkins and Strauser (1999) advocated a "horizontal expansion" (p. 4) of rehabilitation services into corporate America, asserting the need for rehabilitation counselors to view employers as customers in such settings as disability management and employee assistance programs. Chapin (2012) discussed new opportunities in job development and placement for rehabilitation counselors resulting from changes in the meaning of work in contemporary society and in the way work is performed (e.g., telecommuting, technology interface). Hawley, McMahon, Reid, and Shaw

(2000) highlighted potentially burgeoning opportunities for rehabilitation counselors in such professional settings as disability management, addictions counseling, and problem gambling treatment. Taking an alternative point of view, Hennessey (2001) cautioned expansion-minded rehabilitation counselors against expanding the profession into an overgeneralist "jack of all trades, master of none" status. She noted the unique product lines and services that rehabilitation counselors now claim, especially with regard to vocational assessment, job placement, and career planning–and she aptly suggested that those niches had emerged as a result of decades of specialization and focused advocacy on behalf of the profession.

Whether rehabilitation counselors should view themselves as generalists or specialists, there is no doubt that they must continually update their skills and knowledge as new practice domains emerge and traditional practice domains change. Crystal and Espinosa (2012) urged rehabilitation counselors to familiarize themselves with the Affordable Care Act and other health care reform measures to better assist clients in managing their mental and physical health. Wickert, Dresden, and Rumrill (2013) noted that the changing age demographic in America requires rehabilitation counseling and health care professionals to develop proficiencies for working with people who acquire disabilities related to aging (e.g, arthritis, heart disease, visual impairments, hearing impairments, cancer, diabetes, dementia). Atherton and Toriello (2012) described emerging issues in the treatment of substance use disorders that integrate contemporary models of addiction and take into account the increased incidence of addiction to prescription medication that has been observed among rehabilitation clients who are coping with chronic pain. Smith, Dillahunt-Aspillaga and Kenney (2015) presented guidelines for rehabilitation counselors to follow in integrating customized employment for people with intellectual and developmental disabilities into the state-Federal VR program.

The topic of professional identity has also been central to discussions regarding the decision to merge their respective accrediting bodies by the officers representing the Council on Rehabilitation Education (CORE) and the Council for Accreditation of Counseling and Related Educational Programs (CACREP). In this context, Patterson, McFarlane, and Sax (2005) discussed a number of compelling reasons for retaining CORE as a separate entity rather than integrating with CACREP, including emphasizing the unique identity of rehabilitation counselors, maintaining the autonomy of the rehabilitation counseling profession, promoting advocacy and partnerships with people with disabilities, and developing opportunities for accreditation of undergraduate and doctoral rehabilitation education programs. Glenn (2006) provided an alternative perspective in support of the proposed merger of CORE and CACREP and suggested that combining their organizational resources would allow them to be more responsive to the needs of their membership and the students served by these programs. Indeed, the argument in favor of the merger eventually won out, and this writing finds many RCE programs across the United States modifying their curricula, adding courses in mental health counseling, changing the credentials required for RCE faculty members, and formally affiliating with other counseling programs to meet the new demands of joint CORE and CACREP accreditation.

Professional Ethics

In recent years, the once-straightforward topic of professional ethics has emerged as a complicated and controversial issue for rehabilitation educators, researchers, and counselors alike. The requirement that Certified Rehabilitation Counselors (CRCs) obtain 10 continuing education contact hours of ethics training during each five-year certification cycle has created a cottage industry of rehabilitation ethicists who provide, for a fee, in-person consultation and on-line training for practitioners regarding appropriate professional conduct (Cartwright & Hartley, 2016). At the same time, the *Code of Professional Ethics for Rehabilitation Counselors* (Commission on Rehabilitation Counselor Certification [CRCC], 2017) has vastly expanded in recent years, to the point that it is now a 41-page, single-spaced document with ethical standards pertaining to such aspects of our field as the counseling relationship, confidentiality, advocacy and accessibility, professional responsibility, relationships with other professionals, evaluation and assessment, education, evidence-based practice, training, supervision, research, publication, electronic communication, business practices, and procedures for resolving ethical issues. Given the heightened regulation of counselor behavior that our profession has imposed, it should come as no surprise that the subject of ethics currently stands as one of the most widely written-about topics in the field. Rarely is this subject the basis for empirical investigation, but the contemporary rehabilitation literature is replete with narrative literature reviews that call for, describe, and/or interpret ethical standards in various aspects of professional activity.

For example, Burker and Kazukauskas (2010) provided guidance for rehabilitation counselors to abide by the evidence-based practice (EBP) requirements set forth in the 2010 CRCC Code of Ethics. Unfortunately, the profession still lacks consensus agreement concerning the standards and thresholds for considering a practice evidence-based, which makes it difficult if not impossible for practitioners to comply with the EBP ethical standard.

Cartwright and Fleming (2010) discussed multicultural factors related to ethical practice and identified items in the revised *Code of Ethics* that make specific reference to diversity issues in such areas as developing interventions, test selection and interpretation, recruiting and retaining students from diverse backgrounds, and conducting research. Hartley (2012) examined issues of ethics and accountability in rehabilitation counseling practice related to the fact that a sizable proportion of Americans with disabilities live in poverty and must vie for scarce service delivery, living maintenance, and health care resources. Scott (2000) highlighted selected ethical issues germane to addictions counseling. Nunez (2011) enumerated ethical considerations for forensic rehabilitationists who provide expert opinions and testimony in litigation. Case, Blackwell, and Sprong (2016) presented ethical implications related to end of life care for counselors working with clients with terminal illnesses and disabilities. Other rehabilitation ethicists have issued ethical guidelines and interpretations regarding the disclosure of client assessment results (Blackwell, Autry, & Guglielmo, 2001), confirmation bias in clinical judgments about clients (Wright-McDougal & Toriello, 2013), and clinical supervision (Blackwell, Strohmer, Belcas, & Burton, 2002).

Multicultural Competencies and Training Issues

Terms like multiculturalism, cultural diversity, and affirmative action almost always evoke controversies regardless of the context in which those concepts are raised. A number of recent narrative reviews address rehabilitation counselor education and training issues related to multiculturalism. For example, Lewis and Burris (2012) provided recommendations for rehabilitation counselor educators to infuse content regarding the health and employment disparities experienced by members of traditionally underrepresented racial and ethnic groups into preservice training programs. Middleton et al. (2000) collaborated to endorse a set of multicultural competencies that purports to "define a culturally competent rehabilitation counselor" (p. 219). In their holistic approach to multicultural rehabilitation counseling, Stebnicki, Rubin, Rollins, and Turner (2000) offered guidance to rehabilitation educators and agency supervisors who wish to instill multicultural competencies in preservice and practicing rehabilitation counselors. Harley, Alston, and Middleton (2007) discussed the interplay between social justice and rehabilitation counseling to address the marginalization and disenfranchisement frequently experienced by people with disabilities from minority groups. They also provided recommendations for infusing the tenets of social justice into the profession through curricula refinements. Umeasiegbu, Mpofu, and Johnson (2012) provided important global perspectives on disability and rehabilitation, offering multicultural training and direct service recommendations cast within an international context. In another internationally-oriented narrative literature review, Rumrill (2013) compared and contrasted the American and Japanese systems of workforce development and vocational rehabilitation, with an emphasis on the roles and functions of rehabilitation professionals in both societies. Underlying these articles is the notion that the increasing cultural diversity in America and throughout the world requires (a) greater cultural sophistication among rehabilitation counselors in understanding the needs of clients from diverse backgrounds, and (b) new competencies in providing culturally-sensitive and more effective rehabilitation services to meet the needs of these consumer groups.

A number of narrative literature reviews that pertain to multicultural issues highlight the characteristics and/or concerns of rehabilitation consumers from various racial, ethnic, or cultural groups in the United States and provide guidance in the provision of culturally-sensitive rehabilitation services. McKenna and Power (1999) advanced a rationale and method for engaging African American families in rehabilitation planning and service provision. Marshall, Johnson, Saravanabhavan, and Bradford (1992) discussed the rehabilitation needs of Native Americans with disabilities in urban settings. Hampton (2000) examined the rehabilitation needs of Asian Americans and Pacific Islanders with disabilities, and Chen, Jo, and Donnell (2004) discussed obstacles and remedies to the underutilization of vocational rehabilitation and mental health services among Asian Americans. Quinones-Mayo, Wilson, and McGuire (2000) examined cultural considerations that arise in working with Latino populations in the United States. Graf, Reed, and Sanchez (2008) discussed the environmental and cultural factors associated with violence against women with disabilities of Mexican descent and provided recommendations for education of preservice counselors and for culturally sensitive service provision. Marini (2001) addressed cross-cultural counseling issues pertaining to males with acquired disabilities. Mpofu and Harley (2000) and Harley, Mpofu, and Ford (2000) tackled the thorny issue of tokenism among American rehabilitation counselors and rehabilitation agency leaders, respectively. These authors noted that an unavoidable consequence of progressive efforts to increase racial and ethnic diversity among rehabilitation counselors and agency leaders is the perception that race, ethnicity, or, for that matter, disability status is the primary reason behind hiring and promotion decisions rather than the qualifications of applicants.

Other Controversial or Complicated Issues

A variety of other complicated or controversial issues have also been the subject of narrative literature reviews in recent rehabilitation journals. These topics include strategies to move workers with significant disabilities from sheltered workshops to integrated community employment settings (Cimera, 2011), the technology gap between people with and without disabilities (Scherer, 2012), sexual abuse of children with disabilities (Orange & Brodwin, 2005), and men who batter women with disabilities (Peterman & Dixon, 2001). Other recent treatises on controversial or complicated topics include discussions of eugenics, euthanasia, and physician-assisted suicide (Zanskas & Coduti, 2006), right to health care and medical treatment for people with chronic and persistent disabilities (Crystal & Espinosa, 2012), paternalism in community-based efforts to include people with disabilities in public housing and transportation (White, Simpson, Gonda, Ravesloot, & Coble, 2010), and civil rights protections for people with substance use disorders (Atherton & Toriello, 2012).

INFORMATIONAL REPORTS AND "HOW TO" STRATEGIES

One of the most basic, and probably most important, roles of rehabilitation literature is to provide information that can assist educators and practitioners in advancing contemporary standards of best practice. To that end, recent journals in our field are packed with a wealth of informational reports and/or how-to strategies to improve educational programs and services to people with disabilities. We categorize these articles into four broad areas: strategies for practitioners to expand their assessment and service delivery skills, roles and responsibilities of rehabilitation counselors in collaboration with other professionals, strategies to improve training in graduate rehabilitation programs, and informational reports on research methods.

Strategies for Practitioners to Expand Their Assessment and Service Delivery Skills

Many recent articles in rehabilitation journals have presented strategies and guidelines for rehabilitation practitioners to expand their assessment and intervention repertoires. For example, Mpofu, Rosamond, Gitchel, Peterson, and Chou (2012) offered contemporary strategies for person-centered assessments of rehabilitation client's medical, psychosocial, and vocational needs, including a strong emphasis on culturally fair, situational, and ecological evaluation. Bezyak and Clark (2016) described needs assessment strategies to promote physical and mental wellness for college and university students. Olney (2001) presented several communication strategies for rehabilitation counselors to use with persons with severe disabilities to facilitate their self-determination in rehabilitation. She noted that behind each purposeful communicative act is a drive to self-determination, but that, for self-determination to be actualized in rehabilitation, communication partners (e.g., rehabilitation counselors) must learn to apprehend, and respond appropriately to, these messages. Toriello and Keferl (2012) echoed Olney's emphasis on the counselor-client relationship in their recommendations for enhancing consumer autonomy in the rehabilitation process.

Frain, Lee, Roland, and Tschopp (2012) presented strategies to more responsively serve the large numbers of injured combat veterans returning from the Iraq and Afghanistan military theaters. They noted that existing services from state Vocational Rehabilitation agencies and the Veterans Administration do not appear sufficient to meet the complex medical, mental health, and vocational challenges that these veterans face in their efforts to resume civilian life following their injuries. Frain et al. (2012) pointed to the extremely high incidence of traumatic brain injuries among Iraq and Afghanistan veterans as a particularly difficult issue in planning and implementing rehabilitation services. In another "how-to" article regarding military veterans, Smith, Humm, Fleming, Jordan, Wright, Ginger, Wright, Olsen, and Bell (2015) presented a model of virtual reality job interview training for veterans who are coping with post-traumatic stress disorder.

Potts (2005) discussed the importance of social capital in explaining, in part, the high unemployment rates of people with disabilities. She noted that employment options may be expanded by considering social capital, particularly in the form of social networks, as part of a broad-based employment strategy. Potts recommended several strategies for rehabilitation counselors to assist people with disabilities to build more effective social networks to enhance employment. White et al. (2010) aptly noted that the benefits of increasing social capital among people with disabilities go far beyond employment–they suggested that considering social capital as part of the rehabilitation process can yield important and positive outcomes related to physical and mental health, community participation, and overall quality of life for consumers and their families.

Numerous other articles have presented strategies for rehabilitation practitioners to expand their assessment and intervention skills in specific contexts. For example, Scherer (2012) described her cognitive support technology (CST) model for promoting academic and employment success among people with cognitive impairments resulting from traumatic brain injuries, learning disabilities, and multiple sclerosis. The CST approach utilizes universal-access tablet computers such as iPads coupled with cognitive enhancement applications that consumers can download to address such issues as memory, executive functioning, organizational skills, time management, and professional networking.

McHugh, Storey, and Certo (2002) instructed job coaches in the provision of natural supports. Rudstam, Golden, Gower, Switzer, Bruyere, and Van Looy (2014) provided important information on Section 503 of the Rehabilitation Act for rehabilitation professionals whose clients are placed with employers who are Federal contractors. Martinis (2015, p. 221) advanced the "Right to Make Choices" framework for helping young people with disabilities increase their self-determination and avoid guardianship. Koch (2000) advanced a vocational assessment approach rooted in the Americans with Disabilities Act's consumer advocacy requirements. Hagner (2000) identified sound job placement approaches that utilize both primary and secondary labor markets. Bolton (2001b) offered a thorough discussion of instrumentation for measuring vocational rehabilitation outcomes. Moxley, Manela, Finch (2000) discussed the role of program evaluation in effecting organizational change in rehabilitation agencies.

A large number of recent practitioner-focused informational reports pertain to specialized information needed to work more effectively with persons with particular types of disabilities. The following examples represent a small subset of recent informational reports for practitioners. Gordon and Feldman (2002) reviewed the medical, psychosocial, and vocational implications of post-polio syndrome and provided recommendations for rehabilitation assessment and service provision. Wald and Alvaro (2004) reviewed the major psychological factors associated with work-related amputation and provided suggestions for the use of cognitive-behavioral strategies to address these adjustment challenges. Rumrill, Koch, and Wohlford (2013) described the medical and psychological effects of multiple sclerosis and how those effects bear on the provision of vocational services to people with that disease. Koch, Conyers, and Rumrill (2012) described the challenges in case planning and service delivery when working with clients who have rare disorders that are not well-known to medical science. Lustig and Strauser (2001) reviewed the medical, psychosocial, and vocational challenges associated with post-traumatic stress disorder and discussed the implications for rehabilitation planning and vocational development. Hendren (2002) discussed the challenges of Tourette's Syndrome for vocational evaluation and rehabilitation.

Roles and Responsibilities of Rehabilitation Counselors in Collaboration with Other Professionals

Nearly all rehabilitation counselors collaborate with other rehabilitation professionals in providing services, and many counselors work explicitly as part of an interdisciplinary support or service team. Hence, a prominent theme in informational articles over the past few years has been the roles and responsibilities of rehabilitation counselors in collaborating with other professionals. Crystal and Espinosa (2012) described an interdisciplinary case management strategy for rehabilitation counselors working in medical or allied health fields. Balser, Hagner, and Hornby (2000) and Buys and Rennie (2001) detailed models for forming collaborative partnerships between rehabilitation professionals and local business communities. Leech and Holcomb (2000) identified elements of contemporary psychiatric rehabilitation services that serve as inherent impediments to effective interdisciplinary collaboration. Wehman (2013) detailed the interdisciplinary constitution of effective transition teams that provide community living and vocational supports for youth with disabilities. Relatedly, Flannery, Slovic, Treasure, Ackley, and Lucas (2002) developed a process by which vocational rehabilitation professionals can form partnerships with employers, public schools, parents, and other stakeholders to improve employment outcomes for transition-age youth with significant disabilities. Along the same lines, Nittrouer, Shogren, and Pickens (2016) presented established procedures that interdisciplinary teams can use to help young workers with disabilities in formulating their vocational goals and developing effective self-management strategies.

Strategies to Improve Training in Graduate Rehabilitation Programs

Numerous articles in rehabilitation journals provide helpful guidelines for enhancing the quality of training in RCE programs. Davis and Yazak (1998) emphasized the importance of writing across the RCE curriculum, and Riemer-Reiss et al. (2002) discussed the value of professional writing among rehabilitation counseling graduate students. Kampfe, Wadsworth, Smith, and Harley (2005) and Koch et al. (2012) advocated for the infusion of information about aging and disability into the RCE curriculum to help older people with disabilities maintain their economic independence. Wadsworth, Harley, Smith, and Kampfe (2008) provided recommendations for RCE programs to better prepare counselors to assist clients and their families with end-of-life issues by incorporating training specific to these issues in assessment, counseling techniques, advocacy, and professional ethics. Stebnicki (2006) called upon RCE programs to more effectively address spirituality issues in rehabilitation and provided recommendations for infusing spirituality in rehabilitation education and supervision.

Zanskas and Leahy (2007) reviewed the literature on the training needs of rehabilitation counselors entering private sector practice and proposed constructive educational approaches to apply within the CORE curriculum to more effectively prepare for professional practice in these settings. Dallas,

Sprong, and Kluesner (2016) described the principles of universal design for instruction (UDI) and gave strategies for applying UDI in rehabilitation education to provide accessible course content on the basis of individual learner needs. Ehrmann and Herbert (2005) proposed a family-focused interventions course to be incorporated into RCE programs to examine disability from multiple perspectives (e.g., child, sibling, parent).

Informational Reports on Research Methods

Over the years, many articles have been written to introduce readers to various aspects of rehabilitation research such as evidence-based practice (Chronister & Rumrill, 2012), the role of people with disabilities as research partners (Hagner, 2002; White et al., 2010), action research in clinical supervision (Koch & Arhar, 2002), the role of philosophy of science in rehabilitation counseling research (Bellini & Rumrill, 2002), and alternative methods to the scientific approach to rehabilitation counseling research (Stewart, 2002). A 2008 special issue of *Rehabilitation Psychology* (Vol. 53, No. 3) was devoted to advanced research and statistical methods in rehabilitation.

In recent years, several rehabilitation journals have commissioned series of articles on various aspects of scientific inquiry. In those articles, rehabilitation professionals can read current and practical discussions of selected research designs and data analytic techniques including single-subject research (Dixon, 2002), non-parametric statistics (Fitzgerald, Dimitrov, & Rumrill, 2001), structural equation modeling (Merchant, Li, Karpinski, & Rumrill, 2013), conjoint analysis (Chan et al., 2002), differential item functioning (Gitchel, Turner, & Rumrill, 2010), meta-analysis (Bellini, Rumrill, Webb, & Snyder, 1999), and experimental design (Rumrill & Bellini, 1999). Recent stand-alone articles pertaining to specific research methods and issues address such topics as effect size estimates, confidence intervals, and statistical power (Ferrin, Bishop, Tansey, Swett, & Lane, 2007); rehabilitation research ethics (Falvo & Parker, 2000); multiple case study designs and consensual qualitative research analysis (Anderson, Leahy, DelValle, Sherman, & Tansey, 2014); ethnographic research and other qualitative designs (Hanley-Maxwell, Al Hano, & Skivington, 2007); and the Delphi method in rehabilitation research (Vazquez-Ramos, Leahy, & Hernandez, 2007).

EXPLANATIONS OF EMERGING AND IMPORTANT ISSUES

A final category of narrative articles that synthesize existing literature and present new perspectives pertains to the important and emerging issues facing rehabilitation counseling. These articles address such subjects as federal legislation and its implications for people with disabilities, technology, the needs of emerging and/or underserved rehabilitation consumer populations, and international rehabilitation.

Federal Legislation and Its Implications for People with Disabilities

A number of recent narrative literature review articles have addressed new developments in the laws that provide protections and/or funds for direct services for people with disabilities. Rudstam et al. (2014) descried key provisions of the 2014 Workforce Innovation and Opportunity Act (WIOA), which amended and re-authorized numerous aspects of the Rehabilitation Act of 1973. In particular, the WIOA calls for a greater emphasis than ever before on transition into community employment settings for people with disabilities, and closing access to most long-term sheltered workshops by 2016 (Wohl, 2015). The WIOA underscores community employment as the preferred vocational setting for Americans with disabilities (Martinis, 2015; Rumrill & Koch, 2014), and it is expected to result in more widespread availability of supported employment services to people with the most significant disabilities (Rubin et al., 2016).

Crystal and Espinosa (2012) and Wickert et al. (2013) provided narrative descriptions of the 2010 Patient Protection and Affordable Care Act (ACA), which contains several provisions that have important implications for people with disabilities. Not only does the ACA increase access to low-cost health insurance coverage to people who are uninsured and require employers to provide group health insurance coverage for employees who work at least 30 hours per week, it also prohibits health insurance companies from excluding people from coverage based on preexisting conditions. This latter measure holds significant promise for the millions of Americans who are dealing with chronic diseases and health conditions. Also, the ACA prohibits health insurance companies from imposing annual or lifetime "caps" on coverage, a provision that benefits people with the most severe disabilities and the growing population of older individuals who consume an increasing proportion of health care services (Wickert et al., 2013).

Finally, the 2008 Americans with Disabilities Act Amendments Act (ADAAA) has been the subject of narrative literature reviews by a number of authors, including Koch et al. (2012) and Nissen and Rumrill (2014). The ADAAA reversed the trend of narrowing civil rights protections that had resulted from ADA case law over the previous decade (Nissen & Rumrill, 2014). Specifically, the ADAAA added protection for people whose disabilities are temporary in nature; repealed the "mitigating measures" exclusion that had rendered millions of Americans non-disabled under the law as per the Sutton decision and subsequent Supreme Court rulings (currently, only prescription eyeglasses and contact lenses are mitigating measures under the ADAAA that disqualify a person as an individual with a disability); expanded the list of major life activities that can be substantially limited by a person's impairment (especially internal functions that are not readily apparent to others such as those of the endocrine system, normal cell growth, and digestion); reaffirmed that only one major life activity needs to be substantially limited for a person's impairment to qualify as a disability; and issued a list of 13 impairments that are presumed to substantially limit major life activities, thereby qualifying people with those impairments as individuals with disabilities under the law (Job Accommodation Network, 2014; Nissen & Rumrill, 2014). The 13 impairments and the major life activities they are presumed to substantially limit are as follows (Job Accommodation Network, 2014):

- Deafness substantially limits hearing.
- Blindness substantially limits seeing.
- An intellectual disability (formerly mental retardation) substantially limits brain function.
- Partially or completely missing limbs or mobility impairments requiring the use of a wheelchair substantially limit musculoskeletal function.
- Autism substantially limits brain function.
- Cancer substantially limits normal cell growth.
- Cerebral palsy substantially limits brain function.
- Diabetes substantially limits endocrine function.
- Epilepsy substantially limits neurological function.
- Human Immunodeficiency Virus (HIV) infection substantially limits immune function.
- Multiple sclerosis substantially limits neurological function.
- Muscular dystrophy substantially limits neurological function.
- Major depressive disorder, bipolar disorder, post-traumatic stress disorder, obsessive compulsive disorder, and schizophrenia substantially limit brain function.

According to Koch et al. (2012), the ADAAA represents significant progress toward actualizing the original spirit of the ADA, with its reversal of the mitigating measures exclusion and its list of presumptively disabling impairments. Many more people with impairments are now considered individuals with disabilities than was the case following several landmark Supreme Court decisions around the turn of the twenty-first century, decisions that eroded regulatory definitions of disability and, in so doing, undermined the scope of civil rights protections that was promised in the ADA's first iteration in 1990.

Technology

Narrative literature reviews in rehabilitation counseling bear witness to the changing and expanding role that technology plays in contemporary society. Keijer and Breding (2012) noted that the fast pace at which information and communication technology (ICT) has developed has forever changed the way Americans live, work, and communicate. Trends such as miniaturization, on-demand electronic navigation and information-retrieval services, voice recognition, artificial intelligence applications for tablets and smart phones, and voice output will continue to provide opportunities for people to interact with one another in new ways in both virtual and physical environments (Chapin, 2012). Scherer (2012) pointed out that emerging technologies have become an integral part of most tasks in the workplace, even for jobs that previously did not require the use of technology.

Kassberg, Prellwitz, and Lund (2013) described how the widespread use of laptop computers, tablets, and smart phones, which now come fully equipped with ready access to the Internet, enables American workers to exercise tremendous flexibility in the way they do their jobs, including where work is performed; more than three-quarters of American workers telecommute at least part of the time (Chapin, 2012; Strauser, 2013).

Technological advances have created many opportunities for people with disabilities to participate in employment and other aspects of community life, but they also require people with disabilities to stay current in the use of both assistive and general technology if they want to remain competitive in today's dynamic world of work. Unfortunately, many people with disabilities report that they are not proficient in the use of modern technology, often because they cannot afford the latest devices and software programs (Scherer, 2012). Scherer emphasized the utility of general-use technologies such as laptop and tablet computers, smart phones, and hands-free voice activation systems as assistive devices for people with a wide variety of disability-related needs. For people with cognitive impairments resulting from traumatic brain injuries, learning disabilities, and other neurological disorders, Scherer described cognitive enhancement applications or "apps" for tablet computers and smart phones as important aids for improving academic, vocational, and community living outcomes.

Brodwin, Star, and Cardoso (2004) discussed computer-assisted technology for people with a wide range of disabilities. They provided information on alternative input devices (e.g., alternative keyboards, switches, eye tracking devices), alternative input processing aids (e.g., reading and writing aids, electronic reference tools), and alternative output (e.g., motor, visual, auditory, and tactile representation) to facilitate use of computers by people with various disabilities.

To help people with disabilities narrow the technology gap, Scherer (2012) urged rehabilitation professionals to maintain current knowledge of (a) how, where, and with what technology work is done in the diversified global marketplace; (b) general-usage ICT devices and operating systems; and (c) state-of-the-art workplace accommodation strategies that enable people with disabilities to perform job tasks. To the latter end, Rubin et al. (2016) provided a compendium of assistive technology devices and strategeies that help people with a variety of disability-related needs perform personal and social functions. They also described important national-level resources related to workplace accommodations such as the National ADA Centers Network, Abledata, and the Job Accommodation Network.

Needs of Emerging and/or Underserved Rehabilitation Consumer Populations

There is no doubt that one of the most important reasons for the looming changes in the rehabilitation counseling field is the changing needs of our clients and the changing population of people with disabilities. Rehabilitation counselors can expect to provide services to different populations of people with disabilities than were served in past decades. One emerging issue in this regard concerns the needs of women with disabilities. Banks (2008) stressed the importance of culturally relevant services for women with disabilities who are members of traditionally underrepresented racial and ethnic groups. Nosek and Hughes (2003) and Smart (2009) noted that women with disabilities constitute one of the largest, most disadvantaged, and underserved populations in the United States, and that rehabilitation researchers have generally neglected gender-related issues and preferences when designing interventions. Compared to men, women are disadvantaged in regard to socioeconomic status, access to health care, depression, stress, self-esteem, social connectedness, and abuse. These authors also asserted that the life situation of women with disabilities is permeated with attitudinal, social, and economic obstacles to psychosocial well-being.

The issue of violence against women with disabilities has also attracted considerable attention in narrative reviews over the past two decades. Women with disabilities experience emotional, physical, and sexual abuse at similar or higher rates than women in the general population and often experience disability-specific abuse for longer periods of time and from multiple perpetrators, including personal attendants and primary caregivers (Hassouneh-Phillips & Curry, 2002; Glover-Graf & Reed, 2006). As Glover-Graf and Reed noted, numerous empirical studies have indicated extremely high levels of abuse for some categories of women with disabilities. Both of these sets of authors noted that empirical research on abuse of women with disabilities is still in its infancy, and they provided recommendations for rehabilitation counselors regarding practical, public resources to utilize when working with women at risk for abuse. Nosek, Howland, and Hughes (2001) called for the use of more specific definitions in research that distinguish emotional, physical, sexual, and disability-related abuse and concluded that, to increase the capacity of battered women's programs to serve women with disabilities, considerably more needs to be known about interventions that are most effective with this population. Glover-Graf and Reed also provided helpful guidelines for rehabilitation educators to infuse this important topic into rehabilitation education curricula. Other recent rehabilitation scholarship on women's issues has included narrative reviews of the psychosocial and psychospiritual issues facing women with physical disabilities (Nosek & Hughes, 2001, 2003) and female sexuality and spinal cord injury (Miller & Marini, 2004).

The characteristics and needs of people with emerging disabilities is another fertile subject area for recent narrative literature reviews in our field. Koch et al. (2012) defined emerging disabilities as conditions that are either (a) new to medical science, or (b) marked by increased incidence and prevalence in recent years. They described disabilities that are accompanied by pain (e.g., fibromyalgia, cumulative trauma disorders, arthritis, cancer), conditions that are attributable to lifestyle and environmental factors (e.g., diabetes, allergies, asthma, multiple chemical sensitivity), conditions associated with trauma and/or violence (e.g., post-traumatic stress disorder, brain injuries, injuries sustained in military combat), neurodevelopmental disorders (e.g., non-verbal learning disabilities, attention deficit/hyperactivity disorder, Asperger's syndrome, autism), and conditions that increase in incidence as a function of aging (e.g., dementia, sensory impairments, heart disease, orthopedic impairments, various chronic health conditions) as emerging disabilities under that definition. They also noted that rare disorders, that is, medical conditions that affect fewer than 5,000 people in the United States, are increasingly prevalent as medical science develops new and more sophisticated diagnostic procedures.

Wickert et al. (2013) pointed out that people with emerging disabilities often have difficulty seeking medical validation of their illnesses and injuries; being approved for eligibility programs such as state VR services; and accessing disability benefits such as Social Security Disability Insurance,

Supplemental Security Income, and long-term disability insurance. Koch et al. (2012) reviewed recent research on the characteristics of people with emerging disabilities, asserting that people with these conditions are more likely to be female, to be unemployed (and therefore to live in poverty), to experience symptoms that are invisible or not readily apparent to others, to have psychiatric diagnoses, and to abuse substances in comparison to people with what Koch et al. termed traditional disabilities. In terms of substance use disorders, Atherton and Toriello (2012) reported an increased incidence of addiction to prescription medications and increased abuse of heroin and methamphetamine as emerging challenges for rehabilitation professionals who provide chemical dependency treatment services.

International Rehabilitation

A final emergent topic area in recent narrative reviews pertains to international rehabilitation. As Umeasiegbu et al. (2012) noted, international rehabilitation has grown considerably since the *International Decade of the Disabled* and the revision of the *International Classification of Function (ICF)* by the *World Health Organization.* Among the important issues highlighted in international rehabilitation are: (a) the inextricable link between disability and poverty; (b) limited access to trained rehabilitation personnel and resources, particularly in more rural districts; (c) cross-cultural variation in how disability is identified, defined, and assessed; and (d) the recent development of a global disability rights movement that frames disability oppression and disability access as fundamental human rights concerns. The examples that follow suggest that cross-cultural exchanges related to rehabilitation education are essential for our professional knowledge base and that the interest in international rehabilitation will continue to grow. Hampton (2001) described the current status of rehabilitation services in the People's Republic of China. Rumrill (2013) compared and contrasted the American and Japanese systems of vocational rehabilitation and workforce development. Li and Tsang (2002) described applications of the Becker Work Adjustment Profile-Chinese Version for people with developmental disabilities. Mpofu and Harley (2002) drew parallels and lessons from the rehabilitation process in Zimbabwe to address contemporary challenges in the American rehabilitation system. Marshall and Juarez (2002) specified a myriad of rehabilitation and life adjustment issues facing women with disabilities in Oaxaca, Mexico. Graf, Reed, and Sanchez (2008) discussed violence against Mexican and Mexican-American women with disabilities.

SUMMARY

Narrative literature reviews make significant contributions to the theory and practice of rehabilitation counseling. In aggregate, the body of works that bring forth new perspectives from comprehensive analyses of existing research in areas such as those discussed in this chapter has helped the rehabilitation profession to:

1. Build theoretical models to serve as conceptual foundations for empirical research and professional practice;
2. Analyze and, in some cases, reconcile complicated or controversial issues in the lives of Americans with disabilities;
3. Develop the professional knowledge base and important practitioner skills related to the delivery of responsive, effective services in diverse practice settings; and
4. Stay abreast of emerging issues in our dynamic field.

As readers move from reading this text to incorporating research utilization strategies into their own practices as rehabilitation counselors, they will be well-served to remember the important contributions that narrative literature reviews make to the advancement of knowledge and enhancement of practice in rehabilitation counseling.

Chapter 9

ANATOMY OF A RESEARCH ARTICLE AND GUIDELINES FOR CRITIQUE

INTRODUCTION

In this chapter, we examine the sections of a research article and provide guidelines for conducting critical analyses of published works. Drawn from the American Psychological Association's (2013) *Publication Manual* and related descriptions in other research design texts (Bellini & Rumrill, 2009; Goodwin & Goodwin, 2012; Heppner et al., 2015; Kazdin, 2003; Rumrill, Cook, & Wiley, 2010), general descriptions of each component of a research article are followed (section-by-section) by a reprinted article from the rehabilitation literature. We conclude the chapter with a framework that university instructors, graduate students, and rehabilitation practitioners can use in critiquing research articles on the basis of their scientific merits and practical utility.

SECTIONS OF A RESEARCH ARTICLE

The American Psychological Association (2013) presented guidelines for authors to follow in composing manuscripts for publication in professional journals. Most journals in rehabilitation counseling and disability studies adhere to those style and formatting guidelines. In the paragraphs to follow, descriptions of each section of a standard research article are presented: Title, Abstract, Method, Results, Discussion, and References. Following our generalized descriptions of each section, we have reprinted verbatim sections of an empirical article by Cichy, Li, McMahon, and Rumrill (2015). This article is reprinted from a 2015 issue of the *Journal of Vocational Rehabilitation, Volume 42*(3), pages 137–148, with the kind permission of IOS Press.

Title

As with other kinds of literature, the title of a journal article is a very important feature. At the risk of contravening the "You can't judge a book by its cover" maxim, we believe that most articles in rehabilitation journals are either read or not read based upon the prospective reader's consideration of the title. Hence, a clear, concise title that provides the article's key concepts, hypotheses, methods, and variables under study is critical. A standard-length title for a journal article in the social sciences is 12–15 words, including a subtitle if appropriate. Social science indexing systems, which track and categorize journal articles by topic area, rely heavily on titles in their codification systems. Therefore, if authors want other scholars to be directed to their works, they must carefully compose a title that reflects the article without distractive or irrelevant descriptors. Cichy et al. (2015, p. 137) presented the following title, whose 23 words significantly exceed the 12–15 word convention:

> "The Workplace Discrimination Experiences of Older Workers with Disabilities: Results from the National Equal Employment Opportunity Commission Americans with Disabilities Act Research Project."

Before we move into descriptions of the text of a research article, we want to briefly address the concept of technical writing as it applies to the composition of academic manuscripts. Journals adhering to the American Psychological Association's (2013) publication guidelines favor manuscripts that are written in direct, uncomplicated sentences. Editors prefer that text be written in the "active voice" whenever possible. Sentences should begin with their subjects and follow with verbs and objects (e.g., "The researcher conducted an experiment" rather than "An experiment was conducted by the researcher"). In the name of concise communication, extraneous phrases and clauses that add words to the sentence without enhancing the overall statement should be avoided (e.g., "In order to . . . ," "For purposes of . . . ," "As far as . . . is concerned . . ."). Technical writing is also marked by the sparing use of adverbs (e.g., very, somewhat, strikingly) and adjectives that do not serve to further define or specify the terms that they are modifying (e.g., interesting, important, good, noteworthy).

Organization is another critical element of an effectively composed journal article, with multilevel headings serving to guide the flow of text and keep the reader on track. For authoritative information regarding the style and formatting guidelines for submitting manuscripts to most journals in social science fields, readers should consult the American Psychological Association's (2013) *Publication Manual.*

For a more literary perspective on technical writing, readers should consider the following composition guidelines that were first presented in George Orwell's (1946, 1982) *Politics and the English Language:*

1. Never use a metaphor, simile, or other figure of speech which you are used to seeing in print.
2. Never use a long word where a short one will do.
3. If it is possible to cut a word out, always cut it out.
4. Never use the passive (voice) where you can use the active.
5. Never use a foreign phrase, a scientific word, or jargon word if you can think of an everyday English equivalent.
6. Break any of these rules sooner than say anything outright barbarous (p. 170).

Abstract

Next to the title, the abstract is the most widely read section of a journal article (Bellini & Rumrill, 2009). In an empirical article, the abstract should be a succinct, 100–150-word summary of the investigation's key features, including background, objective, methods, results, and conclusions. Results of the study should be summarized in full in the abstract; authors should describe both significant and non-significant findings, not only those which upheld their hypotheses or expectations. The abstract serves as an "advance organizer" for the article, and it should include every important premise, method, and finding of the investigation. Like the "Preface" that commonly introduces readers to full-length textbooks, the abstract provides a thorough, albeit summary, glimpse of the contents of the article. In most instances, the title is what determines whether a reader will read the abstract; the abstract determines whether the reader will read the body of the article. Cichy et al. (2015, p. 137) prefaced their article with the following abstract:

> **Background**: In this study, investigators examined the employment discrimination experiences of older workers (55 and over) with disabilities in comparison to younger adult workers with disabilities. **Objective**: To examine age as a differential indicator of demographic characteristics of the Charging Parties, characteristics of Employers against whom allegations were filed, the discrimination issues alleged to occur, and the legal outcome of allegation investigations. **Methods**: The study utilized data from the Integrated Mission System of the U.S. Equal Employment Opportunity Commission (EEOC). **Results**: Findings indicate that allegations filed by older Charging

Parties were more likely to come from males and Caucasians and to involve more non-paralytic orthopedic, cardiovascular, vision, hearing, endocrinological, respiratory, and other age-related impairments. Allegations filed by older Charging Parties involved fewer mental health concerns, substance use disorders, blood and immune disorders, developmental disabilities, and chronic illnesses such as multiple sclerosis and epilepsy. Allegations filed by older workers were less likely to involve involuntary termination and more likely to involve work assignments, the terms and conditions of employment, layoff, and involuntary retirement. No significant differences in the proportions of allegations were observed related to the size of respondent employers or the outcomes of the EEOC's investigatory process. **Conclusions**: Results suggest that many of the workplace discrimination experiences of people with disabilities are common across age groups, and that partial support is evident for 'double jeopardy' in the treatment of older workers with disabilities. Implications for policy and practice are discussed.

Introduction

Immediately following the abstract, the introductory section of the article sets the stage for the study upon which the article was based. It orients the reader to the problem or issue being addressed, develops the logic and rationale for conducting the investigation, and expresses the empirical hypotheses or research questions. Heppner et al. (2015) suggested that the introduction should answer questions such as why the topic is an important one to study, what previous work bears on the topic, how existing work logically connects to the author's research questions and/or hypotheses, how the question will be researched, and what predictions can be made.

To answer these questions, authors typically address three major elements in the introductory section of an article: (1) The Research Problem, (2) The Framework for the Study, and (3) The Research Questions and Hypotheses (Goodwin & Goodwin, 2012; Heppner et al., 2015). Although we will describe each introductory element in discrete, linear fashion in this text, it is important to point out that many (if not most) authors blend these considerations to fit the flow and logic of their respective manuscripts.

THE RESEARCH PROBLEM. The very first sentences of an empirical journal article should draw the reader's attention to the scope, impact, and current status of the problem or issue being investigated. This initial orientation is most effectively achieved by applying the broadest-possible perspective to the concern. A study of return-to-work rates for injured workers with cumulative trauma disorders in the manufacturing industry might be introduced by citing national statistics concerning the long-term employment outcomes of participants in workers' compensation rehabilitation programs. An article describing the effects of a job placement intervention for adults with visual impairments or blindness might begin with a review of existing literature regarding the employment concerns and experiences of Americans who are blind or visually impaired.

THE FRAMEWORK FOR THE STUDY. The specific theoretical and empirical framework for the particular investigation is typically the second part of the Introduction. Authors summarize existing literature related to the identified problem, and build a logical "case" for a study that addresses gaps or inconsistencies in the literature. The author(s) should present the theoretical or conceptual model that informs the inquiry and provides enough background to enable the reader to appreciate the rationale of the current study. This framework elucidates the purpose of the current study (e.g., to evaluate the effectiveness of a job retention program for women with fibromyalgia), which is then operationalized in the research questions or hypotheses.

THE RESEARCH QUESTIONS AND HYPOTHESES. The Introduction section of a research article typically (or, often) concludes with a statement of the research questions and/or hypotheses that served to guide the study. A more speculative research question tends to be used in descriptive research designs (e.g., surveys, program evaluations, empirical literature reviews; see Chapter 6) or in qualitative studies (see Chapter 7). Examples of research questions could include: "What concerns do college students with disabilities have regarding their future career prospects?" "What are the barriers to community participation faced by Americans with diabetes across regions of the United States?" and "What steps are Fortune 500 employers taking to provide on-the-job accommodations for workers with disabilities?"

The hypothesis, on the other hand, is predictive by design. Its specificity is dependent upon the theory underlying it or previous, relevant research, but it should include the direction of the anticipated results whenever possible. Independent and dependent variables need not be operationalized in theory-based hypotheses (because this is done in the Method section), but the expected relationship among study variables must be clearly articulated. Examples of directional hypotheses could include: "Participation in a cognitive-behavioral stress management program will decrease symptom onset and magnification" "Anxiety, depression, and low self-esteem will be collectively, positively, and significantly related to work interference" and "Rehabilitation counselors will rate people with severe disabilities as less favorable candidates for employment than similarly qualified people with mild or no disabilities."

The introduction presented by Cichy et al. (2015, pp. 137–139)–which effectively blends discussions of the research problem, the conceptual framework of the study, and research questions–is as follows:

The Americans with Disabilities Act (ADA), which prohibits discrimination against qualified individuals with disabilities (McMahon, Edwards, Rumrill, & Hursh, 2005), was passed in 1990 and took effect in 1992. Two decades later, even with the passage of the ADA Amendments Act of 2008, discrimination against those with disabilities persists. Studies show that adults with disabilities are significantly underutilized and underrepresented in the paid labor force (Erickson & Lee, 2007; Erickson, Lee, & von Schrader, 2012). Compared to their non-disabled peers, adults with disabilities have lower labor force participation rates, are less likely to be employed full-time, and face more barriers to reemployment (Burkhauser, Houtenville, & Wittenburg, 2001; Burkhauser & Stapleton, 2003; DeLeire, 2000a, 2000b; Hotchkiss, 2004; Houtenville & Burkhauser, 2005; Jolls & Prescott, 2004). Workers with disabilities are often overrepresented in highly physical, entry level, low-skill occupations where they earn low wages and are most vulnerable to job loss (Kaye, 2009). Further, people with disabilities often report lower participation in organizational decision-making, and receive less training (Schur, Kruse, Blasi, & Blanck, 2009).

Disability and Workplace Discrimination

The bleak employment outcomes for Americans with disabilities are often attributed to negative stereotypes, including the beliefs that they are less skilled, require more supervision, increase health care costs, and have low levels of emotional adjustment (Stone-Romero, Stone, & Lukaszewski, 2006). Employers' persistent stereotypes of people with disabilities promote negative expectations (Stone & Colella, 1996) which have been shown to influence hiring decisions and performance reviews (Ren, Paetzold, & Colella, 2008). These adverse workplace experiences have been the subject of more than 550,000 Equal Employment Opportunity Commission (EEOC) investigations of workplace discrimination filed by people with various disabilities under Title I of the ADA from 1992 through 2011 (Bowe, McMahon, Chang, & Louvie, 2005; McKenna, Fabian, Hurley, McMahon, & West, 2007; Rumrill, Roessler, McMahon, & Fitzgerald, 2005, Van Wieren, Reid, & McMahon, 2008). Indeed, Rumrill and Koch (2014) described workplace discrimination as one of the unifying features of the employment experience for Americans with disabilities.

Age and Workplace Discrimination

Disability aside, extant research provides compelling evidence that older adults are also frequent targets of employment discrimination, with several parallels to the findings observed among workers with disabilities. Older employees are often the first to be fired and the last to be re-hired (Bendick & Brown, 1999; Lahey, 2005; Goldman, Gutek, Stein, & Lewis, 2006). For example, workers over the age of 55 take significantly longer than younger workers to find employment and re-enter the workforce (Rix, 2005; Sargeant, 2001). When employed, older employees often receive fewer opportunities for career advancement (Neumark, 2003) and are frequently perceived as inferior to younger employees (Taylor, Steinberg, & Walley, 2000). Further, older adults, like individuals with disabilities, are often the targets of negative stereotyping. Older workers are perceived as less flexible, less receptive to new technologies or skills, more resistant to change, less alert, less productive, less creative, poor decision-makers, lacking in energy, or deteriorating in intelligence (Gringart, Helmes, & Speelman, 2013; Perrin, 2005; Sargaent, 2001; Taylor & Unwin, 2001). These ageist attitudes contribute to what has been a large body of allegations of age-based employment discrimination under the Civil rights Act of 1964 and the Age Discrimination in Employment Act of 1967 (Bjelland et al., 2010).

Double Jeopardy: Discrimination Experiences of Older Adults with Disabilities

Despite extensive research on both the unique workplace discrimination experiences of individuals with disabilities (Bowe et al., 2005; McKenna et al., 2007; Rumrill et al., 2005, Van Wieren et al., 2008) and older employees (Bendick & Brown, 1999; Lahey, 2005; Goldman et al., 2006), few discrimination studies have examined the intersection between age and disability. Both older adult employees and individuals with disabilities are often the targets of negative stereotypes that result in discriminatory actions (Gringart et al., 2013; Perrin, 2005; Sargaent, 2001; Stone-Romero et al., 2006; Taylor & Unwin, 2001). According to the double jeopardy theory, patterns of inequality often reinforce one another (Beale, 1970; Purdie-Vaughns & Eibach, 2008), such that older employees with disabilities may be doubly disadvantaged by their age and disability status. Bjelland and colleagues (2010), in one of the few studies to explicitly consider this issue, used the U.S. Equal Employment Opportunity Commission (EEOC) Integrated Mission System data to investigate the nature of employment discrimination charges that cite the Americans with Disabilities Act or Age Discrimination in Employment Act individually or jointly. Their examination of jointly filed allegations included only individuals with disabilities who were 40 years of age or older. Although this investigation provided information about the characteristics and circumstances unique to older individuals with disabilities, questions remain. Bjelland et al. focused exclusively on the experiences of older Charging Parties, making no comparison to their younger counterparts. It is conceivable that the shared biases against older adults and individuals with disabilities could contribute to differences in some aspects of the discrimination experiences of older versus younger individuals with disabilities. For example, employer characteristics have been shown to predict discrimination experiences of individuals with disabilities (Rumrill et al., 2005), but it is not known whether that predictive relationship is mitigated by the age of the worker. Other discrimination-related factors may vary according to worker age, as well. For example, certain types of disabilities may increase in prevalence in later life, such as physical or sensory impairments (Smart, 2009), so the workplace discrimination experiences of people with physical or sensory impairments could change as a function of aging.

To address these gaps in the literature, the current study utilized data from the EEOC Integrated Mission System database to examine age differences in several aspects of the EEOC's ADA Title I (employment provisions) investigatory processes. Understanding how, for whom, and under what circumstances the discrimination experiences of older workers with disabilities differ from those of younger workers with disabilities is important for several reasons. The participation rates and total number of older workers in the workforce are expected to continue to increase for the next 20 years (Toossi, 2006). The prevalence of disability increases with age and thus increased numbers of older workers will increase the prevalence of disability in the workplace. Older adults are interested in remaining in the labor force due to both financial necessity and the need to support their retirement as well as for personal fulfillment (Loretto & White, 2006). Previous research emphasizes the strengths of older workers and the benefits of retaining an aging workforce (Magd, 2003; Perrin 2005). Changes in some functional areas, such as vision or reaction times that may emerge with age, are offset by gains in other areas (e.g., caution, experience, wisdom, and leadership skills) (Gunderson, 2003; Shen & Kleiner, 2001). These facts underscore the importance of understanding the discrimination experiences of older workers with disabilities, and of striving to retain and accommodate older workers when possible. Workplace discrimination is a barrier to employment for individuals with disabilities of all ages that has profound implications for individuals' emotional, physical, and financial well-being (Rumrill & Koch, 2014).

Study Objectives

The two objectives of this study were: (1) to document the nature and scope of employment discrimination allegations involving older workers with disabilities, and (2) to compare the discrimination experiences of older workers with disabilities to the experiences of younger workers with disabilities (i.e., young adults and middle-aged workers). Specifically, the current study addressed the following research questions:

1. Do the employment discrimination experiences of older workers with disabilities differ from those of younger workers with disabilities with respect to the demographic characteristics of Charging Parties who file allegations with the EEOC (i.e., gender, race/ethnicity, and type of disability)?

2. Do the employment discrimination experiences of older workers with disabilities differ from those of younger workers with disabilities with respect to the nature of the discrimination alleged to occur (e.g., issues such as hiring, firing, disability harassment, etc.)?

3. Do the employment discrimination experiences of older workers with disabilities differ from those of younger workers with disabilities with respect to employer characteristics, including industry designation, size, and location?

4. Do the employment discrimination experiences of older workers with disabilities differ from those of younger workers with disabilities with respect to the legal outcomes or resolutions of the EEOC investigatory process? These resolutions may be determined to be in favor of the Charging Party (i.e., "With Merit;" discrimination did occur) or in favor of the Employer (i.e., "Without Merit;" discrimination did not occur).

Method

The Method section delineates how the research questions were addressed and/or how the hypotheses were tested. It should provide the reader with sufficient information so that one could replicate the investigation. Because the Method section is the primary source for determining the validity of the study (see Chapter 5), the quality and clarity of this section is generally regarded as the strongest determinant of whether an empirically-based manuscript will be accepted for publication (Heppner et al., 2015).

Although the type and order of sub-sections found in the Method section of a research article vary depending upon the design of the study and the author's judgment related to the flow of text, most articles include descriptions of the study's subjects/participants, instruments/measures/variables, materials, design, and procedures.

SUBJECTS/PARTICIPANTS. According to Heppner et al. (2015), the Method section should include (a) total number of subjects and numbers assigned to groups, if applicable, (b) how subjects were selected and/or assigned, and (c) demographic and other characteristics of the sample relevant to the study's purpose. Some authors also include a description of the population from which the study sample was drawn, an indication of the representativeness of the sample vis a vis the broader population, the circumstances under which subjects participated (e.g., whether they were compensated, what risks they assumed), statistical power analyses, and response rates (if applicable).

INSTRUMENTS/MEASURES/VARIABLES. The Method section must include a detailed description of how all study variables were operationalized, measured, scored, and interpreted. All instruments or measures that were used in sampling, conducting the study, and evaluating results must be specified in terms of content (number of items, response sets), how measures were administered, scoring procedures, relationship to study variables, and psychometric properties (reliability and validity). Authors should also include a rationale for selecting each instrument, i.e., why that instrument was the best choice for measuring a particular construct.

MATERIALS. Researchers should also include a description of any materials that were used to carry out the investigation. Written guides for participants, instructional manuals, media or technology, and scientific apparatus or equipment should be noted in detail. Some authors, especially those who conducted reliability and validity studies with psychometric instruments, include a description of the setting in which the study was executed and data were collected.

DESIGN. One of the most important features of the Method section is a clear description of the design of the study. This is essential because the design serves as the link between (a) the research questions/hypotheses and the scientific procedures used in carrying out the study, and (b) the findings of the study and how these are interpreted. Authors typically label their designs in terms of how variables were manipulated, observed, and analyzed. Thereby, the design is the unifying force in connecting the research objectives to the results and to the knowledge claim that is made. To every extent possible, a direct reference to the hypotheses should be made when authors identify the design of a particular investigation. For example, Rumrill, Roessler, and Denny (1997, p. 7) described their design as follows: "The researchers selected a three-group, posttest-only (experimental) design to assess the intervention's univariate and multivariate effects on (a) self-reported attitudes (situational self-efficacy and acceptance of disability) and (b) participation in the accommodation request process."

PROCEDURES. The most important component of the Method section is the easiest to describe. In chronological order, authors simply list every step they took in developing, administering, and evaluating the study. Beginning with initial recruitment of participants, following the study through collection of the last datum, and including everything in-between, the Procedures subsection should provide the reader with a step-by-step protocol that could serve as a guide for replicating the study. Descriptions of any interventions should be provided in detail, along with summaries of the qualifications of project personnel who were instrumental in executing the investigation. Procedures should also include how the investigation was concluded and a statement of any debriefing or follow-up services provided to participants.

In aggregate, the Method section comprises the most important information found in a research article. Cichy et al. (2015, pp. 139–140) captured the essence of a detailed, concisely written Method section. It follows below:

Data Source

This study utilized the EEOC Integrated Mission System database, which is used to track the filing, investigation, and resolution of workplace discrimination allegations under Title 1 of the Americans with Disabilities Act of 1990 (ADA; McMahon et al., 2005). Several safeguards are in place to maintain confidentiality and to protect the identity of Charging Parties and Employers. First, all identifying information for the Charging Parties has been removed, leaving only information on age, gender, race/ethnicity, and disability status. For Respondents, the only information available is the North American Industrial Classification Standard (NAICS code), number of employees, and location (U.S. Department of Education regional boundaries).

The unit of analysis in the database is an allegation (not a person, Charging Party, or Employer). Only unique allegations that do not involve recording errors or duplications are included in the study dataset. All allegations are limited to those brought under Title I of the ADA due to the wide state-to-state variations in state anti-discrimination statutes based on disability. Allegations that are still being investigated are also excluded.

Further, the current analyses only include allegations filed by those Charging Parties who were 25 years of age or older at the time that the allegation was filed with the EEOC. The final analytic dataset for this study included 79,858 allegations of employment discrimination under ADA Title I that were filed, investigated, and closed by the EEOC between January 1, 2009 (the day that the ADA Amendments Act took effect) and December 31, 2011. Using these recent dates obviates any impact from either the original ADA language (1992–1998) or the confusion in definitions created by the Sutton trilogy of Supreme Court decisions (1999–2008). With an effective date of January 1, 2009, the ADA Amendments Act substantially expanded the anti-discrimination protections available to American workers with disabilities (Toriello, Bishop, & Rumrill, 2012). These allegations were divided into groups on the basis of age including: 1) older workers aged 55 and over ($n=20,030$) and younger adult workers aged 25 to 54 years ($n=59,828$).

Variables in the EEOC Database

Characteristics of the Charging Party. As stated above, the characteristics of the Charging Party include gender (female/male), race/ethnicity (White, African American, Hispanic/Mexican, Asian, and Other), and disability type (39 impairments within the following categories: physical, behavioral, neurological, and sensory impairments).

Characteristics of the respondent. The characteristics of the Respondent include the location/region (New England, Northeast, Mid-Atlantic, Southeast, Midwest, Southwest, Great Plains, Rocky Mountains, Pacific, and Northwest), the industry designation (NAICS code), and number of employees (ranges from 15 to over 500).

Issues. The database includes more than 40 specific employment decisions upon which an ADA Title I allegation can be based. This study mainly focused on 24 types of discrimination identified by the EEOC between January 1, 2009 and December 31, 2011 that are related to job acquisition (i.e., qualification standards, prohibited medical inquiry, testing, hiring, training, and reasonable accommodation), work conditions (i.e., wages, benefits, job classification, assignment, segregated facilities, demotion, promotion, discipline, suspension, intimidation, harassment, and terms/conditions), and job retention (i.e., discharge, constructive discharge, involuntary retirement, layoff, recall, and reinstatement).

Resolution. This refers to the final EEOC determination as to whether or not discrimination actually occurred. Resolutions are classified as Merit, favoring the Charging Party (a determination that discrimination did occur) or Non-Merit, favoring the respondent Employer (a determination that discrimination did not occur).

Data Analysis

To describe the characteristics of the Charging Parties and Employers, the researchers used descriptive statistics such as frequencies and percentages. The age group differences between older workers and younger workers were investigated using z-test for proportions (a non-parametric technique) to compare age group differences for gender, race, and disability types of the Charging Parties; industry designation, location, and size of respondent Employers; allegation issues; and resolution status. All the analyses were conducted using the statistical computer package Stata (2013). As multiple tests were conducted, levels of significance (i.e., alpha values) were set conservatively at .001.

Results

The Results section of a research article should include a complete inventory of all relevant findings obtained by the investigators. In articles that report quantitative studies (see Chapter 6), results are typically presented in two parts: summary, or descriptive, statistics related to participants' performance on whatever measures were taken (e.g., means, standard deviations, frequencies, percentages; see Chapter 3), and statistical analyses related to the specific hypotheses of the study (e.g., analysis of variance, multiple regression, factor analysis; see Chapter 3). We believe that all analyses conducted as part of the investigation should be reported in full, not only those which yielded statistically significant results. The *Publication Manual of the American Psychological Association* (2013) provides considerable guidance related to how statistics should be presented in the Results section, but it does not provide adequate guidelines regarding *what* statistical information should be included. Heppner et al. (2015) identified a pattern in recent counseling literature whereby researchers tend to err on the side of providing too little statistical information. Bellini and Rumrill (2009) expressed the same concern regarding contemporary rehabilitation counseling research. Both sets of authors advocated for more complete presentations of statistical analyses in Results sections, especially regarding effect sizes which permit other researchers to compare findings across studies within a particular content domain.

A quantitative Results section should be limited to the findings obtained by the researcher(s) in the current investigation. Speculation concerning what those findings mean in a larger context is reserved for the Discussion section.

The Results sections of qualitatively oriented articles display much more variety in the content and manner of presentation than is found in quantitative studies. Because the researcher's subjective interpretations help to shape the processes and outcomes of qualitative investigations (see Chapter 7), results are often framed in broad, interpretive contexts. In that regard, the lines between the Results and Discussion sections are often blurred in qualitative research.

Researchers (qualitative and quantitative) commonly use tables and figures to summarize and/or graphically depict their results. There is wide variability in terms of the content and presentation of tables and figures, with the most important universal requirement being easy interpretability for the reader.

Cichy et al. (2015, pp. 140–144; including five tables) presented their results as follows:

Differences in Characteristics of Charging Parties

The first research question concerns the demographic characteristics of ADA Title I Charging Parties who were aged 55 and over versus those who were 25 to 54 years of age. The differences in these characteristics between the two groups are displayed in Table 9.1.

Table 9.1.
Characteristics of Allegations by Charging Party Characteristics

Characteristics	Age ≥ 55 (N = 20,030)		Age < 55 (N = 59,828)		Z	p
	N	%	N	%		
Sex						
Female	10,347	51.7	32,988	55.1	−8.56	<0.001
Race						
White	13,249	66.1	34,316	57.4	21.94	<0.001
African American	4,150	20.7	16,557	27.7	−19.44	<0.001
Hispanic/Mexican	1,819	9.1	6,655	11.1	−8.12	<0.001
Asian	346	1.7	928	1.6	NSD	
Other	466	2.3	1,372	2.3	NSD	
Disability						
Nonparalytic Orthopedic Impairment	1,893	9.5	3,852	6.4	14.28	<0.001
Back Impairment	1,684	8.4	4,647	7.8	NSD	
Heart/Cardiovascular Impairment	1,184	5.9	1,496	2.5	23.20	<0.001
Diabetes	1,123	5.6	2,425	4.1	9.23	<0.001
Depression	919	4.6	4,019	6.7	−10.83	<0.001
Cancer	815	4.1	1,378	2.3	13.23	<0.001
Anxiety Disorder	636	3.2	3,022	5.1	−10.99	<0.001
Hearing Impairment	594	3.0	1,322	2.2	6.05	<0.001
Other Neuro Impairment	579	2.9	1,931	3.2	NSD	
Other Psych Impairment	493	2.5	2,228	3.7	−8.53	<0.001
Vision Impairment	475	2.4	951	1.6	7.23	<0.001
Other Respiratory/Pulmonary Impairment	322	1.6	619	1.0	6.50	<0.001
Manic Depressive Disorder	316	1.6	2,274	3.8	−15.37	<0.001
Asthma	291	1.5	833	1.4	NSD	
Learning Disability	180	0.9	1,197	2.0	−10.37	<0.001
Gastrointestinal Impairment	174	0.9	705	1.2	−3.64	<0.001
Brain/Head Injury-Traumatic	164	0.8	604	1.0	NSD	
Other Blood Disorders	154	0.8	674	1.1	−4.33	<0.001
Multiple Sclerosis	144	0.7	767	1.3	−6.50	<0.001
Kidney Impairment	128	0.6	395	0.7	NSD	
Missing Digits or Limbs	115	0.6	242	0.4	NSD	
Epilepsy	103	0.5	805	1.3	−9.60	<0.001
Allergies	90	0.4	274	0.5	NSD	
Speech Impairment	65	0.3	266	0.4	NSD	
Alcoholism	61	0.3	416	0.7	−6.21	<0.001
Chemical Sensitivities	60	0.3	145	0.2	NSD	

Table 9.1.—Continued

Characteristics	Age ≥ 55 (N = 20,030)		Age < 55 (N = 59,828)		Z	p
	N	%	N	%		
Paralysis	40	0.2	190	0.3	NSD	
Disfigurement	38	0.2	96	0.2	NSD	
Schizophrenia	35	0.2	291	0.5	−5.99	<0.001
Mental Retardation	34	0.2	279	0.5	−5.81	<0.001
Cumulative Trauma Disorder	33	0.2	92	0.2	NSD	
Cerebral Palsy	29	0.1	224	0.4	−5.01	<0.001
HIV/AIDS	19	0.1	491	0.8	−11.16	<0.001
Drug Addiction	17	0.1	324	0.5	−8.58	<0.001
Alzheimer's	12	0.1	2	0.0	5.23	<0.001
Tuberculosis	9	0.0	20	0.0	NSD	
Autism	8	0.0	102	0.2	−4.31	<0.001
Dwarfism	5	0.0	26	0.0	NSD	
Cystic Fibrosis	0	0.0	29	0.0	NSD	

The group of older workers consisted of 20,030 Charging Parties, of which 52% were women, 66% were White, 21% were African American, 9% were Hispanic or Mexican, and 2% were Asian. The five disability types that were most frequently reported by older workers were non-paralytic orthopedic impairment (10%), back impairment (8%), heart or cardiovascular impairment (6%), diabetes (6%), and depression (5%). In contrast, the group of younger workers consisted of 59,828 Charging Parties, of which 55% were women, 57% were White, 28% were African American, 11% were Hispanic or Mexican, and 2% were Asian. The five disability types that were most frequently reported by younger workers were back impairment (8%), depression (7%), non-paralytic orthopedic impairment (6%), anxiety disorder (5%), and diabetes (4%).

Relative to the group of younger workers, proportionally fewer allegations appeared in the group of older workers involving Charging Parties who were female ($Z = -8.56$, $p < .001$), African American ($Z = -19.44$, $p < .001$), and Hispanic/Mexican ($Z = -8.12$, $p < .001$). Proportionally more allegations appeared in the group of older workers involving Charging Parties who were White ($Z = 21.94$, $p < .001$). Proportionally more allegations appeared in the group of older workers involving Charging Parties who had non-paralytic orthopedic impairment ($Z = 14.28$, $p < .001$), heart/ cardiovascular impairment ($Z = 23.20$, $p < .001$), diabetes ($Z = 9.23$, $p < .001$), cancer ($Z = 13.23$, $p < .001$), hearing impairment ($Z = 6.05$, $p < .001$), vision impairment ($Z = 7.23$, $p < .001$), respiratory/pulmonary impairment ($Z =$

6.5, $p<.001$), and Alzheimer's disease ($Z=5.23$, $p<.001$). Proportionally fewer allegations appeared in the group of older workers involving Charging Parties who had depression ($Z=-10.83$, $p<.001$), anxiety disorder ($Z=-10.99$, $p<.001$), manic depressive disorder ($Z=-15.37$, $p<.001$), learning disability ($Z=-10.37$, $p<.001$), gastrointestinal impairment ($Z=-3.64$, $p<.001$), blood disorder ($Z=-4.33$, $p<.001$), multiple sclerosis ($Z=-6.50$, $p<.001$), epilepsy ($Z=-9.60$, $p<.001$), schizophrenia ($Z=-5.99$, $p<.001$), mental retardation ($Z=-5.81$, $p<.001$), cerebral palsy ($Z=-5.01$, $p<.001$), HIV/AIDS ($Z=-11.16$, $p<.001$), alcoholism ($Z=-6.21$, $p<.001$), drug addiction ($Z=-8.58$, $p<.001$), autism ($Z=-4.31$, $p<.001$), and other psychological impairment ($Z=-8.53$, $p<.001$).

Differences in Discrimination Issues

The second research question involves the specific issues or discriminatory actions alleged by Charging Parties 55 years of age or older, in comparison to the issues alleged by Charging Parties 25 to 54 years of age. Descriptive statistics for discrimination issues with respect to job acquisition, working conditions, and job retention are displayed for the two groups in Table 9.2. In both groups, the five discrimination issues most often filed by Charging Parties were discharge (i.e., 31.1% for the group of older workers; 32.6% for the group of younger workers), reasonable accommodation (i.e., 17.0% for the group of older workers; 18.0% for the group of younger workers), terms/conditions (i.e., 11.3% for the group of older workers; 10.4% for the group of younger workers), harassment (i.e., 9.3% for the group of older workers; 9.4% for the group of younger workers), and discipline (i.e., 6.4% for the group of older workers; 6.9% for the group of younger workers). Relative to the group of younger workers, proportionally fewer allegations appeared in the group of older workers involving Charging Parties who encountered involuntary termination of employment status on a permanent basis (i.e., discharge, $Z=-3.78$, $p<.001$). Proportionally more allegations appeared in the group of older workers involving Charging Parties who encountered denial or inequitable terms/conditions ($Z=3.78$, $p<.001$), undesirable work assignments ($Z=4.94$, $p<.001$), layoff ($Z=6.88$, $p<.001$), involuntary retirement ($Z=12.94$, $p<.001$), and unfair qualification standards ($Z=5.11$, $p<.001$). There were no significant differences in proportion between the two groups on the other recorded discrimination issues.

Differences in Characteristics of Respondents

The third research question investigates differences between the two groups in terms of characteristics of respondents (i.e., Employers). Descriptive statistics regarding the size and location of Employers for the two groups are displayed in Table 9.3. Charging Parties in the group of older

Table 9.2.
Differences in Proportion by Discrimination Issues

Issue	Age ≥ 55 (N = 20,030)		Age < 55 (N = 59,828)		Z	p
	N	%	N	%		
Discharge	6,233	31.1	19,479	32.6	-3.78	<0.001
Reasonable Accommodation	3,412	17.0	10,792	18.0	NSD	
Terms/Conditions	2,269	11.3	6,208	10.4	3.78	<0.001
Harassment	1,854	9.3	5,614	9.4	NSD	
Discipline	1,282	6.4	4,121	6.9	NSD	
Hiring	594	3.0	1,784	3.0	NSD	
Assignment	511	2.6	1,179	2.0	4.94	<0.001
Constructive Discharge	479	2.4	1,409	2.4	NSD	
Layoff	403	2.0	795	1.3	6.88	<0.001
Suspension	364	1.8	1,312	2.2	NSD	
Intimidation	309	1.5	1,006	1.7	NSD	
Wages	289	1.4	756	1.3	NSD	
Demotion	280	1.4	740	1.2	NSD	
Promotion	210	1.0	712	1.2	NSD	
Benefits	178	0.9	487	0.8	NSD	
Reinstatement	124	0.6	368	0.6	NSD	
Prohibited Medical Inquiry	119	0.6	362	0.6	NSD	
Involuntary Retirement	99	0.5	36	0.1	12.94	<0.001
Training	88	0.4	206	0.3	NSD	
Recall	57	0.3	121	0.2	NSD	
Job Classification	48	0.2	87	0.1	NSD	
Qualification Standards	29	0.1	23	0.0	5.11	<0.001
Testing	25	0.1	63	0.1	NSD	
Other	774	3.9	2,168	3.6	NSD	

workers most often filed allegations against Employers with 501 or more employees (49.4%), followed in descending order of frequency by Employers with 15–100 employees (26.3%), 201–500 employees (14.6%), and 101–200 employees (9.8%). Similarly, Charging Parties in the group of younger workers most often filed allegations against Employers with 501 or more employees (50.4%), followed in descending order of frequency by Employers with 15–100 employees (26.4%), 201–500 employees (14.1%), and 101–200 employees (9.0%). There were no statistically significant differences between the two groups in the proportions identified for the size of Employers.

Table 9.3.
Characteristics of Allegations by Respondent
Characteristics of Industry Location and Size

Respondent Characteristics	Age ≥ 55 (N = 20,030)		Age < 55 (N = 59,828)		Z	p
	N	%	N	%		
Size						
15–100	5,274	26.3	15,804	26.4	NSD	
101–200	1,953	9.8	5,408	9.0	NSD	
201–500	2,916	14.6	8,435	14.1	NSD	
501+	9,887	49.4	30,181	50.4	NSD	
Region						
New England	308	1.5	720	1.2	3.63	<0.001
Northeast	1,170	5.8	4,051	6.8	–4.61	<0.001
Mid Atlantic	2,537	12.7	6,747	11.3	5.31	<0.001
Southeast	4,870	24.3	15,263	25.5	NSD	
Midwest	3,633	18.1	11,079	18.5	NSD	
Southwest	3,632	18.1	11,222	18.8	NSD	
Great Plains	627	3.1	1,856	3.1	NSD	
Rocky Mountain	561	2.8	1,646	2.8	NSD	
Pacific	2,008	10.0	5,846	9.8	NSD	
Northwest	684	3.4	1,398	2.3	8.29	<0.001

With regard to the location of Employers, Charging Parties in both groups most often filed allegations against Employers in the Southeast (i.e., 24.3% for the group of older workers; 25.5% for the group of younger workers) and least often filed allegations against Employers in New England (i.e., 1.5% for the group of older workers; 1.2% for the group of younger workers). In the group of older workers, proportionally more allegations involved Charging Parties who worked in New England ($Z = 3.63$, $p < .001$), Mid Atlantic ($Z = 5.31$, $p < .001$), and Northwest ($Z = 8.29$, $p < .001$); proportionally fewer allegations involved those who worked in Northeast ($Z = -4.61$, $p < .001$). There were no statistically significant differences between the two groups in the proportions identified for the other locations of Employers.

Represented by frequencies and proportions, descriptive statistics for the industry designations of Employers across the two groups are displayed in Table 9.4. Charging Parties in the group of older workers most often filed allegations against Employers in the educational services field (16.3%); however, Charging Parties in the group of younger workers most often filed allegations against Employers in the manufacturing industry (13.6%). Compared to the group of younger workers, proportionally more allegations appeared in the group of older workers involving respondents who were in educational services ($Z = 15.06$, $p < .001$); health care and social assistance ($Z = 6.42$, $p < .001$); and arts, entertainment, and recreation ($Z = 7.26$, $p < .001$; see Table 9.4) proportionally fewer allegations appeared in the group of older workers involving respondents who were in finance and insurance ($Z = -7.32$, $p < .001$); accommodation and food services ($Z = -10.02$, $p < .001$); professional, scientific, and technical fields ($Z = -6.02$, $p < .001$); information ($Z = -13.61$, $p < .001$); wholesale trades ($Z = -4.34$, $p < .001$); and utilities ($Z = -4.29$, $p < .001$). However, caution is warranted in the interpretation of these results because the variable of industry designation is subject to a high proportion (41%) of missing values in the database for the two age groups.

Table 9.4.
Characteristics of Allegations by Respondent Characteristic of Industry Designation

Industry	Age ≥ 55 (N = 20,030)		Age < 55 (N = 59,828)		Z	p
	N	%	N	%		
Educational Services	1,949	16.3	4,228	12.1	15.06	<0.001
Retail Trades	1,642	13.7	4,486	12.9	NSD	
Manufacturing	1,562	13.0	4,753	13.6	NSD	
Health Care and Social Assistance	1,461	12.2	3,685	10.6	6.42	<0.001
Public Admininstration	1,061	8.9	2,861	8.2	NSD	
Transportation and Warehousing	671	5.6	2,040	5.8	NSD	
Administrative, Support, Waste Management, and Remediation Services	652	5.4	2,015	5.8	NSD	
Finance and Insurance	533	4.4	2,027	5.8	-7.32	<0.001
Accommodation and Food Services	452	3.8	1,946	5.6	-10.02	<0.001
Professional, Scientific, and Technical	407	3.4	1,527	4.4	-6.02	<0.001
Information	335	2.8	1,782	5.1	-13.61	<0.001
Other Services (Except Public Administration)	330	2.8	809	2.3	NSD	
Construction	188	1.6	479	1.4	NSD	
Arts, Entertainment, and Recreation	182	1.5	318	0.9	7.26	<0.001
Wholesale Trades	175	1.5	675	1.9	-4.34	<0.001
Real Estate, Rental, and Leasing	130	1.1	412	1.2	NSD	
Management of Companies and Enterprises	83	0.7	252	0.7	NSD	
Utilities	68	0.6	307	0.9	-4.29	<0.001
Mining	55	0.5	192	0.6	NSD	
Agriculture, Forestry, Fishing, and Hunting	45	0.4	111	0.3	NSD	

Table 9.5.
Differences in Proportion for Merit and Non-Merit Closures

Resolution	Age ≥ 55 (N = 20,030)		Age < 55 (N = 59,828)		Z
	N	%	N	%	
Merit	4,994	24.9	14,835	24.8	NSD
No Cause Finding	13,839	69.1	41,709	69.7	NSD
Administrative Closure	1,197	6.0	3,284	5.5	NSD

Differences in Resolutions

The final research question involves case resolution patterns in ADA Title I allegations. All case resolutions were grouped into two categories: merit resolutions and non-merit resolutions. Merit resolutions include those allegations withdrawn with benefits to the Charging Party, settled with benefits to the Charging Party, successful conciliation, and conciliation failure. Non-merit resolutions include no cause and all administrative closures. Descriptive statistics for the merit and non-merit resolutions are displayed in Table 9.5 for the two groups. The two groups did not significantly differ in the proportions of merit and non-merit resolutions.

Discussion

The Discussion section serves as the researchers' forum to go beyond the current investigation and discuss the contributions of the study findings to existing literature, theory, and professional practices. The first part of a thoughtful Discussion is typically an analysis of the study's results vis a vis the research questions and hypotheses. Researchers should begin with a discussion of whether the hypotheses were upheld, posit possible explanations for those outcomes, and draw implications from the findings back to the research problem that was identified in the Introduction. If the results provide a warrant for modifying or re-testing the conceptual framework upon which the investigation was based, the Discussion section is the place to suggest a reformulation of the underlying theory. Researchers should also include a statement of the scientific limitations of the current study, along with specific recommendations for future research. Finally, the researcher ends the article with a cogent summary of the conclusions, in the most general sense, that can be drawn from the methods and findings of the current study. Some authors use a separate Conclusion section for this purpose.

In their Discussion section, Cichy et al. (2015, pp. 144–146) framed both the results of the study and the major discussion points within the context of the conceptual framework for the investigation and the literature review that were presented in the Introduction section:

> The current study utilized data from the EEOC Integrated Mission System database to understand how, for whom, and under what circumstances the workplace discrimination experiences of older workers with disabilities differ from those of younger adult workers with disabilities. Overall, our findings suggest that the workplace discrimination experiences of older and younger Charging Parties are surprisingly similar in regard to the characteristics of employers against whom ADA Title I allegations are filed and the resolutions of the EEOC investigatory process. The age differences that did emerge from this investigation were indicative of both age differences in disability as well as age differences in the contexts (e.g., issues, industries) where the discrimination was alleged to have occurred. Together, findings provide partial support for the double jeopardy theory as it applies to older workers with disabilities, and they suggest that although some characteristics of the workplace discrimination experiences of adults with disabilities are common for younger and older workers, there are unique contexts where older workers may be more vulnerable than their younger counterparts.

Differences in Characteristics of Charging Parties

In terms of impairment type, it is not surprising that older Charging Parties were more likely to have nonparalytic impairments, cardiovascular disease, diabetes, visual or hearing impairments, cancer, respiratory and pulmonary diseases, and Alzheimer's disease than the comparison group of young adult and middle-aged people. All of these conditions increase in prevalence as a function of age (Sales, 2011; Wickert, Dresden, & Rumrill, 2013). The finding that depression, anxiety, schizophrenia, drug and alcohol addiction, and manic-depressive disorder were less common among the older group is most likely a function of the prevalence and age of onset for these conditions. Compared to younger and middle-aged adults, older adults have a lower prevalence of mental health and substance use disorders (Zarit, 2009). Further, the majority of mental health issues, including depression and anxiety, originate early in life, with the onset typically occurring during adolescence or young adulthood (Andrade et al., 2005; Kessler, Walters, & Wittchen, 2004). The underrepresentation of workers with mental illness in the older Charging Party group may, therefore, simply reflect the fact that at older ages mental illness is less prevalent. Also, shortened life expectancies for people with cerebral palsy, mental retardation (now referred to as intellectual disability), HIV/AIDS, and certain blood disorders (Smart, 2009) mean that proportionally fewer workers ages 55 and over are dealing with those conditions, thus explaining the overrepresentation of those disorders among young adult and middle-age charging parties. People with chronic illnesses such as multiple sclerosis and epilepsy tend to leave the workforce long before retirement age (Nissen & Rumrill, 2014) and therefore do not experience workplace discrimination at the same rate as younger workers with disabilities. Finally, the finding that older charging parties were less likely than younger ones to have learning disabilities and autism probably reflects the fact that those conditions were diagnosed far less frequently in earlier generations than they are today (Koch, Conyers, & Rumrill, 2012).

Differences in Discrimination Issues

The finding that the older Charging Party group was less likely than younger Charging Parties to allege discrimination in the area of unlawful discharge may reflect the increased career maturity that comes with age. Research indicates that Employers value the leadership, work ethic, and reliability of older workers (Magd, 2003; Perrin, 2005) and their records of attendance, punctuality, and productivity compare favorably to younger workers (O'Reilly & Caro, 1994). Hence, older workers with disabilities may be less likely to file ADA Title I allegations related to unlawful termination because they are having fewer performance problems in the first place.

Importantly, though, our findings suggest that older Charging Parties were more likely than younger Charging Parties to allege discrimination related to aspects of working conditions as well as several issues related to maintaining employment (e.g., layoff, involuntary retirement). Together, these findings suggest that older workers with disabilities do encounter double jeopardy (Beale, 1970; Purdie-Vaughns & Eibach, 2008), where their age and disability status, may make them more vulnerable to workplace discrimination, particularly with regard to issues related to remaining in the workforce. Age differences in these issues are supported by previous research, which suggest that older employees are often the first to be downsized and the last to receive opportunities for career advancement (Bendick & Brown, 1999; Goldman et al., 2006; Lahey, 2005; Neumark, 2003).

Similarities and Differences in Characteristics of Respondents

Our findings indicate that both older and younger workers were more likely to bring allegations against Employers with more than 500 employees. This finding is consistent with prior studies of workplace discrimination against workers with disabilities (Rumrill et al., 2005), and it likely reflects that larger Employers hire more employees, including more employees with disabilities (Rubin & Roessler, 2008). Larger Employers may also implement more practices that inform employees about their rights, particularly with regard to employment discrimination (Roessler & Sumner, 1997), and if so such policies are affecting both older and younger workers. Further, across age groups, more charges were filed against Employers in the Southeast and the fewest charges were filed against Employers in New England. This may reflect regional differences in employee rights legislation, workers compensation policies, or the involvement of labor unions to protect the rights of workers.

There were a few differences that did emerge with regard to employer characteristics. Older workers filed significantly more allegations against Employers in the educational services industry; in healthcare and social assistance fields; and in the arts, entertainment, and recreation than younger workers. Workers with disabilities may be able to remain in those fields long enough to encounter double jeopardy, where being an older worker with a disability becomes particularly disadvantageous (Beale, 1970; Purdie-Vaughns & Eibach, 2008). This finding suggests that these industries would benefit from targeted prevention/intervention efforts to improve Employers' responses to older workers with disabilities. It is important, however, to exercise caution in interpreting the differences in industry designations because of the high levels of missing data for this variable.

Similarities in Resolutions

Finally, our findings revealed no significant age differences in merit or non-merit resolutions, suggesting that the results of the EEOC investigatory process are similar for older and younger workers with disabilities. This finding is encouraging because it indicates that investigations of allegations of workplace discrimination are not susceptible to age bias, and that older workers with disabilities are just as likely as their younger counterparts to have ADA Title I allegations resolved in their favor. Still, the fact that only slightly more than one-fifth of all ADA Title I allegations result in merit resolutions for both age groups, even after the effectuation of the ADA Amendments Act, indicates a strong need for people with disabilities of all ages to have accurate information regarding what does and does not constitute workplace discrimination under the law (Nissen & Rumrill, 2014).

Conclusion

Results of this investigation reveal a mix of similarities and differences in the workplace discrimination experiences of older and younger adult workers with disabilities. Specifically, there were no significant age differences in the size of Employers against whom allegations were filed. Regardless of age, more allegations were filed against Employers with 500 or more employees, who both employ more workers with disabilities (on a proportional basis) and are more active in educating employees about their rights. Further, the findings suggest that age is not a factor in the resolution of the EEOC's investigatory process. Together, these findings speak well of the professionalism of EEOC investigators and Employer efforts to implement the ADA for employees and job candidates across the lifespan. These initiatives and advocacy are important because the number of older workers (many of whom have age-related impairments) in the workforce is expected to continue to increase, and the continued employment of older workers has benefits for individuals as well as organizations.

Older workers with disabilities were less likely than their younger counterparts to allege discrimination related to unlawful discharge, suggesting that the strengths older workers with disabilities bring to the workplace (e.g., leadership, work ethic) may prevent them from being terminated. Additional workplace policies, such as intergenerational mentorship programs, could be one strategy to reduce the factors that precipitate unlawful discharge allegations from younger workers with disabilities by providing opportunities for older workers to share their knowledge and experience with their younger counterparts. Importantly, there were issues related to maintaining employment, such as terms/conditions, assignment, layoff, and involuntary retirement, which were more likely to be cited by older Charging Parties, suggesting that these issues require redoubled efforts with respect to ADA training and technical assistance regarding older workers with disabilities. Finally, group differences in the industry designations of employers against whom ADA Title I allegations were filed suggest that ADA training and technical assistance efforts should be tailored to specific industries (e.g., education, health care, the arts) where the incidence of alleged discrimination against older workers with disabilities is especially high.

References

The final section of a research article is always a listing of the references that were cited in the body of the text. References are listed in alphabetical order, according to authors' last names. Most rehabilitation journals require adherence to the American Psychological Association's (2013) guidelines regarding the composition of the References page. The works cited by Cichy et al. (2015) appear in the References section of this book.

GUIDELINES FOR CRITIQUING RESEARCH ARTICLES

It is our hope that understanding the components, organization, and composition of a research article, via the descriptions and examples provided to this point in the chapter, will make preservice and practicing rehabilitation counselors better informed consumers as they read the professional literature. As readers digest the contents of research articles and apply them to their practices, the "anatomy" of empirical reports can serve as a useful rubric for critically analyzing the quality, content, and practical significance of published research. Table 9.6 presents guidelines and specific questions for conducting a section-by-section critique of a rehabilitation research article. Educators are encouraged to modify this framework to meet their students' specific needs in rehabilitation research utilization courses.

SUMMARY

As Chapters 6, 7, and 8 of this book attest, there are many ways to conduct scholarly research and make valuable contributions to the knowledge base of rehabilitation counseling. When composing research reports, it is important for rehabilitation scholars to exercise creativity in their scientific endeavors within the context of prevailing publication guidelines set forth by the American Psychological Association (2013). Specifically, research articles published in most social science journals share in common clear and descriptive titles; 100–150-word abstracts; introductory sections including the research problem, the conceptual framework of the study, and research questions/hypotheses; Method sections including descriptions of the sample, instruments, materials, design, and procedures; full reports of relevant results; discussions of the limitations of the study and implications for future research; and references presented in accordance with the American Psychological Association's style guidelines.

Understanding the sections of a research article helps readers to make decisions regarding the quality and practical significance of research investigations published in the rehabilitation literature. Familiarity with the components of a standard article facilitates the critical analyses that informed consumers of rehabilitation research make as they read reports in an effort to enhance their own practices. By delineating the "anatomy" of a research article and providing a framework for critiquing research reports, we hope that this chapter has prepared readers to assimilate contemporary rehabilitation literature into their professional development and continuing education activities.

Table 9.6.
Guidelines for Critiquing Research Articles

Instructions: Answer the following questions regarding the article,
"_____."

Use examples from the article to support your analyses.

A. Title

1. Did the title describe the study?
2. Did the key words of the title serve as key elements of the article?
3. Was the title concise, i.e., free of distracting or extraneous phrases?

B. Abstract

4. Did the abstract summarize the study's purpose, methods, and findings?
5. Did the abstract reveal the independent and dependent variables under study?
6. Were there any major premises or findings presented in the article that were not mentioned in the abstract?
7. Did the abstract provide you with sufficient information to determine whether you would be interested in reading the entire article?

C. Introduction

8. Was the research problem clearly identified?
9. Is the problem significant enough to warrant the study that was conducted?
10. Did the authors present a theoretical rationale for the study?
11. Is the conceptual framework of the study appropriate in light of the research problem?
12. Do the author's hypotheses and/or research questions seem logical in light of the conceptual framework and research problem?
13. Are hypotheses and research questions clearly stated? Are they directional?
14. Overall, does the literature review lead logically into the Method section?

D. Method

15. Is the sample clearly described, in terms of size, relevant characteristics, selection and assignment procedures, and whether any inducements were used to solicit subjects?
16. Do the instruments described seem appropriate as measures of the variables under study?
17. Have the authors included sufficient information about the psychometric properties (e.g., reliability and validity) of the instruments?
18. Are the materials used in conducting the study or in collecting data clearly described?
19. Are the study's scientific procedures thoroughly described in chronological order?
20. Is the design of the study identified (or made evident)?

Table 9.6.–*Continued*

21. Do the design and procedures seem appropriate in light of the research problem, conceptual framework, and research questions/hypotheses?
22. Overall, does the method section provide sufficient information to replicate the study?

E. Results

23. Is the Results section clearly written and well organized?
24. Are data coding and analysis appropriate in light of the study's design and hypotheses?
25. Are salient results connected directly to hypotheses?
26. Are tables and figures clearly labeled? Well organized? Necessary (non-duplicative of text)?

F. Discussion and Conclusion

27. Are the limitations of the study delineated?
28. Are findings discussed in terms of the research problem, conceptual framework, and hypotheses?
29. Are implications for future research and/or rehabilitation counseling practice identified?
30. Are the author's general conclusions warranted in light of the results?

G. References

31. Is the reference list sufficiently current?
32. Do works cited reflect the breadth of existing literature regarding the topic of the study?
33. Are bibliographic citations used appropriately in the text?

Chapter 10

THE FUTURE OF REHABILITATION RESEARCH

INTRODUCTION

As we enter the final chapter of this text, we hope that readers have been well-acquainted with the past and present of scientific inquiry in rehabilitation counseling. In the first chapter, we discussed the methods, norms, and processes by which scientific knowledge claims are evaluated; the current status of research in social sciences; and the purposes of rehabilitation counseling research. Then, following an examination of the foundational principles of empirical research (Chapters 2–5), we spent three chapters (6, 7, & 8) reviewing selected rehabilitation literature within the context of current practices in research design and methodology. In Chapter 9, we presented the Anatomy of a research article and provided guidelines for evaluating published research. We will devote this final chapter to a discussion of contemporary and emerging issues for rehabilitation researchers, research consumers, and people with disabilities, as we continue in the early decades of the twenty-first century.

This chapter offers our perspective on the past, present, and future of rehabilitation research, organized around the heuristic framework of primary, secondary, and tertiary knowledge claims in rehabilitation, and grounded in our own experiences as researchers, educators, rehabilitation counselors, and research consumers. We cast what we think will be new developments in rehabilitation research in political, regulatory, and (we hope) practical contexts – in the following sequence: (a) the role of theory in contemporary and future rehabilitation research, (b) the topic areas that we regard as most fertile for future inquiry, and (c) the research approaches and strategies that investigators are likely to draw upon in addressing those topics.

A FRAMEWORK FOR ORGANIZING REHABILITATION RESEARCH

Our framework for organizing rehabilitation research efforts in terms of primary, secondary, and tertiary contributions to the knowledge base in rehabilitation counseling is structured by the primary beneficiaries of rehabilitation research—people with disabilities—and the principal goal of federally funded research on disability—enhancing the participation of people with disabilities in society. The categories of primary, secondary, and tertiary research reflect the relative proximity or distance of the knowledge claims generated by contemporary rehabilitation research to the principal beneficiaries and goals of these research efforts. *Primary* research efforts are those that generate new knowledge pertaining directly to the status and/or participation of people with disabilities in society. These studies involve descriptive and predictive studies on the outcomes achieved by people with disabilities, research on psychosocial adjustment to various types of disabilities, evaluation of causal models that explain participation outcomes, and intervention research designed to enhance participation. *Secondary* research efforts operate one step removed from the central focus of rehabilitation and seek to understand the competencies, attitudes, and dispositions of preservice or practicing rehabilitation counselors who work with people with disabilities. Examples of secondary research include the many studies of roles and functions of rehabilitation counselors in different practice settings, practitioner confidence and competence in specific knowledge domains, and the impact of preservice training on rehabilitation counselor attitudes and behaviors. *Tertiary* research efforts contribute knowledge about the professional issues that are relevant to rehabilitation counselors and educators, but they do not center directly on the experiences, perspectives, and concerns of rehabilitation consumers and professionals. Examples of tertiary research include topic areas such as ethics and ethical standards in rehabilitation; clinical supervision in rehabilitation counseling; evaluation of training modalities in rehabilitation education; and the research productivity of rehabilitation educators, researchers, and programs.

Occasionally, studies will integrate more than one "level" or context in an attempt to develop warranted knowledge. For example, an investigation of the employment outcomes achieved by people with disabilities being served by CRC and non-CRC rehabilitation professionals would integrate primary and secondary contexts in the research design. We categorize these cases according to the more proximal context in relation to principal beneficiaries and goals of the research. Hence, the example provided would be *primary* research based on the fact that the knowledge claim pertains to employment outcomes achieved by people with disabilities. Our goals in presenting this heuristic framework are to (a) orient rehabilitation counselors and educators to the different contexts in which rehabilitation research efforts are framed, and (b) ensure that future rehabilitation research becomes ever more relevant to people with disabilities and the goals of rehabilitation.

We believe strongly that nothing is more important to the continued viability of our profession than developing a more thorough understanding of our consumers and, by virtue of that understanding, providing more effective and responsive services in partnership with them. We believe that the rehabilitation counseling profession neglects first-order research topics to our own detriment, with irrelevancy to our principal constituencies being the ultimate peril.

THE ROLE OF THEORY IN REHABILITATION RESEARCH

Theory plays an essential role in the generation of research ideas, and in the development and organization of knowledge within the professional domain of rehabilitation counseling. The history of science teaches us that the advancement of scientific knowledge depends on the development of theory, empirical evaluation of theoretical propositions and models, and refinement of these based on the findings of systematic research programs. In our 2009 edition of this text, we noted that, to advance the scientific bases of rehabilitation counseling, rehabilitation researchers needed to devote more time and energy to theory-driven research programs rather than theory-free investigations. In recent years, an encouraging number of new or revised theoretical models of disability and related constructs have been proposed, including the *International Classification of Function (ICF)* model of disability (Frain et al., 2015), the consumer autonomy and empowerment model (Toriello & Keferl, 2012), the poverty disability model (Strauser, 2013) and the quality of life/disability centrality model (Bishop, 2012). Each of these theoretical models frames disability and the rehabilitation process as a complex interaction of personal, environmental, and systems variables. Each serves to organize and explain hypothesized relationships among personal, environmental, and experiential phenomena in the lives of people with disabilities and/or service providers. It is becoming far more common than in previous decades for rehabilitation investigators to utilize these and other theoretical frameworks to guide the development of their research programs and to design individual studies to test, either wholly or in part, specific theoretical propositions (Bishop, 2012; Roessler, Rumrill, Li, & Leslie, 2015). The continuing development of the scientific basis of rehabilitation counseling is facilitated by (a) explicit evaluation of the theory-based propositions that follow from contemporary theories and models, and (b) the use of empirical findings to revise theories and models so that they better mirror reality. Theory provides the necessary framework for the advancement of scientific knowledge, but knowledge can only be verified incrementally through successive, individual studies that are relatively narrow in scope.

As Serlin (1987) noted, research findings are rarely directly applicable to professional practice. Rather, research contributes to effective practice through the testing, confirmation or disconfirmation, and refinement of causal explanations, which specify what variables are related, how they are related, the nature of the processes that are involved, and the extent to which variable relationships can be generalized across populations, settings, and conditions. Thus, the recent and positive trend toward greater utilization of theories and models in designing and implementing rehabilitation research has the potential to enhance the relevance of research findings to professional practices. Therefore, we challenge rehabilitation scholars to continue to develop even stronger theoretical basis for their empirical investigations and to proceed with efforts toward translating this new knowledge more effectively into professional practice. The growing evidence-based practice (EBP) movement in rehabilitation counseling (Chan, Tarvydas, Blalock, Strauser, & Atkins, 2008) reinforces the reciprocal link among theoretical propositions, empirical research findings, and professional practice by establishing agreed-upon standards for considering specific professional practices "evidence-based" (Leahy, Chan, & Lui, 2014). This movement will provide scientists with stronger warrants for new knowledge claims than has historically been the case in atheoretical investigations. In so doing, it will more rapidly bridge the gap between the profession's need for and utilization of new knowledge, thereby allowing research to keep up with field practice (and, hopefully, vice versa).

Specific rehabilitation research areas that have already begun to benefit from the application of contemporary person-environment interaction models include workplace discrimination, rehabilitation processes and outcomes, family issues in the adjustment to and acceptance of disability, the reciprocal impact of self-perceptions and the perceptions of others in formulating personal responses to disability, and the specific interactions of personal and contextual factors that influence the experiences of people with disabilities across the life span. Moreover, the continued development and testing of theory-based psychosocial and employment-focused interventions have the potential to yield valuable information for both scholars and practitioners about *what* facilitates the achievement of valued social outcomes for people with disabilities and *why*.

Cutting across these various research topics and programs, a stronger focus on the environmental aspects of person-environment interaction models is also needed. Across many of the topic areas described to this point in this book, we need to know what aspects of the environment present barriers (attitudinal, architectural, systems) to the participation of people with disabilities in various life pursuits and what types of environmental accommodations and supports serve to enhance participation. The causal role of the environment in producing disability outcomes is a central tenet of the disability rights movement and is a cornerstone of the service philosophy of rehabilitation counseling, yet the bulk of the research efforts in our field continues to be directed toward understanding the role of the personal dimensions that contribute to the person-environment interaction. A more sophisticated understanding of disability and participation requires greater attendance to the role of the environment and the measurement of barriers and supports.

EMERGING SUBJECT AND TOPIC AREAS IN REHABILITATION RESEARCH

The existing knowledge base in rehabilitation counseling has been built in small increments, with successive studies serving to extend the ones before them along specific lines of inquiry. As we look toward the future, we recognize that the current subject matter of empirical work in our field will be augmented with new research programs designed to build upon what we already know. The progressive, linear approach to developing valid knowledge serves many useful purposes, but it also requires vigilance on the part of scientists to avoid "re-hashing" what has already been done and, thereby, truncating the growth of new knowledge.

Numerous studies have given us a thorough understanding of such phenomena as clinical supervision, employer attitudes toward workers with disabilities, practitioner confidence and competence in specific knowledge domains, the influence of preservice training on counselor behaviors, and the scholarly productivity of rehabilitation faculty. In fairness, these lines of inquiry have served and will continue to serve an important evaluative function for the profession. However, from a global perspective, these research topics represent second- and third-order investigations, one (or more) step removed from the primary foci of rehabilitation research, which are: (a) the interests, skills, values, and experiences of people with disabilities; and (b) how the rehabilitation process facilitates the participation of people with disabilities in all social roles. A peril that inheres in devoting too much energy to secondary and tertiary issues (to the exclusion of primary topics) is that rehabilitation research may be viewed as irrelevant to its primary beneficiaries (i.e., people with disabilities). We need to place the focus of our efforts to generate new knowledge squarely where it belongs—on our clients and consumers. Thus, we still eagerly await the time when rehabilitation researchers devote as much energy to understanding the needs of people with disabilities as is devoted to promoting and preserving the profession of rehabilitation counseling.

Our call for rehabilitation counseling researchers to more explicitly place the primary emphasis of their scientific investigations on the experiences, concerns, perspectives, and outcomes of people with disabilities is consistent with other recent voices in rehabilitation counseling. Koch and associates (Koch, Schultz, Hennessey, & Conyers, 2005; Schultz, Koch, & Kontosh, 2007) conducted two investigations on the perspectives of rehabilitation educators regarding future research directions for rehabilitation counseling. The initial study by Koch et al. used qualitative methods (i.e., focus groups and open-ended internet surveys) with 63 members of the National Council on Rehabilitation Education (NCRE). The rehabilitation educators were asked to (a) reflect on the history of rehabilitation research and specify those research programs that have had the greatest impact on rehabilitation counselor training and practice, and (b) identify the most important research topics for the future. In the second study, a survey instrument—the NCRE Research Priorities Survey—was sent to all members of the NCRE listserv. NCRE members were asked to rank order eight broad categories and 67 specific research topics regarding the rehabilitation issues that warrant further investigation. The data for this second study were analyzed quantitatively and consisted of 88 usable surveys from NCRE members. The formal purpose of these studies was to establish a consensus-driven research agenda for the field to consider.

In the Koch et al. (2005) study, the NCRE members stated that foremost among the knowledge domains that have had the greatest impact on the profession over the past decades was research that has addressed the professional competencies of rehabilitation counselors (e.g., role and function studies, studies on CORE curricula, and studies of training needs of rehabilitation counselors in different work settings. Although we characterize this knowledge domain as secondary research, we acknowledge that this broad research program has been pivotal in developing the empirical foundation of the profession. Research on professional competencies of rehabilitation counselors in various work settings will continue to be relevant in the future as an important means of maintaining solid connections between contemporary practice in rehabilitation counseling and the accreditation of graduate rehabilitation education programs and between professional practice and the certification of rehabilitation counselors.

Other knowledge domains cited by the NCRE members in the Koch et al. (2005) study as having the most significant impact in past decades were vocational rehabilitation outcome studies, research on psychosocial issues in adjustment to disability, research that identified inequities in the delivery of rehabilitation services to persons from minority groups, and intervention studies. Interestingly, four of the five cited research programs with the greatest past impact on the profession are areas that we characterize as primary research.

In the Schultz et al. (2007) study, the 88 NCRE members ranked rehabilitation outcomes, rehabilitation interventions, and consumer involvement in rehabilitation as the highest-priority general categories for future research. All three of these areas pertain to primary research topics according to our criteria. Among the 67 specific research topics, the 13 highest-ranked topics warranting further investigation pertained to primary research as we have defined it, with quality of life for persons with disabilities, consumer job retention, and career advancement for persons with disabilities ranked highest overall.

We are encouraged that the rehabilitation educators who participated in the Koch et al. (2005) and Schultz et al. (2007) studies appear to share our perspective on what constitutes the most important research topics to be addressed in future rehabilitation research, namely, research that pertains directly to the status/participation of people with disabilities in society. We believe that this broad consensus on future research priorities reflects a fundamental agreement among most rehabilitation educators regarding the primary goals and beneficiaries of rehabilitation research. We believe that this consensus reflects the core values of rehabilitation counseling: what we as a profession value in terms of new knowledge and the practice-related values rehabilitation educators seek to instill in their students. That said, these studies were conducted more than a decade before the publication of this third edition of our book; a contemporary investigation of the research priorities of rehabilitation educators is needed to determine whether these priorities have changed in recent years.

More recently, Chronister and Rumrill (2012) suggested a number of rehabilitation research topics that should be investigated in greater depth. Foremost among these fertile lines of inquiry were intervention studies that promote evidence-based practices in the field. Fields such as education, psychology, and medicine have adopted guidelines and standards for research findings that constitute evidence-based practices, and we believe that it would greatly benefit the field of rehabilitation counseling to adopt a set of standards for intervention research that guides preservice training and professional service delivery. Moreover, the Federal government has steadily increased its emphasis on knowledge translation in all of the disability and rehabilitation research programs that it sponsors, so rehabilitation researchers will gain a distinct advantage in their pursuit of federal funding if they develop standards by which knowledge generated in their research investigations can be translated into professional practice.

Koch and Rumrill (2016) also strongly suggested that intervention research be designed to address the unique needs of specific and emerging populations of people with disabilities such as older individuals, combat veterans, people with psychiatric disabilities and substance use disorders, injured workers, and people with disabilities from racial and ethnic minority groups. Koch and Rumrill added to this list of important and understudied consumer populations people with adult-onset chronic illnesses (e.g., multiple sclerosis, lupus, Type II diabetes mellitus, rheumatoid arthritis) and people whose disabilities are either new to medical science or have grown in prevalence in recent years (e.g., multiple chemical sensitivity, asthma, allergies, dementia, autism, fibromyalgia and other primary pain disorders). More research is also needed to evaluate psychosocial interventions and community services that address the unique rehabilitation needs of women with disabilities, as well as interventions to assist people with disabilities in developing more effective social networks to enhance participation (Rubin, Roessler, & Rumrill, 2016; Smart, 2009). Other intervention research studies recommended in recent publications include the use of the Internet as a job placement and career counseling tool (Strauser, 2013), the use of the World Health Organization's International Classification of Functioning framework in vocational rehabilitation (Frain et al., 2015), strategies for helping people with disabilities avail themselves of the expanded civil rights protections set forth in the 2008 Americans with Disabilities Act Amendments Act (ADAAA; Rubin et al., 2016), the validity of self-estimates versus standardized testing in vocational planning and service delivery (Chronister & Rumrill, 2012), and the impact of mentoring and role modeling on the employment and long-term career success of people with disabilities (Hendricks et al., 2015).

In our view, helping people with disabilities develop more effective self-advocacy skills is a priority that cuts across a number of different topic areas and is central to enhancing the civil rights and participation of people with disabilities in various life areas. Hence, we place a high priority on the need for intervention studies that involve targeted training for people with disabilities who wish to invoke their rights to non-discriminatory treatment in the workplace under the ADAAA. Whether they are completing job application forms, participating in employment interviews, requesting reasonable accommodations, or redressing discriminatory conduct to which their employers have subjected them, people with disabilities need to know their civil rights as they apply for, enter, and seek to maintain employment, their recourses if those rights are violated, and specific actions they must take to protect the guarantees of fair and equitable treatment that the ADAAA provides.

Intervention studies are also needed to assist workers with disabilities or their advocates to invoke their federal employment rights under such statutes as the Family and Medical Leave Act, the Affordable Care Act, and the Workforce Innovation and Opportunity Act (Rudstam et al., 2014; Rubin et al., 2016). As with most of their legal rights, people with disabilities have historically been reticent to take advantage of the considerable benefits of these laws, and rehabilitation counselors must develop and evaluate strategies for improving the self-advocacy skills of our consumers with regard to these federal protections.

Given our society's emphasis on fiscal responsibility and professional accountability in our systems of education, health care, government services, and workforce development, it should come as no surprise that we consider outcome research as another major future priority for rehabilitation counseling. Chronister & Rumrill (2012) encouraged future rehabilitation researchers, for example, to develop alternative measures of Status 26 (successfully rehabilitated) closures in the state-Federal Vocational Rehabilitation program such as quality of life and career advancement. We would add that future outcome research should address multidimensional outcomes of the rehabilitation process (e.g., various psychosocial benefits associated with receipt of rehabilitation services, benefits to families, employers, etc.) as well as other valued participation outcomes beyond employment (e.g., participation in community settings, participation in leisure pursuits; Bishop, 2012). Other important emphases for future outcome studies include long-term outcomes in the workers' compensation system and other areas of private-sector rehabilitation (Brodwin, 2016), long-term outcomes of children with disabilities exiting public schools and entering adult life roles (Strauser, 2013; Wehman, 2013), and the continuation of research examining differential rehabilitation outcomes for members of traditionally underrepresented racial and ethnic groups (Lewis & Burris, 2012).

Pursuant to the examination of rehabilitation outcomes for persons with disabilities, we note that the federal government maintains numerous large databases for use in rehabilitation and disability policy research, including the RSA-911 database, the Equal Employment Opportunity Commission's Integrated Mission System database, the Social Security database, and the National Longitudinal Transition database (NTLB2). We observe that these data sets continue to be underutilized as sources for theory-driven research on rehabilitation outcomes and policy in the rehabilitation counseling literature, and we encourage rehabilitation researchers to examine and utilize these sources in their work. Higher quality rehabilitation research will also require improvements in the scope and breadth of required reporting for agencies that manage these databases, thereby enhancing the quality of these data as a tool for theory-driven research.

Consumer involvement in rehabilitation was another highly ranked priority for future research according to the NCRE participants in the Schultz et al. (2007) study, and we agree with our fellow rehabilitation educators that we must develop strategies to ensure that the counselor-client partnership transcends the rhetoric of the classroom and becomes the guiding force in the rehabilitation process. Involving people with disabilities, and all other stakeholders, for that matter, in all aspects of rehabilitation research and service delivery is the only way to ensure that our complementary research and service delivery efforts are fully responsive to their needs. Moreover, as noted by Schultz et al. (2007), the perceived gap between research and practice will only be bridged when people with disabilities and service providers become more active partners in rehabilitation research efforts.

From our own vantage point as rehabilitation educators and researchers, there are a number of areas of scientific inquiry that seem particularly important to the immediate future of rehabilitation counseling. One such area is privatization. Since the first edition of this book was published in 1999, there has been disappointingly little growth in the knowledge base regarding such private-sector phenomena as the validity of life care planning as a rehabilitation service, the efficacy and cost-benefits of disability management programs in industry, factors that influence return-to-work outcomes for injured employees, and applications of vocational assessment and planning strategies in personal injury and workers' compensation litigation.

The knowledge base in rehabilitation counseling always requires systematic and comprehensive evaluations of disability and rehabilitation policy initiatives, especially as the policies and laws that govern our field change over time with new Congresses and Presidential administrations and as a result of case law. Specifically, we need to better understand how the ADAAA complements and intersects with other laws such as the Civil Rights Act, the Family and Medical Leave Act, the Affordable Care Act, state workers' compensation statutes, the Workforce Innovation and Opportunity Act, and the Age Discrimination in Employment Act (Rubin et al., 2016; Rudstam et al., 2014; Strauser, 2013; Wehman, 2013). We need to more thoroughly understand the disability-related provisions of the Social Security Act–especially the Social Security Disability Insurance and Supplemental Security Income programs, Medicaid, Medicare, and Ticket to Work and other work incentives—regarding how these benefits and incentives apply to the services and end goals of the rehabilitation process (Hendricks et al., 2015; Marini, 2003). We need to study and understand the impact of amendments and reauthorizations of the Rehabilitation Act (most notably the 2014 Workforce Innovation and Opportunity Act) and changes in the Rehabilitation Services Administration's programs on rehabilitation counselor training and practice over time. We need to understand how specific disability policy initiatives and generic social policy initiatives have affected people with disabilities in such fundamental areas of life as housing, transportation, leisure and recreation, health care, civic participation, education, employment, financial planning, and access to technology. We need to know whether there is such a thing as the "disability community," or will people with disabilities continue to exist as fragmentary sub-groups divided by medically-derived illness and impairment classifications (American Association of People with Disabilities, 2016)?

At the most basic policy level, we need to know what the term "disability" means in contemporary American society. Is it a medical, economic, social status, or situational phenomenon (Bishop, 2012)? How does the way we classify people and single them out for services affect their stature and standing in our communities (Koch & Rumrill, 2016; Smart, 2009)?

Another burgeoning area for empirical research in rehabilitation in the years to come will be assistive technology. We need to follow developments in this dynamic facet of our field and systematically study the effectiveness, safety, availability, practicality, and use patterns of new devices as they come on the market, as well as consumers' satisfaction with assistive technology devices (Scherer, 2012). We also look for in-depth inquiries into the interactions between medical technology and assistive technology; in that regard, the interface among health care professionals, rehabilitation counselors, rehabilitation engineers, employers, and people with disabilities will be of paramount interest.

Medical science will continue to have major effects on rehabilitation counseling and research. People with catastrophic injuries and illnesses (e.g., spinal cord injuries, traumatic brain injuries, cancer) are living longer than ever before (Hendricks et al., 2015; Wickert et al., 2013), and scientifically-based research to monitor the medical and psychosocial adjustment of those individuals is needed to continue to improve rehabilitation interventions and outcomes. People with congenital conditions such as spina bifida can now look forward to vocational opportunities and career success thanks to medical advances that have vastly extended their life expectancies (Wehman, 2013). People with HIV/AIDS are increasingly being viewed as having a chronic, rather than terminal, disease, a classification that brings with it numerous service, research, and policy implications (Koch et al., 2012). Medical science has also extended life expectancies for the general population, a phenomenon that points to a myriad of scientific and service delivery considerations related to geriatric rehabilitation for people who incur age-related disabilities (e.g., visual impairments, hearing loss, orthopedic impairments, arthritis, cerebrovascular disease; American Association of People with Disabilities, 2016; Koch & Rumrill, 2016; Wickert et al., 2013).

The processes and outcomes of several intervention strategies and professional specialty areas also need to be examined more rigorously. Foremost among these is transition from school to adult living for young people with disabilities—a process that spans one of the most important developmental periods in people's lives. Applied research is needed to assist special educators and rehabilitation counselors to collaborate more effectively in planning and providing comprehensive services to youth with disabilities who exit public schools and enter the world of work, postsecondary educational programs, and other adult roles (Strauser, 2013; Wehman, 2013). Long-term follow-up data are needed to clarify the service needs of transitioning youth with disabilities and practices that best meet those needs. One of the most important areas for future transition research is postsecondary education. With enrollment rates of students with disabilities having more than quadrupled on American college and university campuses since 1978 (Association on Higher Education and Disability, 2016), growing interest has been evident in the transition *to* higher education for these students. Less focus has been evident in the transition *from* college and university programs to competitive careers. Comparisons with non-disabled college graduates find alumni with disabilities at a distinct disadvantage for career-entry and job retention (Hendricks et al., 2015; Hennessey, Roessler, Cook, Unger, & Rumrill, 2006). In-depth inquiry is needed to ascertain the precise nature of the difficulties that people with disabilities have in translating a college education into a successful career.

Effective employment interventions are needed for people with disabilities that focus on expanding the parameters of rehabilitation service delivery. Primarily, this will involve a commitment to understand the career development needs of people with disabilities after their cases have been closed by rehabilitation agencies. Current rehabilitation practice is replete with sophisticated and proven job development and placement strategies to help people with disabilities secure employment (McMahon, 2006; Rubin et al., 2016; Wehman, 2013), but there is a glaring lack of effective career maintenance interventions. Numerous studies over the past several years have documented the poor post-rehabilitation employment outcomes of people with disabilities, and most of these investigations point toward the lack of adequate work adjustment services for employed individuals as a primary reason for workforce attrition (Chapin, 2012; Fraser, Kraft, Ehde, & Johnson, 2006). Researchers need to identify the specific reasons that job retention is so difficult for employees with disabilities and tailor interventions to meet those needs.

EMERGING RESEARCH TECHNIQUES AND STRATEGIES

As rehabilitation researchers apply scientific methods to address those emerging issues discussed to this point in the chapter (and many other issues), it is important to note that the way research is conducted is likely to change just as dramatically as the topics under study will. This section examines a number of trends that we anticipate for the foreseeable future in terms of how science is applied in rehabilitation research.

For example, we are seeing the broad applicability of qualitative research methods in rehabilitation counseling (Niesz, Koch, & Rumrill, 2008). As a means of investigating phenomena that have not been previously examined, identifying variables for theory-building purposes, and providing understanding of the lived experience of disability and rehabilitation that is not possible using quantitative methods, qualitative research will continue to play a vital role in building our profession's knowledge base. Within the qualitative realm, we hope to see a movement toward prolonged engagements with research participants within their natural environments and the application of more rigorous research methods to enhance the credibility of qualitative findings. The grounded theory method of qualitative research (Strauss & Corbin, 1990)–whereby theoretical propositions are developed on the basis of observation and then tested, revised, and refined through prolonged engagement and systematic data analysis–is well-suited to contribute to the theoretical foundation of our profession. Koch et al. (2005) reported that several rehabilitation educators and researchers identified focus groups as a time-efficient and cost-effective qualitative strategy to gather important data in a small-group format. Focus groups have been used in marketing and advertising for many years, and they have recently made their way to the social sciences as a viable means of eliciting the perspectives of stakeholders in such matters as the future directions of rehabilitation counseling research (Koch et al.), the employment concerns of Americans with chronic illnesses (Rumrill, Roessler, Li, Daly, & Leslie, 2015), and the career preparation needs of college and university students with disabilities (Hennessey, 2004).

For rehabilitation researchers who use quantitative research methods, we have seen an encouraging increase in the use of multivariate outcome analyses in recent years. The constructs that underlie clinical practice and service provision in rehabilitation counseling are multidimensional, as are the psychosocial factors that influence clients' participation in the rehabilitation process (e.g., motivation, social supports, socioeconomic status). Therefore, it is important for rehabilitation researchers to evaluate outcomes as they really are—multidimensional, sometimes complicated, dependent upon multiple factors that vary widely among individuals, and falling along a continuum of successfulness—rather than adhering to an "all or nothing" rubric. We need to examine more than one outcome at a time in the vast majority of research contexts. We also need to evaluate complex variable models that more fully incorporate the complex person-environment interaction models that dominate our theoretical conceptualizations of disability and the rehabilitation process rather than focusing on simple variable relationships.

To accomplish these aims, we need to utilize data analytic techniques that are more suited to these tasks. For example, multivariate analysis of variance enables researchers to gauge the interactive effects of different correlated outcomes in a manner that is not possible using univariate analyses. Path analysis and structural equation modeling are data analytic techniques that permit the simultaneous evaluation of theory-driven models of variable relationships in a manner that provides rigorous tests of theory. They also permit the revision of theoretical propositions based on the actual empirical data. We observe that during the past decade there has been increased use of path analysis and structural equation modeling in rehabilitation counseling research, and this increased use parallels a greater emphasis on theory-driven research.

Another multivariate data analytic technique that provides opportunities to more effectively capture the complexity of the real world is multilevel modeling (MLM), also known as hierarchical linear modeling (HLM). MLM is a statistical approach that is appropriate for analysis of "nested" or hierarchically-ordered data, as are often encountered in the rehabilitation service provision process. For example, client outcomes vary as a function of specific client characteristics such as ethnicity, education level, motivation, and so forth. Client outcomes may also vary as a function of rehabilitation counselor competency (the next "level" of data in the hierarchy) and state agency characteristics (e.g., amount of funding, specific agency policies). To adequately "model" the rehabilitation process as it really is requires that these different levels of data be taken into consideration. When we analyze client outcomes at the level of the client only, we may be inappropriately ascribing all the sources of variability in the service provision process to the characteristics of the client, when in fact additional sources may better explain why specific outcomes are achieved. Although to date the use of MTM in the rehabilitation literature has been quite rare, there are a few recent examples of studies that utilize these methods (Matrone & Leahy, 2005; Kwok et al., 2008). Although we advocate here for the use of more sophisticated data analyses in rehabilitation research, we also recognize that sophisticated data analytic techniques are no substitute for a rigorous research design. Quality in the research design, coupled with appropriate data analytic strategies, provides the strongest warrant for a scientific knowledge claim.

Therefore, along with more sophisticated data analytic techniques, rehabilitation researchers should design more studies that are longitudinal in nature. The vast majority of quantitative rehabilitation investigations utilize a cross-sectional approach to data gathering. That is, data are gathered at one point in time and an attempt is made to infer causal relations from this "snapshot in time." However, regardless of the specific data analytic technique used, cross-sectional studies are generally unable to generate strong warrants for causality, given the fact that in these designs the temporal precedence of the causal factor(s) is not established within the data gathering effort. Longitudinal designs may yield much stronger warrants for causal relations precisely because a primary condition of causality—that the cause precedes the effect—is mimicked in the research design. We have observed few examples of longitudinal research designs in recent rehabilitation research, and the development of warranted scientific knowledge in our field has been hindered by this lacking.

For rehabilitation outcomes and other data that are not normally distributed, we recommend that rehabilitation researchers become familiar with non-parametric statistical analyses that permit comparisons among groups on nominally or categorically coded dependent variables. A growing body of literature in our field is devoted to studies that have used chi squares and other non-parametric techniques to analyze important phenomena in the lives of people with disabilities (McMahon, West, Mansouri, & Belongia, 2006; Unger, Campbell, & McMahon, 2006).

One major development in federal policy and rehabilitation counseling practice that has direct bearing on the techniques and strategies of future rehabilitation research is the increased emphasis on consumer involvement over the past several decades. Amendments to the Rehabilitation Act in 1992 and 1998 provided strict guidelines for ensuring that people with disabilities take an active role in all aspects of case planning and service delivery in the VR program (Rubin et al., 2016). Also, there is growing interest among policymakers to involve people with disabilities in all phases of the research process (Rumrill et al., 2010). One such approach to involving people with disabilities in research is known as Participatory Action Research (PAR; Graves, 1991). PAR is defined as "applied rehabilitation research that includes people with disabilities, their families, service providers, scholars, policymakers, and/or other members of the community in the quest of information from the initial conception of the idea through implementation and evaluation of its impact" (19th Institute on Rehabilitation Issues, 1993, p.16). Given the expanded emphasis on consumer involvement in all aspects of research, we expect to see people with disabilities playing an increasingly prominent role in shaping and implementing research projects. By assisting researchers in identifying samples, developing instruments, formulating intervention strategies, analyzing data, reflecting on results, and establishing policy and service agendas, rehabilitation consumers will serve as key consultants and real stakeholders in the investigations designed to address their needs.

One particular PAR approach that has the potential to advance our understanding of the experiences and outcomes of Americans with disabilities while ensuring their active involvement in rehabilitation research is the concerns report methodology (CRM; Schriner & Fawcett, 1988; Schriner, Roessler, & Johnson, 1992). The CRM is a widely-used set of procedures for developing a relevant list of consumer concerns and setting an agenda for needed changes in policy and service delivery based on perceived strengths and problems identified by a particular group of people. This approach has often been applied in rehabilitation research, involving people with disabilities and other stakeholders in identifying prominent concerns, setting priorities among the identified concerns for intervention and change, and establishing plans for implementing needed solutions to high-priority problems.

As partners in CRM research, people with disabilities are involved in selecting items for data collection instruments, determining useful data collection procedures, evaluating significant strengths and weaknesses in existing policies and services, and interpreting results. CRM has proven useful with a number of disability groups, including people with multiple sclerosis (Rumrill, Roessler, Li, Daly, & Leslie, 2015), individuals with traditional and emerging disabilities (Nary, White, Budde, & Vo, 2004), individuals with blindness or visual impairments (Wolffe, Roessler, & Schriner, 1992), individuals with traumatic brain injuries (Roessler & Schriner, 1992), people with spina bfida (Schriner, Roessler, & Johnson, 1993), Deaf people (Schriner, Roessler, & Raymer, 1991), adults with psychiatric disorders (Snyder, Temple, Youngbauer, O'Neil, & Cromwell, 1995), and college students with disabilities (Hennessey et al., 2006; Schriner & Roessler, 1990).

SUMMARY

In an applied social science such as rehabilitation counseling, policy, practice, and scientific inquiry are shaped through an ongoing, reciprocal process. Thus, many of the impending changes in rehabilitation research about which we have speculated in this chapter stem from changes in disability and rehabilitation policy that have an impact on the profession and practice of rehabilitation counseling. Contemporary rehabilitation counselors are subject to new regulations and policy shifts, heightened certification and licensure standards, and pressures to specialize (to name just a few recent and continuing trends). These trends place heavy demands on rehabilitation counselors to update their knowledge in order to continue to effectively serve people with disabilities. Similarly, rehabilitation researchers must stay current with respect to new developments in the field if the contributions that they make to the knowledge base are to be considered meaningful by policymakers, administrators, counselors, employers, and people with disabilities.

This chapter was meant to bring together the observations that we made in preparing the first nine chapters of the book. It reflects our synthesis of contemporary rehabilitation literature, our experiences in teaching and advising graduate-level rehabilitation counseling students, our own research interests and experiences, and the personal perspectives that we have brought to all of those endeavors. By looking ahead in this culminating chapter, we hope that the totality of this volume constitutes a credible and useful look at the past, present, and future of rehabilitation research.

REFERENCES

Abelson, R. (1995). *Statistics as principled argument.* Hillsdale, NJ: Erlbaum.

Accordino, M. P., Porter, D. F., & Morse, T. (2000). Deinstitutionalization of persons with severe mental illness: Context and consequences. *Journal of Rehabilitation, 66,* 16–22.

Adams, M. H. (2000). Online technology leadership. *Journal of Rehabilitation Administration, 24,* 7–13.

Adkins, V. K., Youngbauer, J., & Mathews, R. M. (2000). A validation of a brief instrument to measure independence of persons with head injury. *Journal of Rehabilitation, 66*(3), 51–55.

Agan, J., Koch, L., & Rumrill, P. (2008). The use of focus groups in rehabilitation research. *Work: A Journal of Prevention, Assessment, and Rehabilitation, 31*(2), 259–269.

Agar, M. (1996). *The professional stranger: An informal introduction to ethnography.* San Diego, CA: Academic Press.

Alloway, L. H. (2000). Fibromyalgia syndrome: Symptoms, functional limitations and vocational impediments. *Journal of Applied Rehabilitation Counseling, 31*(3), 38–44.

Alston, R. J. (1992). Wright constructs of psychosocial adjustment to physical disability as a framework for understanding adaptation to chemical dependency. *Journal of Applied Rehabilitation Counseling, 24*(3), 6–10.

American Association of People with Disabilities. (2016). Retrieved January 26, 2016, from http://www.aapd.com/docs/highlights.php

American Counseling Association. (1995). *Code of ethics and standards of practice.* Alexandria, VA: Author.

American Educational Research Association, American Psychological Association, & Council on Measurement in Education. (1985). *Joint technical standards for educational and psychological testing.* Washington, DC: American Psychological Association.

American Educational Research Association, American Psychological Association, & National Council on Measurement in Education. (2015). *Standards for educational and psychological testing.* Washington, DC: American Educational Research Association.

American Psychological Association. (1992). Ethical principles of psychologists and code of conduct. *American Psychologist, 47,* 1597–1611.

American Psychological Association. (1994). *Publication manual of the American Psychological Association* (4th ed.). Washington, DC: Author.
American Psychological Association. (2001). *Publication manual of the American Psychological Association* (5th ed.). Washington, DC: Author.
American Psychological Association. (2013). *Publication manual of the American Psychological Association* (6th ed.). Washington, DC: Author.
American Psychological Association Ethics Committee. (1983). *Authorship guidelines for dissertation supervision.* Washington, DC: Author.
American Rehabilitation Counseling Association. (1988). Code of professional ethics for rehabilitation counselors. *Rehabilitation Counseling Bulletin, 31,* 255–268.
Americans with Disabilities Act of 1990, 42, U.S.C.A. S 12101 et seq. (West 1993).
Anastasi, A. (1992). What counselors should know about the use and interpretation of psychological tests. *Journal of Counseling & Development, 70,* 610–615.
Anderson, C., Leahy, M., DelValle, R., Sherman, S., & Tansey, T. (2014). Methodological application of multiple case study design using modified consensual qualitative research (CQR) analysis to identify best practices and organizational factors in the public rehabilitation program. *Journal of Vocational Rehabilitation, 41*(2), 87–98.
Anderson, W. P., & Heppner, P. P. (1985). Counselor applications of research findings to practice: Learning to stay current. *Journal of Counseling & Development, 65,* 152–155.
Andrade, L., Caraveo-Anduga, J. J., Berglund, P., Biji, R. V., DeGraff, R., Volebergh, W., et al. (2003). The epidemiology of major depressive episodes: Results from the International Consortium of Psychiatric Epidemiology (ICPE) Surveys. *International Journal of Methods in Psychiatric Research, 12,* 3–21.
Angoff, W. H. (1988). Validity: An evolving concept. In H. Wainer & H. I. Braun (Eds.), *Test validity* (pp. 19–32). Hillsdale, NJ: Erlbaum.
Antonak, R. F., & Livneh, H. (1995). Direct and indirect methods to measure attitudes toward persons with disabilities, with an exegesis of the error choice method. *Rehabilitation Psychology, 40,* 3–24.
Araten-Bergman, T., Tal-Katz, P., & Stein, M. A. (2015). Psychosocial adjustment of Israeli veterans with disabilities: Does employment status matter? *Work, 50*(1), 59–71.
Arnold, N., Seekins, T., & Ravesloot, C. (1995). Self-employment as a vocational rehabilitation employment outcome in rural and urban areas. *Rehabilitation Counseling Bulletin, 39*(2), 94–106.
Arokiasamy, C. V. (1993). A theory for rehabilitation? *Rehabilitation Education, 7,* 77–98.
Ary, D., Jacobs, L., & Razavieh A. (1985). *Introduction to research in education.* New York: CBS College Publishing.
Association on Higher Education and Disability. (2016). Retrieved June 6, 2016, from http://www.ahead.org/training/conference/2015_conf/index.php
Atherton, W. L., & Toriello, P. J. (2012). Re-conceptualizing the treatment of substance use disorders: The impact on employment. In P. J. Toriello, M. L. Bishop, & P. D. Rumrill (Eds.), *New directions in rehabilitation counseling: Creative responses*

to professional, clinical, and educational challenges (pp. 282–304). Linn Creek, MO: Aspen Professional Services.

Babbie, E. (1995). *The practice of social research.* New York: Wadsworth.

Baker, S., & Daniels, T. (1989). Integrating research on the micro-counseling program: A meta-analysis. Journal of Counseling Psychology, 36, 213–222.

Baldwin, M. (1997). Gender differences in social security disability decisions. *Journal of Disability Policy Studies, 8*(1–2), 25–50.

Balser, R. M., Hagner, D., & Hornby, H. (2000). Partnership with the business community: The mental health employer consortium. *Journal of Applied Rehabilitation Counseling, 31*(4), 47–56.

Banks, M. (2008). Women with disabilities: Cultural competence in rehabilitation psychology. *Disability and Rehabilitation: A Multidisciplinary Journal, 30,* 184–190.

Barnartt, S., & Altman, B. (1997). Predictors of wages. *Journal of Disability Policy Studies, 8*(1–2), 51–74.

Bat-Chava, Y., & Martin, D. (2002). Sibling relationships of deaf children: The impact of child and family characteristics. *Rehabilitation Psychology, 47,* 73–91.

Bauer, W., & Growick, B. (2003). Rehabilitation counseling in Appalachian America. *Journal of Rehabilitation, 69*(2), 18–24.

Beale, F. (1970). Double jeopardy: To be black and female. In T. Cade (Ed.), *The black woman anthology* (pp. 90–100). New York: Penguin.

Beauchamp, T. L., & Childress, J. F. (1989). *Principles in biomedical ethics* (3rd ed.). New York: Oxford University Press.

Beck, R., Janikowski, T., & Stebnicki, M. (1994). Doctoral dissertation research in rehabilitation: 1990–1991. *Rehabilitation Counseling Bulletin, 38*(1), 3–26.

Beck, R., Janikowski, T., & Stebnicki, M. (1996). Doctoral dissertation research in rehabilitation: 1992–1993. *Rehabilitation Counseling Bulletin, 39*(3), 165–188.

Bellini, J. (1998). Equity and order of selection: Issues in implementation and evaluation of the mandate to serve individuals with the most severe disabilities. *Journal of Disability Policy Studies, 9*(1), 107–124.

Bellini, J. (2001). Implementation and evaluation of the order of selection mandate in state vocational rehabilitation agencies. In P. Rumrill, J. Bellini, & L. Koch (Eds.), *Emerging issues in rehabilitation counseling* (pp. 21–58). Springfield, IL: Charles C Thomas.

Bellini, J. (2002). Correlates of multicultural counseling competencies of vocational rehabilitation counselors. *Rehabilitation Counseling Bulletin, 45*(2), 66–75.

Bellini, J. (2003). Counselors' multicultural competencies and vocational rehabilitation out-comes in the context of counselor-client racial similarity and difference. *Rehabilitation Counseling Bulletin, 46,* 164–173.

Bellini, J., Bolton, B., & Neath, J. (1996). Diagnostic determinants of rehabilitation counselor eligibility decisions. *Journal of Rehabilitation Administration, 20*(2), 93–105.

Bellini, J., Bolton, B., & Neath, J. (1998). Rehabilitation counselors' assessments of applicants functional limitations as predictors of rehabilitation services provided. *Rehabilitation Counseling Bulletin, 41*(4), 242–258.

Bellini, J., Fitzgerald, S., & Rumrill, P. (2000). Perspectives on scientific inquiry: The basics of measurement and statistics. *Journal of Vocational Rehabilitation, 14*(2), 131–143.

Bellini, J., & Rumrill, P. (1999a). Implementing a scientist-practitioner model of graduate level rehabilitation counselor education: Guidelines for enhancing curricular coherence. *Rehabilitation Education, 13*(3), 261–276.

Bellini, J., & Rumrill, P. (1999b). *Research in rehabilitation counseling.* Springfield, IL: Charles C Thomas.

Bellini, J., & Rumrill, P. (2002). Contemporary insights in philosophy of science: Implications for research in rehabilitation counseling. *Rehabilitation Education, 16,* 115–134.

Bellini, J., & Rumrill, P. (2009). *Research in rehabilitation counseling* (2nd ed.). Springfield, IL: Charles C Thomas.

Bellini, J., Rumrill, P., Webb, J., & Snyder, J. (1999). Perspectives on scientific inquiry: Meta-analysis in rehabilitation research. *Journal of Vocational Rehabilitation, 12*(3), 75–78.

Bendick, M. Jr., & Brown, L. E. (1999). No foot in the door: An experimental study of employment discrimination against older workers. *Journal of Aging and Social Policy, 10*(4), 5–23.

Berven, N. L., & Scofield, M. E. (1980). Evaluation of clinical problem-solving skills through standardized case-management simulations. *Journal of Counseling Psychology, 27,* 199–208.

Betz, N., & Weiss, D. (2001). Validity. In Brian Bolton (Ed.), *Handbook of measurement and evaluation in rehabilitation* (3rd ed., pp. 49–76). Gaithersburg, MD: Aspen Publishers, Inc.

Beveridge, S., Craddock, S. H., Liesener, J., Stapleton, M., & Hershenson, D. (2002). Income: A framework for conceptualizing the career development of persons with disabilities. *Rehabilitation Counseling Bulletin, 45,* 195–206.

Bezyak, J., & Clark, A. (2016). Promoting physical and mental health among college students: A needs assessment. *Rehabilitation Research, Policy, and Education, 30*(2), 188–192.

Birk, L. B. (2013). Erasure of the credible subject: An autoethnographic account of chronic pain. *Cultural Studies? Critical Methodologies, 13*(5), 390–399.

Bishop, M. (2004). Determinants of employment status among a community-based sample of people with epilepsy. *Rehabilitation Counseling Bulletin, 47,* 112–120.

Bishop, M. (2005). Quality of life and psychosocial adaptation to chronic illness and disability: Preliminary analysis of a conceptual and theoretical synthesis. *Rehabilitation Counseling Bulletin, 48,* 219–231.

Bishop, M. L. (2012). Psychosocial adaptation to chronic illness and disability: Current status and considerations for new directions. In P. J. Toriello, M. L. Bishop, & P. D. Rumrill (Eds.), *New directions in rehabilitation counseling: Creative responses to professional, clinical, and educational challenges* (pp. 25–53). Linn Creek, MO: Aspen Professional Services.

Bishop, M., Berven, N., Hermann, B., & Chan, F. (2002). Quality of life among adults with epilepsy: An exploratory model. *Rehabilitation Counseling Bulletin, 45,* 87–95.

Bishop, M., Chou, C., Chan, C. C. H., Rahimi, M., Chan, F., & Rubin, S. E. (2000). Wellness promotion for people with disabilities in private-sector rehabilitation: A conceptual and operational framework. *Journal of Rehabilitation Administration, 24,* 57–65.

Bishop, M., Stenhoff, D. M., & Shepard, L. (2007). Psychosocial adaptation and quality of life in multiple sclerosis: Assessment of the disability centrality model. *Journal of Rehabilitation, 73,* 3–12.

Bjelland, M. J., Bruyère, S. M., von Schrader, S., Houtenville, A. J., Ruiz-Quintanilla, A., & Webber, D. A. (2010). Age and disability employment discrimination: Occupational rehabilitation implications. *Journal of Occupational Rehabilitation, 20,* 456–471.

Blackwell, T. L., Autry, T. L., & Guglielmo, D. E. (2001). Ethical issues in disclosure of test data. *Rehabilitation Counseling Bulletin, 44*(3), 161–169.

Blackwell, T. L., Strohmer, D. C., Belcas, E. M., & Burton, K. A. (2002). Ethics in rehabilitation counselor supervision. *Rehabilitation Counseling Bulletin, 45*(4), 240–247.

Bogdan, R. C., & Biklen, S. K. (1992). *Qualitative research for education.* Boston: Allyn & Bacon.

Bogdan, R. C., & Biklen, S. K. (1998). *Qualitative research for education* (2nd ed.). Boston: Allyn & Bacon.

Bolton, B. (1979). *Rehabilitation counseling research.* Baltimore: University Park Press.

Bolton, B. (1986). Comments on Rubin & Rice's recommendations for the improvement of rehabilitation research. *Rehabilitation Counseling Bulletin,* 43–47.

Bolton, B. (2001a). *Handbook of measurement and evaluation in rehabilitation* (3rd ed.). Gaithersburg, MD: Aspen Publishers, Inc.

Bolton, B. (2001b). Measuring rehabilitation outcomes. *Rehabilitation Counseling Bulletin, 44,* 67–75.

Bolton, B., & Akridge, R. (1995). Meta-analysis of skills training programs for rehabilitation clients. *Rehabilitation Counseling Bulletin, 38,* 262–273.

Bolton, B. F., Bellini, J. L., & Brookings, J. B. (2000). Predicting client employment outcomes from personal history, functional limitations, and rehabilitation services. *Rehabilitation Counseling Bulletin, 44*(1), 1021.

Bolton, B., & Brookings, J. (2001). Scores and norms. In Brian Bolton (Ed.), *Handbook of measurement and evaluation in rehabilitation* (3rd ed., pp. 3–28). Gaithersburg, MD: Aspen Publishers, Inc.

Bolton, B., & Parker, R. M. (1998). Research in rehabilitation counseling. In R. M. Parker & E. M. Szymanski (Eds.), *Rehabilitation counseling: Basics and beyond* (3rd ed., pp. 437–470). Austin, TX: Pro-Ed.

Bolton, B., & Roessler, R. (1986). *Manual for the work personality profile.* Fayetteville, AR: Arkansas Research and Training Center in Vocational Rehabilitation.

Borg, W. R., Gall, J. P., & Gall, M. D. (1993). *Applying educational research: A practical guide* (3rd ed.). New York: Longman.

Boschen, K. (1996). Correlates of life satisfaction, residential satisfaction, and locus of control among adults with spinal cord injuries. *Rehabilitation Counseling Bulletin, 39*(4), 230–243.

Boswell, B. B., Dawson, M., & Heininger, E. (1998). Quality of life as defined by adults with spinal cord injuries. *Journal of Rehabilitation, 64,* 27–32.

Boswell, B. B., Knight, S., Hamer, M., & McChesney, J. (2001). Disability and spirituality: A reciprocal relationship with implications for the rehabilitation process. *Journal of Rehabilitation, 67,* 20–32.

Bowe, F. G., McMahon, B. T., Chang, T., & Louvie, I. (2005). Workplace discrimination, deafness and hearing impairment: The National EEOC ADA Research Project, *WORK: A Journal of Prevention, Assessment, and Rehabilitation.*

Brodwin, M. (2016). Rehabilitation in the private for-profit sector: Opportunities and challenges. In S. Rubin, R. Roessler, & P. Rumrill, *Foundations of the vocational rehabilitation process* (7th ed., pp. 465–483). Austin, TX: Pro-Ed.

Brodwin, M., Star, T., & Cardoso, E. (2004). Computer assisted technology for people who have disabilities: Computer adaptations and modifications. *Journal of Rehabilitation, 70*(3), 28–33.

Broussard, S. L., & Crimando, W. (2002). Effects of consumer attributions of disability and race on rehabilitation trainees' predictions of rehabilitation outcomes. *Rehabilitation Education, 16,* 243–254.

Brucker, D. L., & Houtenville, A. (2014). Living on the edge: Assessing the economic impacts of potential disability benefit reductions for Social Security disability beneficiaries. *Journal of Vocational Rehabilitation, 41,* 209–223.

Burgstahler, S. (2001). A collaborative model to promote career success for students with disabilities. *Journal of Vocational Rehabilitation, 16*(3, 4), 209–215.

Burker, E. J., & Kazukauskas, K. A. (2010). Code of ethics for rehabilitation educators and counselors: A call for evidence-based practice. *Rehabilitation Education, 24*(3/4), 101–111.

Burkhauser, R. V., Houtenville, A. J., & Wittenburg, D. (2001). *A user guide to current statistics on the employment of people with disabilities.* Ithaca, NY: Cornell University/Urban Institute, Rehabilitation Research and Training Center for Economic Research on Employment Policy for People with Disabilities.

Burkhauser, R. V., & Stapleton, D. (2003). A review of the evidence and its implications for policy change. In D. Stapleton & R. V. Burkhauser (Eds.), *The decline in employment of people with disabilities: A policy puzzle* (pp. 369–405). Kalamazoo, MI: W. E. Upjohn Institute for Employment Research.

Buros Institute of Mental Measurements. (2005). Publications catalog. Retrieved on April 20, 2005, from www.unl.edu/buros/bimm/html/catalog.html

Buros Institute of Mental Measurements. (2006). *Tests in Print VII* (Edited by L. Murphy, B. Plake, & R. Spies). Lincoln, NE: Author.

Buros Institute of Mental Measurements. (2007). *The Seventeenth Mental Measurements Yearbook* (Edited by K. Geisinger, R. Spies, J. Carson, & B. Plake). Lincoln, NE: Author.

Butts, S., & Shontz, F. (1962). Comparative evaluation and its relation to coping effectiveness. *American Psychologist, 17,* 326 (Abstract).

Buys, N. J., & Rennie, J. (2001). Developing relationships between vocational rehabilitation agencies and employers. *Rehabilitation Counseling Bulletin, 44*(2), 95–103.

Caelli, K., Ray, L., & Mill, J. (2003). 'Clear as mud': Toward greater clarity in generic qualitative research. *International Journal of Qualitative Methods, 2*(2), 1–13.

Calkins, J., Lui, J., & Wood, C. (2000). Recent developments in integrated disability management: Implications for professional and organizational development. *Journal of Vocational Rehabilitation, 15,* 31–37.

Camic, P. M., Rhodes, J. E., & Yardley, L. (2003). *Qualitative research in psychology.* APA: Washington, DC.

Campbell, D. T., & Fiske, D. W. (1959). Convergent and discriminate validation by the multi-trait multi-method matrix. *Psychological Bulletin, 56*(2), 81–105.

Capella, M. E. (2001). Predicting earnings of vocational rehabilitation clients with visual impairments. *Journal of Rehabilitation, 67*(4), 43–47.

Capella, M. E. (2002). Inequities in the VR system: Do they still exist? *Rehabilitation Counseling Bulletin, 45*(3), 143–153.

Carney, J., & Cobia, D. (1994). Relationship of characteristics of counselors in training to their attitudes toward persons with disabilities. *Rehabilitation Counseling Bulletin, 38,* 72–76.

Cartwright, B. Y., & Fleming, C. L. (2010). Multicultural and diversity considerations in the new Code of Professional Ethics for Rehabilitation Counselors. *Journal of Applied Rehabilitation Counseling, 41*(2), 20–24.

Cartwright, B. Y., & Hartley, M. T. (2016). Ethics consultation in rehabilitation counseling: A content of CRCC advisory opinions, 1996–2013. *Rehabilitation Counseling Bulletin, 59*(2), 84–93. doi: 10.1177/0034355215573537

Cartwright, B. Y., Washington, R. D., & McConnell, L. R. (2009). Examining racial microaggressions in rehabilitation counselor education. *Rehabilitation Education, 23*(3–4), 171–181.

Case, J. C., Blackwell, T. L., & Sprong, M. (2016). Rehabilitation counselor ethical considerations for end of life care. *Journal of Rehabilitation, 82*(1), 47–60.

Cassell, J. (1978). *A field manual for studying desegregated schools.* Washington, DC: The National Institute of Education.

Cater, J. K. (2011). Skype a cost-effective method for qualitative research. *Rehabilitation Counselors & Educators Journal, 4*(2), 3.

Chan, F., Shaw, L., McMahon, B., Koch, L., & Strauser, D. (1997). A model for enhancing counselor-consumer working relationships. *Rehabilitation Counseling Bulletin, 41,* 122–137.

Chan, F., Tarvydas, V., Blalock, K., Strauser, D., & Atkins, B. (2008). Unifying and elevating rehabilitation counseling through model-driven, diversity-sensitive, evidence-based practice. *Journal of Applied Rehabilitation Counseling, 39,* 46–50.

Chan, F., Wang, M., Thomas, K., Chan, C., Wong, D., Lee, G., & Liu, K. (2002). Conjoint analysis in rehabilitation counseling research. *Rehabilitation Education, 16,* 179–195.

Chang, H., Ngunjiri, F., & Hernandez, K. A. C. (2012). *Collaborative autoethnography.* Walnut Creek, CA: Left Coast Press.

Chang, H., Wambura Ngunjiri, F., & Hernandez, K. A. C. (2013). *Collaborative autoethnography.* Walnut Creek, CA: Left Coast Press.

Chang, H., Ngunjiri, F., & Hernandez, K. A. C. (2016). *Collaborative autoethnography.* London: Routledge.

Chapin, M. (2012). The role of participation of people with disabilities in the new American workplace. In P. J. Toriello, M. L. Bishop, & P. D. Rumrill (Eds.), *New directions in rehabilitation counseling: Creative responses to professional, clinical, and educational challenges* (pp. 236–254). Linn Creek, MO: Aspen Professional Services.

Chapin, M. H., & Kewman, D. G. (2001). Factors affecting employment following spinal cord injury: A qualitative study. *Rehabilitation Psychology, 46,* 400–416.

Chapin, M. H., & Leahy, M. J. (1999). Factors contributing to rehabilitation counselor success in the private sector in Michigan. *Journal of Applied Rehabilitation, 30*(3), 19–28.

Charlton, J. (1998). *Nothing about us without us: Disability oppression and empowerment.* Berkeley, CA: University of California Press.

Chen, R., Jo, S., & Donnell, C. (2004). Enhancing the rehabilitation counseling process: Understanding the obstacles to Asian-Americans' utilization of services. *Journal of Applied Rehabilitation Counseling, 35*(1), 29–35.

Chibnall, J., & Tait, R. (1990). The Quality of Life Scale: A preliminary study with chronic pain patients. *Psychology and Health, 4,* 283–292.

Chiu, C.-Y., Sharp, S., Pfaller, J., Rumrill, P., Cheing, G., Sanchez, J., & Chan, F. (2015). Differential vocational rehabilitation service patterns related to the job retention and job placement needs of people with diabetes. *Journal of Vocational Rehabilitation, 42*(2), 177–186.

Chronister, J., & Rumrill, P. D. (2012). New directions in rehabilitation research. In P. J. Toriello, M. L. Bishop, & P. D. Rumrill (Eds.), *New directions in rehabilitation counseling: Creative responses to professional, clinical, and educational challenges* (pp. 54–78). Linn Creek, MO: Aspen Professional Services.

Chubon, R. (1990). *Manual for the life situation survey.* Columbia, SC: University of South Carolina, Rehabilitation Counseling Program.

Chubon, R., Clayton, K., & Vandergriff, D. (1995). An exploratory study comparing the quality of life of South Carolinians with mental retardation and spinal cord injury. *Rehabilitation Counseling Bulletin, 39,* 107–118.

Cichy, K., Li., J., McMahon, B., & Rumrill, P. (2015). The workplace discrimination experiences of older workers with disabilities: Results from the National EEOC ADA Research Project. *Journal of Vocational Rehabilitation, 43,* 137–148.

Cimera, R. E. (2011). Does being in sheltered workshops improve the employment outcomes of supported employees with intellectual disabilities? *Journal of Vocational Rehabilitation, 35,* 21–27. doi: 10.3233/JVR-2011-0550.

Cimera, R., Rumrill, P., Chan, F., Kaya, C., & Bezyak, J. (2015). Vocational rehabilitation services and outcomes for transition-age youth with visual impairments and blindness. *Journal of Vocational Rehabilitation, 43*(2), 103–112.

Clarke, N. E., & Crewe, N. M. (2000). Stakeholder attitudes toward ADA Title I: Development of an indirect measurement method. *Rehabilitation Counseling Bulletin, 43,* 58–65.

Cocco, K., & Harper, D. (2002). Substance use in people with mental retardation. *Rehabilitation Counseling Bulletin, 46,* 34–41.

Cohen, J. (1969). *Statistical power analysis for the behavioral sciences.* New York: Academic Press.
Cohen, J. (1988). *Statistical power analysis for the behavioral sciences* (2nd ed.). Hillsdale, NJ: Lawrence Erlbaum Associates.
Cohen, J. (1990). Things I have learned (so far). *American Psychologist, 45,* 1304–1312.
Cohen, J. (1994). The earth is round (p < .05). *American Psychologist, 47,* 997–1003.
Cohen, J., & Cohen, P. (1983). *Applied multiple regression/correlational analysis for the behavioral sciences* (2nd ed.). Hillsdale, NJ: Erlbaum.
Cohen, P., Cohen, J., West, S., & Aiken, L. (2003). *Applied multiple regression: Correlation analysis for the behavioral sciences* (3rd ed.). Hillsdale, NJ: Lawrence Erlbaum.
Collins, J. D., Markham, A., Service, K. Reini, S., Wolf, E., & Sessoms, P. (2015). A systematic literature review of the use and effectiveness of the computer assisted rehabilitation environment for research and rehabilitation as it relates to the wounded warrior. *Work, 50*(1), 121–129.
Commission on Rehabilitation Counselor Certification. (2002). *Code of professional ethics for rehabilitation counselors.* Rolling Meadows, IL: Author.
Commission on Rehabilitation Counselor Certification. (2010). CRC code of ethics. Retrieved from http://www.crccertification.com/pages/crc_ccrc_code_of_ethics/10.php
Commission on Rehabilitation Counselor Certification. (2017). CRC code of ethics. Retrieved from http://www.crccertification.com/pages/crc_ccrc_code_of_ethics/10.php
Conner, C. (2005). *A people's history of science: Miners, midwives, and "low mechanics."* New York: Nation Books.
Conrad, C., Neumann, A., Haworth, J. G., & Scott, P. (1993). *Qualitative research in higher education: Experiencing alternative perspectives and approaches.* Needham Heights, MA: Ginn Press.
Conyers, L. M. (2004). Expanding understanding of HIV/AIDS and employment: Perspectives of focus groups. *Rehabilitation Counseling Bulletin, 48,* 5–18.
Cook, B., Gerber, M., & Murphy J. (2000). Backlash against the inclusion of students with learning disabilities in higher education: Implications for transition from post-secondary environments to work. *Work: A Journal of Prevention, Assessment, & Rehabilitation, 14,* 31–40.
Cook, D., Andrew, J., & Faubion, C. (1998). Rehabilitation education and research productivity. *Rehabilitation Education, 12,* 17–27.
Cook, T. D. (1985). Post-positivist critical multiplism. In R. L. Shotland & M. M. Mark (Eds.), *Social science and social policy* (pp. 21–62). Beverly Hills, CA: Sage.
Cook, T. D., & Campbell, D. T. (1979). *Quasi-experimentation: Design and analysis issues for field settings.* Chicago: Rand McNally.
Corbin, J., & Strauss, A. (2008). *Basics of qualitative research: Techniques and procedures for developing grounded theory* (3rd ed.). Thousand Oaks, CA: Sage.
Corbin, J., & Strauss, A. (2014). *Basics of qualitative research: Techniques and procedures for developing grounded theory* (4th ed.). Thousand Oaks, CA: Sage.
Corey, G., Corey, M., & Callanan, P. (1998). *Issues and ethics in the helping professions* (5th ed). Pacific Grove, CA: Brooks/Cole.

Corey, G., Corey, M. S., & Callanan, P. (2011). *Issues and ethics in the helping professions* (8th ed.). Belmont, CA: Brooks/Cole.

Corring, D. J. (2002). Quality of life: Perspectives of people with mental illness and family members. *Psychiatric Rehabilitation Journal, 25*(4), 350–358.

Cottone, R. (1987). A systemic theory of rehabilitation. *Rehabilitation Counseling Bulletin, 30,* 167–176.

Cottone, R. R., & Emener, W. (1990). The psychomedical paradigm of vocational rehabilitation and its alternatives. *Rehabilitation Counseling Bulletin, 34,* 91–102.

Council on Rehabilitation Education. (1997). *Accreditation manual for rehabilitation counselor education programs.* Rolling Meadows, IL: Author.

Council on Rehabilitation Education. (2007). *Accreditation manual for rehabilitation counselor education programs.* Rolling Meadows, IL: Author.

Council on Rehabilitation Education. (2017). *Accreditation manual for rehabilitation counselor education programs.* Rolling Meadows, IL: Author.

Coyle, C., Lesnik-Emas, S., & Kinney, W. (1994). Predicting life satisfaction among adults with spinal cord injuries. *Rehabilitation Psychology, 39,* 95–112.

Crank, J., & Deshler, D. (2001). Disability eligibility issues and university student assessment outcomes. *Journal of Vocational Rehabilitation, 16*(3/4), 217–226.

Creswell, J. W. (2003). *Research design: Qualitative and quantitative approaches* (3rd ed.). Thousand Oaks, CA: Sage.

Creswell, J. W. (2007). *Qualitative inquiry and research design: Choosing among five approaches* (2nd ed.). Thousand Oaks, CA: Sage.

Creswell, J. W. (2012). *Qualitative inquiry and research design: Choosing among five approaches* (3rd ed.). Thousand Oaks, CA: Sage.

Creswell, J. W. (2014). *Educational research: Planning, conducting, and evaluating quantitative and qualitative research* (5th ed., revised). Upper Saddle River, NJ: Pearson.

Creswell, J. W., & Garrett, A. L. (2008). The "movement" of mixed methods research and the role of educators. *South African Journal of Education, 28*(3), 321–333.

Crewe, N., & Athelstan, G. (1984). *Functional Assessment Inventory Manual.* Minneapolis, MN: University of Minnesota.

Crewe, N. M. (2000). A 20-year longitudinal perspective on the vocational experiences of persons with spinal cord injury. *Rehabilitation Counseling Bulletin, 43,* 122–133.

Cronbach, L. (1988). Five perspectives on the validity argument. In H. Wainer, & H. I. Braun (Eds.), *Test validity.* Hillsdale, NJ: Erlbaum.

Cronbach, L. (1990). *Essentials of psychological testing* (5th ed.). New York: Harper & Row.

Cronbach, L., & Meehl, P. (1955). Construct validity in psychological tests. *Psychological Bulletin, 52*(4), 281–302.

Crystal, R., & Espinosa, C. T. (2012). Individuals with disabilities and the American healthcare system. In P. J. Toriello, M. L. Bishop, & P. D. Rumrill (Eds.), *New directions in rehabilitation counseling: Creative responses to professional, clinical, and educational challenges* (pp. 140–163). Linn Creek, MO: Aspen Professional Services.

Dalgin, R., & Bellini, J. (2008). Invisibility disability disclosure in an employment interview: Impact on employers' hiring decisions and views of employability. *Rehabilitation Counseling Bulletin, 52,* 6–15.

Dallas, B., Sprong, M., & Kluesner, B. (2016). Multiuniversity comparison of faculty attitudes and use of universal design instructional techniques. *Rehabilitation Research, Policy, and Education, 30*(2), 148–160.

Darling, W., Growick, B., & Kontosh, L. (2002). Transferable skills analysis in rehabilitation: Issues in definition and application. *Journal of Vocational Rehabilitation, 17*(3), 217–224.

Davis, A., & Yazak, D. (1998). Writing across the curriculum as an approach to promoting curriculum coherence. *Rehabilitation Education, 12,* 29–43.

Dawis, R. (1991). Vocational interests, values, and preferences. In M. D. Dunnette & L. M. Hough (Eds.), *Handbook of industrial and organizational psychology: Vol. 2* (pp. 833–871). Palo Alto, CA: Consulting Psychologists Press.

Dawis, R. (2005). The Minnesota theory of work adjustment. In S. Brown & R. Lent (Eds.), *Career development and counseling: Putting theory and research to work* (pp. 3–23). Hoboken, NJ; Wiley.

DeLeire, T. (2000a). The unintended consequences of the Americans with Disabilities Act. *Regulation, 23*(1), 21–24.

DeLeire, T. (2000b). The wage and employment effects of the Americans with Disabilities Act. *The Journal of Human Resources, 35,* 693–715.

Dellario, D. J. (1996). In defense of teaching master's level rehabilitation counselors to be scientist-practitioners. *Rehabilitation Education, 10,* 229–232.

Del Valle, R., Leahy, M. J., Sherman, S., Anderson, C. A., Tansey, T., & Schoen, B. (2014). Promising best practices that lead to employment in vocational rehabilitation: Findings from a four-state multiple case study. *Journal of Vocational Rehabilitation, 41*(2), 99–113.

Dembo, T., Leviton, G., & Wright, B. (1975). Adjustment to misfortune: A problem of social-psychological rehabilitation. *Rehabilitation Psychology, 22,* 1–100. (Reprinted from *Artificial Limbs,* 1956, 3, 4–62.)

Denson, C. R. (2000). Public sector transportation for people with disabilities: A satisfaction survey. *Journal of Rehabilitation, 66*(3), 29–37.

Denzin, N. K. (1970). *The research act.* Chicago: Aldine.

Denzin, N. K., & Lincoln, Y. S. (2000). *Handbook of qualitative research* (2nd ed.). Thousand Oaks, CA: Sage.

Devine, E., & Pearcy, J. (1996). Meta analysis of the effects of psychoeducational care in adults with chronic obstructive pulmonary disease. *Patient Education & Counseling, 29,* 167–178.

Diamond, J. (2005). *Guns, germs, and steel: The fates of human societies.* New York: W. W. Norton.

Diener, E., & Crandall, R. (1978). *Ethics in social and behavioral research.* Chicago: University of Chicago Press.

Dillman, D. A. (2000). *Mail and internet surveys: The tailored design method.* New York: Wiley and Sons.

Dimitrov, D., Fitzgerald, S., & Rumrill, P. (2000). Speaking of research: Multiple regressions in rehabilitation research. *Work: A Journal of Prevention, Assessment, and Rehabilitation, 15*(3), 209–215.

Dispenza, F., Viehl, C., Sewell, M. H., Burke, M. A., & Gaudet, M. M. (2016). A model of affirmative intersectional rehabilitation counseling with sexual minorities: A grounded theory study. *Rehabilitation Counseling Bulletin, 59*(3), 143–157.

Dixon, M. (2002). Single-subject research designs: Dissolving the myths and demonstrating the utility for rehabilitation research. *Rehabilitation Education, 16*(4), 331–344.

Dodson, H. B. (2000). Organizational communication online. *Journal of Rehabilitation Administration, 24*, 47–58.

Douglas, J. (1976). *Investigative social research.* Beverly Hills, CA: Sage.

Drew, C. F. (1980). *Introduction to designing and conducting research* (2nd ed.). St. Louis: C. V. Mosby.

Drisko, J. W. (2013). Qualitative data analysis software. In A. E. Fortune, W. J. Reid, & R. Miller (Eds.), *Qualitative research in social work* (2nd ed., pp. 284–306). NY: Columbia University Press.

Drummond, R. (2004). *Appraisal procedures for counselors and helping professionals* (5th ed.). Englewood Cliffs, NJ: Prentice-Hall, Inc.

Duggan, C. H., & Dijkers, M. (2001). Quality of life after spinal cord injury: A qualitative study. *Rehabilitation Psychology, 46*, 3–27.

Dunn, P. (2001). Proprietary rehabilitation: Challenges and opportunities in the new millennium. *Work: A Journal of Prevention, Assessment and Rehabilitation, 17*(2), 135–142.

Edgley, K., Sullivan, M. J., & Dehoux, E. (1991). A survey of multiple sclerosis, part 2: Determinants of employment status. *Canadian Journal of Rehabilitation, 4*(3), 127–132.

Ehrmann, L., & Herbert, J. (2005). Family intervention training: A course proposal for rehabilitation counselor education. *Rehabilitation Education, 19*, 235–244.

Eldredge, G., McNamara, S., Stensrud, R., Gilbride, D., Hendren, G., Siegfried, T., et al. (1999). Distance education: A look at five programs. *Rehabilitation Education, 13*(3), 231–248.

Elliott, T. R., Kurylo, M., Chen, Y., & Hicken, B. (2002). Alcohol abuse history and adjustment following spinal cord injury. *Rehabilitation Psychology, 47*(3), 278–290.

Ellis, C. (2004). *The ethnographic I: A methodological novel about autoethnography.* Rowman Altamira.

Ellis, C. S., & Bochner, A. (2000). *Autoethnography, personal narrative, reflexivity: Researcher as subject.* Communication Faculty Publications.

Emerson, R. M., Fretz, R. I., & Shaw, L. L. (2011). *Writing ethnographic fieldnotes* (2nd ed.). Chicago: University of Chicago Press.

Erickson, W. A., & Lee, C. (2007). Disability status report: United States [Internet]. Ithaca, NY: Cornell University Rehabilitation Research and Training Center on Disability Demographics and Statistics; 2008 [cited 2009 Jul 7]. Available at: http://www.disabilitystatistics.org/

Erickson, W., Lee, C., & von Schrader, S. (2012). *2011 Disability status report: United States.* Ithaca, NY: Cornell University, Employment and Disability Institute.

Fabian, E. S. (1991). Using quality of life indicators in rehabilitation program evaluation. *Rehabilitation Counseling Bulletin, 45,* 2–11.

Fabian, E., McInerney, M., & Santos Rodrigues, P. (2005). International education in rehabilitation: A collaborative approach. *Rehabilitation Education, 19*(1), 15–24.

Fabian, E. S., & Waugh, C. (2001). A job development efficacy scale for rehabilitation professionals. *Journal of Rehabilitation, 67*(2), 42–47.

Falvo, D. R., & Parker, R. M. (2000). Ethics in rehabilitation education and research. *Rehabilitation Counseling Bulletin, 43*(4), 197–202.

Fassinger, R. (1987). Use of structural equation modeling in counseling psychology research. *Journal of Counseling Psychology, 34,* 425–436.

Ferrin, J., Bishop, M., Tansey, T., Swett, E., & Lane, F. (2007). Conceptual and practical implications for rehabilitation research: Effects size estimates, confidence intervals, and power. *Rehabilitation Education, 21,* 87–100.

Fesko, S. L. (2001). Workplace experiences of individuals who are HIV+ and individuals with cancer. *Rehabilitation Counseling Bulletin, 45,* 2–11.

Fielding, N. (2001). Computer applications in qualitative research. In P. Atkinson, A. Coffey, S. Delamont, J. Lofland, & L. Lofland (Eds.), *Handbook of ethnography* (pp. 453–467). Thousand Oaks, CA: Sage.

Fielding, N. G., & Fielding, J. L. (1986). *Linking data.* Newbury Park, CA: Sage.

Finfgeld-Connett, D. (2016). The future of theory-generating meta-synthesis research. *Qualitative Health Research, 26.* doi: 10.1177/1049732315616628.

Fitzgerald, S., Dimitrov, D., & Rumrill, P. (2001). Speaking of research . . . : The basics of nonparametric statistics. *Work: A Journal of Prevention, Assessment, and Rehabilitation, 16*(3), 287–292.

Fitzgerald, S., Rumrill, P., & Hart, R. (2000). Speaking of research . . . : Using analysis of variance in rehabilitation research investigations. *Work: A Journal of Prevention, Assessment, and Rehabilitation, 15,* 61–65.

Fitzgerald, S., Rumrill, P., & Merchant, W. (2015). A response to Harris, Gould, and Fujiura: Beyond scoping reviews—a case for mixed-methods research reviews. *Work, 50,* 335–339.

Flannery, K., Slovic, R., Treasure, T., Ackley, D., & Lucas, F. (2002). Collaboration and partnership to improve employment outcomes. *Journal of Vocational Rehabilitation, 17*(3), 207–216.

Flick, U. (2002). An introduction to qualitative research. Thousand Oaks, CA: Sage.

Floyd, F., & Widaman, K. (1995). Factor analysis in the development and refinement of clinical assessment instruments. *Psychological Assessment, 7,* 286–299.

Forsyth, D. R., & Strong, S. R. (1986). The scientific study of counseling and psychotherapy: A unification's view. *American Psychologist, 41,* 113–119.

Fowler, F. (2002). *Survey research methods* (3rd ed.). Thousand Oaks, CA: Sage.

Frain, M., Bishop, M., Rumrill, P., Tansey, T., Chan, F., Strauser, D., & Chiu, C. (2015). Multiple sclerosis and employment: A research review based on the

International Classification of Functioning. *Rehabilitation Research, Policy, and Education, 29*(2), 153–164.

Frain, M. P., Lee, J., Roland, M., & Tschopp, M. K. (2012). A rehabilitation counselor integration into the successful rehabilitation of veterans with disabilities. In P. J. Toriello, M. L. Bishop, & P. D. Rumrill (Eds.), *New directions in rehabilitation counseling: Creative responses to professional, clinical, and educational challenges* (pp. 255–281). Linn Creek, MO: Aspen Professional Services.

Fraser, R., McMahon, B., & Danczyk-Hawley, C. (2003). Progression of disability benefits: A perspective on multiple sclerosis. *Journal of Vocational Rehabilitation, 19*(3), 173–179.

Fraser, R. T., Kraft, G. H., Ehed, D. W., & Johnson, K. L. (2006). *The MS workbook: Living fully with multiple sclerosis.* Oakland, CA: New Harbinger Press.

Frazier, P., Tix, A., & Barron, K. (2004). Testing moderator and mediator effects in counseling psychology research. *Journal of Counseling Psychology, 51,* 115–134.

Frey, J. H., & Fontanta, A. (1991). The group interview in social research. *Social Science Journal, 28,* 175–187.

Gagne, C., Bowers, A., Russinova, Z., Bloch, P., & McNamara, S. (2010). *Combating prejudice and discrimination through Photo Voice empowerment: Leader's guide.* Boston: University Center for Psychiatric Rehabilitation.

García-Moriche, N., Rodríguez-Gonzalo, A., Muñoz-Lobo, M. J., Parra-Cordero, S., & Fernández-De Pablos, A. (2010). Quality of life in stroke patients. A phenomenological study. *Enfermería Clínica, 20*(2), 80–87.

Gay, L., & Airasian, P. (2003). *Educational research: Competencies for analysis and applications* (7th ed.). Upper Saddle River, NJ: Pearson Education, Inc.

Geertz, C. (1973). *The interpretation of cultures: Selected essays (Vol. 5019).* New York: Basic Books.

Geertz, C. (1983). Thick description: Toward an interpretive theory of culture. In R. Emerson (Ed.), *Contemporary field research: A collection of readings* (pp. 37–59). Boston: Little, Brown.

Gilbride, D., & Stensrud, R. (1999). Expanding our horizons: Using the internet in rehabilitation education. *Rehabilitation Education, 13*(3), 219–229.

Gilbride, D., Stensrud, R., Ehlers, C., Evans, E., & Peterson, C. (2000). *Journal of Rehabilitation, 66*(4), 17–23.

Gilbride, D., Stensrud, R., Vandergoot, D., & Golden, K. (2003). Identification of the characteristics of work environments and employers open to hiring and accommodating people with disabilities. *Rehabilitation Counseling Bulletin, 46*(3), 130–137.

Gilmore, D. S., Schuster, J. L., Timmons, J. C., & Butterworth, J. (2000). An analysis of trends for people with MR, cerebral palsy, and epilepsy receiving services from state VR agencies: Ten years of progress. *Rehabilitation Counseling Bulletin, 44,* 30–38.

Gitchel, D., Turner, R., & Rumrill, P. (2010). Differential item functioning in rehabilitation research. *Work: A Journal of Prevention, Assessment, and Rehabilitation, 36*(3), 351–369.

Glaser, B. G. (1978). *Theoretical sensitivity.* Mill Valley, CA: Sociology Press.

Glaser, B., & Strauss, A. (1967). *The discovery of grounded theory: Strategies for qualitative research.* Chicago, IL: Aldine.

Glass, G. (1976). Primary, secondary, and meta-analysis of research. *Educational Reearcher, 5*(10), 3–8.

Glenn, M. (2006). A rehabilitation educator's perspective on merging accreditation resources. *Rehabilitation Education, 20,* 71–77.

Glenn, M. K., Danczyk-Hawley, C., & Mann, D. (2000). Rehabilitation leadership education online. *Journal of Rehabilitation Counseling, 24,* 25–32.

Glesne, C., & Peshkin, A. (1992). *Becoming qualitative researchers: Introduction.* White Plains, NY: Longman Publishing.

Glover-Graf, N., & Reed, B. (2006). Abuse against women with disabilities. *Rehabilitation Education, 20*(1), 43–56.

Glueckauf, R. L. (2002). Telehealth and chronic disabilities: New frontier for research and development. *Rehabilitation Psychology, 47,* 3–7.

Goldman, B. M., Gutek, B. A., Stein, J. H., & Lewis, K. (2006). Employment discrimination in organizations: Antecedents and consequences. *Journal of Management, 32*(6), 786–830

Goodwin, C. J., & Goodwin, K. A. (2012). *Research in psychology: Methods and design* (7th edition). Hoboken, NJ: Wiley Publications.

Goodyear, R. K., & Benton, S. L. (1986). The roles of science and research in the counselor's work. In A. J. Palmo & W. J. Weikel (Eds.), *Foundations of mental health counseling* (pp. 287–306). Springfield, IL: Charles C Thomas.

Gordon, P., Feldman, D., & Crose, R. (1998). The meaning of disability: How women with chronic illness view their experience. *Journal of Rehabilitation, 62,* 5–11.

Gordon, P. A., & Feldman, D. (2002). Post-polio syndrome: Issues and strategies for rehabilitation counselors. *Journal of Rehabilitation, 68,* 28–35.

Gouvier, W., Systma-Jordan, S., & Maryville, S. (2003). Patterns of discrimination in hiring job applicants with disabilities: The role of disability type, job complexity, and public contact. *Rehabilitation Psychology, 48,* 175–181.

Graf, N., Reed, B., & Sanchez, R. (2008). Abuse against women with disabilities of Mexican descent: Cultural considerations. *Rehabilitation Education, 22,* 31–42.

Graves, W. H. (1991). Participatory action research: A new paradigm for disability and rehabilitation research. *ARCA, 19,* 8–10.

Gray, D., Morgan, K., & Hollingsworth, H. (2001). Independent living and assistive technology: Work context. *Rehabilitation Education, 15*(1), 353–364.

Graziano, K. (2004). The power of teaching and learning with documentary photography and storytelling: A photovoice case study. In *Proceedings of World Conference on Educational Multimedia, Hypermedia and Telecommunications* (pp. 3881–3886).

Grim, L., & Yarnold, P. (1995). *Reading and understanding multivariate statistics.* Washington, DC: American Psychological Association.

Gringart, E., Helmes, E., & Speelman, C. (2013). Development of a measure of stereotypical attitudes towards older workers. *Australian Psychologist, 48,* 110–118.ap

Gross, J. M. S., & Francis, G. (2015). Development and testing of the community employment survey. *Journal of Vocational Rehabilitation, 42*(3), 229–234.

Groves, R., Fowler, F., Couper, M., Lepkowski, J., Singer, E., & Tourangeau, R. (2004). *Survey methodology.* Hoboken, NJ: Wiley Interscience.

Guba, E. G. (1978). *Toward a methodology of naturalistic inquiry in educational evaluation.* CSE Monograph Series in Evaluation, 8. Los Angeles: Center for the Study of Evaluation, University of California.

Guba, E. G., & Lincoln, Y. (1981). *Effective evaluation: Improving the usefulness of evaluation results through responsive and naturalistic approaches.* San Francisco: Jossey-Bass.

Guillemin, M., & Gillam, L. (2004). Ethics, reflexivity, and "ethically important moments" in research. *Qualitative Inquiry, 10*(2), 261.

Gunderson, M. (2003). Age discrimination in employment in Canada. *Contemporary Economic Policy, 21,* 318–328.

Hagner, D. (2000). Primary and secondary labor markets: Implications for vocational rehabilitation. *Rehabilitation Counseling Bulletin, 44*(1), 22–29.

Hagner, D. (2002). Subjects or objects? Participants as research partners. *Rehabilitation Education, 16*(2), 135–148.

Hagner, D., & Helm, D. T. (1994). Qualitative methods in rehabilitation research. *Rehabilitation Counseling Bulletin, 37,* 290–303.

Hahn, H. (1985). Disability policy and the problem of discrimination. *American Behavioral Scientist, 28,* 293–318.

Hammel, J., Magasi, S., Heinemann, A., Gray, D. B., Stark, S., Kisala, P., & Hahn, E. A. (2015). Environmental barriers and supports to everyday participation: a qualitative insider perspective from people with disabilities. *Archives of Physical Medicine and rehabilitation, 96*(4), 578–588.

Hammell, K. W. (2007). Quality of life after spinal cord injury: A meta-synthesis of qualitative findings. *Spinal Cord, 45*(2), 124–139.

Hammersley, M., & Atkinson, P. (2007). *Ethnography: Principles in practice* (3rd ed.). London: Routledge.

Hampton, N. Z. (2000). Meeting the unique needs of Asian Americans and the Pacific Islanders with disabilities: A challenge to the rehabilitation counselors in the 21st Century. *Journal of Applied Rehabilitation Counseling, 31,* 40–48.

Hampton, N. Z. (2001). The evolving rehabilitation service delivery system in the People's Republic of China. *Journal of Rehabilitation, 67,* 20–28.

Hampton, N. Z. (2002). Teaching a vocational assessment course online: Design and implementation. *Rehabilitation Education, 16,* 357–372.

Hampton, N. Z., & Chang, V. (1999). Quality of life as defined by Chinese Americans with disabilities: Implications for rehabilitation services. *Journal of Applied Rehabilitation Counseling, 30*(3), 35–41.

Hanley-Maxwell, C., Al Hano, I., & Skivington, M. (2007). Qualitative research in rehabilitation counseling. *Rehabilitation Counseling Bulletin, 50,* 99–110.

Harley, D. A. (2001). Recognizing and understanding chronic fatigue syndrome: Implications for rehabilitation counselors. *Journal of Rehabilitation, 67,* 22–29.

Harley, D. A. (2002). Disability and rehabilitation in Zimbabwe: Lessons and implications for rehabilitation practice in the U.S. *Journal of Rehabilitation, 68*(1), 26–33.

Harley, D. A., Alston, R., & Middleton, R. (2007). Infusing social justice into rehabilitation education: Making a case for curriculum refinement. *Rehabilitation Education, 21,* 41–54.

Harley, D. A., Hall, M., & Savage, T. A. (1999). Working with gay and lesbian consumers with disabilities: Helping practitioners understand another frontier of diversity. *Journal of Applied Rehabilitation Counseling, 30*(2), 4–12.

Harley, D. A., Mpofu, E., & Ford, H. (2000). Tokenism and the minorities in rehabilitation administration and leadership: Implications for the new millennium. *Journal of Rehabilitation Administration, 24,* 73–79.

Harre, R. (1986). *Varieties of realism: A rationale for the natural sciences.* New York: Blackwell.

Harris, S., Gould, R., & Fujiura, G. (2013). Enhancing rigor in practice of scoping reviews in social policy research: Considerations from a worked example on the Americans with Disabilities Act. *Work, 50,* 324–334.

Hart, D., Zimbrich, K., & Ghiloni, C. (2001). Interagency partnerships and funding: Individual supports for youth with significant disabilities as they move into post-secondary education and employment options. *Journal of Vocational Rehabilitation, 16*(3/4), 145–154.

Hartley, M. T. (2012). Ethics and accountability in rehabilitation: Implications for education, clinical practice, and research. In P. J. Toriello, M. L. Bishop, & P. D. Rumrill (Eds.), *New directions in rehabilitation counseling: Creative responses to professional, clinical, and educational challenges* (pp. 79–94). Linn Creek, MO: Aspen Professional Services.

Hartung, P. (2013) The life-span, life space theory of career. In S. Brown & D. Lent (Eds.), *Career development and counseling* (2nd ed., pp. 83–114). Hoboken, NJ: John Wiley.

Hasnain, R., Sotnik, P., & Ghiloni, C. (2003). Person-centered planning: A gateway to improving vocational rehabilitation services for culturally diverse individuals with disabilities. *Journal of Rehabilitation, 69*(2), 10–15.

Hassouneh-Phillips, D., & Curry, M. A. (2002). Abuse of women with disabilities: State of the science. *Rehabilitation Counseling Bulletin, 45*(2), 96–104.

Havraneck, J. (2000). Rehabilitation counseling: An independent profession. *Rehabilitation Education, 14*(3), 299–300.

Hawley, C., McMahon, B., Reid, C., & Shaw, L. (2000). Rehabilitation counseling and education: Career counseling suggestions for the profession. *Journal of Vocational Rehabilitation, 14*(2), 95–101.

Haworth, J. G., & Conrad, C. F. (1997). *Emblems of quality in higher education: Developing and sustaining high-quality programs.* Boston: Allyn and Bacon.

Hein, S., Lustig, D. C., & Uruk, A. (2005). Consumers' recommendations to improve satisfaction with rehabilitation services: A qualitative study. *Rehabilitation Counseling Bulleting, 49,* 29–39.

Helling, I. K. (1988). The life history method. In N. K. Denzin (Ed.), *Studies in symbolic interaction*. Greenwich, CT: JAI.

Hendricks, D. J., Sampson, E., Rumrill, P., Leopold, A., Elias, E., Jacobs, K., Nardone, A., Scherer, M., & Stauffer, C. (2015). Activities and interim outcomes of a multi-site development project to promote cognitive support technology use and employment success among postsecondary students with traumatic brain injuries. *Neurorehabilitation, 37,* 449–458.

Hendren, G. (2002). Tourette's syndrome: A new look at an old condition. *Journal of Rehabilitation, 68,* 22–29.

Hennessey, M. L. (2001). What is rehabilitation counseling? A student's perspective on professional identity. *Work, 17*(2), 151–156.

Hennessey, M. L., & Rumrill, P. (2003). Treatment fidelity: Enhancing rehabilitation services and research. *Journal of Vocational Rehabilitation, 19*(3), 123–126.

Hennessey, M. L. (2004). *An examination of the employment and career development concerns of postsecondary students with disabilities: Results of a tri-regional study*. Unpublished doctoral dissertation, Kent State University, Kent, Ohio.

Hennessey, M. L., & Koch, L. (2007). Universal design for instruction in rehabilitation education. *Rehabilitation Education, 21,* 187–194.

Hennessey, M. L., Roessler, R., Cook, B., Unger, D., & Rumrill, P. (2006). Employment and career development concerns of postsecondary students with disabilities: Service and policy implications. *Journal of Postsecondary Education and Disability, 19*(1), 39–55.

Heppner, P., Kivlighan, D., & Wampold, B. (1992). *Research design in counseling*. Pacific Grove, CA: Brooks/Cole.

Heppner, P., Kivlighan, D., & Wampold, B. (1999). *Research design in counseling* (2nd ed.). Pacific Grove, CA: Brooks/Cole.

Heppner, P., Kivlighan, D., & Wampold, B. (2007). *Research design in counseling* (3rd ed.). Pacific Grove, CA: Brooks/Cole.

Heppner, P., Wampold, B., Owen, J., Thompson, M., & Wang, K. (2015). *Research design in counseling* (4th ed.). Independence, KY: Cengage Learning.

Herbert, J. (1998). Therapeutic effects of participating in an adventure therapy program. *Rehabilitation Counseling Bulletin, 41,* 201–216.

Hershenson, D. (1996). A system's reformulation of a developmental model of work adjustment. *Rehabilitation Counseling Bulletin, 40,* 2–10.

Hershenson, D. (1998). Systemic, ecological model for rehabilitation counseling. *Rehabilitation Counseling Bulletin, 42,* 40–50.

Hershenson, D. (2000a). Toward a cultural anthropology of disability and rehabilitation. *Rehabilitation Counseling Bulletin, 43,* 150–157.

Hershenson, D. (2000b). The walrus and the carpenter–an oyster's view: A response to Mpofu. *Rehabilitation Education, 14,* 297–298.

Hershenson, D. (2005). INCOME: A culturally inclusive and disability-sensitive framework for ongoing career development concepts and interventions. *The Career Development Quarterly, 54,* 150–161.

Hershenson, D. (2010). Career counseling with diverse populations: Models, interventions, and applications. In E. Szymanski & R. Parker (Eds.), *Work and disability* (3rd ed., pp. 163–202). Austin, TX: Pro-Ed.

Hershenson, D. (2015). The individual plan for retirement: A missing part of plan development with older consumers. *Rehabilitation Counseling Bulletin, 59,* 9–19.

Hill, M. R., Noonan, V. K., Sakakibara, B. M., & Miller, W. C. (2010). Quality of life instruments and definitions in individuals with spinal cord injury: A systematic review. *Spinal Cord, 48*(6), 438–450.

Hill, C. E., Thompson, B. J., & Williams, E. N. (1997). A guide to conducting consensual qualitative research. *The Counseling Psychologist, 25*(4), 517–572.

Hill, C. E., Knox, S., Thompson, B. J., Williams, E. N., Hess, S. A., & Ladany, N. (2005). Consensual qualitative research: An update. *Journal of Counseling Psychology, 52*(2), 196.

Holland, N., Murray, T., & Reingold, S. (1996). *Multiple sclerosis: A guide for the newly diagnosed.* New York: Demos.

Holman Jones, S. (2005). Autoethnography: Making the personal political. In Norman K. Denzin & Yvonna S. Lincoln (Eds.), *Handbook of qualitative research* (pp. 763–791). Thousand Oaks, CA: Sage.

Hood, A., & Johnson, R. (2002). *Assessment in counseling: A guide to the use of psychological assessment procedures* (3rd ed.). Alexandria, VA: American Counseling Association.

Hotchkiss, J. L. (2004). A closer look at the employment impact of the Americans with Disabilities Act. *The Journal of Human Resources, 39,* 887–911.

Houser, R., Hampton, N. Z., & Carriker, C. (2000). Implementing the empowerment concept in rehabilitation: Contributions of social role theory. *Journal of Applied Rehabilitation Counseling, 31*(3), 18–27.

Houtenville, A., & Burkhauser, R. (2005). *Did the employment of people with disabilities decline in the 1990s, and was the ADA responsible? A replication and robustness check of Acemoglu and Angrist (2001).* Ithaca, NY: Cornell University, Rehabilitation Research and Training Center for Employment Policy for Persons with Disabilities.

Howard, G. S. (1985). Can research in the human sciences become more relevant to practice? *Journal of Counseling & Development, 63,* 538–544.

Howie, J., Gatens-Robinson, E., & Rubin, S. (1992). Applying ethical principles in rehabilitation counseling. *Rehabilitation Education, 6,* 41–55.

Huang, I., Cheing, G., Rumrill, P., Bengtson, K., Chan, F., Telzlaff, J., & Snitker, M. (2016). Characteristics of people with disabilities receiving assistive technology services in vocational rehabilitation: A logistic regression analysis. *Journal of Vocational Rehabilitation, 45*(1), 63–72.

Hunt, B. (2011). Publishing qualitative research in counseling journals. *Journal of Counseling and Development, 89*(3), 296.

Hunt, B., Matthews, C., Milsom, A., & Lammel, J. A. (2006). Lesbians with physical disabilities: A qualitative study of their experiences with counseling. *Journal of Counseling and Development: JCD, 84*(2), 163.

Hunt, B., Milsom, A., & Matthews, C. R. (2009). Partner-related rehabilitation experiences of lesbians with physical disabilities: A qualitative study. *Rehabilitation Counseling Bulletin, 52*(3), 167–178.

Hunt, B., & Rosenthal, D. A. (2000). Rehabilitation counselors' experiences with client death and death anxiety. *Journal of Rehabilitation, 66*(4), 44–50.

Hunt, G., Moloney, M., & Evans, K. (2009). Epidemiology meets cultural studies: Studying and understanding youth cultures, clubs and drugs. *Addiction Research & Theory, 17*(6), 601–621.

Hunter, J., & Schmidt, F. (1990). *Methods of meta-analysis.* Newbury Park, CA: Sage.

Iwasaki, Y., & Mactavish, J. B. (2005). Ubiquitous yet unique: Perspectives of people with disabilities on stress. *Rehabilitation Counseling Bulletin, 48*(4), 194–208.

Jenkins, W., & Strauser, D. (1999). Horizontal expansion of the role of the rehabilitation counselor. *Journal of Rehabilitation, 65,* 4–9.

Job Accomodation Network. (2014). *Workplace accomodations: Low cost, high impact.* Retrieved October 31, 2014, from http://AskJAN.org/media/lowcosthighimpact.html

Jolls, C., & Prescott, J. J. (2004, September). *Disaggregating employment protection: The case of disability discrimination* (NBER Working paper). Cambridge, MA: National Bureau of Economic Research.

Jones, G. R. (2000). Partnering online. *Journal of Rehabilitation Administration, 24,* 13–21.

Kalton, G. (1983). *Introduction to survey sampling.* Newbury Park, CA: Sage.

Kampfe, C., & Dennis, D. J. (2000). Counseling for diversity: Application of the house model of social stress. *Journal of Applied Rehabilitation Counseling, 31,* 27–37.

Kampfe, C., Wadsworth, J., Smith, S., & Harley, D. (2005). The infusion of aging issues in the rehabilitation curriculum: A review of the literature. *Rehabilitation Education, 19,* 225–233.

Kassberg, A., Prellwitz, M., & Lund, M. (2013). The challenges of every day technology in the workplace for persons with acquired brain injury. *Scandinavian Journal of Occupational Therapy, 20*(4), 272–281.

Kauppi, D. (1999). Distance education in rehabilitation counseling: From the process that brought us Y2K. *Rehabilitation Education, 13*(3), 207–218.

Kaya, C., Chan, F., Rumrill, P., Hartman, E., Wehman, P., Iwanaga, K., Pai, C., & Avellone, L. (2016). Vocational rehabilitation services and competitive employment for transition-age youth with autism spectrum disorders. *Journal of Vocational Rehabilitation, 45*(1), 73–83.

Kaye, H. S. (2009). Stuck at the bottom rung: Occupational characteristics of workers with disabilities. *Journal of Occupational Rehabilitation, 19*(2), 115–28.

Kazdin, A. (1998). *Research design in clinical psychology* (2nd ed.). Boston: Allyn & Bacon.

Kazdin, A. (2003). *Research design in clinical psychology* (4th ed.). Boston: Allyn & Bacon.

Keany, K., & Glueckauf, R. (1999). Disability and value change: An overview and reanalysis of acceptance of loss theory. In R. Marinelli & A. Dell Orto (Eds.), *The psychological and social impact of disability* (4th ed., pp. 139–151). New York: Springer.

Keijer, U., & Breding, J. (2012). Work life, new technology and employment of disabled people: A twenty year program. *Technology & Disability, 24*(3), 211–218.

Keim, J. (1999). Workplace violence and trauma: A 21st century rehabilitation issue. *The Journal of Rehabilitation, 65,* 16–20.

Keith, T. Z. (2006). *Multiple regression and beyond.* New York: Pearson Education.

Kelley, S., Sikka, A., & Venkatesan, S. (1997). A review of research on parental disability: Implications for research and counseling practice. *Rehabilitation Counseling Bulletin, 41*(2), 105–121.

Kessler, R. C., Walters, E. E., & Wittchen, H. (2004). Epidemiology. In R. G. Heimberg, C. L. Turk, & D. S. Mennin (Eds.), *Generalized anxiety disorder: Advances in research and practice* (pp. 29–50). New York: Guilford.

Ketelaer, P., Crijns, H., Gausin, J., & Bouwen, R. (1993). *Multiple sclerosis and employment: Synthesis report.* Brussels: Belgian Ministry of Labour and Employment.

Kincaid, H. (1996). *Philosophical foundations of the social sciences: Analyzing controversies in social research.* New York: Cambridge University Press.

King, N. (2012). *Doing template analysis. Qualitative organizational research: Core methods and current challenges.* London: Sage.

Kinugasa, T., Cerin, E., & Hooper, S. (2004). Single-subject research designs and data analysis for assessing elite athletes' conditioning. *Sports Medicine, 34*(15), 1035–1050.

Kirsh, B. (2000). Work, workers, and workplaces: A qualitative analysis of narratives of mental health consumers. *Journal of Rehabilitation, 66,* 24–30.

Kitchner, K. (1984). Intuition, critical evaluation, and ethical principles: The foundation for ethical decision in counseling psychology. *The Counseling Psychologist, 12*(3), 43–55.

Klem, L. (1995). Path analysis. In L. Grim & P. Yarnold (Eds.), *Reading and understanding multivariate statistics.* Washington, DC: American Psychological Association.

Kline, W. B. (2008). Developing and submitting credible qualitative manuscripts. *Counselor Education and Supervision, 47*(4), 210–217.

Koch, D. S. (1999). Protections in federal rehabilitation legislation for persons with alcohol and other drug abuse disabilities. *Journal of Applied Rehabilitation Counseling, 30*(3), 29–35.

Koch, L. (2000). Assessment and planning in the Americans with Disabilities Act era: Strategies for consumer self-advocacy and employer collaboration. *Journal of Vocational Rehabilitation, 14*(2), 103–108.

Koch, L. (2001). The preferences and anticipations of people referred to a vocational rehabilitation agency. *Rehabilitation Counseling Bulletin, 44,* 76–86.

Koch, L., & Arhar, J. (2002). Action research in rehabilitation counseling intern supervision. *Rehabilitation Education, 16,* 165–178.

Koch, L., Conyers, L., & Rumrill, P. D. (2012). The nature and needs of people with emerging disabilities. In P. J. Toriello, M. L. Bishop, & P. D. Rumrill (Eds.), *New directions in rehabilitation counseling: Creative responses to professional, clinical, and educational challenges* (pp. 115–139). Linn Creek, MO: Aspen Professional Services.

Koch, L., & Eaton, B. (2005). Multiple chemical sensitivity and rehabilitation planning implications. *Journal of Applied Rehabilitation Counseling, 36*(1), 24–29.

Koch, L., Hennessey, M., Ingram, A., Rumrill, P., & Roessler, R. (2006). Faculty learning communities to promote inclusion of students with disabilities on college and university campuses. *Rehabilitation Education, 20*(3), 191–200.

Koch, L. C., Niesz, T., & McCarthy, H. (2014). Understanding and reporting qualitative research: An analytical review and recommendations for submitting authors. *Rehabilitation Counseling Bulletin, 57*(3), 131–143.

Koch, L., & Rumrill, P. (1998). The working alliance: An interdisciplinary case management strategy for health professionals. *Work, 10,* 55–62.

Koch, L., & Rumrill, P. (1999). Work support tips: The career portfolio as a work supports strategy for people with disabilities. *Journal of Vocational Rehabilitation, 13*(3), 141–147.

Koch, L., & Rumrill, P. (2016). *Rehabilitation counseling and emerging disabilities: Medical, psychosocial, and vocational aspects.* New York: Springer.

Koch, L., Rumrill, P., Roessler, R., & Fitzgerald, S. (2001). Illness and demographic correlates of quality of life among people with multiple sclerosis. *Rehabilitation Psychology, 46,* 154–164.

Koch, L., Schultz, J., Hennessey, M., & Conyers, L. (2005). Rehabilitation research in the 21st Century: Concerns and recommendations from members of the National Council on Rehabilitation Education. *Rehabilitation Education, 19,* 5–14.

Kosciulek, J. (1999). The consumer-directed theory of empowerment. *Rehabilitation Counseling Bulletin, 42,* 196–213.

Kosciulek, J. (2004). Research applications of the Longitudinal Study of the Vocational Rehabilitation Services Program. *Rehabilitation Counseling Bulletin, 47,* 173–180.

Kosciulek, J. (2005). Structural equation model of the consumer-directed theory of empowerment in a vocational rehabilitation context. *Rehabilitation Counseling Bulletin, 49,* 40–49.

Kosciulek, J., & Merz, M. (2001). Structural analysis of the consumer-directed theory of empowerment. *Rehabilitation Counseling Bulletin, 44,* 209–216.

Kosciulek, J. F., & Szymanski, E. M. (1993). Statistical power analysis of rehabilitation counseling research. *Rehabilitation Counseling Bulletin, 36,* 212–219.

Kosciulek, J., & Wheaton, J. (2002). Information technology: An important rehabilitation education tool. *Rehabilitation Education, 16,* 327–329.

Krabbendam, L., & Aleman, A. (2003). Cognitive rehabilitation in schizophrenia: A quantitative analysis of controlled studies. *Psychopharmacology, 169,* 376–382.

Krathwohl, D. R. (1993). *Methods of educational and social science research: An integrated approach.* White Plains, NY: Longman.

Krathwohl, D. R. (1998). *Methods of educational and social science research: An integrated approach* (2nd ed.). White Plains, NY: Longman.

Krefting, L., & Brief, A. (1976). The impact of applicant disability on evaluative judgments in the selection process. *Academy of Management Journal, 19*(4), 675–680.

Kvale, S. (1996). *Interviews: An introduction to qualitative research interviewing.* Thousand Oaks, CA: Sage.

Kwok, O., Underhill, A., Berry, J., Luo, W., Elliott, T., & Yoon, M. (2008). Analyzing longitudinal data with multilevel models: An example with individuals living with lower extremity intra-articular fractures. *Rehabilitation Psychology, 53*, 370–386.

Lahey, J. N. (2005). Do older workers face discrimination? Center for Retirement research. Issue brief, no. 33. Boston: Boston College, Center for Retirement Research.

Lane, F. J., Shaw, L. R., Young, M. E., & Bourgeois, P. J. (2012). Rehabilitation counselors' perceptions of ethical workplace culture and the influence on ethical behavior. *Rehabilitation Counseling Bulletin, 55*(4), 219–231.

LaRocca, N. (1995). *Employment and multiple sclerosis: Current status and recommendations for services.* New York: National Multiple Sclerosis Society.

Leahy, M., Chan, F., & Lui, J. (2014). Evidence-based best practices in the public vocational rehabilitation program that lead to employment outcomes. *Journal of Vocational Rehabilitation, 41*(2), 83–86.

Leahy, M., Chan, F., & Saunders, J. (2003). Job functions and knowledge requirements of certified rehabilitation counselors in the 21st century. *Rehabilitation Counseling Bulletin, 46*, 66–81.

Leahy, M. J., Chan, F., Sung, C., & Kim, M. (2013). Empirically derived test specifications for the certified rehabilitation counselor examination. *Rehabilitation Counseling Bulletin, 56*(4), 199–214.

Leahy, M. J., & Szymanski, E. M. (1995). Rehabilitation counseling: Evolution and current status. *Journal of Counseling & Development, 74*, 163–166.

Leahy, M. J., Szymanski, E. M., & Linkowski, D. C. (1993). Knowledge importance in rehabilitation counseling. *Rehabilitation Counseling Bulletin, 37*, 130–145.

LeCompte, M. D., & Preissle, J. (1993). *Ethnography and qualitative design in education research* (2nd ed.). San Diego: Academic Press.

Leech, L. L., & Holcomb, J. M. (2000). The nature of psychiatric rehabilitation and implications for collaborative efforts. *Journal of Applied Rehabilitation Counseling, 31*(4), 54–62.

Leierer, S., Strohmer, D., Leclere, W., Cornwell, B., & Whitton, S. (1996). The effect of counselor disability, attending behavior, and client problem on counseling. *Rehabilitation Counseling Bulletin, 40*, 82–95.

Leierer, S. J., Strohmer, D. C., Kern, A. M., Clemons-Guidry, D. B., Roberts, K. J., & Curry, K. E. (1998). The effects of counselor disability status and reputation on perceptions of counselor expertness, attractiveness, and trustworthiness. *Rehabilitation Counseling Bulletin, 41*, 278–292.

Leigh, I. W., & Anthony-Tolbert, S. (2000). Reliability of the BDI-II with deaf persons. *Rehabilitation Psychology, 46*, 195–202.

Lemaire, G., Mallik, K., & Stoll, B. (2002). Expanding horizons: A model academic and vocational training program for out-of-school youth with disabilities. *Journal of Rehabilitation, 68*(2), 39–43.

Levine, H. G. (1985). Principles of data storage and retrieval for use in qualitative evaluations. *Educational Evaluation and Policy Analysis, 7*, 169–186.

Lewis, A. N., & Burris, J. L. (2012). The multicultural rehabilitation counseling imperative in the 21st century. In P. J. Toriello, M. L. Bishop, & P. D. Rumrill (Eds.), *New directions in rehabilitation counseling: Creative responses to professional, clinical, and educational challenges* (pp. 164–208). Linn Creek, MO: Aspen Professional Services.

Li, J., Fitzgerald, S. M., Bishop, M., Zhang, H., & Rumrill, P. (2015). Development and cross validation of the home functioning scale for people with multiple sclerosis. *Journal of Vocational Rehabilitation, 42*(2), 115–130.

Li, R. S. Y., & Tsang, H. W. H. (2002). The Chinese version of the Becker Work Adjustment Profile (BWAP-CV) for use by people with developmental disabilities. *Journal of Rehabilitation, 68,* 52–63.

Lincoln, Y. S., & Guba, E. G. (1985). *Naturalistic inquiry.* Beverly Hills, CA: Sage.

Lindstrom, L. E., Flannery, K. B., Benz, M. R., Olszewski, B., & Slovic, R. (2009). Building employment training partnerships between vocational rehabilitation and community colleges. *Rehabilitation Counseling Bulletin, 52*(3), 189–201.

Linkowski, D. (1971). A scale to measure acceptance of disability. *Rehabilitation Counseling Bulletin, 14,* 236–244.

Liss, H. J., Glueckauf, R. L., & Ecklund-Johnson, E. P. (2002). Research on telehealth chronic medical conditions: Critical review, key issues, and future directions. *Rehabilitation Psychology, 47,* 8–30.

Livneh, H. (1991). On the origins of negative attitudes toward people with disabilities. In R. P. Marinelli, & A. E. Dell Orto (Eds.), *The psychological and social impact of disability* (3rd ed., pp. 181–197). New York: Springer.

Livneh, H. (2000). Psychosocial adaptation to cancer: The role of coping strategies. *Journal of Rehabilitation, 66,* 40–49.

Livneh, H. (2001). Psychosocial adaptation to chronic illness and disability: A conceptual framework. *Rehabilitation Counseling Bulletin, 44,* 151–160.

Livneh, H. (2016). Quality of life and coping with chronic illness and disability: A temporal perspective. *Rehabilitation Counseling Bulletin, 59*(2), 67–83. doi: 10.1177/0034355215575180

Livneh, H., & Parker, R. (2002). Psychosocial adaptation to disability: Perspectives from chaos and complexity theory. *Rehabilitation Counseling Bulletin, 49,* 17–28.

Loehlin, J. (1992). *Latent variable models: An introduction to factor, path, and structural analysis* (2nd ed.). Hillsdale, NJ: Lawrence Erlbaum.

Loretto, W., & White, P. (2006). Employers' attitudes, practices and policies towards older workers. *Human Resource Management Journal, 16*(3), 313–330.

Luft, P., Rumrill, P., Snyder, J., & Hennessey, M. (2001). Transition strategies for youths with sensory impairments. *Work: A Journal of Prevention, Assessment, and Rehabilitation, 17*(2), 123–134.

Lundervold, D., & Belwood, M. (2000). The best kept secret in counseling: Single-case (N=1) experimental designs. *Journal of Counseling & Development, 78,* 92–102.

Lustig, D. C., & Strauser, D. R. (2001). The implications of posttraumatic stress disorder on vocational behavior and rehabilitation planning. *Journal of Rehabilitation, 67*(3), 26–31.

Lustig, D. C., & Strauser, D. R. (2007). Casual relationships between poverty and disability. *Rehabilitation Counseling Bulletin, 50,* 194–202.

Lydell, M., Grahn, B., Mansson, J., Baiqi, A., & Marklund, B. (2009). Predictive factors of sustained return to work for persons with musculoskeletal disorders who participated in rehabilitation. *Work, 33*(3), 317–328.

MacCoun, R. J. (1998). Biases in the interpretation and use of research results. *Annual Review of Psychology, 49,* 259–287.

Magd, H. (2003). Management attitudes and perceptions of older employees in hospitality management. *International Journal of Contemporary Hospitality Management, 15*(7), 393–401.

Malterud, K. (2001). Qualitative research: Standards, challenges, and guidelines. *The Lancet, 358*(9280), 483–488.

Mamboleo, G., Kaya, C., Meyer, L., Kamnetz, B., Bezyak, J., & Chan, F. (2015). Vocational rehabilitation services and outcomes for individuals with arthritis in the United States. *Journal of Vocational Rehabilitation, 42*(2), 131–140.

Manicas, P. T., & Secord, P. F. (1983). Implications for psychology of the new philosophy of science. *American Psychologist, 38,* 399–413.

Marini, I. (2001). Cross-cultural counseling issues of males who sustain a disability. *Journal of Applied Rehabilitation Counseling, 32*(1), 36–44.

Marini, I. (2003). What rehabilitation counselors should know to assist Social Security beneficiaries in becoming employed. *Work, 21*(1), 37–44.

Marshall, C., Johnson, M., Saravanabhavan, R., & Bradford, B. (1992). The rehabilitation needs of American Indians with disabilities in an urban setting. *Journal of Rehabilitation, 58*(2), 13–21.

Marshall, C., & Juarez, L. G. (2002). Learning from our neighbor: Women with disabilities in Oaxaca, Mexico. *Journal of Rehabilitation, 68*(3), 12–18.

Marshall, C., Leung, P., Johnson, S., & Busby, H. (2003). Ethical practice and cultural factors in rehabilitation. *Rehabilitation Education, 17,* 55–65.

Marshall, C., & Rossman, G. B. (1989). *Designing qualitative research.* Newbury Park, CA: Sage.

Marshall, C., & Rossman, G. B. (2011). *Designing qualitative research.* Thousand Oaks, CA: Sage.

Martinis, J. (2015). The right to make choices: How vocational rehabilitation can help young adults with disabilities increase self-determination and avoid guardianship. *Journal of Vocational Rehabilitation, 42*(3), 221–228.

Matrone, K., & Leahy, M. (2005). The relationship between vocational rehabilitation client outcomes and rehabilitation counselor multicultural counseling competencies. *Rehabilitation Counseling Bulletin, 48,* 233–244.

Matthews, L. R., Harris, L. M., Jaworski, A., Alam, A., & Bozdag, G. (2014). Function, health and psychosocial needs in job-seekers with anxiety, mood, and psychotic disorders who access disability employment services. *Work, 49*(2), 271–279.

Maxwell, J. A. (1996). *Qualitative research design: An interactive approach.* Thousand Oaks, CA: Sage.

Maxwell, J. A. (2012). *Qualitative research design: An interactive approach* (3rd ed.). Thousand Oaks, CA: Sage.

McCarthy, H. (2003). The disability rights movement: Experiences and perspectives of selected leaders in the disability community. *Rehabilitation Counseling Bulletin, 46,* 209–223.

McCarthy, H., & Leierer, S. J. (2001). Consumer concepts of ideal characteristics and minimum qualifications for rehabilitation counselors. *Rehabilitation Counseling Bulletin, 45,* 12–23.

McDonnall, M. C., O'Mally, J., & Crudden, A. (2014). Employer knowledge of and attitudes toward individuals who are blind or visually impaired as employees. *Journal of Visual Impairment & Blindness, 108*(3), 213–225.

McHugh, S., Storey, K., & Certo, N. (2002). Training job coaches to use natural support strategies. *Journal of Vocational Rehabilitation, 17*(3), 155–163.

McIlveen, P. (2008). Autoethnography as a method for reflexive research and practice in vocational psychology. *Australian Journal of Career Development, 17*(2), 13–20.

McKenna, M. A., Fabian, E., Hurley, J. E., McMahon, B. T., & West, S. L. (2007). Workplace discrimination and cancer. *Work, 29*(4), 313–322.

McKenna, M. A., & Power, P. W. (1999). Engaging the African American family in the rehabilitation process: An intervention model for rehabilitation counselors. *Journal of Applied Rehabilitation Counseling, 30*(3), 12–22.

McMahon, B. (Ed.). (2006). *Workplace discrimination and disability.* Richmond, VA: Virginia Commonwealth University, School of Education and Department of Physical Medicine and Rehabilitation.

McMahon, B. T., Edwards, R., Rumrill, P. D., & Hursh, N. (2005). An overview of the National EEOC ADA Research Project. *Work, 25,* 1–7.

McMahon, B., & Shaw, L. (1999). *Enabling lives.* Boca Raton, FL: CRC Press.

McMahon, B., West, S. L., Mansouri, M., & Belonia, L. (2006). Workplace discrimination and diabetes. In B. McMahon (Ed.), *Workplace discrimination and disability* (pp. 37–48). Richmond, VA: Virginia Commonwealth University.

McMillan, J. (2000). *Educational research: Fundamentals for the consumer.* New York: Longman.

McMillan, J., & Schumacher, S. (1997). *Research in education: A conceptual introduction* (4th ed). New York: Longman.

McMillan, J. J., & Schumacher, S. (2006). *Research in education: Evidence based inquiry* (6th ed.). Upper Saddle River, NJ: Merrill Publishing.

McMillan, J. J., & Schumacher, S. (2009). *Research in education: Evidence based inquiry* (7th ed.). Upper Saddle River, NJ: Pearson.

McReynolds, C. J. (2001). The meaning of work in the lives of people living with HIV disease and AIDS. *Rehabilitation Counseling Bulletin, 44,* 104–115.

McReynolds, C., Koch, L., & Rumrill, P. (2001). Speaking of research: Qualitative strategies in rehabilitation research. *Work: A Journal of Prevention, Assessment and Rehabilitation, 16,* 57–65.

Meade, M., Reed, K., Rumrill, P., Aust, R., & Krause, J. (2016). Perceptions of quality of employment outcomes after multiple sclerosis: A qualitative study. *Journal of Rehabilitation, 82*(2), 31–40.

Meara, N. M., Schmidt, L. D., Carrington, C. H., Davis, K. L., Dixon, D. N., Fretz, B. R., et al. (1988). Training and accreditation in counseling psychology. *The Counseling Psychologist, 16,* 366–384.

Mehnert, T., Krauss, H. H., Nadler, R., & Boyd, M. (1990). Correlates of life satisfaction in those with disabling conditions. *Rehabilitation Psychology, 35,* 3–17.

Merchant, W., Li, J., Karpinski, A., & Rumrill, P. (2013). A conceptual overview of structural equation modeling in rehabilitation research. *Work: A Journal of Prevention, Assessment, and Rehabilitation, 45,* 407–415.

Merton, R. K. (1968). *Social theory and social structure.* New York: Free Press.

Merz, M., Bricout, J., & Koch, L. (2001). Disability and job stress: Implications for vocational rehabilitation planning. *Work: A Journal of Prevention, Assessment and Rehabilitation, 17*(2), 85–95.

Messick, S. (1980). Test validity and the ethics of assessment. *American Psychologist, 35,* 1012–1027.

Messick, S. (1988). The once and future issues in validity: Assessing the meaning and consequences of measurement. In H. Wainer, & H. I. Braun (Eds.), *Test validity* (pp. 33–45). Hillsdale, NJ: Erlbaum.

Middleton, R. A., Rollins, C. W., Sanderson, P. S., Leung, P., Harley, D. A., Ebner, D., et al. (2000). Endorsement of the professional multicultural rehabilitation competencies and standards: A call to action. *Rehabilitation Counseling Bulletin, 43,* 219–240.

Miles, J., & Shevlin. M. (2001). *Applying regression and correlation: A guide for students and practitioners.* London: Sage.

Miles, M. B., & Huberman, A. M. (1994). *Qualitative data analysis* (2nd ed.). Thousand Oaks, CA: Sage.

Miller, J. (2000). *Coping with chronic illness* (3rd ed.). Philadelphia, PA: F.A. Davis.

Miller, E., & Marini, I. (2004). Female sexuality and spinal cord injury: Counseling implications. *Journal of Applied Rehabilitation Counseling, 35*(4), 17–25.

Millington, M. (1997). *The employment expectations questionnaire.* New Orleans: Louisiana State University Medical Center.

Millington, M., & Strauser, D. (1998). Planning strategies in disability management. *Work: A Journal of Prevention, Assessment and Rehabilitation, 10*(3), 261–270.

Minden, S. L., & Schiffer, R. B. (1990). Affective disorders in multiple sclerosis: Review and recommendations for clinical research. *Archives of Neurology, 47,* 98–104.

Moravcsik, A. (2014). Transparency: The revolution in qualitative research. *PS: Political Science & Politics, 47*(01), 48–53.

Moore, C. L., & Feist-Price, S. (1999). Societal attitudes and the civil rights of persons with disabilities. *Journal or Applied Rehabilitation Counseling, 30*(2), 19–25.

Morgan, D. L. (1988). *The Focus Group Kit.* Thousand Oaks, CA: Sage.

Morrow, S. L. (2005). Quality and trustworthiness in qualitative research in counseling psychology. *Journal of Counseling Psychology, 52*(2), 250

Moustakas, C. (1994). *Phenomenological research methods*. Thousand Oaks, CA: Sage.

Moxley, D. P., Manela, R. W., & Finch, J. R. (2000). The role of evaluation in facilitating organizational change in rehabilitation agencies. *Journal of Rehabilitation Administration, 24,* 41–49.

Mpofu, E. (2000). Rehabilitation counseling: Issues in professionalization and identity. *Rehabilitation Education, 14*(3), 199–205.

Mpofu, E., & Harley, D. A. (2000). Tokenism and cultural diversity in counselors: Implications for rehabilitation education and practice. *Journal of Applied Rehabilitation Counseling, 31*(1), 47–58.

Mpofu, E., & Harley, D. A. (2002). Disability and rehabilitation in Zimbabwe: Lessons and implications for rehabilitation practice in the U.S. *Journal of Rehabilitation, 68,* 26–35.

Mpofu, E., Rosamond, M., Gitchel, W. D., Peterson, D. B., & Chou, C. C. (2012). Person-centered assessment in rehabilitation and health care. In P. J. Toriello, M. L. Bishop, & P. D. Rumrill (Eds.), *New directions in rehabilitation counseling: Creative responses to professional, clinical, and educational challenges* (pp. 209–235). Linn Creek, MO: Aspen Professional Services.

Mullins, J., Roessler, R., Schriner, K., Brown, P., & Bellini, J. (1997). Improving employment outcomes through quality rehabilitation counseling (QRC). *Journal of Rehabilitation, 63*(4), 21–31.

Mullins, L. L., Cote, M. P., Fuemmeler, B. F., Jean, V. M., Beatty, W. W., & Paul, R. H. (2001). Illness intrusiveness, uncertainty, and distress in individuals with multiple sclerosis. *Rehabilitation Psychology, 46,* 139–153.

Muncey, T. (2005). Doing autoethnography. *International Journal of Qualitative Methods, 4*(1), 10.

Murphy, S. T., & Salomone, P. R. (1983). Client and counselor expectations of rehabilitation services. *Rehabilitation Counseling Bulletin, 27,* 81–93.

Muthard, J., & Salomone, P. (1969). The roles and functions of the rehabilitation counselor. *Rehabilitation Counseling Bulletin, 13*(1–SP), 81–168.

Nardone, A., Sampson, E., Stauffer, C., Leopold, A., Jacobs, K., Hendricks, D., Elias, E., Chun, H., & Rumrill, P. (2015). Project Career: A qualitative examination of five college students with traumatic brain injuries. *Neurorehabilitation, 37,* 459–469.

Nary, D. E., White, G. W., Budde, J. F., & Hoang Yen, V. (2004). Identifying the employment and vocational rehabilitation concerns of people with traditional and emerging disabilities. *Journal of Vocational Rehabilitation, 20*(1), 71–77.

National Institute on Disability and Rehabilitation Research. (2006). *NIDRR long-range plan for fiscal years 2005–2009*. Washington, DC: Author.

National Institute on Disability, Independent Living, and Rehabilitation Research. (2017). *NIDILRR draft long-range plan for the period 2018–2023*. Retrieved June 2, 2017 from https://www.acl.gov/sites/default/files/news%202017-05/NIDILRR-Long-Range-Plan-DRAFT.pdf

Neath, J., Roessler, R., McMahon, B., & Rumrill, P. (2007). Patterns in perceived employment discrimination for adults with multiple sclerosis. *Work: A Journal of Prevention, Assessment, and Rehabilitation, 29*(3), 255–274.

Nelson, P. A., Dial, J. G., & Joyce, A. (2002). Validation of the Cognitive Test for the Blind as an assessment of intellectual functioning. *Rehabilitation Psychology, 47*(2), 184–193.

Neubert, D., Moon, M., Grigal, M., & Redd, V. (2001). Post-secondary educational practices for individuals with mental retardation and other significant disabilities: A review of the literature. *Journal of Vocational Rehabilitation, 16*(3/4), 155–168.

Neumark, D. (2003). Age discrimination legislation in the United States. *Contemporary Economic Policy, 21,* 217–317.

Niesz, T., Koch, L., & Rumrill, P. (2008). The empowerment of people with disabilities through qualitative research. *Work: A Journal of Prevention, Assessment, and Rehabilitation, 31,* 113–125.

Nightingale, D., & Cromby, J. (1999). *Social constructionist psychology: A critical analysis of theory and practice.* McGraw-Hill Education (UK).

19th Institute on Rehabilitation Issues. (1993). *Consumer involvement and empowerment in all aspects of the rehabilitation process.* Alexandria, VA: Author.

Nissen, S., & Rumrill, P. (2014). Employment and career development considerations. In B. Giesser (Ed.), *Primer on multiple sclerosis* (2nd ed., pp. 362–391). New York: Oxford University Press.

Nittrouer, C., Shogren, K., & Pickens, J. (2016). Using a collaborative process to develop goals and self-management interventions to support young adults with disabilities at work. *Rehabilitation Research, Policy, and Education, 30*(2), 110–128.

Nochi, M. (1998). Struggling with the labeled self: People with traumatic brain injuries in social settings. *Qualitative Health Research, 8,* 655–681.

Northrup, D. (2006). *Health insurance resources: A guide for people with chronic disease and disability.* New York: Demos Medical Publishers.

Nosek, M., Howland, C., & Hughes, R. (2001). The investigation of abuse and women with disabilities: Going beyond assumptions. *Violence Against Women, 7*(4), 477–499.

Nosek, M., & Hughes, R. (2001). Psychospiritual aspects of sense of self in women with physical disabilities. *Journal of Rehabilitation, 67,* 20–28.

Nosek, M., & Hughes, R. (2003). Psychosocial issues of women with physical disabilities: The continuing gender debate. *Rehabilitation Counseling Bulletin, 46,* 224–233.

Nosek, M., & Young, M. (1997). Abuse of women with disabilities. *Journal of Disability Policy Studies, 8*(1/2), 157–175.

Nunez, P. (2011). Ethics in rehabilitation counseling. *Counseling Today, 54*(2), 36.

Oberle, K. M. (2002). Ethics in qualitative health research. *Annals (Royal College of Physicians and Surgeons of Canada), 35*(8 Suppl.), 563–566.

Oestreich, R. P. (2000). Living online. *Journal of Rehabilitation Administration, 24*(1), 57–63.

Oliver, I., & Spokane, A. (1988). Career intervention outcome: What contributes to client gain? *Journal of Counseling Psychology, 35,* 447–462.

Olney, M. F. (2001). Communication strategies of adults with severe disabilities: Supporting self-determination. *Rehabilitation Counseling Bulletin, 44,* 87–94.

Onwuegbuuzie, A., & Daniels, L. (2002). A framework for reporting and interpreting internal consistency reliability estimates. *Measurement and Evaluation in Counseling and Development, 35*(2), 89–103.

Orange, L., & Brodwin, M. (2005). Childhood sexual abuse: What rehabilitation counselors need to know. *Journal of Rehabilitation, 71,* 5–11.

Orb, A., Eisenhauer, L., & Wynaden, D. (2001). Ethics in qualitative research. *Journal of Nursing Scholarship, 33*(1), 93–96.

O'Reilly, P., & Caro, F. G. (1994). Productive aging: An overview of the literature. *Journal of Aging and Social Policy, 6*(3), 39–71.

Orwell, G. (1946, 1982). Politics and the English language. In J. R. Hammond (Ed.), *A George Orwell companion.* New York: St. Martins Press.

Palmer, C. D. (1998). *Self-advocacy and conflict resolution: Requesting academic accommodations at postsecondary education institutions.* Unpublished Doctoral Dissertation, University of Arkansas, Fayetteville.

Park, N., & Ingles, J. (2001). Effectiveness of attention rehabilitation after an acquired brain injury: A meta-analysis. *Neuropsychology, 15,* 199–210.

Parker, R. M., & Patterson, J. B. (2012). *Rehabilitation counseling: Basics and beyond* (5th ed). Pro-Ed.

Parker, R., & Szymanski, E. (1996). Editorial: Ethics and publication. *Rehabilitation Counseling Bulletin, 39*(3), 162–165.

Parker, R. M. (1990). Science, philosophy, and politics in the search for truth in rehabilitation research. *Rehabilitation Counseling Bulletin, 34,* 165–169.

Paterson, J., Hamilton, M., & Grant, H. (2000). The effectiveness of the hierarchic dementia scale in tailoring interventions to reduce problem behaviors in people with Alzheimer's disease. *Australian Occupational Therapy Journal, 47,* 134–140.

Patterson, C. H. (1986). *Theories of counseling and psychotherapy* (4th ed.). New York: Harper & Row.

Patterson, J., McFarlane, F., & Sax, C. (2005). Challenges to a legacy: Retaining CORE accreditation of rehabilitation counselor education programs. *Rehabilitation Education, 19,* 203–214.

Patterson, J. B. (2000). Using the internet to facilitate the rehabilitation process. *Journal of Rehabilitation, 66,* 4–10.

Patton, M. Q. (2002). *Qualitative research & evaluation methods* (3rd ed.). Thousand Oaks, CA: Sage Publications.

Pedazur, E. (1982). *Multiple regression in behavioral research* (2nd ed.). New York: Harcourt College Publishers.

Pedhazur, E. J. (1997). *Multiple regression in behavioral research: Explanation and prediction* (3rd ed.). New York: Harcourt.

Perrin, T. (2005). *The Business Case for Workers Age 50+: Planning for Tomorrow's Talent Needs in Today's Competitive Environment.* Washington: AARP.

Persel, C. S., Persel, C. H., Ashley, M., & Krych, D. (1997). The use of non-contingent reinforcement and contingent restraint to reduce physical aggression and self-injurious behavior in a traumatically brain injured adult. *Brain Injury, 11,* 751–760.

Peshkin, A. (1988). In search of subjectivity—one's own. *Educational Researcher, 17*(7), 17–22.

Peterman, L., & Dixon, C. (2001). Assessment and evaluation of men who batter women. *Journal of Rehabilitation, 67,* 38–46.

Phillips, D. C. (1987). *Philosophy, science, and social inquiry.* New York: Pergamon.

Phillips, D. C. (1992). *The social scientist's bestiary: A guide to fabled threats to, and defenses of, naturalistic science.* Tarrytown, NY: Pergamon Press.

Phillips, D., & Burbules, N. (2000). *Postpositivism and educational research.* Lanham, MD: Rowman & Littlefield.

Pohlman, J., Poosawtsee, Gerndt, K., & Lindstrom-Hazel, D. (2001). Improving work programs' delivery of information and service to workers' compensation carriers. *Work: A Journal of Prevention, Assessment and Rehabilitation, 16*(2), 91–100.

Polkinghorne, D. E. (1991). Qualitative procedures for counseling research. In C. E. Watkins, & L. J. Schneider (Eds.), *Research in counseling* (pp. 163–204). Hillsdale, NJ: Erlbaum.

Popper, K. (1959). *The logic of scientific discovery.* New York: Basic Books.

Popper, K. (1976). The logic of the social sciences. In T. Adorno (Ed.), *The positivist dispute in German sociology.* NY: Harper Torchbooks.

Porter, E., Neysmith, S. M., Reitsma-Street, M., & Collins, S. B. (2009). Reciprocal peer interviewing. *International Review of Qualitative Research, 2*(2), 291–312.

Potts, B. (2005). Disability and employment: Considering the importance of social capital. *Journal of Rehabilitation, 71*(3), 20–25.

Power, P. (2013). *A guide to vocational assessment* (5th ed.). Austin, TX: Pro-Ed.

Prodinger, B., Shaw, L., Laliberte-Rudman, D., & Stamm, T. (2014). Negotiating disability in everyday life: Ethnographical accounts of women with rheumatoid arthritis. *Disability and Rehabilitation, 36*(6), 497–503.

Pro-Ed. (2015). Publications catalog. www.proedinc.com/tests/catalog.html (April 28, 2015).

Puckett, F., & Johnson, K. (2002). IT corner: Accessibility issues for electronic and information technology. *Rehabilitation Education 16,* 373–379.

Purdie-Vaughns, V., & Eibach, R. P. (2008). Intersectional invisibility. *Sex Roles, 59,* 377–391.

Quinones-Mayo, Y., Wilson, K. B., & McGuire, M. V. (2000). Vocational rehabilitation and cultural competency for the Latino populations: Considerations for rehabilitation counselors. *Journal of Applied Rehabilitation Counseling, 31*(1), 19–26.

Rebeiro Gruhl, K. L., Kauppi, C., Montgomery, P., James, S., Phyllis, K. R. G. C. K., & James, M. S. (2012). Consideration of the influence of place on access to employment for persons with serious mental illness in northeastern Ontario. *Rural Remote Health, 12,* 2034

Rehabilitation Services Administration. (1992). *The implications of 504 and the ADA regarding client placement services and pre-employment inquiries by employers.* U.S. Department of Education, Office of Special Education and Rehabilitative Services: Washington, D.C. Retrieved June 1, 2017 from https://www2.ed.gov/policy/speced/guid/rsa/tac-93-01.pdf

Remer, R. (1981). The counselor and research: An introduction. *Personnel and Guidance Journal, 59,* 567–571.

Ren, L. R., Paetzold, R. L., & Colella, A. (2008). A meta-analysis of experimental studies on the effects of disability on human resource judgments. *Human Resource Management Review, 18,* 191–203.

Riemer-Reiss, M. (2000). Vocational rehabilitation counseling at a distance: Challenges, strategies and ethics to consider. *Journal of Rehabilitation, 66,* 11–17.

Riemer-Reiss, M., Kampfe, C., Yazak, D., Larson, A., Troutman, C., & Cantrell, C. (2002). Promoting professional writing among rehabilitation counseling students. *Rehabilitation Education, 16,* 345–355.

Riemer-Reiss, M., & Morrissette P. (2002). Family counseling in vocational rehabilitation education. *Rehabilitation Education, 16,* 277–281.

Riemer-Reiss, M. L., & Wacker, R. R. (2000). Factors associated with assistive technology discontinuance among individuals with disabilities. *Journal of Rehabilitation, 66,* 44–50.

Rix, S. (2005). *Update on the Aged 55+ Worker: 2005.* Washington: AARP Public Policy Institute.

Roberts, P. (1998). *In search of American Sign Language: Language attitudes, beliefs, and knowledge.* Unpublished doctoral dissertation. Kent State University: Kent, OH.

Robinson, W. S. (1951). The logical structure of analytic induction. *American Sociological Review, 16,* 812–818.

Roessler, R. (2002). Improving job tenure outcomes for people with disabilities: The 3M model. *Rehabilitation Counseling Bulletin, 45,* 207–212.

Roessler, R., & Brown, P. (2000). Transition and the community college: A Career Keys model for students with disabilities. *Work: A Journal of Prevention, Assessment, and Rehabilitation, 14,* 23–29.

Roessler, R., & Gottcent, J. (1994). The Work Experience Survey: A reasonable accommodation/career development strategy. *Journal of Applied Rehabilitation Counseling, 25*(3), 16–21.

Roessler, R., Neath, J., McMahon, B., & Rumrill, P. (2007). The relationship of selected supply-and-demand-side factors to forms of perceived discrimination among adults with multiple sclerosis. *Rehabilitation Counseling Bulletin, 50,* 203–215.

Roessler, R., Reed, C., & Brown, P. (1998). Coping with chronic illness at work: Case studies of successful employees. *Journal of Vocational Rehabilitation, 10*(3), 261–269.

Roessler, R., & Rubin, S. E. (1992). *Case management and rehabilitation counseling* (2nd ed.). Austin, TX: Pro-Ed.

Roessler, R., Rubin, S., & Rumrill, P. (2017). *Case management in rehabilitation counseling: A systematic approach* (5th ed.). Austin, TX: Pro-Ed.

Roessler, R., & Rumrill, P. (1994). Strategies for enhancing career maintenance self-efficacy of people with multiple sclerosis. *Journal of Rehabilitation, 60*(4), 54–59.

Roessler, R., Rumrill, P., & Hennessey, M. (2002). *Employment concerns of people with multiple sclerosis: Building a national employment policy.* New York: National Multiple Sclerosis Society.

Roessler, R., Rumrill, P., Li, J., & Leslie, M. (2015). Predictors of differential employment statuses of adults with multiple sclerosis. *Journal of Vocational Rehabilitation, 42*(2), 141–152.

Roessler, R., Rumrill, P., Li, J., & McMahon, B. (2016). The workplace discrimination experiences of people with multiple sclerosis across three phases of Americans with Disabilities Act implementation. *Journal of Vocational Rehabilitation, 45*(1), 27–41.

Roessler, R., Rumrill, P., & Timblin, R. (in press). Qualitative focus group perspectives on high-priority employment barriers facing Americans with multiple sclerosis. *Journal of Vocational Rehabilitation.*

Roessler, R., & Schriner, K. (1992). Employment concerns of people with head injuries. *Journal of Rehabilitation, 58*(1), 17.

Roessler, R. T., & Sumner, G. (1997). Employer opinion about accommodating employees with chronic illnesses. *Journal of Applied Rehabilitation Counseling, 28,* 29–34.

Rogers, E. S., Anthony, W., Lyass, A., & Penk, W. (2006). A randomized clinical trial of vocational rehabilitation for people with psychiatric disabilities. *Rehabilitation Counseling Bulletin, 49,* 143–156.

Romero, M., & Marini, I. (2006). Obesity as a disability: Medical, psychosocial, and vocational implications. *Journal of Applied Rehabilitation Counseling, 37*(1), 21–26.

Rosenthal, D., & Olsheski, J. (1999). Disability management and rehabilitation counseling: Present status and future opportunities. *Journal of Rehabilitation, 65,* 31–38.

Rosenthal, R. (1991). *Meta analytic procedures for social research* (Rev. ed., Vol. 6). Newbury Park: Sage.

Rosenthal, R., & Rosnow, R. L. (1969). The volunteer subject. In R. Rosenthal & R. L. Rosnow (Eds.), *Artifact in behavioral research* (pp. 61–118). New York: Academic Press.

Rosnow, R. L., & Georgoudi, M. (1986). The spirit of contextualism. In R. L. Rosnow & M. Georgoudi (Eds.), *Contextualism and understanding in behavioral science: Implications for research and theory* (pp. 3–22). New York: Praeger.

Rosnow, R. L., & Rosenthal, R. (1989). Statistical procedures and the justification of knowledge in psychological science. *American Psychologist, 44,* 1276–1284.

Rubin, S. E., Matkin, R. E., Ashley, J., Beardsley, M., May, V. R., Onstott, K., & Puckett, F. D. (1984). Roles and functions of certified rehabilitation counselors. *Rehabilitation Counseling Bulletin, 29,* 199–224.

Rubin, S. E., & Rice, J. M. (1986). Quality and relevance of rehabilitation research: A critique and recommendations. *Rehabilitation Counseling Bulletin, 31,* 33–42.

Rubin, S., & Roessler, R. (2000). *Foundations of the vocational rehabilitation process* (5th ed.). Austin, TX: Pro-Ed.

Rubin, S., & Roessler, R. (2008). *Foundations of the vocational rehabilitation process* (6th ed.). Austin, TX: Pro-Ed.

Rubin, S., Roessler, R., & Rumrill, P. (2016). *Foundations of the vocational rehabilitation process* (7th ed.). Austin, TX: Pro-Ed.

Rudstam, H., Golden, T., Gower, W., Switzer, E., Bruyere, S., & Van Looy, S. (2014). Leveraging new rules to advance new opportunities: Implications of the Rehabilitation Act Section 503 new rules for employment service providers. *Journal of Vocational Rehabilitation, 41*(3), 193–208.

Rumrill, P. (1996). *Employment issues and multiple sclerosis.* New York. Demos.

Rumrill, P. (1999). Effects of a social competence training program on accommodation request activity, situational self-efficacy, and Americans with Disabilities Act knowledge among employed people with visual impairments and blindness. *Journal of Vocational Rehabilitation, 12,* 25–31.

Rumrill, P. (2001). Contemporary issues in postsecondary education for students with disabilities: Roles and responsibilities for educators and rehabilitation professionals. *Journal of Vocational Rehabilitation, 16*(3/4), 143–144.

Rumrill, P. (2013). Perspectives on the Japanese and American systems of vocational rehabilitation and work force development. *Work, 45*(2), 237–240.

Rumrill, P., & Bellini, J. (1999). The logic of experimental design. *Journal of Vocational Rehabilitation, 13,* 65–70.

Rumrill, P., & Cook, B. (2001). *Research in special education.* Springfield, IL: Charles C Thomas.

Rumrill, P., Cook, B., & Wiley, A. (2010). *Research in special education* (2nd ed.) Springfield, IL: Charles C Thomas.

Rumrill, P., & Fitzgerald, S. (2001). Speaking of research: Using narrative literature reviews to build a scientific knowledge base. *Work: A Journal of Prevention, Assessment, And Rehabilitation, 16*(2), 165–170.

Rumrill, P., & Fitzgerald, S. (2010). Employer characteristics and discharge-related discrimination against people with disabilities under the Americans with Disabilities Act. *Advances in Developing Human Resources, 12*(4), 448–465.

Rumrill, P., Fraser, R., & Anderson, J. (2000). New directions in home-based employment for people with disabilities. *Journal of Vocational Rehabilitation, 14,* 3–9.

Rumrill, P., & Garnette, M. (1997). Career adjustment via reasonable accommodations: The effects of an employee-empowerment intervention for people with disabilities. *Work, 9,* 57–64.

Rumrill, P., & Hennessey, M. (2001). *Multiple sclerosis: A guide for rehabilitation and healthcare professionals.* Springfield, IL: Charles C Thomas.

Rumrill, P., & Koch, L. (2014). Vocational rehabilitation counseling. In P. Hartung, M. Savickas, & B. Walsh (Eds.), *American Psychological Association Handbook of Career Intervention* (pp. 139–155). San Francisco, CA: American Psychological Association Books.

Rumrill, P., Koch, L., & Wohlford, S. (2013). Job retention and career maintenance strategies for people with multiple sclerosis. *Journal of Vocational Rehabilitation, 39,* 127–135.

Rumrill, P., & Luft, P. (2001). Applications for youth with sensory impairments. In P. Wehman (Ed.), *Life beyond the classroom: Transition strategies for young people with disabilities* (pp. 341–370). Baltimore, MD: Paul H. Brookes.

Rumrill, P., & Luft, P. (2006). Applications for youth with sensory impairments. In P. Wehman (Ed.), *Life beyond the classroom: Transition strategies for young people with disabilities* (pp. 447–474). Baltimore, MD: Paul H. Brookes.

Rumrill, P., Millington, M., Webb, J., & Cook, B. (1998). Employment expectations as a differential indicator of attitudes toward people with insulin-dependent diabetes mellitus. *Journal of Vocational Rehabilitation, 10*(3), 271–280.

Rumrill, P., & Roessler, R. (1999). New directions in vocational rehabilitation: A career development perspective on closure. *Journal of Rehabilitation, 65,* 26–30.

Rumrill, P., Roessler, R., & Cook, B. (1998). Improving career re-entry outcomes for people with multiple sclerosis: A comparison of two approaches. *Journal of Vocational Rehabilitation, 10*(3), 241–252.

Rumrill, P., Roessler, R., & Denny, G. (1997). Increasing confidence in the accommodation request process among persons with multiple sclerosis: A career maintenance self-efficacy intervention. *Journal of Job Placement, 13,* 5–9.

Rumrill, P., Roessler, R., & Koch, L. (1999). Surveying the employment concerns of people with multiple sclerosis: A participatory action research approach. *Journal of Vocational Rehabilitation, 12*(2), 75–82.

Rumrill, P., Roessler, R., Li, J., Daly, K., & Leslie, M. (2015). The employment concerns of Americans with multiple sclerosis: Results from a national survey. *Work: A Journal of Prevention, Assessment, and Rehabilitation, 52*(4), 735–748.

Rumrill, P., Roessler, R., McMahon, B., & Fitzgerald, S. (2005). Multiple sclerosis and workplace discrimination: The national Equal Employment Opportunity Commission Americans with Disabilities Act research project. *Journal of Vocational Rehabilitation, 23*(3), 179–188.

Rumrill, P., Roessler, R., McMahon, B., Hennessey, M., & Neath, J. (2007). Gender as a differential indicator of the employment discrimination experiences of people with multiple sclerosis. *Work: A Journal of Prevention, Assessment, and Rehabilitation, 29*(4), 303–312.

Rumrill, P., Schoenfeld, N., Holman, C., & Mullins, J. (1997). Ecological assessment of the career maintenance needs of employees with diabetes mellitus. *Work, 9*(2), 111–120.

Rumrill, P., Tabor, T., Hennessey, M., & Minton, D. (2000). Issues in employment and career development for people with multiple sclerosis: Meeting the needs of an emerging vocational rehabilitation clientele. *Journal of Vocational Rehabilitation, 14*(2), 109–117.

Sales, A. (2011). *Human growth and development considerations in rehabilitation counseling.* Lake of the Ozarks, MO: Aspen Professional Services.

Salmona, M., & Kaczynski, D. (2016). Don't blame the software: Using qualitative data analysis software successfully in qualitative research. *Forum: Qualitative Social Research, 17*(3), Article 11.

Sargeant, M. (2001). Lifelong learning and age discrimination in employment. *Education and the Law, 13*(2), 141–154.

Schall, C. (1998). The Americans with Disabilities Act: Are we keeping our promise? An analysis of the effect of the ADA on the employment of persons with disabilities. *Journal of Vocational Rehabilitation, 10*(3), 191–203.

Schaller, J., & DeLaGarza, D. (1999). "It's about relationships": Perspectives of people with cerebral palsy on belonging in their families, schools, and rehabilitation counseling. *Journal of Applied Rehabilitation Counseling, 30,* 7–18.

Schaller, J., & Parker, R. (1997). Effect of graduate research instruction on perceived research anxiety, research utility, and confidence in research skills. *Rehabilitation Education, 11,* 273–287.

Scherer, M. J. (2012). *Assistive technologies and other supports for people with brain impairment.* New York: Springer Publishing Company, LLC.

Schnelker, D., & Rumrill, P. (2001). Speaking of research: Program evaluation in rehabilitation. *Work: A Journal of Prevention, Assessment, and Rehabilitation, 16*(2), 171–175.

Schriner, K. (1996). The Rehabilitation Act Amendments of 1992: Initiatives and issues. *Journal of Applied Rehabilitation Counseling, 27,* 37–41.

Schriner, K. F., & Fawcett, S. B. (1988). Development and validation of a community concerns report method. *Journal of Community Psychology, 16*(3), 306–316.

Schriner, K. F., & Roessler, R.T. (1990). Employment concerns of college students with disabilities: Toward an agenda for policy and practice. *Journal of College Student Development, 31,* 307–312.

Schriner, K. F., Roessler, R. T., & Johnson, P. (1992). Employment concerns questionnaire. *Journal of Applied Rehabilitation Counseling, 24,* 32–37.

Schriner, K. F., Roessler, R. T., & Johnson, P. (1993). Identifying the employment concerns of people with spina bifida. *Journal of Applied Rehabilitation Counseling, 24*(2), 32–37.

Schriner, K. F., Roessler, R. T., & Raymer, J. (1991). Employment concerns of deaf university students. *Journal of the American Deafness and Rehabilitation Association, 25*(2), 13–19.

Schriner, K., Rumrill, P., & Parlin, R. (1995). Rethinking disability policy: Equity in the ADA era and the meaning of specialized services for people with disabilities. *Journal of the Health and Human Services Administration, 17*(4), 478–500.

Schultz, J., Koch, L., & Kontosh, L. (2007). Establishing rehabilitation research priorities for the National Council on Rehabilitation Education. *Rehabilitation Education, 21,* 149–158.

Schur, L., Kruse, D., Blasi, J., & Blanck, P. (2009). Is disability disabling in all workplaces? Workplace disparities and corporate culture. *Industrial relations, 48,* 381–410.

Schwandt, T. A. (2001). *Dictionary of Qualitative Inquiry* (2nd ed.). Thousand Oaks, CA: Sage.

Scott, C. G. (2000). Ethical issues in addiction counseling. *Journal of Postsecondary Education and Disabilities, 19*(1), 39–55.

Seelman, K. D. (1997). *Disability research: Accomplishments and recommendations for federal coordination.* A report to Congress from the Interagency Committee on Disability Research. Washington, DC: US Department of Education.

Seelman, K. D. (1998, March). *Change and challenge: The integration of the new paradigm of disability into research and practice.* Speech given at the National Council on Rehabilitation Education Conference, Vancouver, WA.

Serlin, R. C. (1987). Hypothesis testing, theory building, and the philosophy of science. *Journal of Counseling Psychology, 34,* 365–371.

Shadish, W. R. (1995). Philosophy of science and the qualitative-quantitative debates: Thirteen common errors. *Evaluation and Program Planning, 18,* 63–75.

Shaw, L. R., & Tarvydas, V. M. (2001). The use of professional disclosure in rehabilitation counseling. *Rehabilitation Counseling Bulletin, 45,* 40–47.

Shek, D. T., & Lee, B. M. (2007). A comprehensive review of quality of life (QOL) research in Hong Kong. *The Scientific World Journal, 7,* 1222–1229.

Shen, G., & Kleiner, B. (2001). Age discrimination in hiring. *Equal Opportunities International, 20*(8), 25–32.

Silver, C. E., & Lewins, A. (2014). *Using software in qualitative research: A step-by-step guide* (2nd ed.). Thousand Oaks, CA: Sage.

Siperstein, G. N., Heyman, M., Stokes, J. E. (2014). Pathways to employment: A national survey of adults with intellectual disabilities. *Journal of Vocational Rehabilitation, 41*(3), 165–178.

Sleister, S. (2000). Separating the wheat from the chaff: The role of the vocational expert in forensic vocational rehabilitation. *Journal of Vocational Rehabilitation, 14*(2), 119–129.

Smart, J. (1999a). Distance learning in rehabilitation education. *Rehabilitation Education, 13,* 183–186.

Smart, J. (1999b). Issues in rehabilitation distance education. *Rehabilitation Education, 13,* 187–206.

Smart, J. (2005). The promise of the International Classification of Functioning, Disability, and Health (ICF). *Rehabilitation Education, 19,* 191–199.

Smart, J. (2009). *Disability, society, and the individual.* Austin, TX: Pro-Ed.

Smith, M. C., & Glass, G. (1977). Meta analysis of psychotherapy outcomes. *American Psychologist, 32*(9), 752–760.

Smith, M. J., Humm, L. B., Fleming, M. F., Jordan, N., Wright, M. A., Ginger, E. J., Wright, K., Olsen, D., & Bell, M. D. (2015). Virtual reality job interview training for veterans with post-traumatic stress disorder. *Journal of Vocational Rehabilitation, 42*(3), 271–279.

Smith, S. M., & Kampfe, C. M. (2000). Characteristics of diversity and aging: Implications for assessment. *Journal of Applied Rehabilitation Counseling, 31,* 33–38.

Smith, T. J., Dillahunt-Aspillaga, C., & Kenney, C. (2015). Integrating customized employment practices within the vocational rehabilitation system. *Journal of Vocational Rehabilitation, 42*(3), 201–208.

Snyder, J., Temple, L., Youngbauer, J., O'Neil, T., & Cromwell, R. (1995). *Needs conference for underserved consumers with psychiatric disabilities.* Lawrence, KS: Research and Training Center on Independent Living, University of Kansas.

Snyder, P., & Lawson, S. (1993). Evaluating results using corrected and uncorrected effect size estimates. *Journal of Experimental Education, 61,* 334–349.

Spengler, P. M., Stromer, D. C., Dixon, D. N., & Spivy, V. A. (1995). A scientist-practitioner model of psychological assessment: Implications for training, practice, and research. *The Counseling Psychologist, 23,* 506–534.

Spicer, J. (2005). *Making sense of multivariate data analysis.* Thousand Oaks, CA: Sage.

Spradley, J. S. (1979). *The ethnographic interview.* New York: Holt, Rinehart and Winston.

Stata. (2013). *Stata user's guide* (Release 13). College Station, TX: Stata Press.

Stebnicki, M. A. (2000). Stress and grief reactions among rehabilitation professionals: Dealing effectively with empathy fatigue. *Journal of Rehabilitation, 66,* 23–33.

Stebnicki, M. A. (2006). Integrating spirituality in rehabilitation counselor supervision. *Rehabilitation Education, 20,* 115–132.

Stebnicki, M. A., Rubin, S. E., Rollins, C., & Turner, T. (1999). A holistic approach to multicultural rehabilitation counseling. *Journal of Applied Rehabilitation Counseling, 30*(2), 3–12.

Stevens, J. (1996). *Applied multivariate statistics for the social sciences* (3rd ed.). Hillsdale, NJ: Lawrence Erlbaum.

Stevens, S. S. (1946). On the theory of scales of measurement. *Science, 103,* 677–680.

Stevens, S. S. (1951). Mathematics, measurement, and psychophysics. In S. S. Stevens (Ed.), *Handbook of experimental psychology* (pp. 1–49). New York: Wiley.

Stewart, J. (2002). Supplementing the scientific method with alternative approaches to rehabilitation research. *Rehabilitation Education, 16,* 227–236.

Stewart, K., & Williams, M. (2005). Researching online populations: the use of online focus groups for social research. *Qualitative Research, 5*(4), 395–416.

Stodden, R., Whelley, T., Chang, C., & Harding T. (2001). Current status of educational support provision to students with disabilities in postsecondary education. *Journal of Vocational Rehabilitation, 16*(3/4), 189–198.

Stone, D. L., & Colella, A. (1996). A model of factors affecting the treatment of disabled individuals in organizations. *Academy of Management Review, 21,* 352–401.

Stone-Romero, E. F., Stone, D. L., & Lukaszewski, K. (2006). The influence of disability on role-taking in organizations. In A. M. Konrad, P. Prasad, & J. K. Pringle (Eds.), *Handbook of workplace diversity* (pp. 401–430). Thousand Oaks: Sage.

Strauser, D. (2013). *Career development, employment, and disability in rehabilitation.* New York: Springer Publishing Company.

Strauser, D., & Ketz, K. (2002). The relationship between self efficacy, locus of control and work personality. *Journal of Rehabilitation, 68,* 20–26.

Strauser, D., & Lusting, D. C. (2001). The implications of posttraumatic stress disorder on vocational behavior and rehabilitation planning. *Journal of Rehabilitation, 67,* 26–36.

Strauss, A. L. (1987). *Qualitative analysis for social scientists.* Cambridge: Cambridge University Press.

Strauss, A. L., & Corbin, J. (1990). *Basics of qualitative research: Grounded theory procedures and techniques.* Newbury Park, CA: Sage.

Strohmer, D. C., & Newman, L. J. (1983). Counselor hypothesis testing strategies. *Journal of Counseling Psychology, 30,* 557–565.

Strong, S. R. (1991). Theory-driven science and naive empiricism in counseling psychology. *Journal of Counseling Psychology, 38,* 204–210.

Stubbins, J. (1984). Vocational rehabilitation as social science. *Rehabilitation Literature, 4*(11/12), 375–379.

Sullivan, J. R. (2012) Skype: An appropriate method of data collection for qualitative interviews? *The Hilltop Review, 6,* 54–60.

Sumner, G. (1995). *Project Alliance: A job retention program for employed people with chronic illness and their employers.* New York: National Multiple Sclerosis Society.

Swenson, T. S. (2000). Chronic fatigue syndrome. *Journal of Rehabilitation, 66,* 37–48.

Szymanski, E. M. (1985). Rehabilitation counseling: A profession with a vision, an identity, and a future. *Rehabilitation Counseling Bulletin, 29,* 2–5.

Szymanski, E. M. (1993). Research design and statistical design. *Rehabilitation Counseling Bulletin, 36,* 178–181.

Szymanski, E. M., & Hershenson, D. B. (1998). Career development of people with disabilities: An ecological model. In R. L. Parker, & E. M. Szymanski (Eds.), *Rehabilitation counseling: Basics and Beyond* (pp. 327–378). Austin, TX: PRO-ED.

Szymanski, E., & Parker, R. (2010). Work and disability: Basic concepts. In E. Szymanski & R. Parker (Eds.), *Work and disability* (3rd ed., pp. 1–16). Austin, TX: PRO-ED.

Szymanski, E. M., Whitney-Thomas, J., Marshall, L., & Sayger, T. (1994). The effect of graduate instruction in research methodology on research self-efficacy and perceived research utility. *Rehabilitation Education, 8,* 319–331.

Tacq, J. (1997). *Multivariate analysis techniques in social science research: From problem to analysis.* London: Sage.

Tansey, T., Bezyak, J., Chan, F., Leahy, M., & Lui, J. (2014). Social-cognitive predictors of readiness to use evidence-based practice: A survey of state vocational rehabilitation counselors. *Journal of Vocational Rehabilitation, 41*(2), 127–136.

Tansey, T., Kaya, C., Moser, E., Eagle, D., Dutta, A., & Chan, F. (2016). Psychometric validation of the brief resilience scale in a sample of vocational rehabilitation consumers. *Rehabilitation Counseling Bulletin, 59*(2), 108–111. doi: 10.1177/0034355215573539

Tarvydas, V. M., & Cottone, R. R. (2000). The code of ethics for professional rehabilitation counselors: What we have and what we need. *Rehabilitation Counseling Bulletin, 43,* 188–196.

Tawney, J., & Gast, D. (1984). *Single subject research in special education.* Columbus, OH: Merrill Publishing Co.

Taylor, P., Steinberg, M., & Walley, L. (2000). Mature age employment: Recent developments in public policy in Australia. *Australasian Journal on Ageing, 19,* 125–129.

Taylor, P., & Unwin, P. (2001). Age and participation in vocational education and training. *Work, Employment and Society, 15,* 763–779.

Thomas, K. R. (1990). Some observations on the feasibility of establishing the superiority of rehabilitation counselors with master's degrees. *Rehabilitation Counseling Bulletin, 34,* 154–163.

Thompson, B. (1986, November). *Two reasons why multivariate methods are unusually vital.* Paper presented at the annual meeting of the Mid-South Educational Research Association, Memphis, TN.

Thorndike, R. (2005). *Measurement and evaluation in psychology and education* (7th ed.). Upper Saddle River, NJ: Pearson Education, Inc.

Toosie, M. (2009). Labor force projections to 2018: Older workers staying more active. *Monthly Labor Review, 132*(11), 30–51.

Toriello, P., Bishop. M., & Rumrill, P. (2012). *New directions in rehabilitation counseling: Creative responses to professional, clinical, and educational challenges.* Lake of the Ozarks, MO: Aspen Professional Services.

Toriello, P. J., & Keferl, J. E. (2012). A renaissance of consumer autonomy: Moving from self-determination theory to therapy. In P. J. Toriello, M. L. Bishop, & P. D. Rumrill (Eds.), *New directions in rehabilitation counseling: Creative responses to professional, clinical, and educational challenges* (pp. 1–24). Linn Creek, MO: Aspen Professional Services.

Tracey, T., & Glidden-Tracey, C. (1999). Integration of theory, research design, measurement, and analysis: Toward a reasoned argument. *The Counseling Psychologist, 27,* 299–324.

Tracey, T. J. (1991). Counseling research as an applied science. In C. E. Watkins & L. J. Schneider (Eds.), *Research in counseling* (pp. 3–31). Hillsdale, NJ: Lawrence Erlbaum Associates.

Umeasiegbu, V. I., Mpofu, E., & Johnson, E. T. (2012). Disability and rehabilitation in the international context. In P. J. Toriello, M. L. Bishop, & P. D. Rumrill (Eds.), *New directions in rehabilitation counseling: Creative responses to professional, clinical, and educational challenges* (pp. 95–114). Linn Creek, MO: Aspen Professional Services.

Unger, D., Campbell, L., & McMahon, B. (2006). Workplace discrimination and mental retardation. In B. McMahon (Ed.), *Workplace discrimination and disability* (pp. 25–36). Richmond, VA: Virginia Commonwealth University.

Vacha-Haase, T., & Thompson, B. (2004). How to estimate and interpret various effect sizes. *Journal of Counseling Psychology, 51,* 473–481.

Vandergoot, D. (1996). Refashioning vocational rehabilitation services to focus on placement. *Journal of Job Placement, 12,* 12–16.

Van Wieren, T. A., Reid, C. A., & McMahon, B. T. (2008). Workplace discrimination and autism spectrum disorders: The National EEOC ADA Research Project. *Work, 31*(3), 299–308.

Vazquez-Ramos, R., Leahy, M., & Hernandez, N. (2007). The Delphi method in rehabilitation counseling research. *Rehabilitation Counseling Bulletin, 50,* 111–118.

Viermo, V., Krause, C. (1998). Quality of life in individuals with physical disabilities. *Psychotherapy and Psychosomatics, 67,* 317–322.

Vierstra, C., Rumrill, P., Koch, L., & McMahon, B. (2007). Multiple chemical sensitivity and employment discrimination: The National Equal Employment Opportunity Commission Americans with Disabilities Act research project. *Work: A Journal of Prevention, Assessment, and Rehabilitation, 28*(4), 391–402.

Wadsworth, J., Harley D. A., Smith J., & Kampfe C. (2008). Infusing end-or-life issues into the rehabilitation counselor education curriculum. *Rehabilitation Education, 22,* 113–124.

Wald, J., & Alvaro, R. (2004). Psychological factors in work-related amputation: Considerations for rehabilitation counselors. *The Journal of Rehabilitation, 70*(4) 6–15.

Walker, M. L. (1993). Participatory action research. *Rehabilitation Counseling Bulletin, 37,* 2–5.

Ware, J. H., Jr. (1984). Conceptualizing disease impact and treatment outcomes. *Cancer, 15,* 2240–2299.

Wax, R. (1979). Gender and age in fieldwork and fieldwork education: No good thing is done by any man alone. *Social Problems, 26,* 509–523.

Weed, R. O. (2000). Ethical issues in expert opinions and testimony. *Rehabilitation Counseling Bulletin, 43*(4), 215–218.

Wehman, P. (2006). Transition: The bridge to adulthood. In P. Wehman (Ed.), *Life beyond the classroom: Transition strategies for young people with disabilities* (4th ed.), pp. 3–44. Baltimore, MD: Paul H. Brookes.

Wehman, P. (2013). *Life beyond the classroom* (5th ed.). Baltimore, MD: Paul Brookes.

Weitzman, E. A. (2000). Software and qualitative research. In N. K. Denzin & Y. S. Lincoln (Eds.), *Handbook of qualitative research* (2nd ed., pp. 803–820). Thousand Oaks, CA: Sage.

Westbrook, M., Legge, V., & Pennay, M. (1995). Ethnic differences in expectations for Women with physical disabilities. *Journal of Applied Rehabilitation Counseling, 26*(4), 26–33.

Wheaton, J., & Berven, N. (1994). Education, experience, and caseload management: Practices of counselors in a state vocational rehabilitation agency. *Rehabilitation Counseling Bulletin, 38,* 44–58.

Wheaton, J., & Hertzfeld, J. (2002). Ancestry and Severity of Disability: A National Study. *Rehabilitation Counseling Bulletin, 45,* 154–161.

White, G. W., Simpson, J. L., Gonda, C., Ravesloot, C., & Coble, Z. (2010). Moving from independence to interdependence: A conceptual model for better understanding community participation of centers for independent living consumers. *Journal of Disability Policy Studies, 20*(4), 233–240.

White, G., Thomson, R., & Nary, D. (1996). An empirical analysis of the effects of a self-administered advocacy letter training program. *Rehabilitation Counseling Bulletin, 41,* 74–87.

White, G. W. (2002). Consumer participation in disability research: The golden rule as a guide for ethical practice. *Rehabilitation Psychology, 47,* 438–446.

Whyte, W. F. (1991). *Participatory action research.* Thousand Oaks, CA: Sage.

Whitney, M., & Upton, T. (2004). Assistive technology: Unequal access in postsecondary education. *Journal of Applied Rehabilitation Counseling, 35*(1), 23–28.

Wickert, K., Dresden, D., & Rumrill, P. (2013). *The sandwich generation's guide to eldercare.* New York: Demos.

Wilcox, S. L., Oh, H., Redmond, S. A., Chicas, J., Hassan, A. M., Lee, P. J., & Ell, K. (2015). A scope of the problem: Post-deployment reintegration challenges in a National Guard Unit. *Work, 50*(1), 73–83.

Wilson, K., Getzel, E., & Brown, T. (2000). Enhancing the post-secondary campus climate for students with disabilities. *Journal of Vocational Rehabilitation, 14*(1), 37–50.

Wilson, L., Livneh, H., & Duchesneau, A. (2002). Disability services in higher education and rehabilitation counseling: Professional parallelism and a graduate certificate program. *Rehabilitation Education, 16,* 283–293.

Wohl, A. (2015). APSE's public testimony to the Advisory Committee on Increasing Competitive Integrated Employment for Individuals with Disabilities: January 23, 2015. *Journal of Vocational Rehabilitation, 42*(3), 193–194.

Wolffe, K. E., Roessler, R. T., & Schriner, K. F. (1992). Employment concerns of people with blindness or visual impairments. *Journal of Visual Impairment & Blindness, 86,* 185–187.

Wong, R., & Wan, M. (2000). Experience in developing a Transition Employment Program (TEP) for the psychiatric patients in an acute general hospital in Hong Kong. *Work: A Journal of Prevention, Assessment, and Rehabilitation, 14*(3), 229–236.

World Health Organization. (2001). *International Classification of Functioning, Disability, & Health.* Geneva, Switzerland: Author.

Wright, B. (1983). *Physical disability: A psychosocial approach* (2nd ed.). NY: Harper Collins.

Wright, B. (1988). Attitudes and the fundamental bias: Conditions and corrections. In H. E. Yuker (Ed.), *Attitudes toward persons with disabilities.* New York: Springer.

Wright-McDougal, J. J., & Toriello, P. J. (2013). Ethical implications of confirmation bias in the rehabilitation counseling relationship. *Journal of Applied Rehabilitation Counseling, 44*(2), 3–10.

Wusthoff, L. E., Waal, H., & Grawe, R. W., (2014). The effectiveness of integrated treatment in patients with substance use disorder co-occurring with anxiety and /or depression—a group randomized trial. *BMC Psychiatry, 14*(67), 1–12.

Yin, R. K. (1989). *Case study research: Design and methods.* Newbury Park, CA: Sage.

Yuen, J., & Shaughnessy, B. (2001). Cultural empowerment: Tools to engage and retain postsecondary students with disabilities. *Journal of Vocational Rehabilitation, 16*(3/4), 199–207.

Zanskas, S., & Coduti, W. (2006). Eugenics, euthanasia, and physician-assisted suicide: An overview for rehabilitation professionals. *Journal of Rehabilitation, 72*(3), 27–34.

Zanskas, S., & Leahy, M. (2007). Preparing rehabilitation counselors for private sector practice within a CORE accredited generalist education model. *Rehabilitation Education, 21,* 205–214.

Zarit, S. H. (2009). A good old age: Theories of mental health and aging. In V. L. Bengston, D., Gans, N. M. Putney, & M. Silverstein (Eds.), *Handbook of theories of aging* (675–691). New York: Spring Publishing Company.

Zimmet, P. (1995). The pathogenesis and prevention of diabetes in adults. *Diabetes Care, 18*(7), 1050–1064.

Zimmerman, P., Kowalski, J., Niggemeier-Groben, A., Sauer, M., Leonhardt, R., & Strohle, A. (2015). Evaluation of an impatient preventive treatment program for soldiers returning from deployment. *Work 50,* 103–110.

Zunker, V. G. (2015). *Career counseling: A holistic approach* (9th ed.). Boston, MA: Cengage Learning.

INDEX

A

Abstract, 41, 44, 47–48, 59, 133, 199, 218–219, 225, 251, 253–254, 275–276, 286
Accommodations, 33, 107, 118, 146, 150–151, 223–224, 247, 255, 282
Acquired Immunodeficiency Syndrome. See HIV/AIDS.
Adaptive technology. See Assistive technology.
Affirmative action, 237
Affordable Care Act (ACA), 223, 235, 244, 286–287
African Americans, 170
American Counseling Association (ACA), 101, 119
American Educational Research Association, 67
American Psychological Association (APA), 41, 67, 119–120, 251–253, 274–275
  APA Publication Manual, 251, 263
Americans with Disabilities Act (ADA), 32, 146, 241, 252, 256–257, 261
  Title I, 107, 115, 171, 175
Americans with Disabilities Act Amendments Act (ADAAA), 32, 244, 256, 285
Amputation, 216, 241
Analogue studies. See Research validity.
Analysis of covariance (ANCOVA), 85–86, 89–90, 92, 95, 149, 154
Anthropology, 4, 187, 233
A priori, 53, 88, 123, 142, 285
Asian Americans, 238
Assistive technology, 4, 103, 153–154, 171, 174, 177, 247, 288
Assumptions, 5, 18–19, 27, 38, 77, 83–85, 94, 196, 202, 205, 216, 226
  Statistical, 137–138, 142
Attitudes toward persons with disabilities, 39, 128, 134–135
Audit trail, 202
Autism spectrum disorder(s) (ASD), 131
  Also Autism: 131, 245, 248, 265–266, 272, 285
Autonomy, 101, 103–106, 119, 123, 206, 233, 235, 240, 280
Axial coding, 218

B

Beneficence, 101, 102–103, 105, 117, 119, 123. See also Research ethics.
Bias (biases), 8, 10–11, 27, 56, 58, 116, 118, 124, 129, 155, 190, 195, 202–205, 206, 237, 257, 273
  Pre-test, 150
Blindness. See Visual impairments.
Boulder model, 26. See also Scientist-practitioner model.

C

Cancer, 17–18, 231, 235, 245, 248, 264, 265, 271, 288
Career planning, 151, 183, 235
Case study, 115, 163, 173, 175–176, 186, 195, 209, 214–215, 221, 243
Causal comparative designs, 161, 170–172
Cause and effect relationship, 15, 147, 151
Causal relationships, 5, 17–18, 50, 59, 126–127
Centers for Disease Control (CDC), 31
Certified Rehabilitation Counselor (CRC),

5, 41, 115, 118, 174, 220, 236, 279
Cluster analysis, 96
Code of Professional Ethics for Rehabilitation Counselors, 100–101, 105–106, 117, 236
Coding, 115, 199–202, 211, 218, 220–221, 277
Coefficients, 67, 69, 71, 79, 91–92
Cognitive support technology (CST), 176, 240
Coherence, 38, 48, 191, 204, 206, 222–223, 230
Commission for Rehabilitation Counselor Certification (CRCC), 26, 100–102, 105–106, 113, 115–119, 121, 236
Comparative method, 156, 171
Comparison group, 86–87, 104, 116, 118, 128, 137, 154, 271
Conceptual model, 25, 255
Concomitant variation, 146
Confidentiality, 100, 105, 113, 115, 119, 122–124, 197, 207–208, 212, 236, 261
Conflict resolution, 150–151
Consensus building, 8, 34
Construct, 12–13, 25, 36–37, 39–48, 59, 62, 65, 67, 70, 72–75, 93, 96, 98, 127, 129, 133–136, 140, 142–144, 163–164, 168, 171, 188, 219–220, 230, 260, 280, 291. *See also* Latent variable.
Construct validity, 70, 72–73, 98, 133–137, 140–142, 144, 157. *See* Research validity, Validity (psycho-metric).
Consumer advocacy, 241
Consumer Directed Theory of Empowerment (CDTE), 168, 233
Control group, 16, 50, 84–85, 117, 126–129, 147–153, 161, 181–182
Correlation. *See* Methods of statistical analysis.
Correspondence, 19, 79
Council for Accreditation of Counseling and Related Educational Programs (CACREP), 235–236
Council on Rehabilitation Education (CORE), 21, 235
Counseling, vii, 20, 26–27, 29, 31, 89, 101, 104, 131–132, 146, 154, 156, 166–167, 174, 183, 187, 207, 217, 222, 224, 234–238, 242–243, 263, 285

Cronbach's alpha coefficient, 69
Cross-referral, 199
Crux model, 28–29
Cultural diversity, 119, 237–238

D

Declaration of Helsinki, 103, 117
Descriptive studies, viii, 145–146, 172
Developmental disabilities, 149, 155, 178, 235, 249, 254
Diabetes, 43, 167, 176–177, 235, 245, 248, 255, 264–265, 271, 285, 302, 320, 329, 336
Disability Centrality Model, 25, 232, 280
Disability management, 234–235, 287
Disability policy, 104, 211–212, 228, 230, 233, 286, 288
Disclosure, 42–43, 49, 117, 136, 214, 223, 237
Discussion, 15, 20, 33, 39, 53, 55, 73, 101, 120, 127, 142, 192, 197, 199–201, 209, 223, 228, 241, 251, 263, 270–217, 277–278
Distributions, 75–78, 87, 94, 98

E

Effect size, 84–86, 90, 99, 138, 149, 182–184, 243
Eligibility, 163, 166–167, 248
Empowerment, 25, 40, 134–135, 168–169, 233, 280
Employee assistance programs, 234
Employment, 4–5, 22, 39, 42–44, 48, 51, 106, 115, 136, 146, 149, 151–152, 154, 163–167, 170–171, 174–175, 177–179, 187–188, 194, 212, 215, 219–220, 223–224, 227, 235, 239–240, 242, 244, 246, 252–259, 261–262, 266, 272–274, 279, 281, 285–290
Epilepsy, 53, 167–168, 147, 245, 254, 264, 266, 272
Equal Employment Opportunity Commission (EEOC), 115, 253, 256–259, 261–262, 271, 273–274
Equity, 104
Ethics, x, 23, 100–101, 105–106, 113, 117, 119, 123, 178, 195, 208, 234, 236–

237, 242–243, 279
Codes of, 195, 208
Ethics in publishing research, 119
   Accuracy of data, 203
   Authorship credit, 119, 121–122
   Citation and acknowledgment credit, 120
   Ordering of multiple authors, 122
Ethnography, 186, 192, 201, 209–212, 222
Evaluation, 9, 12–13, 21, 25, 28, 30, 36, 40–41, 44, 54, 59–60, 62, 70, 75, 86, 90, 92–93, 98–100, 123, 132–134, 155–156, 166–168, 183–184, 188, 202–203, 229, 233, 236, 239, 241, 279–281, 291, 293
Evidence-based practice, 236, 243, 281
Exogenous variables, 167–168
Experimental condition, 118, 131
Experimental designs, 117, 127, 146, 149–150, 153, 161, 318
   Group comparative, 156
   Pretest-posttest, 90, 149, 152
   Two group, 87, 147, 150, 152, 154, 182
Experimental research, 5, 117, 126, 128, 146–147
Experimenter expectancies, 135
Explanatory studies, 209
Explication and operationalization of constructs, 135
Exploratory studies, 209
Extant data, 113, 170, 228
External validity, 130–132, 136, 140–141, 143, 175. *See* Research validity, xi, 117–118, 124–125, 127, 129, 131, 133–135, 137, 139–143, 149

F

Factor analysis, 85, 92–93, 96, 262
Factorial Analysis of Variance, 89
Family and Medical Leave Act, 286–287
Fidelity, 101, 105, 116, 119, 123, 223
Field experimentation, 6
Field notes, 195, 199, 210–211
Fishing and error rate problem, 138
Formatting, 199, 251–252
Functional Assessment Inventory (FAI), 43

G

Graduate Record Examination (GRE), 67, 70–71, 147,
Grounded theory, 186, 192, 195–196, 209, 217–220, 222, 290
Guidelines for critiquing research articles, 274, 276

H

Hawthorne effect, 137
Heterogeneity, 193
Historical/archival research, 173, 176, 184
HIV/AIDS, 194, 219–220, 265–266, 271, 288, 303
Homogeneity, 84, 94, 193
Human Immunodeficiency Virus, 245. *See* HIV/AIDS.
Hypothesis, 10, 17, 19, 27, 29, 36, 39, 47–48, 80, 96–97, 147, 255
Hypothesis testing, 13, 28, 37, 80–81, 96, 99, 126
   Null, 80–81, 94, 99
   Research, 47, 80, 96, 162
   Statistical, 47, 59, 80–81

I

Ideographic interpretations, 190
Income, 32, 50, 77, 162, 177, 231, 249, 287
Independent living, 3, 174, 176, 183, 231
Indicators, 40–41, 44, 46–47, 49, 73, 91, 93, 97, 135, 140, 168, 171, 232
Introduction section, 255, 271
   Type I errors, 81–82, 99, 139, 142
   Type II errors, 81–82, 99, 139, 142
Inferential statistics, viii, 75–80, 88, 96, 99, 184. *See* statistical issues and analysis.
Informational reports, 229, 239, 241, 243
Informed consent, 57, 103, 105, 113–115, 119, 124
Insight, 83, 191, 195, 228
Institutional Review Boards (IRBs), 107, 113, 116, 124
Instruments (measurement), viii, 11, 39, 42, 46, 48, 61–62, 65, 69, 70–71, 73–75, 93, 121, 132, 139–142, 163, 166, 189–190, 226, 259–260, 275–276, 293

Instrumental utility, 191
Intellectual disability, 113, 245, 271. *See also* Mental retardation.
Internal validity. *See* Research validity.
International Classification of Function(ing), Disability & Health (ICF), 25, 230–231, 249, 280
International Rehabilitation, 244, 249
Intervention/stimulus studies, 145–146, 156, 172
Interview, 42–43, 59, 136, 171, 178, 193–194, 196–198, 200–207, 211, 220–221, 240

J

Journal of Applied Rehabilitation Counseling, 25, 75
Journal of Counseling and Development, 75
Journal of Counseling Psychology, 75
Journal of Rehabilitation, 25, 75, 180
Journal of Rehabilitation Administration, 75
Journal of Vocational Rehabilitation, 25, 251
Justice, 101, 104–105, 118–119, 123, 237. *See also* Ethics.

K

Knowledge claims, 4, 6–7, 9–12, 20, 34, 47, 117, 125–126, 140, 143, 175, 278–279, 281. *See also* Science, Scientific knowledge.
  Authority, 6–8, 20, 34, 198
  Intuition, 7–8, 20, 34
  Personal observation and experience: 6
  Tradition, viii, 6–7, 20, 25, 34, 37, 61, 124, 205
Kuder-Richardson formula, 68

L

Latent variable, 46. *See also* Construct.
Latino populations, 238
Learning disabilities (LD), 240, 246, 248, 272
Life care planning, 287
Linguistic structures, 187
Literature review, 191–192, 271, 276
  Empirical, 179–181
  Narrative, 234, 238, 244
Locus of control, 50, 103, 163–164
Locators, 199
Longitudinal studies, 173, 178, 184
Lupus, 176, 285

M

Managed care, 30
Materials, 141, 259–260, 275–276
Mean, 64, 69, 77–78, 80, 83–88, 95, 98, 138, 149, 160, 181, 182–183, 263
Measurement, vii, 4, 11, 16, 38–39, 45–46, 48, 59, 61–67, 69–76, 79, 84, 89–90, 94, 98, 125, 134–136, 139, 157–158, 163, 166, 168, 181, 282
Measurement and Evaluation in Counseling and Development, 75
Measurement instruments, sources of information on, viii, 11, 39, 48, 61–62, 69–70, 73–75, 139, 163, 166, 181
Measures of central tendency, 77, 98, 99. *See also* Statistical issues and analysis.
Measures of relationship, 78, 99. *See also* Statistical issues and analysis.
Measures of variability, 77, 99. *See also* Statistical issues and analysis.
Median, 77, 98
Member checks, 203, 207
Memos, 195, 200–203, 211
Mental illness, 152, 155, 164, 184, 271. *See also* Psychiatric disabilities.
Mental Measurements Yearbooks (Buros Institute), 74–75
Mental retardation, 177, 184, 245, 265–266, 271. *See also* Intellectual disability.
Meta-analysis. *See* Methods of statistical analysis.
Methods of statistical analysis, viii, 86
  Analysis of Covariance (ANCOVA), 85–86, 89–90, 92, 95
  Analysis of Variance (ANOVA), 52, 85–86, 88–90, 92–93, 95, 99, 138, 149, 262
  Chi Square, 94–95
  Correlation, 15, 68–69, 71, 79, 82, 85, 90, 95, 99, 130, 139, 147, 161–162

Canonical, 92–93, 96, 163
Coefficient, 67, 79, 85, 139, 162
Multiple, 85, 90, 162
Ratio, 86
Simple, 90
Statistic, 78
Factor analysis, 85, 92–93, 96, 262
Factorial analysis of variance, 89
General linear model, 85, 99, 163, 166
Hierarchical multiple regression, 163, 165
Logistic regression, 90–91, 95, 165, 170
Meta-analysis, 86, 180, 182–183, 243
Multilevel modeling, 92, 96, 163, 166, 169, 291
Multiple discriminant analysis, 92, 163, 166, 170
Multiple regression, 16, 52–53, 85–86, 90–93, 95, 99, 163–166, 169, 262
Multivariate analysis, 91–92, 94, 99
Multivariate analysis of covariance (MANCOVA), 92
Multivariate analysis of variance (MANOVA), 92, 95, 138, 291
Non-parametric, 77, 94, 243, 262, 292
Path analysis, 53, 92–93, 96, 163, 166–168, 291
Structural Equation Modeling, 53, 92–93, 163, 166, 168, 243, 291
t-test, 15, 86–88, 93, 95, 99, 181
Mode, 77, 99
Multicultural Competencies, 51, 169, 234, 237
Multiculturalism, 237
Multiple regression, 16, 52–53, 85–86, 90–93, 95, 99, 163–166, 169, 262
Multiple sclerosis, 4–5, 165–166, 172, 175–177, 230, 240–241, 245, 254, 264, 266, 272, 285, 293
National Multiple Sclerosis Society, ix
Multiple treatment interference, 132. *See also* Research validity.
Multivariate analysis. *See* Methods of statistical analysis.

N

National Council on Measurement in Education, 67

National Council on Rehabilitation Education (NCRE), 283–284, 287
National Institute on Disability, Independent Living, and Rehabilitation Research (NIDILRR), ix, 31–33
National Institute on Disability, Independent Living, and Rehabilitation Research (NIDRR), 31–33
National Institutes of Health (NIH), ix, 31
National Research Act, 107, 120
Native Americans, 238
Natural settings, 190
Non-experimental research, 126, 147
Nuremberg trials, 103

O

Objectives, 28–29, 185, 258, 260
Open coding, 218
Operational definitions, 42, 44–48, 59, 133–135. *See also* Hypotheses, Research

P

Parsimony, 24
Participatory Action Research (PAR), 187, 198, 292–293
Path analysis. *See* Methods of statistical analysis.
Peer debriefing, 203, 205
Phenomena, 4, 6, 13–14, 25, 38, 41, 44, 61, 92–93, 170–172, 176, 180, 186–187, 189–195, 197, 201–202, 209–213, 215–216, 218, 220–221, 226–227, 229, 280, 282, 287, 290, 292
Photovoice, 197–198
Plagiarism, 119–121
Population issues, 145
Population validity, 54. *See also* Sampling.
Post-Traumatic Stress Disorder (PTSD), 179, 240–241, 245, 248
Power, 83, 137–139, 142, 145, 148–149, 181, 197–198, 208, 211, 217, 220, 243, 259. *See also* Statistical issues.
Probability, 47, 75, 80, 82–83, 87–88, 96, 99, 137–138, 145, 162, 195
Professional ethics, 23, 234, 236, 242.

See also Code of Professional Ethics for Rehabilitation Counselors.
Psychiatric disabilities, 97, 131–132, 151–152, 176, 198, 285
Psychodynamic theory of attitudes toward disability, 39

Q

Qualitative research, ix, 4, 6, 9, 34, 55, 58, 60, 184–203, 206, 208–212, 215, 220, 222, 225–228, 243, 263, 290. *See also* Research.
  Credibility of findings, 46
Quantitative research, ix, x, 4–5, 11, 15, 34, 36–37, 39, 44, 55, 58, 61, 98, 125, 143, 145–146, 157, 161, 184, 186, 188, 190–193, 202, 206, 209, 225–227, 290. *See also* Research.
Quasi-experimental research, 5

R

Random assignment, 15–16, 127, 129–130, 147, 150–151, 153, 154, 170
Random selection, 130, 221
Reasonable accommodations, 107
References, iv, vii, xii, 66, 75, 251, 274–275, 277
Rehabilitation,
  Research in, vii–xii, 3–36, 38–39, 41–44, 46, 48–52, 54, 56–62, 64, 66, 68, 70, 72–73, 75, 79, 80, 83, 86, 91–92, 94, 98–107, 113, 115–124, 126–127, 129–132, 134, 136, 138, 146, 150–151, 153–156, 160, 163–180, 183–185, 187–189, 194, 198, 211–213, 215, 217, 219–22, 224, 226–244, 246–252, 254–255, 263. 274–275, 277–294
Rehabilitation Act, 32, 241, 244, 288, 292
Rehabilitation counseling, vii–x, 4–5, 20–26, 29, 31, 33–35, 38–39, 41, 44, 50, 59, 61, 80, 83, 86, 91–92, 100–102, 105, 119, 123–124, 136, 138, 153–154, 172–175, 180, 183–184, 187, 189, 217, 220, 228–229, 231, 233–235, 237, 242–243, 246–247, 250–251, 263, 275, 277–284, 286–288, 290–294
  Curriculum, 23, 31, 242
  Education, 26–27, 30, 34–35, 146, 172, 174–175, 224, 233–235, 237, 242, 248–249, 279, 284
  Foundations, 250
  Geriatric, 289
  Roles and functions, 56, 174, 187–188, 231, 238, 279
  Services, 33, 105, 220
Rehabilitation Counseling Bulletin, 25, 41, 75, 180
Rehabilitation counseling practice, 22–23, 25, 38, 41, 59, 101, 136, 174, 233, 237, 277, 292
Rehabilitation counseling research, vii–vii, 3–4, 20–22, 24–25, 31, 33, 50, 83, 86, 91–92, 138, 231, 243, 263, 278, 290–291
  Politics of, 31
  Purposes of, 20, 25, 33, 278
Rehabilitation counselor, x, 3, 5, 12, 20–22, 26–31, 33, 35, 39, 41–43, 56, 75, 91, 100–102, 105–106, 113, 115–118, 146, 155, 166, 169, 174–175, 178, 187–188, 217, 220, 222, 224, 231–242, 248, 250, 255, 279–280, 283–284, 286, 288–289, 291, 294
Rehabilitation counselor education, 26, 30, 146, 175, 224, 233, 234, 237
Rehabilitation Education, 21, 174, 235, 242–243, 248–249, 279, 283–284
Rehabilitation Psychology, 25, 75, 180, 243
Rehabilitation Services Administration, ix, 177, 288
Reliability, viii, 11, 62, 65–71, 73–75, 98, 137, 139–141, 163, 166, 191, 202, 225, 260, 272, 276
  Alternate form, 68
  Coefficients, 67, 69, 71
  Internal consistency, 68
  Interrater, 224
  Standard error of measurement (SEM), 69, 74
Reliability of measures, 139
Representativeness, 54, 58, 60, 66, 73, 193, 259
Research. *See also* Knowledge claims, Science.
  Applied, 153–154, 289
  Categories of, 42
  Competencies, 29

Consequences of, 107
Educational, 57, 67, 178,
Empirical, 12, 37, 42, 59, 97–98, 133, 217, 228, 248, 250, 278, 281, 288
Funding, ix, 26, 30, 104, 117, 222, 285, 291
Legal, 115
Logic of experimentation, 49
Medical, 104, 107, 115, 170, 178
Methodological issues, 189–191
Participants in, 123
Process, xi, 21, 27–28, 32, 36–38, 49, 54, 59, 61, 106, 140–142, 189–190, 199, 202–205, 292
Participatory action (PAR), 187, 198, 292
Purposes of, vii
Questions, xi, 6, 32, 36–37, 40–43, 47, 58, 103, 122–123, 173, 191–194, 209–210, 216, 222, 254–255, 258–260, 275–277
Researcher's role, 189, 208
Role of, vii
   Social sciences, 5, 14, 16, 18–20, 24, 34, 37, 39–41, 45, 47–48, 62–63, 68, 81, 84, 86, 92, 94, 183, 229, 252, 278, 290
Sources of research ideas, vii, 38
Types of, 6, 107, 127, 140, 143, 149, 172
Research ethics. *See* Code of Professional Ethics for Rehabilitation Counselors
Research questions. *See* Research.
Research report, viii, 10, 116, 120, 190, 275
Research validity
   Analogue study (studies), 132, 136, 146, 154–156
   Construct validity of research operations, 133
   External validity, 130–132, 136, 140–141, 143, 175
   Internal validity, 127–131, 133, 140–143, 150, 153, 157, 159
   Order of priority, 142
   Statistical conclusion validity, 83, 127, 137–138, 140–144, 149
Research variables. *See also* Variables.
   Individual difference, 50, 88–89
   Mediator, 52–53
   Moderator, 51–52, 59
Researcher

Bias, 11, 205
Multiple, 201, 203, 205
Reflexivity, 190–191, 204–205
Retirement, 231, 254, 258, 262, 266–267, 272, 274
Rheumatoid arthritis, 176, 211, 285

S

Sample, viii, 37, 41, 44, 48, 54–56, 58, 60–61, 65, 67–71, 74, 76, 79–88, 90–94, 96–99, 108, 114, 115, 118, 130–131, 137–142, 147, 152–153, 157, 164–170, 173, 175–176, 179, 181, 209, 221, 232, 259, 275–276
Sampling, 11, 41, 55–60, 68, 87, 125, 145, 187, 191, 193–195, 221, 226, 259
   Cluster, 55, 57
   Convenience, 57
   Errors, 54–55, 60, 86, 88, 181–182
   Issues, vii, 36, 53
   Narrow stimulus, 135
   Population validity, 54
   Purposeful, 58, 60, 193, 223
   Random, 54–55, 57, 88
   Simple random, 56–57, 60
   Snowball, 194
   Stratified, 56–57, 60
   Systematic, 54–58, 60
   Science, 9–15, 17–20, 22, 31, 34–35, 47–48, 52, 57–58, 60, 83, 92, 101, 103, 105, 138, 145, 154, 187, 212, 228, 241, 243, 248, 252, 275, 280, 285, 288–290, 293
   and Causality, 13
   Goals of, 12–13, 83
   Role of theory, 20, 90, 278, 280
   Status of the social sciences, 18
Scientific control, 145
Scientific knowledge, 4, 8–9, 18, 33–34, 73, 125–127, 133, 143, 278, 280–281, 292
Scientific limitations, 120, 270
Scientist-practitioner model of rehabilitation counselor education, 26–27, 30–31, 35
Selective coding, 218, 220
Self-advocacy, 107, 145, 150–151, 160, 224, 286
Self-care, 183

Self-interview, 205
Significant results, 263
Single operations and narrow stimulus sampling, 135. *See also* Research validity.
Social science, 52, 57, 60, 83, 92, 101, 103, 105, 138, 145, 154, 212, 252, 275, 293. *See* Science, Scientific knowledge, Research.
Social Security Disability Insurance (SSDI), 177, 248, 287
Sociology, 4, 22, 187
Spina bifida, 288
Spinal cord injury (SCI), 22, 54, 225, 248
Standard deviation, 64, 69, 78, 84–85, 99, 138, 182–183
Standard error of measurement, 69, 74
Standard error of the mean, 55
Strategies to enhance professional practice, 229
Statistical analysis, viii, 15, 38, 50, 64, 81–82, 84, 86, 89, 97, 138–139, 141, 169
Statistical conclusion validity, 83, 127, 137–138, 140–144, 149. *See* Research validity.
Statistical issues and analysis
    Descriptive statistics, 75, 98, 195, 262, 266, 268
    Distributions, 75–78, 87, 94, 98
    Effect size, 84–86, 90, 99, 134, 149, 183–184, 243
    Inferential statistics, viii, 75–80, 88, 96, 99, 184, 182
    Measures of central tendency, 77, 98, 99
    Measures of relationship, 78, 99
    Measures of variability, 77, 99
    P-value, 80
    Statistical power, 83, 137–138, 149, 181, 243, 259
    Stimulus, viii, 116, 130–132, 135–136, 141, 145–146, 154–156, 161, 172
    Subjects/participants, 259
Statistical significance, 77, 80–84, 88, 90, 94, 99, 138–139, 147, 154, 181
Structural Equation Modeling, 53, 92–93, 163, 166, 168, 243, 291. *See also* Methods of statistical analysis.
Substance abuse disabilities, 97, 152, 219
Substance use disorders, 152, 164, 235, 239, 249, 254, 271, 285

Treatment, 103
Supported employment, 149, 244
Surveys, 5, 55, 173, 184, 255, 283

T

Tests in print, 75
Theoretical model, 22, 24–25, 96, 168, 232–233, 250, 280
Three M Model, 231
Title, 41, 107, 115, 171, 175, 251–253, 256, 258, 261–263, 270–274, 276
Traumatic brain injury (TBI), 16, 59, 104, 161
Transition services, 174
Treatment group, 16, 84, 86–87, 128, 136–137, 147–148, 150–152, 157, 182
Treatment of human subjects, 101, 105, 119
    Debriefing, 106, 116–117, 203, 205, 260
    Deception, 116–117, 124
    Informed consent, 57, 103, 105, 113–115, 119, 124
    Institutional review procedures, 105, 107
    Privacy and confidentiality, 105, 115, 207
    Withholding treatment, 106, 117, 154
Triangulation, 203, 205
Trustworthiness, 116, 131, 191, 195–196, 202–203, 205–206, 225
Type I & Type II errors, 81–82, 99

U

Universal Design for Instruction, 243

V

Validity (psychometric)
    Construct, 70, 72–73, 98, 133–137, 140–142, 144, 157
    Content, 70–72
    Criterion, 9, 12, 15, 17, 49, 70–73, 91–92, 98, 142, 159, 162–164, 166, 193
Value changes, theory of, 24, 97
Variables
    Categorical, 48, 89
    Continuous, 48, 77, 96
    Dependent, 49–50, 52, 58–59, 85, 90–91, 93, 128, 133, 139, 147–148, 151–152,

161, 163, 170, 255, 276, 292
Environmental, 19
Independent, 16, 49–50, 59, 89–90, 92, 96, 131, 162–163, 165, 170
Latent, 40, 47, 93, 168
Status, 50–51, 59, 89–91, 147
Variance, 52, 64, 78–79, 83–86, 88–90, 92–94, 99, 139–141, 145, 149, 170, 262, 291
Visual impairments, 5, 165, 235, 245, 255, 289, 293
Vocational evaluation, 155–156, 241
Vocational rehabilitation, 5, 22, 25, 51, 56, 91, 103–104, 107, 151, 163–164, 166, 168–169, 174, 177, 215, 221, 230–231, 238, 240–242, 249, 251, 284–286
Vocational Rehabilitation Act, 22

W

Work, 3, 9, 11, 12, 13, 14, 15, 17, 18, 21, 23, 24, 25, 26, 28, 30, 35, 38, 42, 56, 58, 71, 75, 98, 107, 120, 121, 122, 123, 124, 143, 155, 156, 164, 165, 168, 173, 174, 176, 190, 210, 219, 220, 222, 224, 227, 229, 230, 231, 234, 241, 244, 246, 247, 249, 250, 252, 254, 255, 262, 266, 272, 274, 279, 282, 283, 287, 288, 289, 290.
Work Adjustment Theories, 24
Workers Compensation, 254, 273, 286–287
Workforce Innovation and Opportunity Act (WIOA), 244, 246, 287

Find us on:
FACEBOOK.COM/CCTPUBLISHER

facebook®

TO ORDER: www.ccthomas.com • books@ccthomas.com • 1-800-258-8980

Sign up for our e-Newsletter for e-Only Specials! Go to: www.ccthomas.com

FREE SHIPPING ON ORDERS OVER $50! USE PROMO CODE: SHIP50
Available on retail purchases through our website only to domestic shipping addresses in the United States

---

ART-BASED GROUP THERAPY
(2nd Edition)
by Bruce L. Moon
258 pp. (7 x 10) • 26 color illustrations
$38.95 (paper) • $38.95 (ebook)

SPIRITUALITY AS A WORKING MODEL IN BRIEF PSYCHOTHERAPY
by Richard H. Cox
202 pp. (7 x 10) • 11 illustrations
$32.95 (paper) • $32.95 (ebook)

TECHNOLOGY IN MENTAL HEALTH
(2nd Edition)
by Stephen Goss, Kate Anthony, LoriAnn Sykes Stretch, and DeeAnna Merz Nagel
456 pp. (7 x 10) • 12 illustrations • 6 tables
$81.95 (paper) • $81.95 (ebook)

PSYCHIATRIC ASPECTS OF CRIMINAL BEHAVIOR
by Louis B. Schlesinger
280 pp. (7 x 10) • 10 tables
$32.95 (paper) • $32.95 (ebook)

INTRODUCTION TO HUMAN RELATIONS STUDIES
by George Henderson and Wesley C. Long
364 pp. (7 x 10)
$62.95 (paper) • $62.95 (ebook)

COMPUTATIONAL ART THERAPY
by Seong-in Kim
318 pp. (8.5 x 11)
358 (266 in color) illustrations • 37 tables
$49.95 (hard) • $35.95 (ebook) • $14.95 (dload)

INTRODUCTION TO ART THERAPY
(3rd Edition)
by Bruce L. Moon
284 pp. (7 x 10) • 28 illustrations
$37.95 (paper) • $37.95 (ebook)

SPIRITUAL ART THERAPY
(3rd Edition)
by Ellen G. Horovitz
230 pp. (7 x 10)
47 illustrations • 3 tables
$37.95 (paper) • $37.95 (ebook)

ART THERAPY WITH STUDENTS AT RISK
(3rd Edition)
by Stella A. Stepney
344 pp. (7 x 10)
39 (12 color) illustrations • 27 tables
$44.95 (paper) • $44.95 (ebook)

COMBINING THE CREATIVE THERAPIES WITH TECHNOLOGY
by Stephanie L. Brooke
332 pp. (7 x 10)
48 illustrations • 3 tables
$49.95 (paper) • $49.95 (ebook)

CHILDREN IN THE URBAN ENVIRONMENT
by Norma Kolko Phillips and Shulamith Lala Ashenberg Straussner
358 pp. (7 x 10) • 1 illustration
$49.95 (paper) • $49.95 (ebook)

CHOOSING TO LIVE
by Cliff Williams
204 pp. (7 x 10) • 1 illustration
$28.95 (paper) • $28.95 (ebook)

UNDERSTANDING PARENTAL ALIENATION
by Karen Woodall and Nick Woodall
252 pp. (7 x 10)
6 illustrations
$39.95 (paper) • $39.95 (ebook)

PRESCRIPTIONS FOR CHILDREN WITH PSYCHOLOGICAL AND PSYCHIATRIC PROBLEMS *(4th Edition)*
by David F. Bogacki, Ralph F. Blanco, Michael Roberts, Basant Pradhan, Karim Sedky, and Andres Pumariega
278 pp. (7 x 10) • 1 table
$42.95 (paper) • $42.95 (ebook)

PRIMER ON EFFECT SIZES, SIMPLE RESEARCH DESIGNS, AND CONFIDENCE INTERVALS
by Marty Sapp
196 pp. (7 x 10) • 1 illustration • 7 tables
$32.95 (paper) • $32.95 (ebook)

THE HANDBOOK OF CHILD LIFE *(2nd Edition)*
by Richard H. Thompson
642 pp. (7 x 10) • 7 illustrations • 14 tables
$59.95 (paper) • $59.95 (ebook)

CHARLES C THOMAS • PUBLISHER, LTD.